HAYDN

A CREATIVE LIFE IN MUSIC

BY

KARL GEIRINGER

IN COLLABORATION WITH
IRENE GEIRINGER

UNIVERSITY OF CALIFORNIA PRESS

BERKELEY AND LOS ANGELES: 1968

Haydn: *A Creative Life in Music* was originally published by W. W. Norton & Company in 1946. The University of California Press edition includes substantial corrections made in the second revised and enlarged edition, and is published by arrangement with the author and Doubleday and Company, Inc.

ML
410
H4
G4
1968

Reprinted with revisions 1968
by the University of California Press
Berkeley and Los Angeles

HAYDN

A CREATIVE LIFE IN MUSIC

KARL GEIRINGER was born in Vienna and studied at the University of Berlin and the University of Vienna, where he obtained a Ph.D. He came to the United States in 1940 and was naturalized five years later. Between 1930 and 1938 he was curator of the Archives of the Society of Friends of Music in Vienna. He has taught at the Royal College of Music in London, at Hamilton College in Clinton, New York, and at Boston University. At present he is professor of music in charge of graduate studies at the University of California, Santa Barbara. Dr. Geiringer is the author of *Musical Instruments: Their History in Western Culture, Brahms: His Life and Work, The Bach Family, and J. S. Bach, The Culmination of An Era*. He has edited the anthology *Music of the Bach Family* and works by Joseph Haydn in the Collected Edition. Dr. Geiringer was awarded fellowships by the Bollingen Foundation and the Guggenheim Foundation and has received grants from the American Philosophical Society. He was president of the American Musicological Society in 1955 and 1956 and was elected a fellow of the American Academy of Arts and Sciences in 1959.

His wife, Irene Geiringer, is a niece of the psychoanalyist Dr. Wilhelm Stekel. She received a Ph.D. from the University of Vienna, where she studied philosophy and German literature, and has taught German on the university level. Mrs. Geiringer assists her husband in his research and has collaborated in all of his books, concentrating in particular on the biographical sections.

PREFACE

This book represents the results of more than three decades of Haydn research. As curator of the Society of Friends of Music in Vienna, which owns the extensive Haydn collections assembled by C. F. Pohl and E. Mandyczewski, I was invited to contribute a book on the composer. It was published in 1932 to commemorate the bicentenary of Haydn's birth. My Haydn research continued in the following years, and in 1946, after I had moved to the United States, a more extensive work in English appeared. Its first part traced the life and the character of the composer; the second part was devoted to an analysis of his music. The vastness of Haydn's output made it seem advisable to emphasize the main lines of his artistic development and to deal in a more extensive manner only with the works from his period of maturity.

Since the publication of that book, Haydn research has progressed by leaps and bounds as though to make up for precious time lost in the nineteenth century. The vast Esterházy collection of Haydn documents and scores owned at present by the Hungarian National Library was opened up, and I was fortunate in being able to visit it in 1959. The publication of the Collected Edition of Haydn's works made good progress, and in addition a considerable amount of previously unprinted compositions was presented in separate editions. The first volume of a thematic catalogue of Haydn's works dealing with instrumental compositions, as well as several valuable monographs concerned with individual aspects of Haydn research, became available.

Under these conditions I decided to offer the book in a completely revised and substantially enlarged version. In the biographical section a number of recently found letters have been included which afford new insight into the character of the composer and his life at the Esterházy court. The musical section likewise attempts to reflect the present state of Haydn research, incorporating—particularly in the field of the smaller sacred and secular vocal compositions—results of my own investigation. To substantiate the description of the works, a number of music examples have been added; likewise, references to modern publications of the lesser-known Haydn compositions have been presented in footnotes to make the acquaintance with the composer's output easier for the reader. A checklist of the main Haydn autographs known to have survived is included in an appendix.

The author wishes to express his sincere thanks to all those who have generously assisted him in his work. In particular he feels indebted to Dr. Georg Feder, chief of the Haydn Institute in Cologne, and to Dr. Irmgard Becker-Glauch on the staff of that institute; to Dr. Jenö Vecsey, director of the music division in the National Library, Budapest; to Dr. Dénes Bartha, professor at the University, and to Dr. László Somfai, both of Budapest; to Dr. Leopold Nowak, professor at the University and director of the music division of the Austrian National Library, Vienna; to Dr. Heinz Ramge of the Westdeutsche Bibliothek, Marburg; to Mr. Alexander Hyatt King, chief of the music department, British Museum, London; to Mr. François Lesure, chief of the music department, Bibliothèque Nationale, Paris, and Mr. Vladimir Fedorov of the Bibliothèque du Conservatoire, Paris; to Dr. Harold Spivacke, chief of the music division, and Mr. William Lichtenwanger, reference librarian, Library of Congress, Washington, D. C.; to Mr. Frank Campbell, assistant chief, music department, New York Public Library.

Valuable help was also given by my friends, Mr. H. C. Robbins Landon, Buggiano (Pistoia); Professor O. E. Deutsch, Vienna; Professor J. P. Larsen, Copenhagen; Dr. h.c. Anthony van Hoboken, Ascona; Mr. Herbert Weinstock, New York. The publishing houses of Doblinger and Universal-Edition in Vienna and Bärenreiter-Verlag, Kassel, kindly furnished their numerous Haydn publications.

My wife, Dr. Irene Geiringer, who for many years has participated in all my research, was also my collaborator in the present venture, dealing in particular with the biographical section.

Karl Geiringer

Santa Barbara, California

CONTENTS

PART ONE

LIFE

THE HAYDNS AND THE KOLLERS

The question of Joseph Haydn's origin has been much disputed. No less than four different theories have been put forward; all are interesting and merit examination, although they fail to furnish a complete solution of the problem. The families of Haydn's parents had their homes in eastern Lower Austria, north of the large Neusiedler Lake, a district of many different races. Since 1533, besides the predominant German element, a large number of Croats have settled in this district, and from the adjacent Hungarian border there has come, through the centuries, a steady stream of Hungarian immigrants. The Slav ethnologist, Dr. Franz Kuhač,[1] has contended that Haydn's family was by race Croatian, that the names of Haydn and Koller (the family name of the composer's mother) were both Croatian, and that many of Haydn's melodies bear a close resemblance to Croatian folk songs. Undue publicity was given to this theory by Sir Henry Hadow, who declared in both the *Oxford History of Music* and Grove's *Dictionary of Music and Musicians*[2] that Haydn was a typical Croatian composer. On the other hand, the Hungarian historian Elemér Schwartz, has attempted to prove Haydn's Hungarian descent.[3] He bases his theory on the fact that the

[1] This champion of the importance of Croatian art had, incidentally, the purely German name of Koch, which he changed later to the Slav form of Kuhač.

[2] Hadow's statements are to be found in the "Haydn" articles of the second and third editions of Grove's *Dictionary of Music and Musicians*. See also Henry Hadow, *A Croatian Composer* (London, 1897).

[3] In the daily publication *Magyaroág* (Budapest, April 10, 1932).

village of Tadten (Hungarian: Tétény), where Haydn's great-grandfather lived before he moved to Hainburg, was predominantly Hungarian in the seventeenth century. In 1659 the Bishop of Raab wrote about Tadten: "All the members of the parish are Hungarian Lutherans, with the exception of a few German houses."[4] There has even been an attempt by the Slav philologist Dedaelus to claim a gypsy origin for Haydn. This induced Ernst Fritz Schmid to make elaborate genealogical researches, tracing the family names in German districts back to the Middle Ages and studying the lists of inhabitants in the respective villages.[5] According to his final conclusions there can be no doubt that the Haydn and Koller families were of German origin.

But blood and race alone do not determine one's nationality. By race Haydn was a German, by nationality an Austrian. He lived in a melting pot of races, a country in which cultural elements from both central and eastern Europe were fused together. It was quite natural that he should be familiar with the way of life of the Croats and the Hungarians. He heard their music from his childhood and attended their festivities; he admired their artistic craftsmanship and the color of their holiday garb. With the instinct of genius he absorbed all these impressions and brought them to life in his music. The inner enrichment that he owed to his acquaintance with the different cultures of Austria and Hungary was more than a minor factor in making him the great artist he was.

Great composers often have someone of artistic or intellectual leanings among their ancestors. Joseph Haydn, one of the most independent spirits of musical history, was exceptional also in this respect. Going back to his great-grandfathers on both sides, we fail to find among them a single musician or even a man who pursued any kind of intellectual occupation. They all toiled with their hands as vinegrowers, farmers, wheelwrights, or millers. They were hardworking, honest men whose infinite diligence, patience, and pertinacity succeeded in raising them from extreme

[4] *"Parociani omnes sont lutherani hungari praeter aliquot domos Germanos."*

[5] E. F. Schmid, *Joseph Haydn . . .* (Kassel, 1934).

poverty to well-ordered circumstances and esteemed positions in the community. This they achieved under the most difficult conditions, for war raged almost continuously in that part of central Europe during the seventeenth and eighteenth centuries. The little section of eastern Austria where the Haydn family lived lies close to the Hungarian border. It was feebly fortified and thus fell easily to any nation that chose to make war on Austria. Haydn's great-grandfather, the wagonmaker Kaspar Haydn, and his wife lost their lives when the town of Hainburg was captured by the Turks in 1683. Of the house and possessions acquired with heartbreaking toil only ruins were left to their one surviving son, Thomas. But less than seven years later Thomas had already built himself a new house and had been nominated a "citizen" of Hainburg. This meant definite progress, for his father had started his career at Hainburg as a modest *Burgknecht*, a day laborer with a permanent domicile.

On the other side, Haydn's maternal grandfather, the farmer Lorenz Koller, after witnessing as a boy of eight the ravages wrought by the Turkish invasion, lost all his possessions in 1704 when the *Kuruczes*, the peasant army of the anti-Habsburg Hungarian party, plundered the border village of Rohrau. One year later he rebuilt his house, only to see it go up in flames a second time when, in 1706, the Hungarians returned. But Lorenz Koller was not a man to give up. Again and again he started from the beginning, and so good was his progress that in 1713 he was offered the office of *Marktrichter* (a magistrate supervising peace and propriety in the village), a position in which his son-in-law, the father of Joseph Haydn, was to succeed him.

As to Haydn's parents, the information supplied by documents is supplemented by stories based on the master's own accounts. Haydn's mother, Maria Koller, was born on November 10, 1707, to the sound of cannon firing against the *Kuruczes* who were attempting another assault on the village of Rohrau. Her father died when she was eleven years old. She became a cook for the lords of Rohrau, the Counts of Harrach, and in their castle she saw something of the way of life of the Austrian nobility. The kitchen staff comprised nine persons, for whom a yearly salary of a thousand florins was budgeted. Menus preserved in the archives of the castle show that the Harrachs demanded high culinary skill from their cooks. Maria had to handle such delicacies as tortoises and crayfish and had an abundance of material at her disposal. We are told, for example, that something like eight thousand eggs, two hundred capons, and three hundred chickens were delivered annually to the castle by the inhabitants of Rohrau as part of their duties to their patron. It must have been quite a change for Maria Koller when, in 1728 at the age of twenty-one, she left the castle to marry the wagonmaker Mathias Haydn. Although she brought her husband a dowry of one hundred and twenty florins and an "honest outfit" (according to the marriage contract), every penny had to be accounted for in the little house, especially when there was a large family to rear. Maria bore her husband twelve children, but six of them died in infancy. Her famous son often testified to Maria's excellent housewifely qualities. She was scrupulously clean and neat, an indefatigable worker; and these were the qualities that she stressed in bringing up her children. She was deeply religious, this being a characteristic trait of the family. We know that her father bequeathed eighty-eight florins to the church, a considerable sum for the modest people of Rohrau. It was Maria Haydn's great dream to see Joseph's talents devoted to the Catholic Church, and she never overcame her disappointment at his preference for the irresponsible life of a musician to that of the sacred profession of a priest. Haydn often lamented that his dear mother did not live to see him succeed; before he got his first post, Maria Haydn, worn out by a life of ceaseless toil, had died in 1754, at the age of forty-seven.

Haydn's father, Mathias Haydn, was born on January 31, 1699, in the town of Hainburg, a son of the wheelwright Thomas Haydn. Only two years after the infant's birth, Thomas died, leaving a widow of thirty with six sons, the eldest being barely twelve. In those troubled times, with war and plague threatening the population, the widow Katharina Haydn naturally sought male support, and four months after her husband's death she married Mathias Seefranz, also a wheelwright. She bore him four children, among them Juliane Rosine, whom we shall meet again as the wife of the schoolmaster Franck. Seefranz, who later became a member of the Hainburg council, was a rather difficult and quarrelsome person, and life with him may not have been easy for his young stepsons, who were all learning the family trade under his instructions. In 1717 Mathias Haydn finished his apprenticeship and set out on the traditional travels of the journeyman, which brought him as far as Frankfort on the Main. When he came home, he brought with him a harp, which someone had taught him to play. Although he could not read a note, it was his great delight to accompany himself on the harp when he sang his favorite folk tunes in a pleasant tenor voice. In 1727 Mathias decided to settle down in the nearby town of Rohrau, remaining at the same time a member of the Hainburg guild of wheelwrights. Why his choice fell on this rather uninviting little market town is not known, but it is not unlikely that the person of his future bride attracted him to it. In 1728 Mathias Haydn and Maria Koller were married, and for twenty-six years they lived happily together. But Haydn's father was certainly no sentimentalist. When his good wife died, the man of fifty-five did not hesitate to marry his servant girl of nineteen.

Mathias lived in Rohrau in a cottage built by himself, and from the outset was fairly prosperous. It has been the custom of Haydn's biographers to stress the extreme poverty of his father, and judging from the appearance of the house in which the Haydns lived throughout their lives, this attitude seems to be justified. The little low-roofed, thatch-covered cottage is bound to fill us with pity, and we all feel like Beethoven, who on his deathbed, when shown a picture of the Haydn house, exclaimed, "Strange that so great a man should have been born in so poor a home!" For all that, Mathias Haydn was by no means a poor man, and he could probably have built himself a much better house if he had felt his cottage to be inadequate. Several of the bills that he made out have been preserved, and it is known that he was given plenty of work and was not paid badly by the Counts of Harrach for making wheels, repairing wagons, and painting houses. From the taxes he paid we see that he ultimately had his own wine cellar, his own farmland, and some cattle. The high esteem in which he was held is proved by his nomination to succeed his father-in-law in the office of *Marktrichter,* which he filled from 1741 to 1762. The list of his duties is imposing, but only a few can be mentioned here. He was responsible for the good conduct of the population and had to keep a sharp lookout for adultery or excessive gambling. He had to see that people went to church and did not break the Sunday rest. It was his job to allot among the inhabitants of Rohrau the labor required by the patron, Count Harrach, and he was responsible for keeping the local roads in good repair. On Sundays at six in the morning he had to report on all such matters to the count's steward.[6] Every two years an open-air meeting of the whole community took place at which the *Marktrichter* rendered a detailed account of the work done during the past period. To be at the same time a wagonmaker, farmer, vinegrower, wine producer, and important official and to carry out all these duties well was no small matter. Mathias Haydn must have been as efficient as he was diligent.

No personal documents of Haydn's parents or any of his forebears have been preserved. No portraits, letters, or diaries have come down to us. Nevertheless we know that it was not a mean heritage that they passed on to their great offspring. A deep religious sense, a stubborn tenacity of purpose, and a passionate desire to rise in the world are qualities that we find in his ancestors. Combined with them were a great pride in good craftsmanship, a warm love of the soil, and a healthy streak of sensuality. Indeed, it might be said that this heritage gave Joseph Haydn the very qualities necessary for the life he was to lead.

[6] These early hours were kept during the period from April to September. In the other months the *Marktrichter* did not have to report until 8 AM once every fortnight.

CHAPTER 1

ROHRAU AND HAINBURG

1732–1740

Rohrau, Haydn's hometown, is by no means an attractive place. The surrounding country is flat and marshy (as may be inferred by the name, which means reedy meadow), and the houses in the little township are mainly low, thatched cottages built of clay. Life is not easy there, for the Leitha River, which at Rohrau forms the border between Austria and Hungary, has an unpleasant tendency to flood the countryside; and in the hot dry summers, fires frequently play havoc with the thatched houses. The Haydn house, for instance, was burned in 1813, 1833, and 1899, but it was always carefully restored to its original form.

Franz Joseph[1] Haydn, the second child of Mathias and Maria, was born on March 31, 1732, and baptized on April 1.[2] His earliest childhood would have been spent like that of any Austrian peasant boy but for one important difference. His musical talent began to show itself at a very early age, and many anecdotes are extant about it. In the evenings, when work was done, his father and mother used to sit by the fireplace and sing their favorite folk tunes to the accompaniment of the harp proudly han-

---

[1] The Haydns, like many other families, used to call their children by their second names. Cf. Johann Michael Haydn, known as Michael Haydn.

[2] There is some difference of opinion about the date of Haydn's birth, as both March 31 and April 1 were mentioned by members of the family. Haydn himself always maintained that it was March 31, and the unpublished diary of the master's friend J. C. Rosenbaum (preserved in the Vienna National Library) states that the birth took place at 4 PM.

dled by Mathias. Little Sepperl, as the boy was called in
the Austrian fashion, joined in with perfect intonation and
a beautiful voice, attracting the attention of all the neighbors. Before long the boy's ambition went further. He
wanted to play an instrument as his father did, and having
seen the schoolmaster perform on a violin, he took two
sticks and pretended that they were a violin and a bow.
Thus he accompanied the songs, keeping time with amazing accuracy. People began to comment on Sepperl's
strange behavior, and in the hearts of his parents there
stirred a hope that one day their son might rise to a position far above theirs. Perhaps he would work with his
brains instead of his hands; perhaps he would become a
schoolmaster or even, as his mother fervently hoped and
prayed, a priest. The auspices seemed good, for Sepperl
showed a deep religious faith that was never to desert him.
Both parents must have felt dimly that the poor little
village could not offer sufficient opportunities for the education of their eldest son. Then one day a cousin, Johann
Mathias Franck, the husband of Mathias Haydn's step-
sister, Juliane Rosine Seefranz, came from Hainburg to pay
the Haydns a visit. He was the school principal as well as
the precentor of the Church of St. Philip and St. James in
Mathias' native town. In the eyes of the wheelwright and
the former cook, he was a person of indisputable authority.
Franck soon noticed Sepperl's musical talent and suggested
taking the boy to Hainburg, where he could get a proper
education, mainly in music. This offer was not wholly
prompted by unselfish motives, however, for any payment
Franck might receive for Sepperl's board and tuition would
be a most welcome addition to his meager budget.[3] At
first Maria Haydn objected, for she wanted Sepperl to be
trained for the priesthood. Thereupon Franck argued that
if the boy should decide later to take holy orders, his musical education would be most helpful. Still his mother hesitated, for he was not yet six years old and she knew that if
he left home her chances of seeing him would be few, for

[3] Just what sum was paid by Haydn's parents is not known;
Schmid mentions that as late as 1760 Mathias owed Franck
thirty florins.

traveling was practically impossible for a woman as busy
as she. But finally the parents decided to accept Franck's
offer, feeling that they were unable to give the boy a
fitting education in Rohrau. It was certainly the best thing
they could have done for Joseph. His intellect was craving
nourishment that his native village could not provide. To
satisfy it seemed imperative, much more imperative than
that he should be given loving care and understanding. So
Sepperl at the age of five-and-a-half[4] was sent away, never
to return to Rohrau except for rare, short visits. All close
contact with his father and mother ceased, and gradually
the thoughts of the narrow life he had shared with them
at home became tender memories, mellowed by distance
and nostalgia. When Haydn, as an old man, told his biographers about his youth, he described his mother—who had
surrendered her child while he was still an infant—as "having always given the most tender care to his welfare." And
when in 1795 the then world-famous composer visited
Rohrau to see the monument erected in his honor by
Count Harrach, he knelt down and kissed the threshold of
the humble cottage he had shared with his parents for less
than six years.

Rohrau once left behind, Sepperl breathed a very different air and saw a new and different landscape. Gone was
the dreary monotony of the marshes, and the boy's eyes
could hardly take in all the new sights that he saw on his
way. There were many relics of times past to admire, for
in this part of Austria the Romans had built important
cities. In the middle of the plain stands a gigantic trium-
phal arch, now called the "Heathen Gate," and not far
from it are the remains of the city of Carnuntum, which
witnessed the coronation of Septimius Severus as Roman
emperor. Even if Sepperl did not understand the historical
meaning of such monuments, he could not help being
thrilled by the lovely surroundings of the city he was approaching.

At Hainburg the mountains slope down steeply to the

---

[4] Haydn's exact age when he left Rohrau is a matter of conjecture. It seems likely that the departure occurred sometime
between his fifth and sixth birthdays.

imposing Danube and, covered with rocks or dense woods
among which appear the ruins of the castle that gave the
city its name, they make a picturesque background to the
little town. Even today the visitor to Hainburg feels that
he is back in the Middle Ages. The ancient, enormous
gates through which the city is entered still stand, and
next to one of them, the Vienna Gate, Haydn's grandmother lived. Imposing walls and towers testify to the part
that Hainburg once played as a fortress against foes from
the East, and within the gates are beautiful baroque fa-
çades and the interesting Church of St. Philip and St.
James. Truly Sepperl had entered a new world.

Here his artistic and intellectual curiosity found full
satisfaction. It was fortunate for him that by old Hainburg
custom Franck's duties were much more numerous than
those that a schoolteacher of the present time would be
willing to undertake. With the aid of two assistants paid
by him, he had to instruct some eighty children in reading, writing, arithmetic, singing, and prayers; he was in
charge of the church music, playing the organ himself and
directing the singers and instrumentalists, who by south-
German tradition took part in every service. In addition,
Franck had to keep the church register, look after the
church clock, and ring the bells both for the services and
for special occasions such as thunderstorms or fires. To
many of these activities little Sepperl was introduced without delay. The daily schedule of the six-year-old boy became very crowded indeed. School began at seven in the
morning and lasted for three hours, after which all the
children went to Mass, some participating as altar boys.
At eleven they went home for their noonday meal, and
from twelve to three there was school again. For the rest
of the day, there was the study of homework and, what
was most important of all, very extensive musical instruction. We do not know exactly which instruments Haydn
studied with Franck, but he himself wrote in his autobiographical sketch:[5] "Our Almighty Father had endowed
me with so much facility in music that even in my sixth
year I stood up like a man and sang Masses in the church

[5] Published in 1778 in *Das gelehrte Oesterreich. Ein Versuch.*

choir and I could play a little on the clavier and violin."
Furthermore, Georg August Griesinger in the biography
based on direct information from Haydn, states that he
studied the "kettledrum as well as other instruments."
How he learned to play the drum at the age of six was
told by another contemporary biographer, the painter Albert Christoph Dies, and is quoted here as evidence of the
child's peculiar gift for self-instruction:

> It was in the Week of the Cross [May 11–18],
> when many processions take place, that Franck was
> in great distress because of the death of his drummer.
> He thought of Joseph; the boy should learn to play
> the instrument at once. He showed Joseph how to
> make the strokes and left him alone. Joseph took a
> little basket, such as peasants use for baking bread,
> covered it with a cloth, placed his contrivance on an
> upholstered chair, and drummed with such enthusi-
> asm that he did not notice the flour pouring out of
> the basket and ruining the chair. He was scolded, but
> his teacher was easily appeased when he saw to his
> amazement that Joseph had already become a per-
> fect drummer.[6]

So the boy proudly marched in the procession. The
instrument was strapped upon a hunchback to make it
possible for the little fellow to play it. What a comical
sight this pair must have been—the hunchback in front
with the kettledrum on his back, little Haydn following,
beating his drum and probably not always aiming quite
straight. When Haydn showed an English orchestral musician how to play the timpani fifty years later, he may
have remembered with amusement his own first efforts
with these instruments. As regards other instruments mentioned by Griesinger, though Haydn probably did not
learn to play them properly, he certainly had ample opportunity to become acquainted with them. The standards

---

[6] If this had really happened, it would show Haydn as an
extremely precocious child. Learning to play the timpani in a
very short time using a basket covered with a limp cloth in lieu
of the resilient surface of a real drum would require genius.

of the music directed by Franck were not too low. The inventory of the church instruments included, for example, as many as eight trumpets and eight violins. Although on ordinary Sundays the music was confined to a four-part chorus, two violins, and organ (the ensemble still used in Haydn's first Mass), on festive occasions a violoncello, double bass, trumpets, horns, and timpani were added. Franck had a rather extensive collection of manuscript music, which he even lent to the churches of larger cities. It is not unlikely that he made his gifted little pupil copy music for him; in this way Haydn may have become familiar at an early age with the sacred music of the period.

Apart from the ordinary routine, in itself interesting enough for the lad, there were special occasions when even a small town like Hainburg displayed the baroque splendor so dear to the Austrian heart. In 1738 the Roman Catholic Church arranged a *jubileum universale*. For two weeks, to the accompaniment of an abundance of music that must have kept young Sepperl tremendously busy, prayers were said for a victory over the Turks. Another great event was the solemn entry of the imperial Commissary Cetto a Cronstorff into Hainburg on May 2, 1739. He came to witness the election of the city councilors, and little Hainburg wanted to pay every possible honor to the guest from Vienna. He was received at the Vienna Gate by the city judges and councilors and conducted in state to the church. Before the portal stood trumpeters and drummers in their red cloaks and the civil guard resplendent in their uniforms. To the sound of fanfares the commissary entered the church, where Franck directed a motet *Veni Sancte Spiritus* before the Mass and a *Te Deum* after it. On the following day the elections took place, followed by another solemn church service. To the sound of impressive fanfares the names of the new councilors were announced from the high altar, among them, to Joseph's pride, that of Mathias Seefranz, the second husband of his grandmother and the father-in-law of Franck. Two months later Hainburg celebrated with all the splendor it could afford the peace concluded between Austria and France. Besides such outstanding events, there were the many great feast days of the Catholic Church, and the processions then held followed age-old tradition, the Almighty being entreated to protect the people and their holdings from thunderstorms, hail, frost, and other disasters. In all these little Sepperl took an active part and they must have made a deep impression on his fertile brain. Particularly attractive was Corpus Christi day, the feast day of the guilds, among them that of the wheelwrights. Masters were admitted and journeymen discharged, all with the solemn ritual that Haydn's grandfather, father, and uncles had witnessed in this very place. To Sepperl's joy, in 1738, his own father attended a meeting in order to bind a new apprentice. Such occasional contacts with his parents meant much to the little boy who, in spite of a life filled with new discoveries, must often have felt homesick.

It is necessary now to reveal another side to the Hainburg picture, one that was much less pleasant. The Francks were very poor. On his modest salary, consisting mainly of allowances in kind, the school rector had to support a steadily growing family. Juliane Franck seems to have lacked the housewifely qualities of Haydn's mother. Her home was never kept in good order and she was already so busy with her two infant daughters, who were joined by a son in November 1739, that she saw in her nephew of six not a child needing love and care, but a useful helper with the housework. Sepperl did not resent doing the tasks she set him, but he did suffer from the neglect of his person. He, who had been trained by his mother in unimpeachable cleanliness and order, lost his neat appearance. The few clothes he possessed were not washed and mended very often. Dies relates that when talking of Hainburg, as an old man Haydn said: "I could not help perceiving, much to my distress, that I was gradually getting very dirty, and though I thought rather highly of my little person, I was not always able to avoid stains on my clothes, of which I was dreadfully ashamed—in fact, I was a regular little ragamuffin." At that time Haydn also began to wear a wig "for the sake of cleanliness." His meals were insufficient, and he admitted in later years that he got from his strict teacher "more floggings than food." Regarding the floggings, we should not blame Franck too much; they were the customary method of education. For instance, Schmid tells us of an "Instruction for the Schoolmaster" in which the Hainburg Council admonished the rector to refrain from pulling out the hair of his pupils, but to keep them strictly in order with the cane.

Still, if we balance the two sides of Haydn's life at Hainburg the final result was certainly favorable. Haydn got what he most needed, extensive musical instruction. Furthermore, he was endowed by nature with a rare combination of gifts, wiry resilience, and a contented disposition. Hardships never made him bitter and never broke him. In spite of being hungry and dirty, in spite of the rough treatment occasionally meted out to him, Sepperl was happy. Throughout his life, whenever Franck's name was mentioned, Haydn had words of praise for his first teacher. "I shall be grateful to that man as long as I live for keeping me so hard at work," he said to Griesinger. In his house Haydn piously kept a portrait of Franck which he left in his last will, together with one hundred florins, to his teacher's daughter, Anna R. Schimpel.[7]

Little Sepperl progressed fast, but after a time Hainburg had given him all it had to offer. To stay longer within its medieval walls would have meant a retarding of his artistic and intellectual growth. Fortunately some natural law appears to direct the artistic destiny of a genius and lead him to the path best suited for his art, even though it may not contribute to his personal happiness.

Karl Georg Reutter the younger, court composer and newly appointed choirmaster at the famous Cathedral of St. Stephen in Vienna, went on a tour in search of good choristers, in the course of which he visited Hainburg and stayed at the house of the pastor, Anton Johann Palmb. On hearing of Reutter's quest, Palmb recommended young Haydn, whose "weak but sweet voice" he had noticed. The rest of the story is best told in the words of Giuseppe Carpani:[8]

[7] See Johann R. von Lucam, "Haydn und die beiden Originalportraits seiner Eltern," *Wiener Allgemeine Zeitung* (1852).
[8] *Le Haydine* (1812).

Reutter gave him a tune to sing at sight. The precision, the purity of tone, the spirit with which the boy executed it surprised him; but he was more especially charmed with the beauty of the young voice. He remarked that the lad did not shake (trill) and smilingly asked him the reason. The boy replied promptly: "How can you expect me to shake when my cousin does not know how to himself?" "Come here," said Reutter, "I will teach you." He took him between his knees, showed him how he should produce the notes in rapid succession, control his breath, and agitate the palate. The boy immediately made a good shake. Reutter, enchanted with the success of his pupil, took a plate of fine cherries and emptied them into the boy's pockets. [According to Dies, he also gave Sepperl a piece of money.] His delight may be readily conceived. Haydn often mentioned this anecdote to me, and added, laughing, that whenever he happened to shake he still thought he saw those beautiful cherries.

Reutter offered to take Sepperl to Vienna as a chorister at St. Stephen's and to give him a thorough musical education if his parents would consent to it. A meeting was quickly arranged, and Sepperl's father and mother were overjoyed with Reutter's promise that he would look after their boy. It was agreed that Sepperl should go to the imperial capital when he reached his eighth year. Reutter urged him to practice singing scales and solfeggios in the meantime so as to develop his voice. As Franck was unable to teach Sepperl anything of the kind, the boy himself found a practical method and with characteristic diligence and ambition worked so hard that he made good progress.

The last few months before his departure were filled with joyous anticipation and passed quickly. Haydn was all impatience; he could hardly wait to see with his own eyes the wonders of the Austrian capital and to begin the musical training that Vienna's great cathedral had to offer.

CHAPTER 2

AT ST. STEPHEN'S

1740–1749

There is one building in Vienna that never fails to fill even the least sensitive inhabitant of the Austrian capital with awe and amazement: the Cathedral of St. Stephen. This Gothic church is so full of power, so imbued with the mystery of life in all its aspects, whether lofty or humorous, that it would be impossible ever to know it completely or to plumb its profundities. The outside of the cathedral displays a bewildering variety of high slender buttresses, gargoyles in the form of dragons, and countless statues of the great of the Church and of the House of Austria. The big south tower of St. Stephen's is the distinctive feature of Vienna. From its top, more than four hundred feet above the ground, one can look east far into the Hungarian plain, north toward the Danube and the fertile fields of Moravia, west and south toward the green Vienna woods and the foothills of the Alps. Although the outside of the church is entirely medieval, there are many baroque decorations and altars inside. In the typical Austrian manner, purity of style is completely lacking, but the daring mixture of old and new is in good taste and works of the fourteenth to eighteenth centuries succeed in being beautifully harmonious. In this imposing cathedral the imagination is never at rest. Every step brings new surprises and wonders, and the whole building is filled with a sense of great mystery, always eluding one, always leading one further. This Gothic architecture seems to lift one from earth into higher and more spiritual spheres, filling the soul of even the most matter-of-fact person with awe. How great must

have been the effect of St. Stephen's upon the highly imaginative child whose constant resort it was for nine years.

While the surroundings in which Haydn dwelt in Vienna
were all that he could have expected, and even more,
closer acquaintance with the man in whose hands his
fate lay proved sadly disappointing. Georg Reutter[1] lived
with the six choirboys, a subcantor, and two preceptors in
the *Cantorei* house next to the cathedral. He was entirely
responsible for the pupils' education and musical training,
as well as for their board, for which he received a yearly
sum of twelve hundred florins from the city of Vienna.
Unfortunately the man who had so generously filled Sepperl's pockets with cherries at Hainburg had turned into a
stern principal who provided the boys with even less and
poorer food than Sepperl had received from his impecunious
relatives in Hainburg. Dies relates: "Joseph's stomach had
to get accustomed to continuous fasting. He tried to make
up for it with the musical academies [concerts that the
choir gave in the houses of the Viennese nobility], where
refreshments were offered to the choristers. As soon as
Joseph made this discovery, so important for his stomach,
he was seized with an incredible love for academies. He
endeavored to sing as beautifully as possible so as to be
known and invited as a skilled performer, and thus to find
occasions to appease his ravenous hunger." But the insufficient food was not the worst, for "it seemed as if they
wanted to starve the mind as well as the body." To Reutter
the boys were merely choristers. He saw that they became
expert singers and sight readers; he also made them learn
to play the clavier and the violin, but he was not interested
in their general education, and they received no instruction in musical theory. Sepperl lacked any encouragement
or help in his groping attempts at composition. Once Reut-

[1] There were two Viennese composers of this name. Georg
Reutter, the father (1656–1738), was choir director of St. Stephen's and court organist. His son, J. A. Karl Georg (1708–
1772), was Haydn's teacher. It is not always easy to distinguish
between the compositions of the father and those of the son.
See Norbert Hofer, "Die beiden Reutter als Kirchenkompo-
nisten," a thesis manuscript (Vienna, 1915)

ter found him writing a *Salve Regina* in twelve parts, for at
that time the boy thought that to write good music he had
only to fill a page with plenty of notes. The Kapellmeister
merely laughed mockingly and exclaimed: "Oh, you silly
child, aren't two parts enough for you?" But he made no
attempt to show Sepperl how to work out these two parts,
contenting himself with advising the boy to arrange the
motets he sang in church. The diligent, ambitious lad must
certainly have followed his teacher's advice, but it is doubtful that Reutter ever deigned to correct his efforts. Haydn
said later that he had had no more than two lessons from
the Kapellmeister during the many years he stayed with
Reutter, who could have taught him so much.

The younger Reutter was, in fact, a very fertile and
experienced composer. His music was distinguished by
brilliance, harmonic richness, and excellent instrumentation. Burney, it is true, characterized his work by the terse
comment, "great noise and little meaning," but even if
this opinion (which was by no means shared by the Viennese public) was correct, Reutter's good workmanship
could have been of immense help to young Haydn. The
fact that the Kapellmeister did not choose to give such assistance was not because of any animosity toward Haydn;
he was simply too busy. Ambition and continual lack of
money turned him into that unpleasant type of man who
accumulates appointments as a confirmed pluralist. In 1731
he became court composer, seven years later conductor at
St. Stephen's, and thus head of the choir school. These two
positions should have been sufficient, but Reutter, who was
knighted in 1740 by the Emperor Charles VI, succeeded
in also being appointed second court conductor in 1747. A
fourth job was added in 1756. In addition to its main ensemble of vocalists and instrumentalists, St. Stephen's had
a special band and choir that performed in a smaller chapel
adorned with a miraculous painting of the Virgin which
was said to shed real tears. Reutter was not satisfied until
he became leader of this ensemble as well. Thereafter he
managed, by intrigue and clever handling of the persons
responsible, still further to consolidate his position at court,
until he was appointed first court conductor in 1759. It

was difficult, of course, for one man to fill so many offices well and as he was naturally more interested in his duties at court, he neglected St. Stephen's. C. F. Pohl[2] quotes a reprimand of the city council that "the church music was becoming worse and worse, thus leading to inattention and even disgust instead of gracious Christian edification." Reutter's income from various sources must have been considerable, and to it was added the unusually high salary of thirty-five hundred florins paid to his wife, the excellent court singer Therese Holzhauser. Even so, he kept the boy choristers on the shortest possible rations.

Lack of a thorough musical education, however, did not mean lack of work for the boys, and therein lay Haydn's salvation. The choristers' duties were very heavy; they had to take part every day in two full choral services (High Mass and Vespers), besides innumerable extra appearances on feast days, especially during Holy Week, and at festivities, private academies, funerals, processions, and even in Latin shows given by the Jesuits.[3] Reutter's double duties brought, as a great advantage, repeated invitations to court, where the singers of St. Stephen's and the court chapel joined forces. The practical musical knowledge that the impressionable boy derived from these various performances was enormous. He became thoroughly acquainted with the sacred music of such contemporary composers as Caldara, Fux, Reutter, Tuma, Ziani, Palotta, and Bonno, and he also heard many secular works. According to Johann Friedrich Rochlitz, Haydn once said: "Proper teachers I have never had. I always started right away with the practical side, first in singing and in playing instruments, later in composition. I listened more than I studied, but I heard the finest music in all forms that was to be heard in my time, and of this there was much in Vienna. Oh, so

[2] *Joseph Haydn* (Leipzig, 1878–1882), Vol. I, p. 41.
[3] The *Wiener Diarium* mentions a performance in the Jesuits' Theater on December 16, 1743, when a Latin drama on the Emperor Constantine with music by Reutter was performed by a cast of two hundred, including the pupils of the Jesuit College, St. Stephen's, and other institutions. The show was attended by the Empress Maria Theresia and the highest nobility and clergy.

much! I listened attentively and tried to turn to good account what most impressed me. Thus little by little my knowledge and my ability were developed."[4]

In addition to these rich musical impressions, baroque Vienna offered many thrilling sights. Young Haydn would certainly not have shared the opinion of Lady Mary Wortley Montagu, who in 1716 wrote from Vienna: "The processions I see very often are a pageantry, as offensive, and apparently contradictory to all common sense, as the pagodas of China."[5] He was too much of an Austrian and a Catholic to be anything but elated by the lavish display of color and sound on festive occasions. One unforgettable experience was the jubilee of Vienna's cardinal archbishop Sigismund von Kollonicz in 1749 to celebrate the fiftieth year of his priesthood, when an enormous procession of clergy and dignitaries marched solemnly into the cathedral, which was lighted by myriads of candles. Archbishops, bishops, and prelates assisted at High Mass, all dressed in the most ornate robes and carrying gorgeous wreaths on their arms. Cardinal Kollonicz' wreath was of pure gold, a present from the Empress Maria Theresia, and the chalice he used was adorned by a magnificent wreath wrought in silver, a gift from the Queen of Portugal. The imperial family was carried to the building in golden sedan chairs and accompanied by the Knights of the Golden Fleece, the ambassadors, and the high nobility, all resplendent in robes of gold and silver encrusted with precious stones.[6] Surely such magnificence must have made any pageant that Sepperl had seen in Hainburg seem mean in comparison.

In connection with such processions, the boys from St. Stephen's frequently took part in outdoor performances. Thus, in honor of St. John, music was performed on brilliantly illuminated boats lying in the Danube Canal opposite the saint's statue, while on St. Nepomuk's Day an evening performance of a Reutter oratorio was given on

[4] *Für Freunde der Tonkunst* (1832), IV, p. 274.
[5] See the letters of Lady Mary Wortley Montagu in Everyman's Library (1906).
[6] See *Wiener Diarium* (1749).

the beautifully decorated Vienna "High Bridge" in the presence of a distinguished audience.

Young Haydn greatly enjoyed outings of any kind, for in spite of the beauty of St. Stephen's, its atmosphere could at times be oppressive. Sepperl had the natural craving of any healthy boy for exercise and fun, and even the very rigid discipline of the *Cantorei* did not prevent him from breaking loose occasionally. Once the choir was ordered to sing before the Empress Maria Theresia at her newly erected castle of Schönbrunn. The scaffolding had not yet been removed, and what was more natural than for the boys to climb on it with shouts of delight and laughter? Angrily the empress appeared at a window and commanded the noisy group to get down immediately, threatening a good thrashing to anyone seen there again. The next day Joseph could not resist the temptation. Alone he climbed to the top and was duly observed by the empress, who instantly ordered the Kapellmeister to give this "fairhaired blockhead" the proposed punishment.

Not often, however, did Joseph displease Her Majesty. Usually she was well satisfied with his execution of important solos, which she was qualified to judge, being herself, like most of the Habsburgs, a well-trained musician. (It was reported that her beautiful singing made the famous male contralto Senesino burst into tears.) Altogether, young Haydn, during his first years at St. Stephen's, was very successful, though he never created a sensation. Again, as at Hainburg, he was too busy, and too interested in everything to be unhappy. But from 1745 on, things seemed to grow steadily worse. Slowly the voice of the boy approaching puberty began to deteriorate. This became all the more noticeable as a newcomer had joined St. Stephen's choir school, a fine soprano with the remarkable compass of three octaves. This voice belonged to Joseph's brother, Michael,[7] who had joined the *Cantorei* in 1745 at the age of eight. At first Joseph was delighted to have a member of his family with him and felt very proud when

---

[7] Johann Michael Haydn, a gifted composer in his own right, was born on September 14, 1737, at Rohrau. Cf. Hans Jančik, *Michael Haydn* (Vienna, 1952).

he was ordered to instruct his younger brother in various
subjects. Michael showed outstanding gifts and seemed
even more brilliant than Joseph. He learned rapidly, and
before long he played the organ so well that for the payment of a few pennies he acted as deputy for the cathedral's organist. He also showed initiative by organizing
among his schoolmates a club for the detection of plagia-
rism in their own compositions. We do not know what
Joseph's feelings were, for he was not the man to dilate on
such personal matters to his biographers. It seems highly
unlikely, however, that his "pleasure" in Michael's presence, mentioned by the contemporary writers, could have
persisted when his young brother snatched all the laurels
from him. Joseph was given no more solos after the empress had complained about his "crowing like a cock";
instead they were entrusted to Michael. In point of fact,
Michael earned from the imperial couple applause such as
had never been given to Joseph. It was customary for the
empress to celebrate annually the festival of St. Leopold,
the patron saint of Lower Austria, in the magnificent
nearby monastery of Klosterneuburg. In 1748, when the
imperial chapel, enlarged by St. Stephen's choir, had the
task of executing the music for this festive occasion, Michael sang a *Salve Regina* so admirably that the emperor
and empress received the boy in a special audience, compli-
mented him, and gave him twenty-four golden ducats.
Asked by Reutter what he would do with such a fortune,
Michael answered: "Half of it I'll send my father, who has
just lost a cow. The other half please keep for me until my
voice breaks too." Reutter agreed, but he never bothered
to give the money back.

According to Haydn's pupil, Ignaz Pleyel, Reutter, noticing Joseph's distress about his breaking voice, hinted
that there was a means of preserving the fine quality of
his singing. Quite a few castrati still had good positions in
the imperial chapel, and Joseph could imitate their example if he would submit to castration. Fortunately, Mathias
Haydn, hearing about this plan, rushed to Vienna to put
a stop to any such project.

More and more Joseph Haydn became useless to St.

Stephen's as a singer. Had Reutter bestowed any thought on the welfare of the boy who for nine years had given him such valuable service, he might of course have employed him as a violinist until his voice had regained its strength. But Reutter was no sentimentalist and did not have a good memory of promises given long before to anxious parents. On the other hand, Joseph himself made no suggestions. Was it shyness or lack of initiative that kept him waiting dumbly for the inescapable catastrophe? Or did the instinct of genius prompt him to give up the familiar routine of life at the *Cantorei* and try for something entirely new? The latter seems more likely, though the boy himself may not have been conscious of such tendencies. He spent his days in great unhappiness, and it must have been a relief when at last the blow fell. A pretext was provided by none other than the victim himself. Joseph, always keen on playing practical jokes, could not resist testing a new pair of scissors by cutting off the pigtail of a fellow chorister. When Reutter heard about it, he exclaimed: "You will be caned on the hand." Joseph, seventeen years old, thought such punishment unbearable and rashly cried: "I would rather leave the *Cantorei* than be caned." This was the opportunity for which Reutter had been waiting. "Of course you will be expelled," he answered, "after you have been caned." And so it happened. On a cold November day in 1749, Haydn, with three ragged shirts and a worn coat as his sole possessions, without money, without any recommendation, was turned out into the street to fight for his existence.

CHAPTER 3

"MAKING SOMETHING OUT OF NOTHING"

1750–1759

The writers of the eighteenth century are full of praise of Vienna as a musical center. Dr. Burney, after visiting it in 1772, wrote: "Vienna is so rich in composers, and incloses within its walls such a number of musicians of superior merit, that it is but just to allow it to be, among German cities, the imperial seat of music, as well as of power." And the Prussian court conductor, J. F. Reichardt, declared: "The court made music with passion and the Austrian nobility was perhaps the most musical that ever existed." The Empress Maria Theresia, following a firmly established tradition in the Habsburg family, was enormously interested in music and the stage. Although not a composer herself, as were many of her ancestors,[1] and in her struggle for the very existence of her empire unable to spend money for music as lavishly as her predecessors did, she saw to it that artists of the very first rank were invited to Vienna and engaged for academies and festive occasions at court. The high nobility of the country followed the example of the imperial dynasty. They vied with each other in establishing their own excellent orchestras. The academies, such as those which Prince Joseph Friedrich von Hildburghausen arranged with his own band

[1] Ferdinand III, Leopold I, Joseph I, and Karl VI all composed sacred music, while Maria Theresia once jokingly called herself the oldest virtuoso in Europe because her father had made her sing on the stage when she was but five years old. See Burney, *The Present State of Music in Germany,* . . . (London, 1773–1775), I, 206 et seq.

in the exquisite palace built by the great architect Johann Fischer von Erlach, were of the very highest standard.

From 1750 onward the middle class also began to become more interested in music. Public concerts were inaugurated, following the model of the Paris Concerts Spirituels, and before long they enjoyed great popularity. The love of the Viennese for spectacles found satisfaction in its two theaters, the Theater nächst der Burg, in which mainly opera was played, and the Theater nächst dem Kärntnerthor, which concentrated on German and French plays. Under the Habsburgs, Vienna became a center of the reigning Italian opera of Naples. On the other hand, the city was also the first to witness, in 1762, the birth of Gluck's musical drama. Great attention was also given to the art of the ballet, which was to achieve in this century a summit of perfection under the great ballet master Noverre. Such native composers as Fux, Wagenseil, Dittersdorf, Reutter, and Starzer added a specifically Austrian touch to the colorful picture of Vienna's music culture during the reign of Maria Theresia.

Bearing all this in mind, one might be inclined to regard as fortunate any young and gifted musician ambitious to make his way in Vienna of 1749. Surely, one would think, some one of the aristocratic music lovers who spent such enormous sums on the cultivation of this passion must have discovered young Haydn's talent and given him the opportunity to develop it. In reality nothing of the kind happened. Haydn, as he bitterly complained in his autobiographical sketch, "had to eke out a wretched existence for eight whole years" before his luck began to change. The reasons for this predicament are clear enough. When he left St. Stephen's, he did not play any instrument more than moderately well (even on the violin, his favorite, he was, as he said, not "a conjuror"), his voice for the time being was nonexistent, and his compositions were groping attempts lacking any theoretical foundation. He was miserably dressed, unattractive in appearance, and on account of his secluded life in the *Cantorei*, unused to the great world and therefore shy and uncouth. What could such a destitute young musician do? Scholarships did not exist in the eighteenth century. Help from his family was neither given nor expected.[2] His parents might have considered assisting him if Joseph had followed his mother's ardent desire and taken holy orders. The young man, however, for all his innate faith and the strong ties that bound him to the Catholic Church, never seriously considered this possibility. With the tenacity that had made his grandfather Lorenz Koller rebuild his house again and again after each devastation, young Haydn clung to his intention. He wanted to be a musician—not merely a mediocre performer, but a real composer. Therefore the position of a musical valet, which was very common in the eighteenth century, when a footman had to be able to play in his master's chamber music,[3] made no appeal to and was not sought by him. It would take up too much of his time and not bring about the artistic development for which he craved. On the other hand, Haydn fully realized how sadly unprepared he was for the career he had chosen. He needed a good teacher of theory, or at least sufficient time for self-instruction. There seemed only one way open to him: to support himself by odd musical jobs and to spend all the time and energy he had left on the improvement of his musical knowledge. It was a long and tortuous way, a way filled with privations, but it led him to his ultimate goal.

When the young musician left St. Stephen's in November 1749, he did not even know where to spend the night. At this critical point he was first helped, characteristically enough, by one who himself was not much better off. As he wandered desperately through the chilly streets, Haydn chanced upon a man he knew slightly, Johann Michael Spangler, a singer in the Church of St. Michael and a private teacher. When Spangler heard of Joseph's misfor-

[2] Just at the most critical time, Haydn's parents had to use all their resources to provide a dowry for their eldest daughter, Franziska, who married the baker J. Vieltzwiser on February 8, 1750.

[3] A typical advertisement in the *Wiener Zeitung* (1789) states: "Wanted by nobleman a servant who plays the violin well and is able to accompany [on his instrument] difficult piano sonatas."

tune he invited him to share the poor garret where he lived with his wife and a baby boy nine months old. The homeless lad accepted this generous offer with relief. A roof was found, and now he had only to earn his food (for here the impecunious singer was unable to help). Slowly Joseph began to make connections. He played at dances, he made arrangements of compositions for various instruments, he took pupils for miserably small fees. Most of all, he went *gassatim*, which means that he took part in serenades. Like Italy, old Austria had a great fondness for open-air music at night, and many musicians were needed to fill the continuous demand. An eighteenth-century Viennese almanac[4] gives a lively description of this custom:

On fine summer nights you may come upon serenades in the streets at all hours. They are not, as in Italy, a mere matter of a singer and a guitar. Here serenades are not meant for declarations of love, for which the Viennese have better opportunities. Such night music may be given to a trio or a quartet of wind instruments, and works of some extent may be played. The evening before the name day of some fair lady will produce a lot of this kind of entertainment; and however late a serenade is given, all windows are soon filled and in a few minutes the musicians are surrounded by an applauding crowd.

Haydn made the best use of this fashion. He earned a little money this way and drew from the rich well of Viennese folk music, which has been a source of inspiration to Mozart, Beethoven, Schubert, Brahms, and many others.

In this way he somehow got through the first difficult months, but he was aware that this state of affairs could not and must not last. In the Spanglers' crowded garret it was impossible for him to undertake the serious studying upon which he was determined. On the other hand, Frau Spangler was expecting another baby, and after its arrival there simply would be no room for him.[5] In the

[4] *Wiener Theater-Almanach* (1794), p. 173.
[5] The child was Maria Magdalena, born September 4, 1750. In 1760 Haydn engaged her as a singer for Prince Esterházy.

spring of 1750, as a temporary escape from his problems,
he joined a party of pilgrims to the miraculous shrine of
the Virgin at Mariazell, a beautifully situated village in
Styria that was, and still is, frequented by crowds of wor-
shipers. By this time, apparently, he was in full command
of his voice, for he introduced himself to the choirmaster,
Father Florian Wrastil, as a former chorister of St. Stephen's
and asked to be admitted to the choir. His shabby appearance did not inspire confidence, and apparently Father
Wrastil had had unfortunate experiences with other traveling musicians; so he rudely sent him away. Thereupon
Haydn stole into the church choir, snatched a vocal
part out of a singer's hand, and sang the solo with
such perfection that "all the choir held their breath to
listen." The choirmaster repented; young Haydn was invited to stay with him for a week. During this time he was
able to enjoy the exquisite, and for him unfamiliar, sensation of getting all the food he wanted. He returned to
Vienna well rested, full of confidence in his ultimate success, and even with a little cash collected from the musicians of Mariazell. Before long this confidence bore fruit.
A tradesman and *Marktrichter* in Vienna (a sort of colleague of Mathias Haydn) by the name of Anton Buchholz
decided to help the young musician to pursue his studies
and lent him unconditionally one hundred and fifty florins,
a sum which must at that time have seemed enormous
to Haydn. In 1801 the composer wrote in his will: "To
Fräulein Anna Buchholz, one hundred florins, inasmuch as
in my youth her grandfather lent me one hundred and
fifty florins when I greatly needed them, which, however,
I repaid fifty years ago." If the date mentioned is correct,
Haydn must have repaid the loan as early as 1751, a year
after he had received it. It seems more likely, however,
that Haydn merely wanted to imply that it had not taken
him long to square his debt. Maybe he was helped in such
attempts by two legacies that came his way in these critical years: seventy-seven florins paid to him as to the other

---

She performed the soprano solo in the first performance of his
Il ritorno di Tobia in 1775. Her husband was Haydn's good
friend, the tenor Karl Friberth.

five Haydn children on the death of his mother in 1754, and sixty-one florins on the death of his maternal grandmother in 1756.

Now Haydn was in a position to leave the good Spanglers and settle down in a room of his own. He chose, of course, the cheapest place available. It was a garret, partitioned off from a larger room, in the old Michaelerhaus near Vienna's ancient Romanesque Church of St. Michael. His neighbors in the attic were a cook, a journeyman printer, a footman, and a house-stoker who tended the fires in the house of some wealthy man. To all outward appearances the new lodgings were anything but pleasant. Indeed, Haydn's early biographers did their utmost to stress the hardships he endured there. Karl Bertuch wrote: "He lived on the sixth story, and his room in the garret had neither stove nor window; in winter his breath froze on his coverlet, and the water that he fetched himself from the spring in the morning for washing was frequently changed into lumps of ice before his arrival in these elevated regions."[6] Such drawbacks were, however, of no great consequence to a youth like Haydn. Here he was, as he said, "too happy to envy the lot of kings," for he had at last the privacy he craved for his studies and he was the proud owner of an "old, worm-eaten clavier." His Mass in F major, written at the beginning of the 1750s, reflects this state of mind, but also shows his artistic immaturity. Haydn now set about to fill the big gaps in his theoretical knowledge. He devoured Johann Joseph Fux's famous *Gradus ad Parnassum*, Johann Mattheson's *Der vollkommene Kapellmeister*, and David Kellner's *Unterricht im Generalbass*. The copies he used have been preserved, and their numerous annotations reveal the passion with which young Haydn threw himself into the study of these subjects.

Perhaps even more important than these manuals was his discovery of the first six keyboard sonatas by Philipp Emanuel Bach, which opened a new world to him. "I did not leave the clavier," he said to Dies, "until I had mastered them all," and to Rochlitz he remarked: "Innumera-

[6] See *Journal des Luxus und der Moden* (Weimar, 1805).

ble times I played them for my own delight, especially when I felt oppressed and discouraged by worries and always I left the instrument gay and in high spirits."[7]

One of the reasons for Haydn's reactions was the strong emotional appeal emanating from the works of the "Hamburg Bach." Up to then he had been familiar with the gay and superficial idiom of the musical rococo; here he found compositions that deeply stirred and excited him. "Who knows me well," he was later to remark, "must have found out that I owe a great deal to Emanuel Bach, that I have understood and diligently studied him." As a matter of fact, no other composer except Mozart influenced him as much as the north-German master.

But while the works of Philipp Emanuel Bach opened new vistas to the young musician, it was only natural for him to maintain connection with Austrian folk music, and in 1752 this resulted in his first dramatic attempt. The story is best told in the words of Bombet—Stendhal[8]—based on the report of Haydn's friend Giuseppe Carpani:

> Haydn composed for his amusement, a serenata for three instruments, which he performed with two of his friends in different parts of Vienna. The Kärntnerthor-theater was at that time directed by Kurz-Bernardon, a celebrated harlequin who amused the public with his puns and drew crowds to the theater by his originality. He had, moreover, a handsome wife; and this was an additional reason for our nocturnal adventurers to perform their serenade under the harlequin's window. Bernardon was so struck with the originality of the music that he came down into the street to ask who had composed it. "I did," replied Haydn boldly. "Come upstairs." Haydn followed the comedian, was

[7] Rochlitz, *Für Freunde der Tonkunst* (1832), IV, p. 274. Rochlitz was in personal contact with Haydn.

[8] In 1814 Marie-Henri Beyle (writing mostly under the pseudonyms of L.-A.-C. Bombet or Stendhal) published his *Lettres écrites de Vienne, en Autriche, sur le célèbre compositeur, Joseph Haydn.* This was actually a translation, with very slight adaptations, of Carpani's *Le Haydine* (1812). It was translated into English in 1817, and an American edition appeared in 1839.

introduced to the handsome wife, and redescended
with the libretto of an opera, entitled *The Limping
Devil* [*Der krumme Teufel*]. The music, composed in
a few days, had a brilliant success. But a nobleman,
who probably was not handsome, suspected that he
was being ridiculed under the name of the "Limping
Devil" and caused the piece to be prohibited. Haydn
often said that he had had more trouble in devising
a mode of representing the motion of the waves in a
tempest shown in this opera than he afterward had in
writing fugues with a double subject. Bernardon, who
had spirit and taste, was difficult to please and there
was also another obstacle. Neither of the two authors
had ever seen either sea or storm. How can a man
describe what he knows nothing about? Bernardon,
all agitation, paced up and down, while the composer
was seated at the harpsichord. "Imagine," said he,
"a mountain rising and then a valley sinking, and then
another mountain and another valley; the mountains
and the valleys follow rapidly one after the other."
This fine description was of no avail and in vain did
the actor add thunder and lightning. At last, young
Haydn, out of all patience, extended his hands to the
two ends of the harpsichord, and bringing them in a
glissando rapidly together, he exclaimed: "The devil
take the tempest!" "That's it, that's it," cried the har-
lequin, springing upon his neck and almost stifling
him. Many years later when Haydn crossed the Straits
of Dover in bad weather, he laughed during the whole
of the passage, remembering the storm in *The Limping Devil*.

While most of the lessons Haydn gave were just "a
miserable mode of earning daily bread," one played an important part in his career. As luck would have it, there
lived on the third floor of the old Michaelerhaus the great
Italian writer, Pietro Metastasio, poet laureate of the Habsburgs since 1730 and author of numerous operatic librettos
that were set to music by a greater number of operatic

composers than those of any other librettist. According
to Dr. Burney, who was Metastasio's first biographer, the
Italian poet's writings "contributed more to the refine-
ment of vocal melody, and consequently of music in general, than the joint efforts of all the great composers in
Europe." The great man shared his apartment with the
family of a Spanish friend, Nicolò de Martinez, and was
greatly interested in the education of his two daughters.
In particular the elder one, Marianne (born on May 4,
1744), was the apple of his eye, and he bestowed the
greatest care on the development of her outstanding musical talent. Somehow Metastasio must have noticed Haydn.
Perhaps in quiet nights the sounds of the clavier on which
the young man was improvising penetrated from the miserable garret down to Metastasio's elegant apartment. He
decided to engage the unknown youth as piano teacher for
Marianne, then ten years old. For three years Haydn
worked daily with the girl, receiving free board in exchange for his labors, and there is no doubt that he learned
a great deal himself while studying with so unusual a
pupil, whose subsequent achievements as pianist, singer,
and composer earned her election to the famous Philharmonic Academy of Bologna and were praised by all Viennese musicians. (Even Mozart played piano duets with
her.)[9] Besides, Haydn was naturally brought into contact
with the gentle Metastasio, whose "simplicity and deco-
rum" (Burney) may have exercised a good influence on
the young teacher's demeanor. The lessons with Marianne
had, moreover, another result of still greater importance.
She received singing instruction from the famous Italian
composer and singing teacher Niccolò Porpora, who lived
in Vienna from 1753 to 1757. Haydn acted as accompanist in these lessons, and thus had the good fortune to
meet the "patriarch of melody." Porpora was then seventy

[9] As a mature master Haydn still maintained contact with
Marianne Martinez. They both appear in an album belonging
to Mozart's pupil Babette Ployer. Haydn wrote into it the canon
he had composed for Oxford University; Marianne contributed
an Italian canzonetta. Cf. R. Tenschert, "Frauen um Haydn"
(Vienna, 1946).

years old, and had probably forgotten his own early struggles, about which Carpani tells the following amusing
story:

In the time of Charles VI [father of Maria The-
resia], the celebrated Porpora lived at Vienna, poor
and unemployed. His music did not please the imperial connoisseur, being too full of trills and mordents.
Hasse wrote an oratorio for the emperor, who asked
him for a second. He entreated His Majesty to permit Porpora to execute it. The emperor at first refused
saying that he did not like that capering style; but,
touched by Hasse's generosity, he at length complied
with his request. Porpora, having received a hint from
his friend, did not introduce a single trill into the
whole oratorio. The emperor, surprised, continually
repeated during the rehearsal: "It is quite a different
man; here are no trills!" But when they came to the
fugue, which concluded the sacred composition, he
observed that the theme began with four trilled notes.
Now you know that in fugues the subject passes from
one part to another, but does not change. When the
emperor, who was said never to laugh, heard in the
full height of the fugue this deluge of trills, which
seemed like the music of some enraged paralytic, he
could no longer maintain his gravity, and laughed,
perhaps for the first time in his life. It was the beginning of Porpora's fortune.

Those days were passed, and now Porpora was "sour
beyond all that can be imagined" (Carpani). This did not
deter Haydn. Here was an excellent teacher within his
grasp and he did not mean to let the opportunity slip
away. He asked for permission to become Porpora's accompanist in order to study his method, and in exchange
he offered menial service. Porpora accepted and took
Haydn to the fashionable baths of Mannersdorf, where
they were both to stay in the house of the Venetian ambassador, Pietro Correr, whose mistress was Porpora's devoted pupil. In this favorite summer resort Haydn seems
to have met various prominent composers like Gluck,

Wagenseil, and Bonno and attended the academies of the Prince of Hildburghausen. He was, however, much more interested in the "old bear," whom he served diligently, "cleaning his shoes, beating his coat, and arranging his antique periwig." The treatment he received was not very good, for the choleric Italian was quite fluent with his tongue and active with his hand, but Haydn did not really resent being called a "blockhead" or a "beast" or receiving sundry cuffs as long as Porpora was willing to correct his valet's compositions. When he left the maestro, after three months, he had improved enormously in singing and in Italian, which he could write in later years nearly as well as German, and had learned, as he said, "the genuine fundamentals of composition."

While Joseph was thus acting as a valet to Porpora, his brother Michael was treading the path toward a successful career. Just as he had outshone Joseph at St. Stephen's, so now he seemed to show more ability than his elder brother. After leaving the Vienna cathedral and eking out his existence by odd jobs as his brother was doing, he was engaged, at the age of twenty, as conductor to the Bishop of Grosswardein in Hungary. Joseph must have felt deeply impressed and somewhat shaken when he heard this news, for he remembered only too well in what utter poverty he had lived when he was twenty. Even now, five years later, he had nothing to show his father that could match Michael's success. Considerations of this kind, however, did not really discourage him. They only strengthened his determination to persevere; and though he could not display visible proofs of success, he felt that he was steadily climbing upward, that he was, in his own words, "making something out of nothing."[10] Slowly he began to gain admission to the only circle in eighteenth-century Vienna that could assure a composer's fortune, that of the nobility. The charming Countess Thun, after coming across one of Haydn's sonatas, wanted to meet the composer, about whom she probably had heard from her relative,

[10] According to Dies, Haydn said once: "Young people can learn from my example that something can come out of nothing. What I am is all the result of the direst need."

Count Harrach, the lord of Rohrau, in whose castle Haydn played chamber music on occasional visits to his native village.[11] When Joseph first stood before her, she was somewhat shocked by his appearance. Could this under-sized, dark-complexioned youth with a face pitted by small-pox, a large aquiline nose, and legs too short for his body, really be the creator of such lovely and graceful tunes? But a closer inspection revealed a noble forehead and dark gray eyes sparkling with humor and kindness which somehow made the countess forget the young man's gen-eral ugliness, awkward manners, and shabby clothes. When she had made sure that she was not being tricked by an impostor, Countess Philippine Aloysia Thun began to study the clavier and singing with Haydn. This meant a decisive step forward as the Thun family, thanks to their good relations to the leading musicians of the time, could do a great deal for a young unknown composer. We can imagine what zeal Haydn displayed in the instruction of his high-born pupil and it seems likely that he was successful. Perhaps the Countess' recommendation helped him to estab-lish another important contact. He was invited by the ardent music lover Karl Joseph von Fürnberg, to his country home, Weinzierl, to take part in chamber music performances. Haydn spent a delightful time in the hospitable little castle, charmingly situated in a hilly country and offering a splen-did view of mountains six thousand feet high. There three other musicians joined him: his host's steward, the local pastor, and the violoncellist Albrechtsberger (not identical with the famous teacher of Beethoven, but possibly related to him). For this group Haydn wrote his first string quartets, which were received with so much praise in Fürnberg's circle that he was encouraged to continue along this line.

From this time on, Haydn's situation improved con-tinually. The number of his pupils grew,[12] he raised his

[11] Cf. L. Nowak, *Joseph Haydn*, 2d ed. (Vienna, 1959), p. 82.

[12] Among them were Abund Mikysch, choral director of the Brothers of Mercy, and Father Robert Kimmerling, of the Bene-

fees, and other engagements filled his time. He worked from sixteen to eighteen hours a day. "At daybreak he took the part of first violin at the church of the Fathers of the Order of Mercy;[13] thence he repaired to the chapel of Count Haugwitz, where he played the organ; at a later hour he sang the tenor part at St. Stephen's; and last, having been on foot the whole day, he passed a part of the night at the harpsichord" (Carpani). And so it went on from day to day.

At last he was able to harvest the fruits of such concentration. In 1758, Fürnberg recommended him to the Bohemian Count Ferdinand Maximilian von Morzin and Haydn was engaged as music director and *Kammercompositeur*. Not only socially, but also financially this was a great step forward. Now he was paid two hundred florins a year, besides receiving free board and lodging. Both the count and his wife, the beautiful Countess Wilhelmine, were great lovers of music. They had their own orchestra of about sixteen musicians which played in the winter in Vienna and in the summer at Lukaveč, their country house in Bohemia. The new responsibilities paved the way for Haydn toward a great artistic development. It was at Lukaveč that his first symphony was composed and its performance earned him great applause. Haydn, conducting it in the traditional way from the harpsichord, had no idea that at this moment his fate was being decided for the following thirty years. Among the audience sat a man who thought it worthwhile to make note of the name of this young composer. He was the Prince Paul Anton Esterházy.

---

dictine order, subsequently connected with the Monastery of Melk. Cf. Nowak, op. cit., p. 125.

[13] According to Griesinger, he received for this work a yearly salary of sixty florins.

CHAPTER 4

THE HONORABLE OFFICIAL OF
A PRINCELY HOUSE

1760–1766

Very little is known about Haydn's life with Count
Morzin, but one little episode mentioned by Griesinger is
not without significance. The countess was a good singer
and it was Haydn's duty to accompany her on the piano.
Once, while she was leaning over him to look more closely
into the music, her neckerchief became unfolded, whereupon Haydn stopped playing, as if struck by lightning.
Reprimanded by the fair countess, he exclaimed naïvely,
"But, Your Highness, who would not lose his head over
this?" There can be no doubt that the composer's interest
in the fair sex began to develop much more strongly once
he had outgrown his artistic apprenticeship and gained a
modest foothold on the social ladder. He felt that the time
had come to consider marriage seriously. The events leading to this fateful step are unfortunately rather obscure
and contemporary statements contradict each other. The
only fact established beyond doubt is that Haydn did not
marry the girl of his choice. Among his pupils in Vienna
were the daughters of a hairdresser, Johann Peter Keller.
Haydn fell in love with one of these girls, but his feelings
were apparently not reciprocated and Therese, whose family was deeply religious, entered the Convent of St.
Nicholas of the Order of the Clares under the name of
Sister Josepha. For the ceremony of her profession, Haydn
offered an organ concerto in C major. This work as well
as the *Salve Regina* of 1756, possibly also written for her,
are the earliest compositions extant that bear a date in his
hand. Maybe these youthful works hold a special signifi-

cance for Haydn because of their personal implications and were therefore carefully preserved by him.

Haydn did not stop visiting the Keller family, and when he entered the service of Count Morzin and his financial position was much improved, the hairdresser naturally tried to secure the promising young artist for another member of the family. There was an elder daughter, thirty-one years old and so much less attractive than Therese that there seemed little prospect of her entering the state of holy matrimony. We do not know what pressure the Kellers brought to bear on Haydn, but unfortunately they succeeded, and the composer took a wife who was probably the most unsuitable life partner that he could have chosen. His blindness and passivity are hard to understand, for it is known that he was a keen judge of human nature, and many recorded facts prove his skill and shrewdness in dealing with other people. It seems most likely he was prompted by reasons similar to those that Mozart expressed in a letter to his father before he married. Mozart had suffered a fate not very different from Haydn's. After falling passionately in love with the singer, Aloysia Weber, and being jilted by this "false coquette," Mozart felt induced to marry her sister Constanze. Here is the explanation he gave to his father:

> The voice of nature speaks as loud in me as in others, louder perhaps, than in many a big strong lout of a fellow. I cannot possibly live as do most young men in these days. In the first place, I have too much religion; in the second place, I have too great a love for my neighbor, and am too honorably minded to seduce an innocent maiden; while in the third place, I have too much care for my health. . . . I can think of nothing more necessary to my disposition than a wife, inclined as I am to quiet domesticity more than to revelry. A bachelor, in my opinion, is only half alive.[1]

Haydn, too, felt that he needed marriage, and the partner herself did not seem of such great importance to him

[1] Letter of December 15, 1781.

now that the one who really mattered was inaccessible. So, though Maria Anna Aloysia Apollonia was three years his senior, not good-looking, not pleasant, and not interested in music, he married her on November 26, 1760. In so doing he made a disastrous mistake—possibly the greatest mistake of his life. He expected marriage to provide him with a comfortable, peaceful home and with children, for whom he felt a great fondness. Neither of these hopes was fulfilled. Maria Anna was quarrelsome, jealous, bigoted, not even a good housekeeper, and Haydn reproached her particularly for being very wasteful. As to progeny, Haydn once remarked to Griesinger: "My wife was unable to bear children, and for this reason I was less indifferent toward the attractions of other women." What irritated him most, however, was his wife's utter lack of appreciation of his work. "She doesn't care a straw whether her husband is an artist or a cobbler," he exclaimed indignantly. Members of Haydn's orchestra even said that Frau Haydn, out of pure mischief, liked to use the master's manuscript scores as linings for her pastry or for curl papers. Hadyn must have felt a diabolical pleasure when he came across the following poem by Lessing, for which he composed a canon:

> If in the whole wide world
> But one mean wife there is,
> How sad that each of us
> Should think this one is his!

It would not be entirely fair to put all the blame for the couple's domestic misery on Frau Haydn, whose position, indeed, was not an easy one. That she was unable to grasp the importance of her husband's creative work was, after all, not her fault. She was not made that way, and if Haydn had tried to know her better before their marriage, he would have found that music meant nothing to her. In her own peculiar way, Maria Anna may have been fond of her husband. It is known, for instance, that she cared so much for a certain portrait of Haydn by Ludwig Guttenbrunn that she brought it with her when taking the cure at Baden and did not want to part with it even when it was required for copying. Haydn, it must be admitted, interpreted her behavior in a less flattering way, declaring that the reason his wife liked the picture so much was because Guttenbrunn had once been her lover. Be that as it may, unless she was quite indifferent toward her husband, Frau Haydn must have suffered agonies of jealousy throughout her married life. She could not forget that Haydn had cared deeply for her younger and prettier sister. That she was right in this respect is proved by the fact that as late as 1801 he remembered his first love in his will.[2] Quite apart from that, the sight of her husband, whose inflammable nature she knew, working constantly with the attractive singers of his ensemble was not easy for this plain woman to bear. The difference between their ages further aggravated the situation. Haydn, who had developed with extreme slowness, was unusually young for his age, while Frau Haydn, according to the views of the time, felt and behaved like an elderly matron while still in her middle thirties. The way each of them spent money proved to be another source of irritation. Frau Haydn may have been as much annoyed at her husband's supporting scores of his poor relatives as he was at his wife's liberality toward the clergy. There is no doubt that in this unhappy union both partners suffered deeply. Frau Haydn found consolation in her church, to which she gave freely of her love and devotion. Haydn, deprived of the comforts of a cheerful home, put all the forces of his being into the service of his art.

Soon after the marriage, at the very time when Haydn became aware of his fatal error, all his energies fortunately were required to cope with a new situation. Count Morzin found himself in financial difficulties and decided to give up his expensive orchestra. Haydn was left with-

[2] He describes her as "ex-nun." In the course of Emperor Joseph II's reform activities, the St. Nicholas convent had been dissolved and Josepha forced to return to secular life. As we learn from the last will of Haydn's wife, who also left her sister a legacy, the latter had become engaged in social work for the poor.

out a position, though not for long. Prince Paul Anton Esterházy, hearing of Morzin's troubles, remembered Haydn's charming symphony, and realized that now he could secure this musician for his court at Eisenstadt. As he already had a conductor, old Gregorius Joseph Werner, Prince Esterházy offered the young composer the post of assistant conductor. Haydn accepted with enthusiasm.

Here was a patron of infinitely greater importance than Count Morzin. The Esterházys stood at the very top of the powerful Hungarian nobility. They were the oldest and wealthiest magnates of the country and had the longest record of zeal in the promotion of music and the fine arts. The first member of the family of barons to be raised to the rank of Prince of the Holy Roman Empire had been Paul (1635–1713), who, a staunch supporter of the House of Habsburg, was largely instrumental in promulgating the law that made the Austrian monarch hereditary King of Hungary. Paul was a great Maecenas. He acquired a magnificent picture gallery for his castle of Forchtenstein and established his own band of music in his residence at Eisenstadt. He was also a composer, and in 1711 published a series of church hymns with orchestra written for all the holidays of the ecclesiastical year. The grand scale on which he liked to organize his enterprises is clearly illustrated by the account of a pilgrimage that he had his subjects make to the shrine at Mariazell in 1692. It consisted of no less than 11,200 persons, who walked for six days, among them members of the high nobility, clergy in ornate robes, girls with golden crowns on their heads, musicians, and banner bearers. Under Prince Paul's reign the splendid castle of Eisenstadt was erected. In this magnificent baroque building with proud towers at the four corners there were no less than two hundred rooms for guests and a beautiful reception hall adorned with frescoes. The building also contained a chapel, a library, and a picture collection (which was acquired in 1860 by the Hungarian State and served as basis for the Budapest Museum of Fine Arts). Great care was given to the planning of the immense park surrounding the castle and it abounded in artificial waterfalls, ponds, grottoes, and beautiful trees.[3]

Prince Paul's successors continued the tradition established by this Maecenas, at the same time consolidating their enormous wealth. (At the beginning of this century the Esterházy estate comprised twenty-nine lordships, with twenty-one castles, sixty market towns, and four hundred and fourteen villages in Hungary alone, besides several lordships in Lower Austria and a county in Bavaria.) Prince Paul Anton (1710–1762) began his reign in 1734. He had a genuine love of music and played the violin and violoncello himself. During his travels through Italy and Germany he had collected a great number of manuscript scores, and he had a detailed catalogue of them made in 1759 by the violinist Champée. His duties at first made it impossible for the prince to plan for the improvement of the Esterházy orchestra, functioning, since 1728, under the leadership of Gregorius Joseph Werner. For some years Paul Anton was ambassador at the Court of Naples, besides taking a very active part in the wars that Austria fought during the reign of Maria Theresia. Twice he supplied his sovereign with a complete and well-equipped regiment of hussars. As a reward, he was given the rank of a field marshal. When at last, at the end of the 1750s, the prince was able to settle down at Eisenstadt, he showed that he had a perfect understanding of what was needed to raise the standard of music-making at his court. New musicians were engaged, among them the excellent tenor Karl Friberth, who was destined to become one of Haydn's great friends, and, one year later, the soprano singer Anna Maria Scheffstoss. The prince's most important act, however, which has awarded him a permanent place in the history of music, was his engagement of Joseph Haydn. The contract was concluded on May 1, 1761, and that interesting document, which has

[3] The park built on the slopes of the Leitha hills was changed several times according to the fashion of the period. In 1754 it was arranged in the style of the gardens at Versailles, while in the nineties of that century it was reorganized in the English fashion.

been preserved in the Esterházy archives, is quoted here in full:

This day (according to the date hereto appended) Joseph Heyden, native of Rohrau in Austria, is accepted and appointed Vice-Kapellmeister in the service of His Serene Highness Paul Anton, Prince of the Holy Roman Empire, of Esterházy and Galantha, etc., subject to conditions here following:

1. Whereas the Kapellmeister at Eisenstadt, namely Gregorius Werner, having devoted many years of true and faithful service to the princely house, is now, on account of his great age and infirmities, unfit to perform the duties incumbent on him, it is hereby declared that the said Gregorius Werner, in consideration of his long services, shall retain the post of Kapellmeister, and the said Joseph Heyden as Vice-Kapellmeister shall, so far as regards the music of the choir, be subordinate to the Kapellmeister and receive his instructions. But in everything else relating to musical performances, and in all that concerns the orchestra, the Vice-Kapellmeister shall have the sole direction.

2. The said Joseph Heyden shall be considered and treated as a member of the household. Therefore His Serene Highness is graciously pleased to place confidence in his conducting himself as becomes an honorable official of a princely house. He must be temperate, not showing himself overbearing toward his musicians, but mild and lenient, straightforward and composed. It is especially to be observed that when the orchestra shall be summoned to perform before company, the Vice-Kapellmeister and all the musicians shall appear in uniform, and the said Joseph Heyden shall take care that he and all the members of his orchestra follow the instructions given, and appear in white stockings, white linen, powdered, and with either a queue or a tiewig.

3. Whereas the other musicians are referred for directions to the said Vice-Kapellmeister, he shall there-

fore take the more care to conduct himself in an exemplary manner, abstaining from undue familiarity and from vulgarity in eating, drinking, and conversation, not dispensing with the respect due to him but acting uprightly and influencing his subordinates to preserve such harmony as is becoming in them, remembering how displeasing the consequences of any discord or dispute would be to His Serene Highness.

4. The said Vice-Kapellmeister shall be under obligation to compose such music as His Serene Highness may command, and neither to communicate such compositions to any other person, nor to allow them to be copied, but he shall retain them for the absolute use of His Highness, and not compose for any other person without the knowledge and permission of His Highness.

5. The said Joseph Heyden shall appear daily in the antechamber before and after midday, and inquire whether His Highness is pleased to order a performance of the orchestra. On receipt of his orders he shall communicate them to the other musicians, and take care to be punctual at the appointed time, and to ensure punctuality in his subordinates, making a note of those who arrive late or absent themselves altogether.

6. Should any quarrel or cause of complaint arise, the Vice-Kapellmeister shall endeavor to arrange it in order that His Serene Highness may not be incommoded with trifling disputes; but should any more serious difficulty occur, which the said Joseph Heyden is unable to set right, His Serene Highness must then be respectfully called upon to decide the matter.

7. The said Vice-Kapellmeister shall take careful charge of all music and musical instruments, and be responsible for any injury that may occur to them from carelessness or neglect.

8. The said Joseph Heyden shall be obliged to instruct the female vocalists, in order that they may not forget in the country what they have been taught with much trouble and expense in Vienna, and, as the said Vice-Kapellmeister is proficient on various in-

struments, he shall take care himself to practice on all that he is acquainted with.

9. A copy of this agreement and instructions shall be given to the said Vice-Kapellmeister and his subordinates, in order that he may be able to hold them to their obligations therein laid down.

10. It is considered unnecessary to detail the services required of the said Joseph Heyden, more particularly since His Serene Highness is pleased to hope that he will of his own free will strictly observe not only these regulations, but all others that may from time to time be made by His Highness, and that he will place the orchestra on such a footing, and in such good order, that he may bring honor upon himself and deserve the further favor of the prince his master, who thus confides in his zeal and discretion.

11. A yearly salary of four hundred florins to be received in quarterly payments is hereby bestowed by His Serene Highness upon the said Vice-Kapellmeister.

12. In addition, the said Joseph Heyden shall board at the officer's table, or receive a half-gulden per day in lieu thereof.

13. Finally, this agreement shall hold good for at least three years from May 1, 1761, with the further condition that if at the conclusion of this term the said Joseph Heyden shall desire to leave the service, he shall give His Highness six months' previous notice of his intention.

14. His Serene Highness undertakes to keep Joseph Heyden in his service during this time, and should he be satisfied with him, he may look forward to being appointed Kapellmeister. This, however, must not be understood to deprive His Serene Highness of the right to dismiss the said Joseph Heyden at the expiration of the term, should he see fit to do so.

Duplicate copies of this document shall be executed and exchanged.

Given at Vienna this first day of May, 1761.

Ad mandatum Celsissimi Principis,

JOHANN STIFFTELL, *Secretary*

The number and variety of the duties expected from Haydn are staggering. No great conductor today has to do one half of what was required of Haydn. Three different spheres of activity were entrusted to him. He was conductor, which meant daily practice with orchestra and singers and very frequent performances; he had to compose a great part of the enormous amount of music performed; finally, he was an important officer of administration, uniting in his person the positions of librarian, supervisor of instruments, and chief of the musical personnel. All this Haydn did, and he performed his duties extremely well. That he succeeded as a composer far beyond Prince Esterházy's fondest hopes need not be emphasized here. As a conductor, playing the violin or the harpsichord, he was outstanding too. There is a humorous report that his face while conducting was so expressive that society snobs who wanted to demonstrate their understanding of music just "dexterously placed themselves in a situation where they could see Haydn and regulate by his smile the ecstatic applause by which they testified to their neighbors the extent of their own rapture." Despite the important duties entrusted to him and despite unceasing creative work, he also found time to carry out tasks of a more practical nature, which he executed with the conscientiousness typical of a descendant of diligent farmers and wheelwrights. He supervised the work of the copyists, occasionally even taking a hand himself, and, according to Griesinger, he liked to tune his own clavier. He also saw to it that old instruments were repaired at the lowest possible cost. As chief of personnel, Haydn revealed his innate tact and good nature and even this part of his duties was performed with a skill not granted to other great composers. (One remembers Handel's fights with the members of his opera company and Bach's difficulties in Leipzig.) Haydn's task was by no means easy and often he had to mediate quarrels among the musicians. The Esterházy archives report, for instance, a settlement between the oboist Zacharias Pohl and the cellist Xaver Marteau[4] con-

4 *Acta Musicalia,* fasc. I, 50; first reproduced by A. Valkó in

cluded in Haydn's presence and doubtless thanks to his intervention. During a brawl in the castle tavern, Marteau had knocked out the oboist's right eye with his ring and now had to undertake to pay Pohl a compensation of forty-nine florins and forty-three kreutzer in monthly install-ments. The act of December 21, 1771, explicitly remarks that the cellist did not inflict damage on the oboist inten-tionally, a remark that reflects the conductor's conciliatory attitude. Altogether the Esterházy archives supply a mov-ing testimonial to Haydn's concern for the welfare of his subordinates. Once[5] he reminded the princely secretary that the cellist Marteau had not been supplied with the firewood, candles, and lodging money the prince had promised Haydn to allow the musician, an oversight that was quickly remedied.

In the year 1774 a correspondence occurred between the prince and his administrator regarding the unauthor-ized absence of certain musicians; it was decided to with-hold a part of their salary for every day missed. On this occasion the prince, apparently familiar with Haydn's tactics, wrote to the administrator: "Do not reveal any-thing of this to Kapellmeister Haydn."[6] But it was im-possible to keep Haydn in darkness about such actions and the conductor sent the following appeal to his patron:[7]

As Your Serene Highness ordered a month's salary to be withheld from the musicians Marteau, Specht, and Chorus, I take the liberty humbly to remind Your Gracious Highness that recently while in Vienna I asked Your Serenity to grant a few days leave to Marteau, to which I received gracious consent. Mar-teau only absented himself longer because he wanted

---

Haydn Emlékére. Zenetudományi Tanulmányok (Budapest, 1960). Henceforth quoted as *Valkó II*.

[5] Letter dated January 9, 1772, to Secretary Scheffstoss. *Acta Musicalia*, fasc. I, 51; first reproduced by A. Valkó in *Kodály Zoltán 75 születésnapjárov* (Budapest, 1957). Henceforth quoted as *Valkó I*.

[6] *Acta Musicalia*, fasc. XX, 1372 (*Valkó II*).

[7] Copy made by E. Marton, preserved in Vienna National Library.

to copy a few new concertos and have his instrument repaired. As to [the oboist] Chorus, time was too short to notify Your Serene Highness in advance that Dr. Bertrand (who had prescribed a change of air because of Chorus' constant indisposition) let the musician accompany him at no cost. I therefore ventured to give permission. Regarding [the viola-player] Specht, his mother-in-law suddenly fell ill at Neustadt and I allowed him to go there for the three days when he was not needed for church service. I therefore beg to submit to Your Serene Highness my humble and most devoted petition not to inflict this financial punishment on them, and for this high favor I remain as long as life lasts with the most profound submissiveness,

Your Serene Highness' most obedient and humble
HAYDN

We don't know the result of this entreaty, but feel inclined to believe in its success. Haydn even went so far as to endeavor to dissuade the prince from carrying out an order of dismissal. A letter like the following[8] may have changed the patron's mind, especially in view of its final remark:

Your Noble Serenity graciously let me know recently that the present rent-collector Frantz Nigst was found to be expendable as violinist and that the same was true of Joseph Diezl, tenorist, wherefore I was ordered to have the former return his two uniforms. Regarding Nigst, may I submissively state and confess that in the operas produced up to now he was the only one to take proper care of the second violin part; therefore, should he be dismissed, I would live in fear of possible errors occurring unless Your Serene Highness was willing to engage another second violinist or have one come from Vienna for our opera performances, as my second violin would be merely handled

[8] *Acta Musicalia*, fasc. I, 47 (*Valkó I*).

by the horn-players Frantz and May, which is not enough. It is true, of course, that if the whole band goes to the Esterháza castle next year, Nigst could not constantly be with them because of his duties at the rent office in Eisenstadt, but I would humbly suggest to have him called to Esterháza, should a visit by the Imperial Court or other august personages occur. I therefore submissively petition Your Serene Highness also henceforth to grant to Nigst the yearly fifty florins as well as the winter and summer clothes (in which he has already served). . . . On the other hand, if the whole band leaves for Esterháza, Joseph Diezl is especially needed in the choir loft [of Eisenstadt] so that the regular church service can be held by him, his preceptor, and the choirboys. I hear from various sides that he cannot possibly subsist on his salary as schoolteacher, and I therefore most humbly petition Your Highness graciously to allow him enough for his livelihood.

In the next days I will obediently submit to Your Serene Highness a few new [Baryton-] Trios. I most humbly commend myself to Your Highness' favor and grace and remain,

Your Serenity's most obedient servant
JOSEPHUS HAYDN

Eisenstadt, 22 December 1768

This letter was sent to the princely secretary, Scheffstoss, for approval, and Haydn added the following characteristic remark:

Should anything in the above seem inadvisable to you, kindly let me know by return. I flatter myself that through this petition and your confirmation regarding these men's characters His Highness will be favorably impressed. Should this not be the case, I cannot be blamed for loving my neighbor.

All this makes it understandable that his musicians loved their "Papa," as they came to call him. The nickname must not, however, lead to the conception that Haydn was in any way easygoing. While he did his utmost to intercede with the prince on behalf of personal misdemeanors, he was certainly adamant as far as the musical activities were concerned. The instructions he wrote down for the execution of his *Applausus* at the Monastery of Zwettl (see page 266 f.), where he could not attend rehearsals, show very vividly to what extent he insisted on the clearness and accuracy of every detail, and how well he knew what mistakes the musicians were likely to make.

Work at the Esterházy court required getting along with a number of subordinates to the prince, and it cannot be denied that Haydn, despite his diplomatic skill, met with difficulties time and time again. As he remarked in 1791, when this type of life lay far behind him: "I had a gracious prince, but sometimes I was forced to be dependent on base souls."[9] An episode of this kind which took place in 1765 is revealed by a document in the Esterházy archives. A dispute arose between the princely administrator, Rahier, and Haydn, who intervened regarding a punishment meted out to a musician. Thereupon the administrator complained to the prince, and Haydn, receiving a reprimand from his patron, wrote a lengthy letter of explanation, which, despite the routine flowery phrases inserted, manages to take an energetic stand for the writer's rights.[10] It reads:

The letter Your Serene Highness sent me on the 8th was received with the most submissive respect, and I learned from it that Your Illustrious Serenity was displeased by my protesting to Herr von Rahier, with all due respect, against the arrest of the flautist Frantz Sigl. . . . However, nothing could be achieved with the administrator and I even had to see the door slammed in my face and hear him threatening us all with detention. Likewise Friberth, who did not lift his hat to Herr von Rahier (certainly owing to an

[9] Letter to Marianne von Genzinger of September 17, 1791.
[10] *Acta Musicalia,* fasc. I, 49 (*Valkó I*).

oversight), is anxiously hiding from the administrator and now out of fear of detention does not dare go home. The administrator asserts that Friberth acted rudely toward him and must accept his punishment. But I testify together with all the other musicians that when the administrator threatened everybody with detention—and this without any justification—Friberth merely remarked that he had no other master but His Serene Highness, Prince Esterházy. I myself said to the administrator that if he should feel that he had suffered a personal insult, he ought to take the matter up with His Serenity, but he answered that the administrator was his own judge and would inflict the penalty himself. Everybody is very disturbed about this, and to respectable people such treatment seems very hard to take. We hope that Your Serene and Gracious Highness will not entertain intentions of this kind and will graciously prevent a procedure whereby anyone can be his own judge without distinguishing between guilty and innocent ones.

As Your Serene Highness is doubtless aware, the commands of the aforementiond administrator have always been properly carried out by me, and whenever I receive through him orders from Your Gracious and Serene Highness I will be intent on executing them. Therefore, if the administrator has complained about me on this account, that was due only to his angry pen. Moreover, Your Serene and Noble Highness will be graciously aware that *I cannot serve two masters* and cannot accept and submit to the administrator's commands, for Your Serenity Yourself once said to me: henceforth he ought to come to me first, for I am his master.

This gives me confidence that Your Serene Highness will not consider ungraciously my most submissive report, but will regard me and the whole band with gracious eyes and afford us fatherly protection, as everyone else is treating us with ill will. In the hope of further marks of favor from Your Serene and Noble

Highness, I remain for life, with the most submissive respect,

Your Serene and Gracious Highness' very obedient and humble

JOSEPHUS HAYDN

Eisenstadt, 9 September 1765

We do not know how the prince reacted, but from a letter written by Rahier on September 13 we learn that the dispute was settled with the conductor and Friberth, and that the administrator asked his patron not to take any further steps. Apparently Haydn was too shrewd to continue a quarrel with the powerful official.

The documents reprinted here, especially the contract, deserve our interest for various reasons. Modern readers may be shocked to see a genius treated not much better than a servant. Imagine a composer in the throes of inspiration having to wait twice a day, at certain hours, in the prince's antechamber, to receive his patron's orders; or having to compose whatever the prince wishes; and who, even in his appearance, had to conform absolutely to the instructions of His Serene Highness. It would, however, be wrong to view such regulations from the vantage point of the twentieth century. Haydn himself, at least at that time, considered them matters of course. Composing to order was the usual practice of every musician of his time; it was only with Beethoven that the attitude of musicians began to change. To await the commands of so exalted a personage as Prince Esterházy, who used to say, and prove by action, that what the emperor did he too could do, was not humiliating for a man who had only recently risen from the depths of poverty. As regards Haydn's clothes, Griesinger remarked: "Mathias Haydn lived to experience the joy of seeing his son in the princely blue uniform braided with gold."[11] Haydn himself probably felt much the same way. The only point in the contract that the composer must have considered unfair was the stipulation that all his compositions were to belong to Prince Esterházy and that he was not to compose for anyone else. Haydn,

[11] Mathias Haydn died on September 12, 1763.

however, soon succeeded in modifying this condition. Apparently, a kind of gentleman's agreement was reached between Haydn and his princely patron; for shortly after his appointment, the composer's works began to be distributed outside the court of Eisenstadt and later he derived a substantial and steadily growing income from the sale of his compositions to publishers.

When Haydn arrived in Eisenstadt, the Esterházy orchestra was still rather small, but in that year various musicians joined it, among them, as its most important member, the outstanding violinist Luigi Tomasini (born in 1741), whom Prince Paul Anton brought from Italy to Eisenstadt as a valet in 1757. The unusual musical talent of the youth induced the prince to send Tomasini to Venice in 1759 to pursue musical studies, which apparently were highly successful. The new Vice-Kapellmeister may have been responsible for the engagement of the eminent violoncellist Joseph Weigl. These two artists, hardly more than twenty years old, together with the new conductor, brought a breath of fresh air into Eisenstadt's musical life, and it was not easy for the head conductor, Gregorius Werner, to adapt himself to the altered conditions. Old Werner was a most conservative musician who excelled in sacred compositions in the polyphonic style.[12] His works required outstanding musicianship from his performers without giving them grateful tasks. (It was the kind of music characterized in Vienna by the comment "noble but dull.") A composer so deeply rooted in the past considered everything new to be a symptom of decline. For Haydn's music Werner had nothing but derision, and he called the newcomer a "mere fop" or "a scribbler of songs." Still, he could not help noticing the great esteem enjoyed by the Vice-Kapellmeister, whose salary, raised one year after his appointment to six hundred florins, exceeded considerably

[12] The old composer had long since lost the sense of humor shown in such burlesque compositions of his younger years as *The Old Clothes Market of Vienna*, *The Election of a Village Justice*, and *A New and Very Curious Musical Instrumental Calendar*, all published in 1748.

his own four hundred and twenty-eight. Naturally enough, the old man grew more and more embittered.

The Esterházy archives preserve a letter by Werner of October 1765[13] uttering serious complaints about young Haydn's negligence and urging the prince to give the strictest commands to remedy the situation. Thereupon the prince issued the notorious *Regulatio Chori Kissmartoniensis* (Kismarton being the Hungarian name for Eisenstadt) in which Haydn was rebuked for the "indolence and lack of discipline among the musicians" and at the same time ordered "to apply himself to composition more diligently than heretofore," a remark that must strike anybody looking at the composer's output as entirely unjustified.[14] However, it did not take Haydn very long to change his patron's attitude, for as early as January 4, 1766, the prince asked his administrator to pay the composer twelve ducats as a sign of approval of three new pieces just submitted.

Werner could not help observing that his accusations had not paid off. He retired as much as possible from court, concentrating on composing sacred music. Between 1761 and 1766, the year of his death, he wrote no less than sixteen Masses, five *Salve Regina,* and eight other sacred works. Haydn, on his side, treated the head conductor with the great respect that he really felt for him. Many years after Werner's death when the "scribbler of songs" stood at the summit of his fame, he arranged six of Werner's fugues for string quartet and had them published by Artaria "out of sincere esteem for this celebrated master." Nevertheless, in spite of his esteem, the young Vice-Kapellmeister managed to take complete charge of the whole musical organization and to increase its size whenever there was a chance to do so. In this he was helped by the prince who took over the leadership after the death (at the age of forty-eight) of Paul Anton on

[13] *Acta Musicalia,* fasc. I, 84 (*Valkó II*).

[14] H. C. Robbins Landon conjectures that this reprimand was responsible for Haydn's decision to start on his draft catalogue. (Cf. *The Collected Correspondence and London Notebooks of Joseph Haydn,* London, 1959, p. 6.) This is a document of greatest significance for posterity, and it makes us forgive the prince for his unwarranted outburst.

March 18, 1762, and who far surpassed his predecessor in his passion for music and in his Medicean dream of creating a center of culture at his court. Haydn's new patron was Prince Nicolaus the Magnificent, as he was called because of his love of splendor and display. For nearly thirty years these two men were destined to live together in a unique sort of companionship. Outwardly the prince was the personification of wealth; his coat covered with diamonds was a sensation in many capitals of Europe. The man who wore it was certainly worth knowing. Goethe, who saw the prince in 1764, professed a "particular sympathy for him" and described him as "not tall, but well built, vivacious and distinguished, and at the same time without haughtiness and coldness." Prince Nicolaus often showed himself to be generous and kindhearted, and as these qualities were combined with a true feeling for music, he was in many respects the ideal patron for a composer, especially one able to put up with his employer's autocratic manner.

Two instances may serve to throw light on conditions prevailing at the Esterházy court. The archives preserve a letter that the administrator wrote to the prince on January 24, 1769,[15] reporting that the tenor Karl Friberth was about to marry the newly engaged singer Magdalena Spangler and that as His Highness had forbidden them to marry, they were to leave the princely service. The administrator had therefore ordered Haydn to have the couple return all clothes supplied for their service at court. Evidently the prince assumed the right to grant or refuse his employees permission to be married and expected such decree to be final. In this case the matter, fortunately, seems to have been settled amicably, for the two singers, although married, remained at the Esterházy court until 1776, when they moved to Vienna, where Friberth obtained a position as music director of a church. We may assume that Haydn helped to placate the prince; naturally he was eager to do so, as Magdalena Spangler was the daughter of the man who had granted him asylum at the

[15] *Acta Musicalia*, fasc. 1526, fol. 191 (*Valkó II*).

critical moment when he had been expelled from St. Stephen's (see page 28). On other occasions, however, the prince acted with greatest severity. When, on October 24, 1776, Dittersdorf's opera *Il finto pazzo per amore* was produced, the tenor Benedetto Bianchi decided to play a joke on his partner, Catharina Boschwa, and twice lifted her skirt with a cane without her noticing it. Her husband, who was in the audience, complained to the prince, whereupon Bianchi was jailed for two weeks, publicly given fifty lashes, and ordered to apologize for his irresponsible behavior at the next performance.[16]

On May 17, 1762, Prince Nicolaus made his solemn entry into Eisenstadt with the splendor that was to characterize the numerous festivities of the years to come. For the occasion, Haydn had the task of composing an Italian operetta, *La marchesa Nepola*, most of which has been lost. A special stage was erected for this performance in the castle's big hall, and a painter, Bon, took charge of producing the decorations. By July 1, Bon was given permanent employment, on condition that his wife and daughter should sing in the choir. Even more splendid was the pompous celebration of the marriage of Prince Nicolaus' son to Countess Erdödy in 1763, when Eisenstadt, as the *Wiener Diarium* stated, saw "greater festivities and more exalted personages than ever before." Haydn wrote for the wedding his pastorale *Acide* and appeared at the performance in the new Esterházy uniform of crimson and gold. During the next year the prince had to attend the coronation of Archduke Joseph as Holy Roman Emperor at Frankfort. Nicolaus—the Magnificent in the true sense of the word—outshone every other ambassador by arranging a "fairylike" (Goethe) illumination of a main street in celebration of the great event. Before going to Frankfort, Prince Nicolaus had been in Paris. The beauty and splendor of Versailles made a deep impression on him and when he returned home he decided to create a Versailles of his own in Hungary.

[16] Cf. Mátyás Horányi: *Das Esterházysche Feenreich* (Budapest, 1959), p. 106.

CHAPTER 5

AT ESTERHÁZA

1766–1779

The castle of Esterháza, which Prince Nicolaus built after his return from France, was a typical product of the eighteenth century. It reflected the attitude toward life adopted by the high aristocracy when neither trouble nor money was spared to satisfy a whim. Prince Nicolaus the Magnificent, having seen the Palace of Versailles, decided to rival the King of France. In choosing a site for his country seat, he went out of his way to find the place that would present the greatest obstacles to his plan. The Esterházy family owned a little hunting lodge at Süttör near the large lake known as the Neusiedler See. The lake had overflowed the surrounding country, producing a huge swamp covering no less than sixteen square miles. It was a desolate place, filled with mud as far as the eye could see. Every sort of insect abounded there, and fever was a permanent guest. There Nicolaus had lived after leaving the Austrian army as a lieutenant field marshal. When he succeeded his elder brother as ruler of the Esterházy estate, he decided to erect his Versailles in this very place. Recollections of his former, much more modest way of life at Süttör may have influenced him, but perhaps he was influenced still more by the thought that he, the Magnificent, would triumph over nature at its worst. So the swamps were cleared, canals were dug, a magnificent dam was built, and after tremendous difficulties and the expenditure of something like eleven million florins (more than five million dollars), the castle of Esterháza came into existence in 1766. A large, richly illustrated book was devoted solely to the description of its wonders.[1] A few selections from it may help to give an idea of the place where Haydn was to spend so much of his time during the following twenty-five years.

The castle is in Italian style, without visible roof, surrounded by a beautifully proportioned stone gallery. Most valuable are two rooms used by the prince. One of them contains ten Japanese panels in black lacquer adorned with golden flowers and landscapes, each of which cost more than a thousand florins. The chairs and divans are covered with golden fabric. There are also some extremely valuable cabinets and a bronze clock that plays the flute. In the second room, richly adorned with golden ornaments, is another gilded clock with a canary on top that moves and whistles pleasant tunes when the clock strikes, as well as an armchair that plays a flute solo when you sit on it. The chandeliers are made from artistically wrought rock crystal. In the library there are seventy-five hundred books, all exquisite editions, to which novelties are being added daily. It also contains numerous manuscripts and many excellent old and new engravings by the best masters. The picture gallery is liberally supplied with first-class original paintings by famous Italian and Dutch masters which fill the eye of the connoisseur with delight and admiration.

In an alley of wild chestnut trees stands the magnificent opera house. The boxes at the sides open into charming rooms furnished most luxuriously with fireplaces, divans, mirrors, and clocks. The theater easily holds four hundred people. Every day, at 6 PM, there is a performance of an Italian *opera seria* or *buffa* or of German comedy, always attended by the prince. Words cannot describe how both eye and ear are delighted here. When the music begins, its touching delicacy, the strength and force of the instruments

---

[1] *Beschreibung des hochfürstlichen Schlosses Esterháss im Königreich Ungarn* (Pressburg, 1784). Its author was probably Prince Nicolaus himself.

penetrate the soul, for the great composer, Herr
Haydn himself is conducting. But the audience is also
overwhelmed by the admirable lighting and the de-
ceptively perfect stage settings. At first we see the
clouds on which the gods are seated sink slowly to
earth. Then the gods rise upward and instantly vanish,
and then again everything is transformed into a delightful garden, an enchanted wood, or, it may be, a
glorious hall.

Opposite the opera house is the marionette theater,
built like a grotto. All the walls, niches, and apertures
are covered with variegated stones, shells, and snails[2]
that afford a very curious and striking sight when they
are illuminated. The theater is rather large and the
decorations are extremely artistic. The puppets are
beautifully formed, and magnificently dressed; they
play not only farces and comedies, but also *opera
seria*. The performances in both theaters are open to
everyone.

Behind the castle is the park. Everyone entering it
stands still in amazement and admiration at the majestic sight, for it fills the soul with rapture. The park
was built after the prince's own designs, and is without doubt the most gorgeous example of its kind in the
whole kingdom. Art and nature are here combined in
an extremely noble and magnificent way. In every corner there is something to attract the eye—statues,
temples, grottoes, waterworks; everywhere are the
glory of majesty, gentle smiles of nature, joy, and delight!

At the gates stands the princely guard consisting
of one hundred and fifty grenadiers, very handsome
and finely trained men, mostly six feet tall. Their uniform is a dark blue coat with red flaps and lapels,
white tie, white vest and trousers, and black bearskin
cap with yellow visor.

Only a few of the splendors are described here. There

[2] The rocaille style applied here was made fashionable by
Louis XV.

were also marvelous hothouses and orangeries and immense game preserves in the park, while the castle boasted one hundred and twenty-six richly gilded and paneled guest rooms and two exquisite halls for entertainments—the parade hall, decorated entirely in white, and the *sala terrena*, tiled with white marble and overflowing with art treasures. This latter hall was used for music on festive occasions. Truly Nicolaus the Magnificent had achieved something worthy of his name. It must have given him real satisfaction when he read in the *Letters of a Traveling Frenchman* by Risbeck: "In France, there is perhaps no place, except Versailles, that equals this castle in splendor."

Esterháza proved to be for the prince much more than a passing whim. The more he improved it, the more attached he became to this, his own, creation. Planned first as a summer resort, Esterháza became the prince's residence for the greater part of the year. Eisenstadt, though much more healthful and richer in natural beauties, was completely eclipsed by the new castle. The prince returned to the old residence for a short sojourn during the winter, spending the rest of it in Vienna, but as soon as spring approached he moved back to his beloved new castle. The unpleasantly damp climate, not greatly changed even by the canals he built, did not appear to affect Prince Nicolaus nor did he suffer from the "vexatious, penetrating north wind" that caused Haydn much discomfort. As long as he could be at Esterháza, busily engaged in some new scheme and enjoying the excellent music and theater performances provided there, he was the best of patrons and the most charming host to the exalted visitors he liked to entertain.

A great staff had to be engaged to fulfill the prince's dream of a cultural center. There were two painters, Johann Basilius Grundmann and (from 1771) Pietro Travaglia,[3] who painted the portraits of the family, adorned the castle with frescoes, and designed the stage scenery. There were also a librarian, a director of the picture gallery, landscape gardeners for the constantly

[3] Travaglia also painted parts of the decorations for the performance of Mozart's *La clemenza di Tito* at Prague.

growing park, and a great number of employees connected with the two theaters. The marionette theater was
entrusted to the pantomime master Bienfait, to P. G.
Bader, and (up to 1778) to J. K. von Pauersbach, who
supplied the librettos. The dialogue for the puppets was
usually recited by actors from one of the well-known
troupes whom the prince used to hire for several months at
a time. After Werner's death, Haydn had become Kapellmeister in 1766, and eventually he engaged excellent
singers, mostly from Italy or, at least, trained by Italian
masters. Among the male singers Friberth, Dichtler,
Specht, Braghetti, Moratti, Lambertini, Jermoli, Griessler,
Bianchi, Totti, Ungricht; among the women, Weigl,
Dichtler, Spangler, Cellini, Prandtner, Jermoli, Boschwa,
Puttler, Ripamonti, Zannini, Valdesturla, and the Bologna
sisters deserve mention because they appeared in Haydn's
operas. The ballet was for some years in the hands of
Ludovico Rossi. The orchestra was made up of from sixteen to twenty-two players whose artistic qualities more
than compensated for the smallness of their number.
Haydn saw to it that only highly promising musicians
were engaged, and it can be imagined how they developed under the continual training of so able a conductor.
At the first desk throughout Haydn's stay at Esterháza
sat Luigi Tomasini, a great favorite of the prince, and also
of the Kapellmeister, who used to remark that no one
(himself included) could play his string quartets like his
"brother Luigi." Of the violoncellists, Haydn's friend Joseph
Weigl[4] stayed from 1761 to 1769, when he joined the
Vienna court orchestra; his colleagues, Franz Xaver Marteau and Anton Kraft, maintained the same high standard.
The prince could afford always to choose the best, as the
salaries he paid were even higher than those offered by
the imperial court at Vienna.

That the musical world was aware of the artistic standard maintained at Esterháza is shown by a remark of the
Gotha Theater-Calender for 1778: "The orchestra consists

---

[4] Haydn was godfather to Weigl's son, Joseph. who became
famous as the composer of German *Singspiele*, including *Die
Schweizer-familie*. See also page 145.

of thirty players, mostly virtuosos, and therefore ranks among the most excellent ensemble groups."

This costly staff of musicians and artists was kept constantly busy by the prince. Apart from two concert academies a week (and it should not be forgotten that concert programs in the eighteenth century were much longer than they are today), there was chamber music in His Serene Highness' private apartments, with Nicolaus often taking part himself. The prince was a passionate lover of the baryton (see page 246), a now obsolete instrument related to the viola da gamba. The baryton is extremely hard to play; this may be why the ambitious prince preferred it to the violin or violoncello. He became quite an adept player and Haydn could hardly keep pace with his patron's demands for new baryton compositions. To give the prince a pleasant surprise, Haydn began secretly to practice playing the baryton and when he had acquired some skill, offered to show his art to the prince. To his disappointment, his attempt was received with icy indifference, and he realized that his patron wanted him only to compose for the baryton, not play it. Likewise, when the cellist Kraft played baryton duets with the prince, all the solos had to be planned so that there were no great technical difficulties, for they were to be executed by the prince and not by Kraft. As Nicolaus remarked: "It is no credit to you to play better than I do; it is your duty." At times changes had to be made in Haydn's compositions so as to make them acceptable to the august baryton player. This is illustrated by the following, very typical letter[5] addressed to the prince, which also throws light on the conductor's manifold concerns:

[undated, but marked "Received 5 December 1766"]

The most welcome arrival of my patron's name day (which may Divine Grace let Your Serene Highness spend in perfect well-being and happiness) causes me not only to offer to Your Serenity in dutiful submission six new divertimenti, but also to kiss the hem of your robe for graciously presenting us with our new

[5] *Acta Musicalia,* fasc. I, 53 (*Valkó I*).

winter clothes, which a few days ago were handed to us. May I add that despite Your Highness' most regrettable absence, we ventured to wear them for the first time at the celebration of High Mass on Your Highness' name day. Order was given to me to have bound the twelve divertimenti I composed. But as Your Highness sent me a few of them to be changed and I had not noted these alterations in my score, I venture to ask to let me have the first twelve pieces for three days and later also the others, so that, with all alterations entered, they may be carefully copied and bound. May I also submissively inquire in what manner Your Serene Highness wishes them to be bound?

Incidentally, the two oboists report to me (a statement I have to corroborate) that their instruments are deteriorating because of old age and do not stay on pitch any longer. I therefore submissively mention that there is a Master Rockobauer in Vienna who, in my opinion, is best qualified in this field. Although this master is constantly engaged in such tasks, he would at present manage to produce a pair of fine and durable oboes with an extra piece of tube (allowing all the necessary notes to be sounded), for which work the best price would be eight ducats. May I expect Your Serene Highness' gracious consent to acquire the two urgently needed oboes at the above-mentioned price.[6]

Hoping for Your Noble Highness' favor and grace
I remain, your most obedient
HAYDN

Frequently the ordinary routine was interrupted by the visit of some distinguished guest and preparations for such an occasion had to be made a long time ahead. These visits usually lasted for three days filled to the brim with concerts, theater and marionette performances, masked

[6] Apparently Haydn's advice was not heeded. The Esterházy archives merely mention payments to Rockobauer for the purchase of woodwind mouthpieces and repair of an English horn.

balls, and hunting. An outstanding event was the visit of
the Empress Maria Theresia herself in 1773. The *Wiener
Diarium* and a special booklet[7] afford detailed accounts
of the festivities, a résumé of which is given here as an
example of the entertainments provided amid the marshes
and swamps of Hungary:

On her arrival the empress and her retinue were es-
corted in fifteen of the prince's magnificent carriages
through the park, the wonders of which Maria Theresia
could not sufficiently admire, though she was used to a
beautiful park in the French style at her own residence
of Schönbrunn. In the evening Haydn's burletta *L'infedeltà delusa* was performed, which so impressed the imperial guest that she was overheard to say: "If I want to
enjoy a good opera, I go to Esterháza" (a remark that
before long was repeated all over Vienna). The performance was followed by a masked ball in the luxuri-
ous hall of the castle. Then the empress was taken to
the Chinese pavilion, whose mirror-covered walls reflected
countless lampions and chandeliers flooding the room with
light. On a platform sat the princely orchestra in gala attire and played under Haydn's direction his new symphony, "Maria Theresia" (No. 48), as well as other music.
The empress then retired to her magnificent suite, while
her retinue continued to enjoy the masked ball until dawn.
The next day a great banquet took place in the *sala terrena*, during which the virtuosos of the orchestra demon-
strated their skill. In the afternoon the empress attended a
performance of Haydn's opera *Philemon and Baucis* in the
marionette theater[8] and she was so fascinated by it that
four years later she had the complete outfit sent to Vienna
for some special festivities. After the "souper" the august
guests watched huge fireworks planned by the pyrotechnist

[7] *Relation des fêtes données à Sa Majesté l'Impératrice . . .
le 1er et 2e 7bre 1773.* Published by Ghelen (Vienna).

[8] The empress must have liked the ending, for out of clouds
dazzlingly rose the Habsburg coat of arms held by Justice,
Wisdom, Leniency, and crowned by Fame, with figures in Hungarian attire symbolizing Obedience, Diligence, and Loyalty
kneeling before it and praising the empress in song.

Rabel, their variety and brilliance surpassing all expectations. Afterward, the prince took the monarch to an immense open space, which was hung with multicolored lights forming artistic designs. Suddenly, about a thousand peasants appeared in their beautiful Hungarian or Croatian costumes and performed national dances to the entrancing tunes of their own folk music. The next morning the empress left after distributing costly presents. Haydn received a valuable gold snuffbox filled with ducats. He was proud to have impressed Her Majesty not merely as a musician, for during her stay he succeeded in killing with one shot three grouse that were graciously accepted for the empress' table. During the festivities, emphasis was laid on Chinese artifacts, which at that time enjoyed a great vogue. At the masked ball, Chinese decorations prevailed and even the princely musicians appeared in gorgeous Chinese robes. Among the countless treasures amassed at Esterháza, the newly erected Chinese pavilion particularly impressed the empress. The prince, however, waved aside her praise with the airy remark that this was merely a "bagatelle," a designation henceforth applied to the exquisite building.[9]

Entertainment of this kind took place once a year or even more frequently, and most of Haydn's operas were written for such occasions. For visitors who would enjoy a more robust form of entertainment than appealed to the empress, the prince took care not to neglect the comic element in arranging his plans. In 1775, for example, when an Austrian archduke and archduchess visited Esterháza, a whole country fair was set up in the park with quack doctors, mountebanks, cheap-jacks, and stalls and booths. There the guests had all the fun they desired and the merry mood was heightened by an entrancing parody of Gluck's *Alceste* in the marionette theater. No less than fourteen hundred guests attended the masked ball arranged in honor of the exalted visitors. Again peasants were invited to dance and sing, each village appearing with its own flag and band, and as the prince liberally

⁹ Cf. Horányi, op. cit., p. 16.

provided food and drinks for the villagers, a hilarious mood prevailed.

Time never hung heavy on the hands of Prince Esterházy's retainers. But in spite of the interesting work under the leadership of their beloved "Papa," in spite of the good salaries they received, the musicians were often much discouraged when their stay at Esterháza dragged on and on far into the autumn. The prince, who never hesitated to adorn the park with a new and expensive monument, and who spent about six thousand florins on the production of the marionette opera *Dido*, saw no necessity for providing living quarters ample enough to house his musicians and their families. All the instrumentalists and singers, all the actors, painters, copyists, and some of the servants, had to live in a single moderate-sized building. In 1772 the prince therefore gave strict orders that no musician was to bring his wife or children to Esterháza. Only Haydn, Friberth, Dichtler, and Tomasini were exempted from this rule. Three rooms were reserved for the Kapellmeister, whereas two musicians generally had to share a single chamber. By paying the married members an extra fifty florins for the expenses incurred in keeping the double households, the prince felt that he had settled the matter generously enough, and it did not trouble him that these husbands had to live for the greater part of the year away from their families. The musicians felt differently. According to Griesinger: "The affectionate husbands appealed to Haydn to help them. Haydn decided to write a symphony [Hob. I:45, known under the name of "Farewell" symphony] in which one instrument after the other ceases to play. The work was executed as soon as an occasion presented itself, and each player was instructed to put out his candle when his part was ended, seize his music, and leave with his instrument tucked under his arm. The prince instantly understood the meaning of this pantomime and the next day he gave the order to leave Esterháza."

The biographer fails to tell us what happened in the following years. Surely Haydn was not always able to invent something new to humor the prince. The musicians actually had to give in or accept a position elsewhere, which many did. The Kapellmeister himself was tied to Esterháza just as closely as his subordinates. He once complained in a letter to a friend[10] about how difficult it was for him to obtain even a short leave: "It is scarcely credible, and yet the refusal is always couched in such polite terms as to render it utterly impossible for me to urge my request." Haydn had to resort to diplomacy to achieve results. His tactics are illuminated by the following letter[11] to the princely secretary Anton Scheffstoss. Here the petition for leave is clothed in a report of the praise given to Haydn by a famous master, and thus was calculated to be pleasing to the vanity of his august patron, who certainly was also inclined to believe that the singers in his service were far superior to those employed in Vienna:

Eisenstadt, 20 March 1768

Doubtless you are aware that last year I set to music with all the power at my disposal the highly respected hymn called Stabat Mater, and I sent my music to the great and world-famous Hasse out of the desire that if I had failed adequately to express the most valuable words, this might be remedied by the Master, so successful in all his compositions. Contrary to my merits, this outstanding artist honored me with inexpressible praise and desired nothing more but to hear my work performed by a proper ensemble of musicians. But as there is a great lack of singers of both sexes in Vienna, I venture to present through you my humble petitions to His Serene Highness to allow me, Weigl, and his wife, as well as Friberth, to leave next Thursday for Vienna in order to promote the honor of our most gracious prince through performances by his servants on Friday afternoon at the

10 Letter to Marianne von Genzinger, May 30, 1790. The English version of this and various other Haydn letters quoted herein is partly based on the translation by Lady G. M. Wallace (London, 1867).

11 *Acta Musicalia,* fasc. I, 56 (*Valkó I*).

Brothers of Mercy. Saturday night we would be back
in Eisenstadt. Should His Highness thus command, I
would send up someone else instead of Friberth. Dearest Monsieur Scheffstoss, do please expedite my petition. I remain with profound respect,

> Your most devoted servant
>   HAYDN

P. S. My compliments to all the gentlemen. The promised divertimento will certainly be handed this week
to His Highness.

Mrs. Weigl, who from 1760 to 1769 sang soprano parts
in the church choir, was the secretary's daughter, and we
may therefore assume that he helped to obtain the requested leave. Such an event was a rarity, however, and
most of Haydn's trips were made officially in the retinue
of the prince. Thus, on March 22, 1770, the Esterházy
ensemble successfully performed Haydn's opera *Lo speziale* in the house of a Viennese nobleman, Freiherr von
Sumerau, and followed it a few days later by a concert. In
1775 Haydn conducted in the capital the first performance
of his oratorio *Il ritorno di Tobia* for the Tonkünstlersocietät, a charitable institution for assisting destitute musicians and their families. The performance was up to the
Esterházy standard, as Haydn brought with him three
singers as well as Tomasini and Marteau. This was the
first occasion on which Haydn sought the approval of a
large audience in a capital city. Its success was notable.
The public was enchanted, and after the deduction of expenses, almost two thousand florins remained for charitable
purposes. Some of the critics were very enthusiastic. The
K.k.priv.Realzeitung der Wissenschaften declared: "Nature and art were so delicately interwoven in this work
that the audience had to love the one and admire the
other. The choruses especially displayed a fire to be found
previously only in Handel's compositions."[12]

The great success of *Il ritorno di Tobia* may have been
responsible for the request sent to Haydn in 1776 to write

[12] April 6, 1775, p. 218.

an autobiographical sketch for Lucca's publication *Das gelehrte Oesterreich*, a sort of Austrian *Who's Who*.[13]

In spite of Haydn's steadily growing fame, which was spreading beyond his native country, praise of his music was by no means unanimous in Vienna. A strong movement against him was led by people who either envied him his excellent position or did not understand his style. Dr. Burney's quotation from a letter that a friend from Hamburg wrote him about Haydn in 1772 reveals exactly the attitude of many Viennese musicians. "His mixture of serious and comic is disliked, particularly as there is more of the latter than the former in his work and, as for rules, he knows but little of them." That was the way Maria Theresia's co-regent and subsequent successor, Joseph II, felt. For him, Haydn's music was just "tricks and nonsense," and this dictum did not make the Kapellmeister from Esterházy popular at the Viennese court. It is not surprising, therefore, that when Haydn tried to penetrate further into these circles, he was roughly rebuffed. In 1776, after the Archduke Ferdinand had returned from Esterháza with a glowing account of what he had heard and seen there, Haydn was commissioned to compose the opera *La vera costanza* for Vienna. He did so, but when he went to the capital to rehearse with the singers, such a flood of intrigues was let loose against him that he withdrew his work in disgust, leaving the field to Pasquale Anfossi, who had composed music to the same libretto. Three years later Haydn's opera was performed at Esterháza.

Even when dealing with the Tonkünstlersocietät, which was so greatly indebted to him for his *Il ritorno di Tobia*, Haydn had good reason for anger. To obtain a kind of insurance for himself and his wife, Haydn applied to the society for admission in 1778, depositing the amount of three hundred florins requested from him as a nonresident. The society, however, was not satisfied and asked him to sign an agreement pledging himself to supply compositions of importance whenever required. Haydn, highly indig-

[13] Parts of this article have been quoted in the earlier chapters of this book.

nant, declined this offer as being incompatible with his
duties toward Prince Esterházy, remarking with a fire
rarely to be found in his letters: "The fine arts and the
beautiful science of composition cannot bear any fetters;
soul and spirit must be free," whereupon the Societät
calmly refused to enroll him among their members.[14]

Incidents of this kind made Haydn appreciate more and
more the advantages of his life at Esterháza. As he once
remarked to Griesinger: "My prince was always satisfied
with my works. Not only did I have the encouragement of
constant approval, but as conductor of an orchestra I could
make experiments, observe what produced an effect and
what weakened it, and was thus in a position to improve,
to alter, make additions or omissions, and be as bold as I
pleased. I was cut off from the world; there was no one
to confuse or torment me, and I was forced to become
original."

It is true that from the middle of the seventies his duties
steadily increased. As D. Bartha and L. Somfai pointed
out in a valuable recent study,[15] 1776 marked a decisive
change in Esterháza's cultural life that greatly affected
Haydn's responsibilities. The prince, who up to then had
used his fine theater mainly for dramatic performances
by traveling theatrical troupes, decided to allot opera a
prominent place. In earlier years opera had been presented
only for special festive events, the composition of the work
always being entrusted to Haydn. Now Esterháza was to
have a repertoire of Italian operas by renowned contemporary composers. Several reasons may have induced the
prince thus to change his policy. The fact that Italian
opera was being stressed at the imperial court in Vienna
after a pause of several years certainly constituted an important factor. Moreover Nicolaus the Magnificent appar-

[14] Mozart's petition for admission in 1785 was equally unsuccessful. Although he had played repeatedly for the society,
they insisted on his presenting his certificate of baptism before
they would make him a member. Mozart apparently neglected
getting this document from Salzburg, and thus his petition was
left pending. Cf. O. E. Deutsch, *Mozart, die Dokumente seines
Lebens* (Kassel, 1961), p. 209.

[15] *Haydn als Opernkapellmeister* (Budapest, 1961).

ently was now less interested in performing on the baryton and preferred to spend his leisure hours attending good operatic performances. With his customary largess, he purchased a sizable number of Italian opera scores and had new singers engaged in 1776. Haydn, though relieved from the continual necessity of supplying new baryton compositions for his patron, had his hands full conducting operas twice a week in the period from February to November or December, novelties appearing between four and eight times per season. Besides coaching the singers and the orchestra and supervising the copying of the material, in most cases Haydn felt obliged to make considerable changes in the works so as to adapt them to the specific requirements of the Esterházy court. The orchestra pit was small and held only about twenty musicians; as a rule clarinets, trumpets, and timpani were not available, and Haydn had to arrange the scores accordingly. On the other hand, he liked to enrich the orchestration of an opera by giving to violin II and viola more important parts and adding wind instruments such as oboes and horns where the original used strings only. At Esterháza no chorus was available, and if choral numbers could not be entrusted to a group of soloists, they had to be omitted. Apart from cuts necessitated by the limitations of his ensemble, Haydn did not hesitate to shorten considerably most of the operas performed, and even had no compunction about changing the form of a number if he felt it to be overlong. Similar motives may have been responsible for his alterations of tempo. Haydn made it a habit to accelerate slow numbers, changing, for instance, larghetto to andante con moto, and once even andante maestoso to allegro vivace.[16] Also, intricate coloraturas occasionally were omitted.

Whether the many cuts and the accelerations of tempo were entirely owing to the taste of the conductor or were owing rather to that of his patron cannot be ascertained today. However, one would think it likely that Haydn himself reacted with impatience to the hollowness and long-windedness so often present in Italian *opera seria*. On the

[16] An aria in Salieri's *La fiera di Venezia*. Cf. Bartha-Somfai, op. cit., p. 55.

other hand a few works like Paisiello's *Il barbiere di
Siviglia*, Martin's *L'arbore di Diana*, and Sarti's *Didone
abbandonata* seem to have been accepted by him without

The majority of the works performed required, however,
a great deal of work before they were ready for production.
Thus a tremendous new responsibility was entrusted to
Haydn. Prince Esterházy, conscious of the increased demands made on his music director, expressed his appreciation by concluding a new contract with Haydn under greatly
improved terms.[17] The 14 stipulations of the original document (*cf.* p. 45) are now reduced to six. The original salary
of 400 florins is increased to 782 fl. 30 Xr. and delivery of
certain quantities of wine, firewood, grain, meat (including
a whole pig), salt, lard, candles, vegetables, and forage for
two horses is guaranteed. Most significant is also the omission of the old clause according to which all compositions by
Haydn were to belong solely to the Prince who was the
only one entitled to commission music from him. Although
Haydn had managed not to be fettered by the old restric-
tion, he could not but be pleased that the new contract
accorded him a more dignified position.

No one was more aware of Joseph Haydn's good fortune
at the Esterházy court than his brother Michael. The positions of the two brothers now had changed. Michael had
been appointed music director and concertmaster to the
Archbishop of Salzburg (the patron of Leopold Mozart and
his son Wolfgang) in 1762, a position in which he remained
until 1800. The archbishop was not so devoted to music or
in any way so generous as Prince Esterházy. Michael's
annual salary was only three hundred florins, and though it
was doubled when he had reached the summit of his career,
these six hundred florins were no more than Joseph had
received after a single year of service with the Esterházys.
As a composer also, Michael was more and more eclipsed by
Joseph. He felt, however, that he had just as great a talent
as his elder brother and once exclaimed: "Give me an
encouraging hand, like that lent to my brother, and I will
not fall behind him."

[17] *Cf.* Joseph Haydn, *Gesammelte Briefe und Aufzeichnungen*,
ed. Dénes Bartha, Kassel, 1965.

Although this was far from the truth—Michael's talent could never have competed with Joseph's genius—it cannot be denied that Haydn's life in the service of Prince Nicolaus gave him just the opportunities he needed for his artistic growth. The very monotony of the daily routine, the lack of diversions of any kind, which probably would have been unbearable to an artist like Mozart, helped him to find himself. At Esterháza he was by no means deprived of intellectual and artistic stimulation; the performances of the traveling dramatic troupes offered, for instance, works by Goethe, Lessing, and Shakespeare, the last still a rarity in this part of the world. The "originality" attained at Esterháza therefore did not mean that Haydn was unaware of the great spiritual and artistic movements of the time. Indeed, this period offered very interesting proof of Haydn's sensitiveness to contemporary trends.

The eighteenth century was the age of rationalism. Religion, culture, and art—everything was governed by the intellect. But before long a reaction set in. In all countries Jean-Jacques Rousseau, with his motto of "return to nature," called forth a storm of opposition to things purely intellectual. The result was a new attitude toward the arts, the first traces of which can be found in England. Edward Young showed in 1759, in his *Conjectures on Original Composition,* that the man of genius creates not by means of his intellect, but with the aid of divine inspiration. A scintilla of this inspiration can be seen in the folk song. When, in 1765, Bishop Thomas Percy published his collection of old English and Scotch ballads under the title *The Reliques of Ancient English Poetry,* everyone began to be deeply interested in folk songs. Laurence Sterne wrote his humorous works, one of which, *A Sentimental Journey through France and Italy* (1768), revealed the poesy of the human heart and made the word "sentimental" the great fashion of the time. This movement, which in Germany was called *Sturm und Drang* (Storm and Stress), was not limited to literature. We find it in the music of that time, in compositions by Dittersdorf and Mozart, and especially in Haydn's works. A trend toward deepening and intensification of the emotional content had been noticeable in his output even earlier. Encouraged by the prevailing tendency to express darker moods, Haydn followed this line to such an extent that one may even speak of a "romantic crisis" in his music, reaching its climax in the works of 1771 and 1772. The passion and melancholy breaking forth in many compositions of this period were apparently not owing to external occurrences or to a specific unhappy experience. If anything in Haydn's personal life was responsible for these unrestrained outbursts, it was not the excess, but rather the starvation of his emotional life. Here lay the danger in his existence at Esterháza. His wife meant nothing to him; friends like Tomasini, Weigl, and Friberth, while very pleasant comrades, were receivers rather than givers in their relation to him. So all the emotional forces of which he was capable inundated his music, sometimes almost marring its artistic quality. What Haydn needed for full mastery in his art was the inner enrichment supplied by vital human contacts.

CHAPTER 6

LOVE AND FRIENDSHIP

1780–1790

In 1779, Prince Esterházy engaged an Italian violinist, Antonio Polzelli, and his wife, Luigia, a mezzo-soprano. Neither proved very satisfactory. The violinist suffered from poor health and often could not fulfill his duties; his wife, with the help of much coaching from Kapellmeister Haydn, was able to master only roles of secondary importance. Although their salaries were comparatively small—each received four hundred and sixty-five florins a year, whereas others, such as the singer Mathilda Bologna, had a salary of one thousand florins—the prince felt that their performances did not justify even this expenditure. Their contract was due to expire at the end of 1780, but even before that date they were told that their services would no longer be required. In spite of this, the Polzellis stayed on, receiving their former salaries, even though the consumptive Antonio in time disappeared from the orchestra and was not even mentioned in the list of its members. For once the prince did not insist on his wishes being carried out, for it became clear to him that if he wanted a contented Kapellmeister, he must put up with the presence of Luigia Polzelli.

The singer was only nineteen, and thus twenty-eight years younger than Haydn. She was a typical Italian brunette, with dark vivacious eyes, an oval face, an olive complexion, and a graceful figure. Her marriage with the aged and infirm Antonio was most unhappy. Haydn understood her plight only too well. The helplessness of the young singer roused all his protective instincts, and before long his sympathy grew into a deep passion. He seemed to feel that the miseries that for years he had suffered in his union with Maria Anna absolved him from any obligation to his marriage vows.

We know practically nothing about Luigia. No portrait of her is in existence, and we have to imagine what picture we can of her from the dry description in a passport issued many years later. Her character remains equally obscure; in fact, the only thing we know is that, in later years, after her husband's death, the widow continually asked for and received Haydn's financial assistance. This shows her, of course, in not a very pleasant light, but it does not prove—as many biographers seem to assume—that Luigia had submitted to Haydn's love ten years before for mercenary motives. It is known that women were often attracted by Haydn. The composer himself admitted it, sarcastically adding that his good looks could not have been responsible for it. There is no reason why Luigia should not have succumbed to the strong personality and abounding vitality of her musical mentor or why she should not have loved him genuinely.

Today we cannot ascertain whether Luigia was worthy of the love of a man like Joseph Haydn. Probably she was not, just as Aloysia Weber was not worthy of that of Wolfgang Amadeus Mozart. Nevertheless, at the time when Haydn was deeply in love, Luigia gave him what he needed, and by awakening his emotional life played an important part in his development. It seems doubtful that Haydn ever could have achieved the artistic maturity that his works of the 1780s reveal so splendidly if his passion for the Italian singer had not opened to him new vistas of life.

We do not have any letters from the time when their love was at its peak, but other documents throw light on Haydn's feelings for the young singer. Luigia had but a small mezzo-soprano, a type of voice for which the current Italian operas offered little scope. Haydn went out of his way to help her overcome these shortcomings. He transposed arias for her to adapt them to her range; he also subtly enriched their orchestral garb so as to make

the music sung by her more attractive. In the scores preserved in the Esterházy archives one can follow his pre-
occupation with Luigia's problems. Typical is his action in
the case of Gazzaniga's opera *La vendemmia*.[1] Here Luigia
had to sing a cavatina with a comparatively high tes-
situra. Haydn had the piece transposed a third down so
as to make it more easily accessible to her range. Apparently he also noticed during rehearsals that Luigia
found it difficult to hit correctly the aria's first note, as
the voice part started without any instrumental introduction. To help her, he inserted three forte chords played by
the orchestra at the beginning of the cavatina, a device he
did not use when the same tune was sung subsequently
by two more experienced singers. As Luigia's voice was
inferior to those of the other opera singers employed,
Haydn found it impossible to entrust a leading part to
her. Except for the somewhat more important role of Silvia
in his own opera *L'isola disabitata*, she played mostly
minor parts such as chambermaids. In order to improve
this situation, Haydn wrote special arias for her, tailored
for her vocal capacities and revealing her talent at its best.
These were inserted into the respective operas in which
she held small parts, and the exquisite pieces thus assured her success. The first of these "insertion arias" was
provided for Anfossi's opera *La Metilde ritrovata*, in which
Luigia represented the chambermaid Nannina. The Esterházy archives preserve five such "insertion arias" definitely
composed for her, and five others rearranged for her, but
we have reason to assume that in reality many more pieces
were especially composed for Luigia.

That the providing of such arias was a work of love is
proved by the quality of these delightful pieces and still
more by the fact that Haydn, burdened with countless responsibilities, still managed to find time for such labors. It
is true that he occasionally contributed an "insertion aria"
for another singer in order to improve an opera. Yet no
other of his singers was as frequently favored as Luigia.

Operatic life at Esterháza was certainly gaining in in-

[1] Cf. Bartha-Somfai, op. cit., p. 51, 001.

tensity and every year witnessed a number of first performances (see p. 72). Even after a fire had destroyed the theater in 1779, opera performances were not cut down, but merely transferred to the marionette theater. Particularly impressive was the repertoire in 1786. One hundred and twenty-five opera performances took place then, seventeen different works being presented alternately, among them eight novelties. Almost every year changes occurred in the vocal personnel and Haydn had to engage and subsequently to train new singers. Some of them brought operatic scores with them from Italy, and thus the Esterházy repertoire reflects the prevailing taste among the supporters of Italian opera. At Esterháza twelve works by Cimarosa, ten each by Anfossi and Paisiello, five by Dittersdorf, four by Guglielmi, three each by Traetta, Salieri, and Zingarelli, were performed in the period from 1776 to 1790. Naturally enough under these circumstances Haydn had no opportunity to compose many operas himself, and we find his creative work in this field more and more curtailed by his duties as opera conductor. In this period he wrote but three operas. *La fedeltà premiata* originated in 1779 to celebrate the opening of the new theater at Esterháza. There followed *Orlando paladino*, intended for the visit of Grand Duke Paul of Russia and his wife, the Grand Duchess Maria Fedorovna (a visit that was canceled, whereupon Haydn's opera was presented on his patron's name day, December 6, 1781). In 1784 he composed *Armida*, his last opera written for Prince Esterházy. It is noteworthy that these two very last operas enjoyed the greatest success at court, a success exceeding that of his previous dramatic works. *Orlando* was played thirty times through the seasons 1782–1784. *Armida* received twenty-one performances in 1784, seventeen in 1785, seven in 1786, and remained in the repertoire in succeeding years.

Studying the casts of the various operatic performances, one notices that Luigia Polzelli was quite active during the eighties, but did not appear on the stage in 1783. This was because of her pregnancy. A son, Aloysius Antonio Nicolaus, was born to her on April 22, 1783. Rumor persisted that he was Haydn's son. Probably this will never be clearly proved, but the imputation cannot be definitely rejected. In the Polzelli family his paternity was taken for granted, and Antonio's daughter did not hesitate to describe herself as Haydn's granddaughter when making an appeal for help in the *Musikalisches Wochenblatt* of December 31, 1875. Haydn himself never made a statement about this matter. He took a loving interest in Antonio as well as in Luigia's elder son, Pietro, born in 1777 in Bologna, but did not differentiate between the two. If anything, he rather preferred the elder. He taught them both music, watching with pleasure the unfolding of their talents, gave them much financial assistance, and helped them to obtain their first appointments.[2] After their mother ceased to mean much to Haydn, the two Polzelli boys were still sure of the master's unfailing sympathy. He certainly had the feelings of a father for both, and he made this so clear that even Frau Haydn, in spite of her hatred for Luigia, was resigned to this state of affairs and received Pietro Polzelli for a prolonged stay in her home "very kindly."[3]

Absorbed though Haydn was in his personal affairs through his love for Luigia, these years brought him another experience of equal or perhaps even greater importance. He met Wolfgang Amadeus Mozart, who had moved from Salzburg to Vienna in 1781. Naturally they had known of each other before this; now, however, a very close personal friendship was established between them that grew stronger from year to year.

It is difficult to conceive of two personalities funda-

[2] Pietro Polzelli, known as Pietrucchio, after working as second violinist in a Vienna orchestra, died at the age of nineteen from tuberculosis. Antonio Polzelli entered the Esterházy orchestra in 1803 and became its music director in 1813. Later he turned to agriculture, working as an estate agent for various Hungarian magnates. In 1826 he was knighted in Rome. Through speculations and lawsuits he lost his fortune and returned to music, dying as a music teacher in Budapest in 1855. Various compositions show him as a talented disciple of Haydn.

[3] Postscript by Haydn to one of Pietro's letters to his mother dated October 22, 1792.

mentally more different than these two great men. Mozart
developed with amazing rapidity. Haydn's progress was
incredibly slow. Indeed, at the age of thirty-six (Mozart
died at this age) Haydn had written hardly any important
compositions. In person Mozart was the typical artist,
his moods undergoing rapid changes from buoyant gaiety
to deep melancholy, from fits of temper to an almost femi-
nine gentleness. Haydn was of a rather even temperament,
mostly calm and gay, and had a great sense of humor. Mozart was a born dramatic composer and a brilliant virtuoso
on both the piano and violin; thus he gained tremendous
success as a performer. Haydn's gifts as a composer for the
stage were limited; he preferred to conduct his own works
inconspicuously from the harpsichord and was free from
any ambition to gain laurels as a soloist. There was little
sense of order and regularity in Mozart's life, and he had
no understanding of the value of money. Haydn's existence
throughout the greater part of his life had something of an
automatic precision; neatness and regularity were indispensable to him; in financial matters he was a match for
his publishers and he left considerable property at his
death, while Mozart died a pauper.

Perhaps the very differences between these two men of
genius drew them to each other. Had they constantly lived
together they might have got on each other's nerves, but
as they did not visit each other very frequently, every
meeting became an event. Haydn was fascinated by Mozart's quicksilver personality, while Mozart enjoyed the
sense of security that Haydn's steadfastness and warmth
of feeling gave him.

But for both of them, their artistic relations far tran-
scended in importance their personal contacts. At the time
of their first meeting, Mozart was twenty-five, Haydn forty-
nine, but the older composer who had developed so slowly
and the younger master who had grown so rapidly had
much to impart to each other. Whenever Haydn went to
Vienna he had the joy of attending chamber music performances at Mozart's home. In 1785, Leopold Mozart
visited his son and Wolfgang's new string quartets were
played for Haydn by the composer, his father, and the

two barons Tinti. Then Haydn took Leopold Mozart aside and said to him: "I tell you before God as an honest man that your son is the greatest composer known to me either in person or by reputation. He has taste and, what is more, the most profound knowledge of composition."[4] Mozart would not accept this praise for himself, but insisted that it was solely from Haydn that he had learned how to write string quartets. To acknowledge this to the musical world, he published in 1785 six quartets dedicated to his "beloved friend Haydn," expressing his deep gratitude in touching words. But he went much further than that, for he allowed no one to say anything against Haydn in his presence. Typical indeed was his reply to Leopold Koželuch, teacher of the pianoforte at the Vienna court. This composer, on hearing a daring passage in one of Haydn's quartets, remarked somewhat contemptuously: "I would never have written that." Whereupon Mozart replied: "Nor would I! And do you know why? Because neither you nor I would have had so excellent an idea." And on another occasion he exclaimed to Koželuch: "Sir, even if they melted us both together, there would still not be stuff enough to make a Haydn." This attitude was reciprocated by Haydn. After the Vienna premiere of *Don Giovanni,* sundry passages were criticized in his presence and he exclaimed: "I cannot settle this dispute but this I know: Mozart is the greatest composer that the world possesses now." And when someone expressed surprise at a daring disregard of the rules of harmony in Mozart's quartet in C major, he replied sharply: "If Mozart wrote it so he must have had a good reason for it." Other examples could be mentioned to illuminate the deep respect each composer felt for the other. Not only reports and anecdotes, but their works themselves testify to this. When the older master created his "Sun" quartets in 1772, the younger felt inspired to work in the same field, the result being compositions that in some respects follow Haydn's model. Then a considerable pause occurred in Haydn's quartet composition, and the same was true of Mozart's.

[4] Letter from Leopold Mozart to his daughter Nannerl, dated February 14, 1785.

But when Haydn had presented his "Russian" quartets, "written in a new and special way," Mozart composed the six exquisite quartets that he dedicated to Haydn.

As to Haydn, Mozart's influence is mainly noticeable in the late works, and we shall have to mention the name of the Salzburg master frequently when discussing Haydn's output in the 1790s. Before that, the young friend's operas had helped the older composer to clarify the limitations of his own talent. A few passages from letters may illustrate this. In his dealings with the Artaria publishing house, Haydn often boasted of his operas. On May 27, 1781, he remarked, for instance, about his *Fedeltà premiata*: "I do assure you that no such work has hitherto been heard in Paris or perhaps in Vienna either." On March 1, 1784, he wrote: "Yesterday my *Armida* was played for the second time with general applause. They say it is my best work up to now." But when he became acquainted with Mozart's *Nozze di Figaro, Così fan tutte,* and *Don Giovanni,* his own achievements in this field appeared to him in a new light. In December 1787 a great admirer from Prague, by the name of Roth, asked him to write an opera for Prague (as Mozart had done) and Haydn answered:

> You wish me to write an *opera buffa* for you. Most willingly if you are desirous of having a vocal composition of mine for yourself alone; but if it is with the idea of producing it on the stage at Prague I cannot comply with your wish, all my operas being too closely connected with our personal circle [Prince Esterházy's, in Hungary], so that they could never produce the proper effect, which I have calculated in accordance with the locality. It would be very different if I had the invaluable privilege of composing a new opera for your theater. But even then I should be taking a big risk, for scarcely any man could stand comparison with the great Mozart.
>
> Oh, if only I could explain to every musical friend, and to the leading men in particular, the inimitable art of Mozart, its depth, the greatness of its emotion, and its unique musical conception, as I myself feel

and understand it, nations would then vie with each other to possess so great a jewel within their frontiers. Prague ought to strive not merely to retain this precious man, but also to remunerate him; for without this support the history of any great genius is sad indeed, and gives very little encouragement to others to adopt a musical career, and for lack of this support many promising talents are lost to the world. It enrages me to think that the unparalleled Mozart has not yet been engaged by some imperial or royal court. Do forgive this outburst—but I love that man too much.[5]

Such an "outburst" was indeed a rarity for Haydn. It proves how much Mozart's welfare meant to him, that he was willing to disparage his own achievements if by so doing he could put the genius of his colleague in the right light.

That Mozart could exert so strong an impact on the older master testifies to Haydn's broadmindedness and flexibility. Even as a man of fifty he was by no means set in his ways. Fundamentally there was an amazingly small difference between the youth who twenty-five years previously had devoured manuals on music while nearly starving in his Vienna garret and the master who by now had achieved world fame.

World fame it was indeed that came to Haydn while he worked in the solitude of Esterháza. His name traveled far beyond the borders of his country, and in the whole of Europe there was hardly a music lover who did not know of, and admire, the works of Joseph Haydn.

The first indications of the composer's widespread reputation came from Spain. As early as 1779 the poet Yriarte wrote glowing praise of his music in the poem *La música*. Two years later King Charles III of Spain sent Haydn a golden snuffbox set with diamonds. What pleased the recipient perhaps even more than the gift itself was the manner in which it was presented. The secretary of the Spanish

[5] The letter was first published by Franz Xaver Niemetschek in his *Lebensbeschreibung des K. K. Kapellmeisters Wolfgang Amadeus Mozart* (Prague, 1798), p. 51.

Legation went to Esterháza for the sole purpose of hand-
ing over the royal gift and expressing his monarch's great
esteem for Haydn's music—a ceremony that must have afforded keen satisfaction to both the composer and his ambitious patron. What the Spanish court thought of Haydn
is also reflected in the attitude of the composer Luigi Boccherini, who was serving as chamber composer to the In-
fante Don Luis in Madrid. Boccherini admired Haydn's
music to such an extent that the Neapolitan violinist
Giuseppe Puppo nicknamed him "Haydn's wife." Spain
was also responsible for the composition of a work to which
Haydn himself attached the greatest importance, *The
Seven Last Words of Our Saviour on the Cross.* In his
preface to the score of the work published by Breitkopf
and Härtel in 1801, Haydn wrote:

About fifteen years ago I was requested by a canon
of Cádiz to compose instrumental music on *The Seven
Last Words of Our Saviour on the Cross.* It was customary at the cathedral of Cádiz[6] to produce an oratorio every year during Lent, the effect of the performance being not a little enhanced by the following
circumstances. The walls, windows, and pillars of the
church were hung with black cloth, and only one large
lamp hanging from the center of the roof broke the
solemn obscurity. At midday the doors were closed
and the ceremony began. After a short service the
bishop ascended the pulpit, pronounced the first of
the seven words (or sentences) and delivered a dis-
course thereon. This ended, he left the pulpit and
prostrated himself before the altar. The pause was
filled by music. The bishop then in like manner pronounced the second word, then the third, and so on,
the orchestra following on the conclusion of each dis-

[6] A. van Hoboken, *Joseph Haydn,* I (Mainz, 1957) (henceforth abbreviated as "Hob."), p. 845, remarks that the exercises
took place in a church situated in the grotto Santa Cueva,
which the priest Marqués de Valde-Inigo had decorated. It was
the marqués who conceived the idea of commissioning a composition for the Passion from Haydn, asking Father Don Fran-
cisco Micón, known to Haydn, to serve as intermediary.

Plate 1. Joseph Haydn, by T. Hardy. London, 1792.

Plate 2. Vienna around 1740. Oil painting by Bernardo Belot[

own as Canaletto. (Kunsthistorisches Museum, Wien.)

Plate 3. The house in Rohrau, lower Austria, where Haydn was born. Oil painting by W. Kröpsch, 1829. (Gesellschaft der Musikfreunde, Wien.)

Plate 4. Esterháza Castle. Engraving by Fernkorn, 1784.

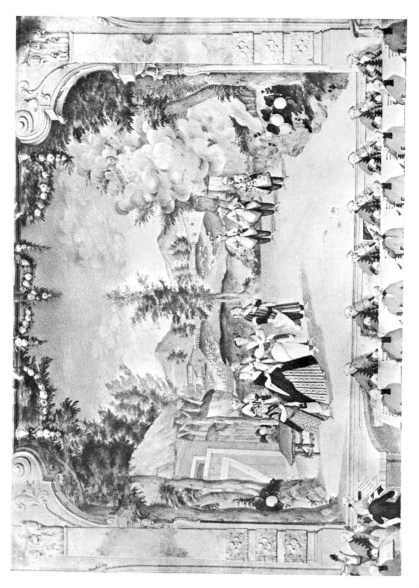

Plate 5. An opera performance at Esterháza Castle (probably the last scene from Haydn's *L'incontro improvviso*). The composer is conducting from the harpsichord. Anonymous oil painting.

Plate 6. J. Haydn, beginning of the String Quartet Op. 74 No. 3. (Autograph, Deutsche Staatsbibliothek, Berlin).

Plate 7. St. Stephen's Cathedral, Wien.

Plate 8. Haydn's square piano, his baryton,
and his bust (without a wig) by A. Robatz.
(Gesellschaft der Musikfreunde, Wien.)

Plate 9. The Bergkirche in Eisenstadt
where Haydn's last Masses had their first performance.
A monument to the composer, who was buried in this church,
is visible under the choir, at left.

Plate 10. Title page of
the original edition of
Haydn's *The Seasons.*

Plate 11. Prospect of London in the eighteenth century by Bowles.

Plate 12. Autograph letter of Haydn to J. P. Salomon, dated May 18, 1799.
(Gesellschaft der Musikfreunde, Wien.)

Plate 13. Joseph Haydn in the uniform
of an Esterházy court official.
Oil painting by J. B. Grundmann (around 1768).

Plate 14. Prince Nicholas Esterházy (the Magnificent).
Anonymous oil painting.

Plate 15. View of the Esterházy castle in Eisenstadt from the garden side.

course. My composition was subject to these conditions, and it was 'no easy matter to compose seven adagios to last ten minutes each, and succeed one another without fatiguing the listeners.

However, Haydn overcame these difficulties and he was justified in writing to the English publisher William Forster:[7] "Each word is expressed by purely instrumental means in such a way as to make the most profound impression on even an inexperienced listener's soul." The work won instant success and was before long played and printed in other countries. Thus, as early as 1793 the first performance took place in the United States.[8] The Spanish canon, incidentally, used an original way to present the honorarium. Haydn received a little box from Cádiz. Upon opening it, he saw to his surprise a chocolate cake. Angrily he cut into it, and found it filled with gold pieces.

France shared its neighbor's admiration for Haydn's music. In 1781 the composer could report to his Vienna publisher, Artaria: "Monsieur Le Gros, director of the Concerts Spirituels, wrote me a great many nice things about my *Stabat Mater* which had been given there [at Paris] four times with great applause; so this gentleman asked permission to have it engraved. They made me an offer to engrave all my future works, on very advantageous terms, and are much surprised that my compositions for the voice are so singularly pleasing." In 1784 another society, the Concerts de la Loge Olympique invited Haydn to write six symphonies specially for them, an invitation to which we owe the famous Paris symphonies (Nos. 82–87). The triumphant success of these works induced one of the society's directors, the Comte d'Ogny, to commission three more symphonies from Haydn (Nos. 90–92). Haydn's prestige in France is also reflected in a remark made to Adalbert Gyrowetz when this composer discovered that one of his own works was circulating in Paris under Haydn's name. "One answered Gyrowetz," the composer

---

[7] Letter of April 8, 1787.
[8] See M. D. Herter Norton, "Hadyn in America," *Musical Quarterly* (April 1932).

reports in his autobiography, "that he should consider it a great honor to have his symphonies taken for works by Haydn." As a matter of fact, enterprising French publishers like Nadermann and Sieber published a sizable amount of alleged "Haydn works" that were not contributed by the composer, a method by no means unusual in that era.

The year 1781, which brought Haydn the letter from Monsieur Le Gros and the present from the King of Spain, also saw the beginning of the master's direct connection with England. The eminent violinmaker William Forster applied to the British ambassador in Vienna for help in securing Haydn's works for his newly established publishing house. The ambassador, General Jermingham, was successful, and within six years Forster published no less than one hundred and twenty-nine works by Haydn, among them eighty-two symphonies, for which he paid considerable sums. Forster's example was followed by the firm of Longman and Broderip. When the Professional Concerts was founded in 1783, Lord Abingdon tried to induce Haydn to take over its direction. Haydn declined, as giving up the service of his prince appeared to be out of the question, and he knew that leave of absence would certainly not be granted to him by his patron. So the directors of the Professional Concerts had to be satisfied with a less famous musician, who opened the series with a Haydn symphony. That rumors persisted regarding Haydn's visit to England is revealed in a note from the north-German town of Königsberg appearing in April 1783 in Cramer's *Magazin für Musik*. It also testified to Haydn's fame in Germany: "Mr. Joseph Haydn, who in his exquisite sonatas has given to many a clavierist an antispasmodic against grief and misfortune, certainly would not take it amiss that the large number of yearning violinists dares hereby most submissively to ask him to bear them in mind and to regale them with some violin sonatas. As to the labor expended by the great artist, is it not payment enough when any violinist offers to the good man his sincere gratitude? According to newspaper reports, Haydn has undertaken a trip

to England. Crowned with laurels and, if his merits are
sufficiently rewarded, paid in good guineas, he will return
to his affectionate and admiring fatherland. Should this
note then come into his hands, he might fulfill the wishes
of the German violinists, who hold him in so great respect."

Haydn, though unable to accept the invitation to London, did not find it easy to give up any plan of this kind,
and as the years went by, it became more and more al-
luring. On April 8, 1787, he wrote to Forster[9] in London
that he hoped to see him personally at the end of the
year, and on July 19, 1787, he outlined to the London
impresario John Gallini terms under which he would come
to London.[10] We cannot ascertain whether this was meant
seriously. In all likelihood Haydn derived some satisfaction from toying with such plans while being tied firmly
to his duties at Esterháza. Meanwhile he kept in touch
with his English admirers.

A particularly enterprising publisher, John Bland, took
the trouble to travel from London to Esterháza to obtain
new works and to persuade Haydn to visit England. The
master presented Bland with two autographs. One was the
cantata *Arianna a Naxos*, the other the string quartet Op.
55, No. 2. About the latter work Bland used to tell an
amusing story, which brought it its peculiar nickname of
the Razor quartet. He said that he visited Haydn just when
the master, while shaving with a very blunt razor, exclaimed in despair, "I would give my best quartet for a
good razor." Bland rushed to his own room and brought
back his own excellent set of razors. Haydn was delighted
and scrupulously kept his promise, for the Razor quartet
was certainly among the best he had written.[11]

[9] Cf. H. C. Robbins Landon, *The Collected Correspondence
and London Notebooks of Joseph Haydn* (London, 1959),
p. 59.

[10] Ibid., p. 66.

[11] Though this sounds not improbable, the story may have
originated in Bland's imagination. Van Hoboken remarks quite
rightly (p. 414) that the quartet was not published by Bland,
and the autograph is lost.

Nor was England the only foreign country that invited the master. In Italy also Haydn was a great favorite. The Philharmonic Society of Modena elected him a member in 1780, thus putting to shame the Viennese Tonkünstlerso-cietät. In 1786, King Ferdinand IV of Naples, a passionate lover of music, commissioned several concertos for his favorite instrument, the lira organizzata (see p. 317). The works that Haydn wrote satisfied the king so completely that he urgently invited the composer to visit his court. Haydn felt much inclined to do so, and in the aforementioned letter to Forster he remarked: "I hope to see you personally at the end of the year, but since I have not heard from Mr. Cramer [London impresario] up to now, I shall accept an engagement to go to Naples this winter."

All in all, royalty was gracious to the son of the wheelwright. Friedrich Wilhelm II of Prussia, an excellent violoncello player,[12] after receiving from Haydn the Paris symphonies, sent him a magnificent diamond ring worth three hundred ducats. Haydn was delighted with the gift and thanked the monarch by dedicating the string quartets Op. 50 to him. He made a habit of wearing the ring when he composed an important work. Carpani even declares that when the master forgot to put on the ring, no ideas came to him.

Another royal admirer of Haydn was the Russian Grand Duchess and subsequent Empress Maria Fedorovna, who took lessons from him while visiting Vienna in 1782, and as late as 1805 sent him a valuable ring in thanks for his new songs for three and four voices. Such proofs of success naturally gave Haydn a great deal of gratification. But his fame did not in the least turn his head. He remained the same kind, simple man whose "eyes beamed with benevolence" (Dies), and he never forgot his humble origin. "I have had intercourse with emperors, kings, and many a great personage," he remarked once to Griesinger, "and have been told by them quite a few flattering things. For all that, I do not care to be on intimate terms with such persons and prefer to keep to people of my own station."

[12] Mozart wrote for the king his last three quartets; Beethoven dedicated the two violoncello sonatas, Op. 5, to him.

The aim of keeping his distance from the highborn is illustrated in a letter of July 28, 1787, to G. A. Kreusser, conductor to the Elector of Mainz.[13] Here the composer employed a servility of expression that we find not at all in keeping with the fame he enjoyed at that time:

> I take the liberty of asking you kindly to hand with my deepest submission the present two symphonies to His Serenity, your most gracious Prince, and as His Illustrious Highness desired to know the cost of all the music sent so far, I venture most obediently to mention the expense of fifty florins for the copying and one hundred talers for my undeserving self. Should this request in any way whatever seem offensive to your most gracious Prince, I won't demand a penny. I consider myself fortunate indeed merely to be favored by His Serene Highness' condescension in listening to my humble efforts.

We may assume that the elector found Haydn's demands reasonable, he being aware of the value the "humble efforts" of the renowned master represented.

Naturally enough, Vienna could not but be influenced by the attitude of the whole musical world. The publishing firm of Artaria and Company entered into a close business connection with Haydn and did much to promote the master's fame in his own country. In 1781, when Artaria published a collection of pictures of the greatest men of the time, they included the portrait of Haydn by Johann Ernst Mansfeld.[14] The composer was, as he wrote to them, "exceedingly pleased," and the prince "was even more delighted."[15] Although certain court circles in Vienna still maintained their old attitude, the number of Haydn's friends in Vienna steadily increased. They belonged mostly to the lower aristocracy or to the wealthy middle classes

[13] Cf. *Zeitschrift für Musik* (1938), p. 1328.

[14] It was reproduced in 1784 in the *European Magazine*, London, with a biography of the "Celebrated composer."

[15] Letter of June 23, 1781. Cf. F. Artaria and H. Botstiber, *J. Haydn und das Verlagshaus Artaria* (Vienna, 1909).

whose role in Austria's musical life was acquiring more and more importance.

Among them were the sisters, Franziska and Marianne von Auernbrugger, to whom Haydn dedicated six piano sonatas, and about whom he wrote to Artaria:[16] "The approval of the Misses von Auernbrugger is most important to me, as their style of playing and their genuine insight into music equal that of the greatest masters. Both deserve through public newspapers to become known in all Europe."

An important personality was the high official Franz Bernhard von Kees, and in his home orchestral concerts of amateurs regularly took place under the host's direction. The catalogue of Haydn symphonies compiled for von Kees was used in 1805 as a valuable source by Haydn and his helper Johann Elssler for his own list (see p. 215). Both Mozart and Haydn considered it an honor to have their new works performed in the von Kees house, and we understand their attitude when we read in a letter from Mozart to his father[17] that his symphony had been executed by forty violins, ten violas, eight violoncellos, and all the wind instruments doubled. Another friend was Hofrat Greiner, who chose the texts for Haydn's songs. As we learn from the memoirs of Greiner's daughter, his house was also frequented by Mozart, Salieri, Paisiello, and Cimarosa. Moreover Haydn liked to visit the Anglo-Italian composer, Stephen Storace, at that time living in Vienna, and his sister, the gifted Nancy, who sang the role of Susanna at the first performance of *Le nozze di Figaro*. The Irish singer Michael Kelly tells us in his *Reminiscences* of a chamber music party in Storace's home, when the quartets were played by no lesser masters than Haydn, Dittersdorf, Mozart, and Vanhall, while Paisiello and the Italian poet, Abbate Casti, were among the listeners. As Kelly remarks: "A greater treat, or a more remarkable one, cannot be imagined. . . . After the musical feast was over, we sat down to an excellent supper and became joyous and lively in the extreme."

[16] Letter of February 25, 1780.
[17] Letter of April 11, 1781.

There was also the music-loving merchant, Johann Michael Puchberg, who besides being an unfailing friend to Mozart (which of course spoke in his favor from Haydn's point of view), helped Haydn with financial matters. Puchberg and Haydn were the only people whom Mozart invited to the first rehearsals of *Così fan tutte*.

It was probably on the recommendation of Mozart and Puchberg, both ardent Freemasons, that in 1785 Haydn joined the highly reputed Masonic lodge, *Zur wahren Eintracht*. This he apparently did for the pleasure of associating with men of high culture. On January 24, 1785, he was voted in "by unanimous and delighted consent" and he was initiated on February 11. Apparently Haydn experienced some disappointment at this meeting, for he never attended another one, and in 1787 his name was removed from the membership list. While Haydn felt in tune with the humanitarian precepts of his fellow Masons, he may have been too deeply rooted in the Catholic faith and liturgy to concern himself seriously with the Masonic religious ideas.

Despite his numerous Viennese friends there was, with the possible exception of Mozart's home, no place in the city that proved so attractive to Haydn as the house of Peter L. von Genzinger, a very successful doctor who had been Prince Esterházy's physician for many years. Both the doctor and his charming wife, Marianne, an excellent singer and pianist, were real friends of music. On Sundays the musical elite of Vienna used to assemble at the Genzingers' home for performances of the first quality. Haydn attended these gatherings whenever he was in Vienna, and they meant a great deal to him. There he found an atmosphere that seemed like the fulfillment of his old dreams: a comfortable, pleasant home; a woman of high culture who took the keenest interest in every one of his new compositions and who at the same time was so thoughtful a hostess that she prepared his favorite dishes; children gifted for music whom he could guide. The Genzinger home offered him all that he had missed throughout his married life. He basked in this congenial atmosphere, only to feel all the more strongly the misery of his lonely existence when he returned to Esterháza.

Fortunately for us, letters were exchanged between Haydn and Marianne von Genzinger after she had sent him in January 1789 a pianoforte arrangement of an andante from one of his symphonies which she had made herself, and which, according to Haydn, was an excellent piece of work. Among the personal documents that have come down to us from Haydn, there is probably nothing more important than his letters to Marianne.[18] The master ordinarily found it difficult to get away from the florid and stilted style of his time. When he wrote to Marianne, however, the words seemed to come from his heart and they convey to the reader the impression that he is actually hearing Haydn talk to his dear friend. Most revealing is the long letter that he wrote to his "much esteemed and kindest Frau von Genzinger" on February 9, 1790, after a visit to Vienna:

> Well here I sit in my wilderness; forsaken, like some poor orphan, almost without human society, melancholy, dwelling on the memory of past glorious days. Yes, past, alas! And who can tell when those happy hours may return—those charming meetings where the whole circle has but one heart and one soul—all those delightful musical evenings that can only be remembered and not described? Where are all those inspired moments? All gone—and gone forever. You must not be surprised, dear lady, that I have delayed writing to express my gratitude. I found everything at home in confusion; for three days I did not know whether I was Kapellmeister or "Kapell-servant." Nothing could console me; my apartment was all in confusion; my pianoforte, which I formerly loved so dearly, was perverse and disobedient, and irritated rather than soothed me. I slept little, and even my dreams persecuted me, for when I fell asleep and was under the

[18] They are preserved in the National Library, Vienna, and were first published in T. von Karajan, *Joseph Haydn in London* (Vienna, 1861).

pleasant illusion that I was listening to *Le nozze di Figaro*, the blustering north wind woke me and almost blew off my nightcap. I lost twenty pounds in weight in three days, for the effects of the good fare at Vienna had disappeared on the journey back. Alas! alas! thought I to myself, when forced to eat at the tavern a slice of a fifty-year-old cow instead of your admirable beef, an old mutton with turnips instead of a ragout with little forcemeat balls, a tough grill instead of a Bohemian pheasant, Hungarian salad instead of good juicy oranges, and dry apple fritters instead of pastry. Alas and alas, thought I to myself, would that I now had many a tidbit that I despised in Vienna! Here in Esterháza no one asks me, "Would you like chocolate with or without milk? Will you take coffee with or without cream? What can I offer you, my good Haydn? Will you have vanilla ice or strawberry?" If only I had a piece of good Parmesan cheese, particularly in Lent, to enable me to swallow more easily the black puddings! Today I gave our porter a commission to get me a couple of pounds.

Forgive me, dear lady, for taking up your time in this, my very first letter, by so wretched a scrawl and such stupid nonsense; you must forgive a man spoiled by the Viennese. Now, however, I begin to accustom myself by degrees to country life, and yesterday I rehearsed for the first time, and somewhat in the Haydn style, too.

No doubt you have been more industrious than myself. The pleasant adagio from the quartet has probably now received its true expression from your fair fingers. I trust that my good Miss Peperl [Marianne's daughter] may be reminded of her master by often singing the cantata *Arianna a Naxos*, and that she will pay particular attention to distinct articulation and correct vocalization, for it would be a sin if so fine a voice were to remain shut up in her chest. I beg, therefore, for a frequent smile, or else I shall be much vexed. I also advise master François [the eldest son] to cultivate his musical talents. Even if

he sings in his dressing gown, it will do well enough,
and I will often write something new to encourage
him. I again kiss your hands in gratitude for all the
kindness you have shown me, and am unchangeably
while life lasts,

Yours, etc.
HAYDN

Soon after this letter was written an event occurred that
was bound to increase Haydn's depression. Princess Maria
Elisabeth, the wife of his patron, died on February 25,
1790. Haydn described the gloomy atmosphere at Esterháza in the following letter, which also shows that he kept
his friend informed of what was happening to him:

March 14, 1790

Most valued, esteemed, and kindest Frau von Genzinger,

I ask your forgiveness a million times for having so
long delayed my answer to your two charming letters.
This has been caused not by negligence (a sin from
which may Heaven preserve me so long as I live),
but by the pressure of business that devolved upon
me on behalf of my gracious prince in his present melancholy condition. The death of his wife has overwhelmed the prince with such grief that we have
been obliged to use every means in our power to rouse
him from his profound sorrow. I therefore arranged
for the first three days a selection of chamber music,
but no singing. The poor prince, however, the first
evening, on hearing my favorite adagio in D, was affected by such deep melancholy that it was difficult
to dispel it by other pieces. On the fourth day we had
an opera, on the fifth a comedy, and afterward our
daily theater as usual. I also commanded them to
study Gassmann's old opera *L'amor artigiano*, as our
master had recently expressed a wish to hear it. I
composed three new arias for it which I will shortly
send you, not on account of their beauty, but to demonstrate my industry. You shall receive the new sym-

phony I promised in April, so that it may be performed
at the Keeses' music party.

You must now permit me to kiss your hands grate-
fully for the rusks you sent me, which came exactly
at the right moment, when I had just finished the
last of the others. That my favorite *Arianna* has been
successful at Schottenhof[19] is delightful news to me,
but I recommend Miss Peperl to pronounce her words
clearly, especially in the phrase *che tanto amai.*

As I feel sure, dear lady, that you take an interest
in everything that concerns me (far greater than I deserve), I must let you know that last week I received
a present of a handsome gold snuffbox, of the weight
of thirty-four ducats,[20] from Prince Öttingen-Wallerstein, accompanied by an invitation to pay him a visit
this year, the prince defraying my expenses. His Highness is desirous of making my personal acquaintance
(a pleasing fillip to my depressed spirits). Whether I
shall be able to make up my mind to the journey is
another question.

I beg you to excuse this hasty scrawl.

I am always, etc.

HAYDN

P.S. My dutiful compliments to Your Grace's husband, your relatives, and the von Hacker family.—
I have just lost my faithful coachman; he died on the
twenty-fifth of last month.

The question has often been asked whether Haydn was
in love with Marianne von Genzinger. It is not easy to
answer. Marianne certainly showed no more than friendliness in her letters. They leave indeed the impression in
one's mind that she was always on guard to convey by her
words nothing but great esteem. We do not know what lay
behind it. Haydn exhibited less reserve. That he maintained such friendly relations with her but not with Dr.
Genzinger is hinted by his mentioning merely in a post-

---

[19] The Genzingers' residence.
[20] Haydn does not mention that the snuffbox also contained
fifty ducats.

script his "dutiful compliments to Your Grace's husband";
clearly his letters are meant only for her. Once he went
so far as to exclaim:[21] "I have so much to say and confess
to you, from which no one but yourself can absolve me."
And in the same letter he employs a revealing method of
punctuation by adding after the customary respects to the
doctor: "I kiss Your Grace a thousand times—on the hands."

It would not be surprising if Haydn had been in love
with this charming admirer of his art who, at the time
when these letters were exchanged, was only in her middle
thirties. When writing a sonata specially for her, he called
her attention in particular to the adagio and added, "It
has a deep significance that I will analyze for you when
opportunity offers." On another occasion, when a letter that
he had written to her went astray and they suspected that
it had been stolen by some curious person, Haydn reassured
his friend in the following words:[22]

> You need be under no uneasiness, dear lady, as re-
> gards either the past or the future, for my friendship
> and esteem for you (warm as they are) can never be-
> come reprehensible because I have always in mind
> my respect for your elevated virtues, which not only I,
> but all who know you, must reverence. Do not let this
> deter you from consoling me sometimes by your
> charming letters, as they are so needed to cheer me
> in this wilderness and soothe my deeply wounded
> heart. Oh, that I could be with you, dear lady, even
> for a quarter of an hour, to pour forth all my sorrows,
> and to receive comfort from you!

This letter gives a clear picture of what Marianne meant
to him. Here was a woman to whom he could "pour forth
his sorrows," who understood and comforted him.

But why should Haydn have needed comfort at that
time? Why was "his heart deeply wounded"? To all outward appearances he was leading a highly satisfactory existence. His fame by far exceeded anything he might have
hoped for in his proudest dreams; indeed probably no liv-

[21] Letter of June 20, 1790.
[22] Letter of May 30, 1790.

ing composer had a more widespread reputation. He had an excellent and well-paid position. His health was good, his productivity in fullest bloom. The unhappiness of his married life was a burden he had become used to carrying, and all the more so since he and his wife now mostly lived apart. Still, many remarks in his letters point to an increasing moodiness and dissatisfaction, which always are ascribed to the same reason. In his autobiographical sketch of 1778, he had proudly said of his position: "Kapellmeister to His Highness Prince Esterházy, in whose service I hope to live and die." Now he wrote:[23] "I am doomed to stay at home. What I lose hereby, Your Grace can certainly realize. It is indeed sad always to be a slave. Yet Providence decrees it so. I am a poor creature." Other similar outbursts could be mentioned, showing that Haydn had ceased to be happy at Esterháza. It was natural for him to long for Vienna, where he could enjoy the inspiring company of Mozart and the wonderful sympathy of Marianne von Genzinger. Moreover, the various invitations to foreign countries that reached him were a great temptation and made the master increasingly restless. But these were only symptoms of a more deeply rooted trouble. Haydn had outgrown Esterháza. The problems that had confronted him in his position there had ceased to interest him. Even his attachment to his patron had somewhat diminished. Like a person of half his age, Haydn, now a man of nearly sixty, craved for change, new tasks, new experiences. With the sure instinct of genius he felt that the immense creative forces still slumbering in him could be released only by a clean-cut break with the way of life that for nearly thirty years had been dear to him.

[23] Letter of June 27, 1790.

CHAPTER 7

SWEET LIBERTY

1790–1792

When Haydn was writing his melancholy letters during the spring and summer of 1790, he could not have guessed how soon the dreary monotony of Esterháza would become only a memory. In the autumn of that year things began to happen with a speed that he had never experienced before. Prince Nicolaus, the patron whom Haydn had faithfully served for twenty-eight years, died on September 28, 1790, thus removing the fundamental reason for his staying at Esterháza. Fortunately for Haydn and for the history of music, Prince Anton, who succeeded Prince Nicolaus, did not share his father's interests. He immediately dismissed all the musicians with the exception of Haydn, Tomasini, and a few instrumentalists who were to carry on the church services. Haydn's old patron and friend had bequeathed to him a yearly pension of a thousand florins, to which Prince Anton added four hundred florins, thus keeping the master nominally in his service, but at the same time leaving him perfectly free to do whatever he wished. Haydn jumped at this opportunity and without making any further plans, rushed off to Vienna. Indeed, he was so anxious to get away from Esterháza that he left behind most of his belongings. Hardly had he moved into an apartment in the house of his friend, Nepomuk Hamberger, when various offers were made to him. Prince Anton Grassalkovics, a son-in-law of Haydn's deceased patron and also a great lover of music, wanted him to come to his court at Pressburg. Such an offer naturally did not tempt Haydn, as it would have meant exactly the same kind of life he had been leading at Esterháza. King Ferdinand IV of Naples, who had come to Vienna for the triple marriage of two of his daughters and a son to members of the Habsburg family, repeated his former invitation with great urgency. While Haydn was still weighing the pros and cons of this proposition, he was swept off his feet by the bearer of a third proposal. One day a stranger appeared in his room and introduced himself with the blunt words: "My name is Salomon. I have come from London to fetch you; we shall conclude our accord tomorrow." In fact, a detailed agreement was instantly worked out by Salomon that stipulated considerably better terms than Haydn himself had outlined in 1787 in his letter to Gallini (see p. 89). He was to receive three hundred pounds for a new opera to be written for the king's theater, the same sum for six new symphonies, two hundred pounds for the copyright of them, another two hundred for twenty new smaller compositions to be performed by him at twenty concerts, and a guarantee of two hundred pounds for a benefit concert. As advance on these twelve hundred pounds Salomon proposed to deposit five thousand florins with the Viennese bankers, Fries and Company.

Italy or England, which was it to be? Haydn was confronted by a crucial problem. For many years he had cherished the dream of traveling to the classical land of opera. Again and again he had suggested such a trip to his patron, always to be put off with some excuse or other. Now, however, when the decision rested entirely with himself, Italy seemed much less glamorous. His interest in composing operas had waned considerably—partly because of the supremacy of Mozart's masterpieces—and he felt keenly that instrumental music was his particular language. In this field, England with its large, excellently trained orchestras was definitely the leader. Moreover, there was the question of personal freedom, which had become extremely vital for Haydn. At the court of a king, he would again have to wait in antechambers, conform to strict etiquette, and in short be treated once more as an upper servant. So Haydn chose England in spite of all the problems connected with such a venture. In a way, to go to

England required more courage than a journey to Italy; it was, to a far greater extent, a step into the unknown. Haydn spoke and wrote Italian fluently and was used to working with Italian singers. But he did not know a word of English, and had no chance of becoming even slightly conversant with it before reaching that country. The journey itself was more complicated, too, for it entailed the dreaded crossing of the Channel, which, even a hundred years later, deterred a less intrepid nature, that of Johannes Brahms, from accepting an honorary degree at Cambridge. In Haydn's time, crossing the Channel was certainly no minor venture, even for people brought up near the sea. There was the tragicomic experience of Dr. Burney, for instance. After leaving Calais on a stormy December day he had been "so nearly annihilated by his sufferings," that on arriving at Dover he had not enough energy left to move. Some time later, when he came out of his torpor, he found himself, to his unspeakable horror, on the way back to France. Haydn may have heard stories of this kind. Even if he had not, his Viennese friends did not restrain themselves from pointing out all the dangers awaiting a man fifty-eight years old starting for the first time on a great journey. But all their Cassandra-like cries were in vain, for the very novelty of the prospective experiences attracted Haydn. He was brimful of energy, in excellent health, and felt himself able to cope with any difficulty. So, when Mozart exclaimed, "Oh, Papa, you have had no education for the wide world, and you speak so few languages," Haydn answered serenely, "But my language is understood all over the world."

In his attitude Haydn was greatly sustained by Salomon, who became Haydn's shadow in his anxiety not to lose this invaluable prize. They got on very well together, in Vienna as well as in London, so that at a much later date Haydn spoke of Salomon as his "dearest friend." It therefore seems appropriate to say a few words about the artist who played an important part in the history of music by taking Haydn to England.

Johann Peter Salomon was born in 1745 at Bonn, the birthplace of Beethoven, and it is worthy of record that

for some time the Salomons shared a house with the Beethoven family. In 1816, Beethoven wrote to Ferdinand
Ries: "Salomon's death grieves me deeply, for he was a
noble-minded man whom I remember well ever since I
was a child." Salomon was an eminent violinist who filled
various positions in Germany and, in 1781, went to England, where he soon won success and a great reputation.
A correspondent of the *Berliner Musikzeitung*,[1] after praising Viotti as the greatest living violinist in Europe, declared
that Salomon almost equaled him as a virtuoso, though not
as a composer. In 1786, Salomon began to give subscription concerts, competing with the older series of the Professional Concerts. He had been an ardent admirer of Haydn
for a long time, and it was for these concerts that he
wanted to engage the master. It chanced that he was at
Cologne, on his way to Italy, when he heard of Prince
Nicolaus Esterházy's death. Taking the next coach, he
rushed to Vienna and carried Haydn off in triumph.

Despite Haydn's eagerness for the great adventure, it
was by no means easy for him to tear himself away from
Vienna, where he was bound by so many ties. There was
Marianne von Genzinger, whom he had so greatly pined
for at Esterháza. How delightful it was now to go regularly to her lovely home, to have long and friendly chats,
and to make music together! Haydn's sad feelings on leaving this cherished companion could not be better expressed
than in the "Farewell Song" for a lady friend, which until
recently has been considered one of his compositions.[2]
Words like "now when we have just begun to know each
other well we have to part" and "think of me when sea
and land are between us," with their tenderness and gentle
melancholy, might well have been uttered by the com-

[1] June 29, 1793.
[2] The piece appears in practically every edition of Haydn's
songs. A printed collection of Lieder by Leopold Koželuch preserved in the National Library of Vienna contains, however, a
simpler version of the song, thus casting grave doubts on
Haydn's authorship of the composition. (According to information supplied by Dr. A. van Hoboken; see also preface and
Kritischer Bericht by Paul Mies in Joseph Haydn *Werke* XXIX/1
Lieder. Munich, 1960.)

poser himself. We can conjecture that Haydn, becoming acquainted with the song, revised it and sang it to his friend in this improved form.

It was probably easier to leave Luigia Polzelli, for whom his passion had somewhat subsided. Luigia, of course, had also lost her position at Esterháza and moved to Vienna. Her husband, who had been failing rapidly, died in a hospital a few months after Haydn's departure. She depended mainly on Haydn's financial support, and would have liked very much to go to England with him. But this was out of the question for so mediocre a singer, and Haydn much preferred to get engagements for her in Italy.

Finally there was the parting from his beloved Mozart. They spent the last day together, both deeply moved. When they said good-bye, Mozart exclaimed with tears: "I am afraid, Papa, this will be our last farewell." Neither of the friends could guess the terrible truth in these prophetic words.

On December 15, 1790, Haydn and Salomon set forth on their journey, which was made as rapidly as possible because the manager was eager to start the preparations for his subscription series. Only two stops of any length were made, one at Munich, the other at Bonn, where, according to Griesinger, Haydn was received cordially and introduced to the court orchestra, of which young Beethoven was a member. On New Year's Eve the travelers arrived at Calais, and Haydn, in a short note to Marianne, described himself as "very well, although somewhat thinner, owing to fatigue, irregular sleep, and eating and drinking so many different things." Appropriately enough it was on New Year's Day that Haydn started his life in England. The journey itself seems to have been but moderately unpleasant and, unless Haydn was boasting to his friend, this elderly man, who had never seen the sea before, had stood on firmer sea legs than most of his fellow passengers. Anyway this is how he described the great event to Marianne:[3]

I must now tell you that on New Year's Day, after

[3] Letter of January 8, 1791.

attending early Mass, I went on board at 7:30 AM, and at five in the afternoon arrived safe and well at Dover, for which Heaven be praised! During the first four hours there was scarcely any wind and the vessel made so little way that in that time we went only one English mile. Fortunately toward eleven-thirty such a favorable breeze began to blow that by four o'clock we had come twenty-two miles. I remained on deck during the whole passage, in order to gaze my fill at that huge monster, the ocean. So long as there was a calm I had no fears, but when at length a violent wind began to blow, rising every minute, and I saw the boisterous waves rushing on, I was seized with slight alarm, and a little indisposition likewise. But I overcame it all and arrived safely in harbor without being actually sick. Most of the passengers were ill and looked like ghosts. I did not feel the fatigue of the journey until I arrived in London, but it took two days before I could recover from it. But now I am quite fresh and well, and occupied in looking at this mighty and vast town of London, its various beauties and marvels causing me the most profound astonishment.

Haydn's "astonishment" can well be imagined. What his young friend, the Czech composer, Adalbert Gyrowetz, expressed in his autobiography (written in the third person) may also reflect the older master's attitude: "The first moment Gyrowetz stood on English soil, he felt as if he were seeing a new world. Everything was different: a different air, a different architecture, different regulations, different customs, the highest degree of cleanliness in everything, and quite different people." And Gyrowetz had traveled a great deal through Italy and France, whereas Haydn had never before been beyond a small section of his own country, a territory corresponding in area approximately to that of the state of Connecticut.

It was not only the strangeness of English life that made Haydn's head whirl; it was also the size of London and its enormous traffic. The figures relating to London's population interested him tremendously. We find twice in his diary[4] a remark that in thirty-one years thirty-eight thousand houses had been built in London, that in 1791, twenty-two thousand persons died in this city, that it consumed annually eight hundred thousand cartloads of coal and kept four thousand carts for cleaning the streets. London fascinated and at the same time frightened him. "The noise in the streets and the cries of the common people selling their wares" seemed "unbearable" to him. As to the traffic, we can well imagine what Haydn felt if we refer to a letter that Horace Walpole wrote in 1791 to Miss Berry:

> Though London increases every day, the town cannot hold all its inhabitants, so prodigiously is the population augmented. I have twice been going to stop my coach in Piccadilly, thinking there was a mob, but it was only nymphs and swains sauntering. The other morning I was stopped five times before I reached Northumberland House, for the tides of coaches, chariots, and phaetons are endless. Indeed, the town is so extended that the breed of chairs is almost lost, for Hercules and Atlas could not carry anybody from one end of this enormous capital to the other.

Added to these difficulties was the strange tongue. Perhaps Haydn was right in assuming that he, with his music, could make himself understood everywhere, but it was another matter for him to understand others. This elderly man with the soul of a youth was filled with insatiable curiosity regarding all aspects of English life and he did

[4] There exist three diaries (or notebooks) from the English visits. Two, preserved by the National Library, Vienna, refer to his first stay; one, in the Mozarteum, Salzburg, refers to the second. There must have existed also a second notebook of the second visit, from which Griesinger and Dies quoted excerpts, but it cannot be traced today. Large sections of the first two notebooks are translated in H. E. Krehbiel, *Music and Manners* (New York, 1898). The third diary is reprinted by H. E. Engl in *Haydns handschriftliches Tagebuch* (Leipzig, 1909). Landon, op. cit., p. 251 ff., translates and reprints all three notebooks.

not like at all being left out of anything. John Taylor in
his *Records of My Life* describes a dinner party at the
house of the singer Madame Mara which was attended by
the satirist Dr. John Wolcot (Peter Pindar), and the violoncellist, John Crosdill,[5] and continues:

> Before the wine was removed, Mr. Salomon arrived
> and brought Haydn with him. They were both old
> friends of Madame Mara. Haydn did not know a word
> of English. As soon as we knew who he was, Crosdill
> proposed that we should celebrate the arrival of
> Haydn with "three time three." This proposal was
> warmly adopted and commenced, all parties except
> Haydn standing up. He heard his name mentioned,
> but not understanding this species of congratulation,
> stared at us in surprise. He was so confused by this
> unexpected and novel greeting that he put his hands
> before his face and was quite disconcerted for some
> minutes.

Incidents like that must have happened often enough.
Haydn, of course, did his best to study English and in the
spring mornings he used to walk in the woods alone with
his English grammar,[6] but for him to follow and take part
in the conversations of his new English friends was a continuous strain.

The numerous old acquaintances that Haydn renewed
in London were a great help. The British capital attracted
artists and virtuosos from all corners of the earth. When
Haydn visited there, it was one of the most important
centers of music (although the British composers of the
time could not compare with those of Vienna). The most
eminent musicians flocked to England, received great honors and excellent salaries, and helped to build up a musical
life which, in volume at least, was quite dazzling. Many of
these artists had been in Vienna, and with them Haydn
naturally established contact.

Mention has already been made of Adalbert Gyrowetz,

[5] Crosdill was the violoncello teacher of the Prince of Wales.
[6] Letter to Marianne dated September 17, 1791.

whom Haydn had met years before at the private concerts of their common friend, Hofrat von Kees.[7] Gyrowetz had arrived in London two years before Haydn; he was a great success and moved freely in society. According to his autobiography, he helped Haydn by introducing him to the right people.

There was also Gertrude Elisabeth Mara, a singer of German origin who had captivated London by the "irresistible fire, dignity, and tenderness of her vocal appeal" (Gardiner) at the Handel Festival of 1784. Madame Mara had been in Vienna in 1780, after escaping from Prussia, where King Friedrich II had held her almost as a captive because of his enthusiasm for her art. Haydn admired her and was glad to have Salomon engage her for appearances at his own concerts.

The distinguished Croatian violinist, Giovanni Mane Giornovichi, who according to Dittersdorf, played "with art and heart," was also known to our master from his participating in the von Kees concerts.

One of the most successful pianists in London was Muzio Clementi. Haydn had probably met him in 1782, when Clementi had gone to Vienna for his contest with Mozart on the pianoforte. Clementi apparently was fond of Haydn, for he presented him with a goblet made of cocoanut shell adorned with rich silver ornaments.

Haydn also had friendly relations with the Czech pianist Jan Ladislav Dussek, who lent him his own excellent piano when the master moved to a more rural apartment in Lisson Grove. In a charming letter to Dussek's father,[8] Haydn described the son as "one of the most upright, moral, and, in music, most eminent of men."

Stephen and Nancy Storace were delighted to meet Hadyn again. He had visited them and played chamber music at their home in Vienna. The master's diary, in men-

[7] Gyrowetz describes his first meeting with various masters at the von Kees house as follows: "Haydn smiled a bit roguishly, Dittersdorf was serious, Albrechtsberger quite indifferent, Giornovichi somewhat somber though noblehearted, and Mozart the kindest of all."

[8] Letter of February 26, 1792.

tioning a dinner with them on June 3, 1792, adds the obscure remark "sapienti pauca," which may have meant that
the food offered was not too plentiful. Among the Storaces'
circle of friends was Michael Kelly, the Irish tenor, returned
to London from Vienna, where he had sung Don Basilio
and Don Curzio at the premiere of *Le nozze di Figaro*.
He probably was not a great creative musician—this is implied at least by Sheridan's remark that "Kelly composed
his wines and imported his music"—but he was a pleasant
companion, and Haydn could chat with him about their
various mutual friends in Vienna.

Another man who, though not personally known to
Haydn, had been corresponding with him for some time,
was the great musicologist, Dr. Charles Burney. He wel-
comed the master with an enthusiastic poem, and one of
Haydn's first visits was to Chelsea College, where the English scholar held the post of organist.

Such was the circle of fellow musicians who gathered
around Haydn, a circle that was to be greatly widened
during the following eighteen months. And there was always Salomon, who helped Haydn get a footing in the
strange and fascinating new world into which he had been
plunged. To find one's way through the intricacies of London's musical life, with all its different currents and undercurrents, was indeed not easy and Haydn needed Salomon's guidance. A preview that appeared in the *Morning
Chronicle* on December 30, 1790, may help us to get some
idea of the number of musical events in the British capital:

> The musical arrangements now being made promise
> a most harmonious winter. Besides two rival opera
> houses a Concert [meaning a whole series] is planned
> under the auspices of Haydn, whose name is a tower
> of strength, and to whom the amateurs of instrumental
> music look as the god of the science. Of this concert
> Salomon is to be the leader and Madame Mara the
> principal singer.
> The Professional Concerts under the able conduct-
> ing of Cramer, are to be reinforced by Mrs. Billing-
> ton, assisted occasionally by Mr. and Mrs. Harrison.

The Ancient Concerts under the patronage of Their Majesties will continue soon after the queen's birthday, with Cramer as their leader and Storace as the principal singer. The Ladies' Subscription Concerts are to be continued as usual on Sunday evenings by permission (we hope) of His Grace the Archbishop of Canterbury.

There will be oratorios twice a week at the theaters of Drury Lane and Covent Garden during Lent.

These, with the Academy of Ancient Music will constitute the principal public musical entertainments of this winter.

Five different subscription series of orchestral concerts—an amazing quantity of music to be offered to a city of less than a million inhabitants. And all this was eagerly absorbed. Most of the concerts were crowded; thus, on the very day when Haydn's sensational first concert took place, oratorio performances in the two theaters also had very full houses. Present-day historians might find the artistic standard of the London audiences of 1791 not high enough —Marion Scott, for instance, in her delightful study *Haydn in England*[9] warns us against mistaking quantity for quality. Anyway, it cannot be denied that the Londoners of Haydn's time loved music very much and that it was natural for them to hear a good deal of it and, if we may believe Gyrowetz,[10] also to perform it. To be sure, the element of competition played some little part in rousing the public's interest in the various concerts. There was, for instance, a fierce rivalry between the English and the Italian opera (Covent Garden versus the Pantheon), between the Professional Concerts and the Salomon series, rivalries in which the press took a very active part. But this was a common occurrence in the eighteenth century, and London certainly took such matters no more passionately than

[9] *Musical Quarterly* (1932).

[10] He writes in his autobiography: "The girls are mostly musical and either well versed in the pianoforte or in singing, and know how to spend their evenings very pleasantly in this way. The men, however, are slightly or not at all musical, but they love to listen to music."

Paris did. Leaving aside those snobs who went to the concerts only for the sake of fashion or faction, enough sincere
music lovers remained to give Haydn the satisfaction of
being truly valued and understood.

Returning to that memorable New Year's Day of 1791,
when Haydn set foot on English soil, we find the master
spending his first night at 45 High Holborn, the home of
John Bland, owner of the Razor quartet. Haydn's host received him with open arms and good pea soup (which
meant much to our master, for in a letter to Marianne he
pined for her delicious soups). Mrs. Bland may have somewhat disconcerted this lover of female beauty at first sight
for she was "short and fat, pitted with smallpox and on the
whole the most inharmonious-looking person that can be
imagined."[11] Later, however, Haydn may have learned to
share the general verdict that "when she sang, she threw
a charm and magic on all she did that was perfectly entrancing."

The next day Haydn moved to a "neat, comfortable,
though very dear" lodging provided by Salomon in the
house where he himself lived (18 Great Pulteney Street,
Golden Square). The Italian landlord was an excellent
cook, and Haydn would have liked to enjoy the meals he
offered in the sole company of Salomon, so as gradually to
get his bearings. This was not to be, however, for Salomon
had paved the way for Haydn extremely well. The newspapers made much of his arrival, and when Haydn wrote
to Marianne on January 8, he confessed that he had "already dined out six times" in this first week and that he
could be invited every day if he chose.

With a certain naïve pride Haydn describes his social
life in a letter to Prince Esterházy,[12] significant in that its
tone definitely deviates from that of former letters to the
princely patron. Here Haydn is incomparably less submissive, and one has the impression that in 1791 it would
not have occurred to him to employ such an expression as

[11] Henry Phillips, *Musical and Personal Recollections* (London, 1864).

[12] *Acta Musicalia*, fasc. I, 55 (*Valkó I*). The letter is dated
January 8, 1791.

"kissing the hem of the princely coat," which was used by him in 1766. Thus, just eight days after his arrival in England the process of detaching himself from the way of life known to him for thirty years had begun. He wrote:

I report respectfully that despite very poor weather and many bad roads throughout the journey I have arrived safe and sound in London on January 2. My arrival caused a great sensation and forced me to move on the very same evening to larger quarters. I am so burdened with visitors that I will hardly be able to reciprocate within six weeks. Both ambassadors called, that is, Prince Castelcicala of Naples and Baron von Stadion. I also had the privilege of having dinner with them at six in the evening.

The new opera libretto I have to compose is entitled *Orfeo*, in five acts, and I will get it one of these days. It is said to be quite different from that used by Gluck. The prima donna is Madame Lops of Munich, a pupil of the great Mingotti, seconda donna is Madame Capelletti, primo homo the famous Davide. The opera is only for three persons, Madame Lops, Davide, and a castrato who is said to be not very outstanding. Moreover, it is to contain many choruses and ballets and great changes of scenery.

In a fortnight the first opera, *Pirro*, by Paisiello will be presented. The concerts will start only next month, on February 11, about which I will later dutifully report to Your Highness, and meanwhile I remain, Your Serenity's

Respectful and most obedient
HAYDN

I venture respectfully to kiss the hands of the most beautiful Princess, Your Highness' charming wife, as well as of Princess Marie and Her Highness' husband.

My address for the time being is: No. 18 Great Pulteney Street, Golden Square, London.

Besides making social contacts Haydn was eager to get a true impression of English musical life. He attended various concerts, at which great honors were bestowed on the illustrious guest, and the impressions he received from the size and quality of the English orchestras were responsible for various alterations he made in the works he had brought with him.

Eighteen days after his arrival he made his real debut in society. He was invited to the court ball given in honor of the queen's birthday, and to the amazement of the guests was greeted very respectfully by the Prince of Wales, though he had not yet been presented at court. Haydn was very favorably impressed by this "handsomest man on God's earth," as he once described him to Marianne.[13] Indeed, the appearance of the future George IV must have been dazzling even to one used to Prince Esterházy's splendor, for on this occasion he wore diamonds worth some eighty thousand pounds. The next day Haydn's interest in the prince was heightened further, for when he was invited to take part in one of the famous musical evenings at Carlton House, the residence of the prince, he found that his host possessed "an extraordinary love of music, and a great deal of feeling."[14] The chamber music, played by Haydn, Salomon, and Giornovichi, and sung by the Italian tenor Davide, took place in the small music room, the "jewel" of Carlton House. Again Haydn's impressions may best be expressed in the words of Horace Walpole: "In all the fairy tales you never were in so pretty a scene. Madam, I forgot to tell you, how admirably all the carving, stucco, and ornaments are executed, but whence the money is to come, I conceive not—all the tin mines in Cornwall would not pay a quarter."

The prince's gigantic debts were known even to Haydn. He mentioned the fact to Marianne, adding anxiously: "*Nota bene*, this is *entre nous*." He need not have worried on this account, as the prince's financial problems were a common topic of conversation. But although His Royal

[13] Letter dated December 20, 1791.

[14] The following story mentioned by Pohl in *Mozart und Haydn in London* (Vienna, 1867) proves the prince's musical aptitude. When he was three years old, he heard the violinist F.-H. Barthélemon and was so impressed by the "harmonics" the artist produced that he exclaimed: "There must be a flute hidden in the violin," and eagerly tried to find its hiding place.

Highness was generally considered to be "above a low
attention to pecuniary matters"[15] Haydn was one of the
very few musicians rewarded adequately for his work.
Following the advice of English friends, he sent on his return to Vienna to the commissioners of Parliament a bill
for one hundred guineas as the honorarium for twenty-six
appearances at Carlton House and obtained prompt payment.

Haydn, by the way, seems also to have enjoyed the fare
offered by his royal host. Anyway, he took pains to note
in his diary the recipe of the Prince of Wales's punch as
follows: "one bottle champagne, one bottle burgundy, one
bottle rum, ten lemons, two oranges, a pound-and-a-half
of sugar."

While the master was starting on an extremely successful social career under the auspices of the Prince of Wales,
he was at first prevented from appearing in public in his
real capacity. Salomon, though most eager to open his
concert series at the earliest possible moment, found himself
unable to carry out his intention. For the first concert he
had engaged the singer, Giacomo Davide, the "first tenor
of his time," as Lord Mount-Edgcumbe described him.
Signor Davide, however, was under contract to make his
first public appearance in the Italian opera at the King's
Theater and as (for reasons to be mentioned later) that
performance could not take place, Salomon was twice
forced to postpone his concert. This was most fortunate
for the rival enterprise, the Professional Concerts, which
started on February 7. Considerately a symphony and a
quartet by Haydn were performed and the composer received a free ticket of admission to all the concerts. Haydn
went and declared that he had never heard a symphony
of his played so well. In spite of this exchange of courte-
sies, Salomon's rivals were not above circulating rumors
injurious to the visiting composer. Remarks could be overheard or read in certain newspapers that Haydn, although
undoubtedly a great composer, was after all an old man
whose powers were exhausted and who was bound to

[15] Letter of Lady Montagu, the "Queen of the Bluestockings,"
dated June 4, 1795.

disappoint the high expectations of British friends of music. Haydn could not help being aware of such undercurrents. He tried not to let them discourage him, and with characteristic persistence, used the extra time to rehearse most carefully, playing important passages to the orchestra on the violin and gradually imbuing them with a perfect understanding of his ideas and wishes.

When the great day finally came, he swept the London audience completely off its feet. The concert took place on March 11, 1791, at the famous Hanover Square rooms, the scene of so many great events in music. Opened in 1775 by Johann Christian Bach, they were destined, after Haydn's triumphs, to witness the spectacular appearances of Liszt, Rubinstein, Mendelssohn, Joachim, and many others. Haydn's audience was a very brilliant one: the ladies all in hoops, the gentlemen in full dress with swords, the solo performers preceded by the sword-bearer who girded them in front of the audience with a special weapon. The artists Salomon had engaged were of the first class and earned much applause. The climax was reached with Haydn's new symphony in D major (No. 96). At the special request of the composer, it was played as the first number of the second part, Haydn hoping that by that time the many latecomers would be in their seats. The orchestra was much stronger than the Esterházy ensemble. It contained some forty players, including sixteen violins, four violas, three violoncellos, and four double basses. Salomon was the leader, playing on a Stradivarius instrument that had previously belonged to Corelli, and Haydn conducted from the harpsichord. Dr. Burney attended the concert and described the reaction of the public in the strongest words he could think of, speaking of Haydn's "electrical effect on all present" and of "such a degree of enthusiasm as almost amounted to frenzy." The slow movement of the symphony had to be encored, and this made Haydn so proud that he asked Griesinger to record this "unusual occurrence." To Luigia Polzelli he reported[16] the fact adding that, he was told, such a thing had never before happened in London. "Imagine," he

[16] Letter of March 14, 1791.

wrote, "what it means to hear this from an Englishman's lips!" March 11 definitely assured Haydn's success in English musical life, and it is significant that the *Morning Chronicle* ended its report with the words: "We cannot suppress our very anxious hope that the first musical genius of his age may be induced by our liberal welcome to take up his residence in England."

The succeeding concerts of the series, taking place from March to June, were a continuous triumph; the peak was reached with Haydn's benefit concert on May 16, when he earned three hundred and fifty pounds, almost double what had been guaranteed to him.

The brilliant success won in the Salomon concerts had far-reaching consequences. It increased Haydn's confidence in himself enormously. He had, of course, before his journey to London, received numerous proofs of his outstanding reputation in various countries. Still, it is one thing to read an enthusiastic letter and another to experience directly the response of a huge and brilliant audience. This was a novel sensation for the master, used to performing his works mostly to a very small and intimate circle of musical connoisseurs. The frenzied applause he was given by the exacting audience of the world's largest capital did not go to his head; it was only a challenge for him to offer London the very best he could give. Haydn's creative powers were taxed to the utmost, and the result took the form of the twelve London Symphonies (six of them written for his first stay in London, six for his second) in which Haydn's music for orchestra attained its very climax. For these masterworks the musical world has to thank London; it is indeed doubtful that Haydn's genius would ever have unfolded so brilliantly without the stimulus of his English adventures.

On the other hand, Haydn's presence in London gave British music an inspiration and impetus of the greatest value which ultimately reached far beyond the frontiers of Great Britain. Musicians who had the privilege of playing under him or, at least, of becoming acquainted with the master's interpretation of his own works, traveled from London to the New World, taking with them an insight

into how Haydn's works should be performed. There is a
direct line from Haydn to such pioneers of American musical life as Graupner, Menel, Hewitt, and Bergmann.

Haydn's triumph was crowned, so to speak, at the in-
stigation of the faithful Dr. Burney, when he was invited
in July 1791 to the Oxford Commemoration in order to
receive the honorary degree of Doctor of Music. Unlike
Brahms, who received a similar invitation from Cambridge,
Haydn went and was immensely feted. Three concerts
took place on this occasion with brilliant soloists, among
them "little Clement," for whom Beethoven was to write
his violin concerto. As a thesis Haydn was obliged to offer
a new symphony. The work in G major (No. 92), composed in 1788 for the Comte d'Ogny, was chosen, and
thenceforth was named the Oxford symphony. Later
Haydn sent the university as his "exercise" a three-part
canon cancrizans, *Thy Voice, O Harmony.* Haydn felt
strange in his doctor's gown of cherry-and-cream-colored
silk, which he had to wear for three days. But he was not
above a bit of naïve pride. "I only wish my Viennese friends
could have seen me," he wrote to Marianne. In his diary
he commented on the event in these words only: "I had to
pay one-and-a-half guineas for the bell peals at Oxforth
[sic] when I received the doctor's degree, and half a guinea
for renting the gown. The journey cost six guineas." This
matter-of-fact statement is not surprising, as Haydn never
expressed any personal feelings in his notebook, but confined himself to jotting down mere facts. A letter to Marianne on the event mentioned by Haydn apparently did
not reach her. To his biographer, Dies, however, Haydn
stressed the importance of the degree, to which he owed,
as he declared, "much, I might say everything, in England;
for thanks to it I met the first men and was admitted to the
most important houses." Although this seems to be somewhat exaggerated, it is certain that this man, who still
remembered so well how he had striven desperately as a
penniless youth to instruct himself in all that Reutter had
failed to teach him, felt satisfaction in signing his letters
with the words "Doctor zu Oxford." After being acclaimed
as a fellow scholar by one of the oldest universities of the

world, Haydn easily could disregard those critics in the German-speaking countries who had found his music too light and not learned enough.

Strangely there is no comment in Haydn's notebook on the exquisite buildings of Oxford. Perhaps he was too much occupied with rehearsals and social functions to take in all the beauty around him. That he observed such things when traveling in a more leisurely way is shown by his account of Cambridge, which he visited in November of the same year:

> Each university has at the back of it a very roomy and beautiful garden, besides stone bridges, in order to afford passage over the stream that winds past. King's College Chapel is famous for its carvings. It is all stone and so delicate that nothing more beautiful could have been made of wood. It has already endured four hundred years, yet everybody judges its age at about ten years because of the firmness and peculiar whiteness of the stone.

At this time, when Haydn was reaping the greatest triumphs as a symphonic composer, his efforts in the domain of opera were doomed to failure. In accord with his contract with Sir John Gallini, he worked during the first part of his stay in London on the opera *L'anima del filosofo*, based on a book by Badini. He had completed the work (having written one hundred and ten pages, hardly less than the scores of all the first six London Symphonies) when it turned out that Gallini was unable to perform the opera for reasons beyond his control. The old Italian opera at the Pantheon was supported by the king, and the management exerted all its influence to prevent a second Italian opera from ·being established in the King's Theater. Although the Prince of Wales espoused Gallini's cause, the Pantheon's adherents pointed out that two Italian opera houses were not needed. Haydn's opera was to be performed in May, but after long controversies Gallini was refused a license for opera altogether. When Haydn was conducting the first rehearsal, officials appeared and forced him to stop after forty measures had been played. Gallini had to be content with arranging entertainments of music and dancing, using the soloists he had engaged. Frequently Haydn's music, such as the chorus "The Storm" (on words by Peter Pindar, pseudonym for John Wolcot), was included. There was now no opportunity for a performance of *L'anima del filosofo*; nevertheless Gallini paid the agreed sum for the composition. The composer naturally regretted having spent so much time on this work, but it seems that he was not especially interested in it, for he never had it performed elsewhere. As for Gallini, who had paid three hundred pounds without being able to produce the opera, no pity need be wasted on him, for in spite of various accidents during his career as a manager he left the tidy sum of £150,000 when death took him in 1805.

Although Haydn's creative output in the field of opera came to an abrupt end in England, it was there that he received the incentive to enter a new field. Here again we have to thank London for a most decisive influence on Haydn's work.

In 1784 a Handel Commemoration on a gigantic scale took place in Westminster Abbey, celebrating the centenary of that master's birth. Its success was so great that similar performances were arranged in the three succeeding years. Then an interval of four years followed, after which a Handel Festival of the same kind took place in May 1791, with Haydn among the enraptured audience. William Gardiner gives a lively description of the scene:

> On entering the Abbey I was filled with surprise at the magnitude of the orchestra; it rose nearly to the top of the west window and above the arches of the main aisle. On each side there was a tier of projecting galleries and I was placed in one of these. Above us were the trumpeters and appended to their instruments were richly embossed banners worked in silver and gold. We had flags of the same description which gave the whole a gorgeous and magnificent appearance. The arrangement of the performers was admirable, particularly that of the sopranos. The young ladies were placed upon a framework in the center of

the band in the form of a pyramid, as you see flower-pots set up for a show. This greatly improved the musical effect. The band was a thousand strong, ably conducted by Joah Bates upon the organ. The orchestra was so steep that it was dangerous to come down and some accidents occurred, one being of a ludicrous nature. A person falling upon a double bass, as it lay on its side, immediately disappeared; nothing was seen of him but his legs protruding out of the instrument. For some time no one could assist him for laughing. Haydn was present at this performance and with the aid of a telescope, which had been placed on a stand near the kettledrums, I saw the composer near the king's box. The performance attracted persons from all parts of Europe and the demand for tickets was so great that in some instances a single one was sold for twenty pounds.

The female fashions of the day were found highly inconvenient, particularly the headdresses, and it was ordered that no caps should be admitted of a larger size than the pattern exhibited at the Lord Chamberlain's office. As everyone wore powder, notwithstanding a vast influx of hairdressers from the country, such was the demand for these artists, that many ladies submitted to have their hair dressed the previous evening and sat up all night to be ready for the early admission in the morning.

We do not know how familiar Haydn was with Handel's oratorios before he went to England, but certainly he had never heard anything like the performance in Westminster Abbey. Although Hadow contends that the number of 1068 performers frequently mentioned is exaggerated, it must have been gigantic. Listening to the immortal masterworks performed by the enormous musical body in one of the loveliest churches of the world, feeling the veneration with which Handel's music was received "in a silence almost devotional" (Mount-Edgcumbe) by an audience taught by their king to see in this music the most sublime achievement, Haydn was so deeply moved that at the

"Hallelujah" chorus he burst into tears, exclaiming: "He is the master of us all." He was tremendously impressed at finding Handel's oratorios still so alive in the hearts of the English people, and he may have conceived at that time the plan of trying his hand at this form.

On another occasion in the following year, Haydn was deeply stirred by great choral masses. This time he wrote in his diary: "No music has ever moved me so much in my life as this devout and innocent one," which is the only emotional utterance in the entire notebook. Haydn referred here to the annual meeting of the charity children at St. Paul's Cathedral, when he heard four thousand children sing a hymn by the organist of the cathedral, John Jones. (Haydn's profound emotion was shared, many years later, by Hector Berlioz and his companion, the tenor Louis-Gilbert Duprez, who "wept and raved.")

Truly, England had revealed to Haydn what human voices in great numbers can accomplish. The consequences of such experiences were to manifest themselves later when he again had firm ground under his feet. At the moment he was unable to start on any new experiment in composition, for he was too much absorbed by the various aspects of the fascinating new country, which he was determined to explore as fully as he possibly could. Through the summer and autumn, when concert activities had ceased, he traveled and visited and had a wonderful time. This does not mean that he stopped working, for he had to prepare for the next season, but that he was free to go wherever he pleased without asking anybody's permission and to indulge in any passing whim. In a way it was the first vacation for this man of fifty-nine. The following outburst in a letter[17] to Marianne is characteristic: "Oh, my dear good lady, how sweet is some degree of liberty! I had a kind prince, but was obliged at times to be dependent on base souls. I often sighed for release and now I have it in some measure. I am quite sensible of this benefit, though my mind is burdened with more work. The consciousness of being no longer a bond servant sweetens all my toil."

Some of the visits Haydn paid at this time are mentioned

[17] Letter of September 17, 1791.

in his diary. For instance we find the following entry: "In the month of August I journeyed at noon in an East India merchantman with six cannon. I was gloriously entertained. In this month, too, I went with Mr. Fraser on the Thames from Westminster Bridge to Richmond, where we had dinner on an island. We were twenty-four persons and a band of music." (How Haydn, with his deep love of nature, must have enjoyed the picnic in such a beautiful spot!)

For five weeks he was "very well entertained" in the house of the rich banker, Mr. Brassey, teaching his daughter at the same time. His hosts, with typical English tact, left him alone as much as he chose, and Haydn describes his life to Marianne in these words: "I have been residing in the country, with a banker, whose heart and family resemble the Genzingers' [what higher compliment could he pay to the Brasseys?], and where I live as if I were in a monastery." After the noise of London, which caused him much suffering, the quiet and peace of the English country must have done him a great deal of good. Unfortunately a letter from his patron caused him some worry. Prince Esterházy complained of his long absence, and exacted, as Haydn described it, "his speedy return in the most absolute terms" because he wanted him to compose an opera for a fete planned in honor of the emperor. Haydn could not comply with the request because he had already concluded a contract with Salomon for the coming season. He had to inform the prince accordingly, which was not easy for a man used to obeying every demand coming from an Esterházy, and he expected his dismissal and the cancelation of his pension. None of this happened, however, as even an unmusical Esterházy like Prince Anton was too conscious of the renown that his connection with the world-famous composer gave him to desire to sever it.

In September, Haydn again took up his residence in London, but as during the months before the New Year concert life was almost stagnant, he frequently interrupted his work to make visits and trips to the country or to attend important official functions. His diary devotes a long description to the dinner of the new lord mayor on November 5, which he attended, sitting at the second table with Mr. Silvester, the "greatest lawyer and first alderman of London." Haydn was naturally interested in the music played on this occasion, and his comments are not very flattering, though quite amusing. Mentioning the small hall where he first watched the dancing, he wrote:

Nothing but minuets are danced in this room; but I could not stay longer than a quarter of an hour. First, because of the heat caused by so many people being crowded into so small a room; secondly, because of the wretched dance music, two violins and one violoncello composing the whole orchestra. The minuets were more Polish than German or Italian. Then I went into another room that looked more like a subterranean cave. There the dance was English and the music was a little better because there was a drum that drowned the blunders of the fiddlers. I went on to the great hall where we had dined; here the music was more tolerable. The dance was English but only on the elevated platform where the Lord Mayor and the first four members had dined. The other tables were all occupied again by men who, as usual, drank right lustily all night long. The most singular thing of all, however, was the fact that a part of the company danced on without hearing a note of the music, for first at one table, then at another, some were howling songs and some drinking toasts amid the maddest shrieks of Hurrah! Hurrah! and the waving of glasses.

Very different is the description of the three days during which Haydn stayed at Oatlands, the castle where the Duke of York was spending his honeymoon. The bride of seventeen was a daughter of the music-loving King Friedrich Wilhelm II of Prussia (whose beautiful ring Haydn valued so much). It gave her the greatest pleasure to meet the composer whose music she knew quite well and Haydn was received in the most gracious way by the young couple as well as by the Prince of Wales, who was responsible for the invitation. He wrote about it to Marianne:[18]

[18] Letter of December 20, 1791.

The duchess is the most charming lady in the world, possesses much intelligence, plays the piano, and sings very pleasingly. She remained beside me from ten o'clock at night, when the music began, until two hours after midnight. No compositions were played but Haydn's. I directed the symphonies at the piano. The sweet little lady sat close beside me at my left hand and hummed all the pieces from memory, having heard them often in Berlin. The Prince of Wales sat on my right and accompanied me very tolerably on the violoncello. They made me sing, too. The Prince of Wales is having me painted just now[19] and the portrait is to be hung in his private sitting room.

The same month Haydn visited Sir Patrick Blake at Langham, but in spite of having traveled a hundred miles, he left after three days to attend the performance of Shield's comic opera *The Woodman* at Covent Garden. The magnet that drew him was the celebrated singer Mrs. Billington, whom Kelly described as "an angel of beauty and the St. Cecilia of song." These words faithfully reflect the verdict of the majority of Londoners, at least of the male sex. In point of fact, Sir Joshua Reynolds painted Elizabeth Billington as the saintly musician. Haydn, according to the report of Carpani, visited the artist while he was working on the picture and pointed out that a strange mistake had been made: "You have painted her listening to the angels, but you should have represented the angels listening to her." Although the story in this form is inaccurate, as the portrait was painted in 1790 before Haydn arrived in England, it is not unlikely that he made the remark when seeing the completed picture. Nice compliments like that were what endeared Haydn to the ladies. When a scandalous book, the so-called *Memoirs of Mrs. Billington*, appeared, his diary commented indignantly on the "shameless exposure" and continued: "It is said that her character is far from faultless, but nevertheless, she is

[19] Haydn's portrait by John Hoppner is now in the collection of Buckingham Palace.

a great genius, and all the women hate her because she is
so beautiful."

Haydn's caustic report on the performance itself is rather
interesting:

> She [Mrs. Billington] sang timidly this evening but
> very well. The first tenor has a good voice and a fairly
> good style but he uses the falsetto to excess. He sang
> a trill on high C and ran up to G. The second tenor
> tried to imitate him but could not master the change
> from the natural voice to the falsetto; besides he is
> very unmusical. He creates a new tempo, now three-
> quarter then two-quarter, and cuts his phrases wher-
> ever he pleases. But the orchestra is used to him. The
> common herd in the galleries, as is the case in all thea-
> ters, is very impertinent and the performers are
> obliged to give encores according to its noisy wishes.
> The parterre and all the boxes frequently have to ap-
> plaud a great deal to secure a repetition but they
> succeeded this evening with the duet in the third act,
> which is very beautiful. The dispute lasted nearly a
> quarter of an hour before the parterre and boxes tri-
> umphed and the duet was repeated. The two perform-
> ers stood in a fright on the stage, now retiring, now
> again coming to the front. The orchestra is sluggish.

Haydn's admiration for Reynolds' St. Cecilia by no
means made him less sensitive to other beautiful women.
Among the music that the master took back from England
was a song, which he commented upon: "This song is by
Mrs. Hodges, the loveliest woman I ever saw in my life,
and a great pianoforte player." Again, when Haydn visited
his great admirer Mr. Shaw in December 1791, he found
his hostess to be the most beautiful woman he ever saw.
How pleased he must have been when he noticed that
this attractive lady had prepared a special homage for him.
She, her daughters, and all the ladies present "wore on
their headdresses a pearl-colored band embroidered in gold
with the name of Haydn, while Mr. Shaw wore the name
worked on the ends of his collar in the finest steel beads"
(Diary). One can well imagine how Haydn basked in this

atmosphere of beauty and admiration and how he repaid it in his particular way. Perhaps he sat down at the pianoforte and sang gay songs to them, with the humor that English people could appreciate so well.[20]

There were certainly quite a few such innocent friendships with beautiful women, but they did not prevent the inflammable master from enjoying a more significant romance as well. This time the story can be followed only in the letters of the lady. Haydn copied them faithfully into his notebook, but what happened to the originals is not known. It may be that the lady wanted them returned to her when Haydn left England. None of the master's answers has been traced, nor is there any further mention of the affair in his diary, except for a note of the lady's address. Many years later, Haydn showed the letters to Dies and remarked: "They are letters from an English widow in London who loved me. Though sixty years old, she was still lovely and amiable and in all likelihood I should have married her if I had been single." There must be an error in this statement, committed by either Dies or Haydn, whose memory at that time was not as good as it had been. Haydn indeed was sixty when he became attached to the widow, but his partner was certainly considerably younger. She was a Mrs. Schröter, the widow of Johann Samuel Schröter, who had been music master to the queen and the first exponent of skilled pianoforte playing in England. Dr. Burney, mentioning the musician Schröter in Rees's *Cyclopedia*, described his wife as "a young lady of considerable fortune." As Schröter was about thirty-eight when he died in 1788, his wife would have been approximately eighteen years his senior to conform to Dies's description and certainly not "a young lady" when she married him. It seems more likely that the amiable English widow was about the same age as Marianne von Genzinger. The two ladies had in common a great love of music, and whereas Marianne arranged Haydn's works for the piano, Mrs. Schröter did copying for the composer. Here the similarity ends, however, for the English widow did not

[20] According to Gyrowetz, it was this singing that made Haydn so popular with his English hosts.

show any of Marianne's reserve. There is preserved, for instance, the following love letter, copied in the original spelling from Haydn's diary:

My D[eare]st
Inclosed I send you the verses you was so kind as to lend me, and am very much obliged to you for permitting me to take a copy of them. Pray informe me how you do, and let me know my D[ear] L[ove] when you will dine with me. I shall be happy to see you to dinner either to morrow or Tuesday whichever is most convenient to you. I am truly anxious and impatient to see you and I wish to have as much of your company as possible: indeed my D[eare]st H[aydn] I feel for you the fondest and tenderest affection the human heart is capable of, and I ever am with the firmest attachment my D[eare]st Love
      Most Sincerely, Faithfully and most affectionately
                                                    Yours
Sunday Evening June 10   792

After the last Salomon concert, Mrs. Schröter wrote:

My D[ear]:
I can not close my Eyes to sleep till I have returned you ten thousand thanks for the inexpressible delight I have received from your ever Enchanting compositions and your incomparably charming performance of them. Be assured my D[ear] H[aydn]: That among all your numerous admirers no one has listened with more profound attention, and no one can have such high veneration for your most brilliant talents as I have. Indeed my D[ear] L[ove] no tongue can express the gratitude I feel for the infinite pleasure your Music has given me, accept then my repeeted thanks for it, and let me also assure you, with heartfelt affection, that I shall ever consider the happiness of your acquaintance as one of the chief Blessings of my life, and it is the Sincere wish of my heart to preserve to cultivate and to merit it more and more. I hope to hear you are quite well. Shall be happy to see you to

dinner and if you can come at three o'clock it would give me great pleasure, as I should be particularly glad to see you my D[ear] before the rest of our friends come. God bless you my D[ear]: I ever am with the firmest and most perfect attachment

Yours

Wednesday night June 6th $\overline{92}$

Mrs. Schröter liked to mother the master a little. She was always inquiring about his sleep and his health, and on April 19, 1792, she wrote: "I am told you was five hours at your Study's yesterday; indeed my D[ear] L[ove] I am afraid it will hurt you. . . . I almost tremble for your health, let me prevail on you my much-loved H[aydn] not to keep to your Study's so long at one time. My d[ear] love if you cou'd know how very precious your welfare is to me I flatter myself you wou'd endeavor to preserve it, for my Sake as well as your own."

This sounds as if the lady were pretty sure of Haydn's affection, and indeed there is no reason to assume that the master did not respond to the lovely widow's feelings. According to the letters, Haydn must have been a fairly frequent visitor at No. 6 James Street, Buckingham Gate, and the music lessons that first took him there probably soon were considered unimportant.

During the time that Haydn was living through this delightful romance, he regularly exchanged letters with his old love, Luigia Polzelli. It cannot be denied that they are ardent in tone. Once he remarked: "I esteem and love you as I did on the very first day. I am very sorry for you and it pains me terribly that I cannot do more for you. But be patient, perhaps the day will arrive when I can show you how much I love you."[21] And another time he exclaimed: "Oh, my dearest, you will always live in my heart. Never, never, shall I forget you, my beloved."[22] Luigia was at that time in Italy and very eager to go to London, where her sister was living. This of course was the last thing that Haydn wanted, for both personal and

[21] Letter of October 13, 1791.
[22] Letter of January 14, 1792.

professional reasons. It seems probable that in order to dissuade her and at the same time extinguish her innate (and probably well-founded) jealousy, Haydn expressed more passion than he really felt. He sent her money in answer to her requests and gladly declared himself willing to have her elder son, Pietro, join him in London.

Evidently the situation was emotionally none too easy for Haydn, and it was further aggravated by sundry venomous letters from his wife, for apparently she also had got wind of Haydn's recent successes with the fair sex. In a letter to Luigia, Haydn reacted with these strong words: "My wife, that infernal beast, wrote me so many things that I was forced to answer that I was never coming back. To this letter she paid attention."[23]

Although there were enough entanglements of the heart to disturb Haydn during the second part of his sojourn in London, they were of minor importance compared with the strain that he labored under at that time in his artistic career. The Professional Concerts twice sent a deputation to the master with the object of inducing him by the offer of a much higher salary to go over to their camp. When they found that nothing could shake Haydn's determination to keep his word to the man who had brought him to England, they changed their tactics. Rumors began again to circulate against Haydn, to such an extent that they reached even the ears of such good Viennese friends as Hofrat von Kees and Marianne von Genzinger. Finally the bomb exploded; the English public was informed that, in view of Haydn's advanced age and inability to create important new music, the Professional Concerts had had the good fortune to engage his young pupil, the outstanding composer, Ignaz Pleyel. Musical London was tremendously stirred by this news and violent partisanships were formed. All drawing rooms rang with heated discussions as to who was the better composer, Haydn or Pleyel. Today it is not easy to envisage the "murderous harmonious war" (Haydn) between the two composers in the right light. Very few people play music by Pleyel, whom we know only as the founder of a celebrated pianoforte factory, an

[23] Letter of January 14, 1792.

improver of the mechanism of the harp, and the first publisher to produce a complete edition of Haydn's quartets. In the eighteenth century, on the other hand, many people valued Pleyel's compositions very highly, especially those written in the earlier part of his life. Even Mozart wrote about Pleyel's first quartets that "they are very well written and very agreeable. It will be a happy thing for music if, when the time arrives, Pleyel should replace Haydn for us."[24] One cannot therefore blame the London public too much for taking the contest between Haydn and Pleyel seriously and awaiting the outcome with eager anticipation.

What satisfied the English sense of "fair play" was that Haydn and Pleyel remained personally on the best of terms. The day after Pleyel's arrival they dined together; they spent New Year's Eve in each other's company; they attended each other's concerts, and Pleyel, according to Haydn, displayed so much modesty that he gained his teacher's goodwill anew. But in spite of this pleasant personal relationship between the two contestants, which Haydn, worldly wise and shrewd as he was, would have kept up under any circumstances, the old master must have felt deeply hurt by the whole matter. Even if Pleyel, who perhaps had gone to London unaware of the implications of his engagement, was not to blame, it was an insult to consider the young musician worthy of entering into competition with Joseph Haydn, an insult of which Haydn was fully aware, though he rarely showed it. For instance there is the story told by John Taylor of a dinner with Haydn, Salomon, and Dr. Wolcot. The last was tactless enough to praise Pleyel's "genius" in the most enthusiastic terms. Haydn, at first, graciously agreed. Finally the doctor's rapture was too much for him and he remarked "with considerable warmth": "But I hope it will be remembered that he was my pupil." And once he wrote to Marianne: "Pleyel's presumption is criticized everywhere."

Pleyel had one advantage; he was an unusually prolific composer. As Haydn informed Marianne: "He brought with him a number of new compositions, which were,

[24] Letter to his father dated April 24, 1784.

however, written long ago! He accordingly promised to produce a new work every evening. On seeing this, I could easily perceive that a lot of people were dead set against me, so I also announced publicly that I would likewise give twelve different new pieces. In order to keep my promise and to support poor Salomon, I must be the victim and work perpetually. I do feel it, however, very much. My eyes suffer most, and I have many sleepless nights."[25] In another letter he exclaimed: "Never in my life have I written so much in one year as during the last, and it has indeed utterly exhausted me."[26] There are more complaints about being quite worn out with fatigue. The amazing thing is that nothing of this weariness can be felt in the works Haydn wrote under this strain, the Surprise symphony being one of them.

The London audience, in spite of the preceding venomous campaign against the composer, could not help being completely overwhelmed by these works. In the concert of February 24, two movements of the symphony in D (No. 93) were encored and the *Morning Chronicle* declared: "The concert was exceedingly spirited and, by the overture [symphony] of the matchless Haydn, was distinguished above all common competition." Of the concert on March 16, 1792, the *Morning Herald* reported: "There has hardly ever been a more beautiful musical treat than the fifth performance of Salomon's Concert. No less than six Pieces of Haydn were performed, exhibiting a richness and variety of genius that far exceed all modern Composers." On the sixth evening, the enthusiasm of the Londoners reached a climax when the Surprise symphony had its first rendering. And so it went on, a series of triumphs for Haydn. On April 24 he wrote to Marianne: "In spite of the great opposition of my musical enemies, who are so bitter against me, more especially leaving nothing undone with my pupil Pleyel this winter to humble me, still, thank God! I may say that I have kept the upper hand." When the twelve concerts for which he had contracted were over (one day before the tenth, the indefatigable master had conducted

[25] Letter of March 2, 1792.
[26] Letter of January 17, 1792.

his own most successful benefit concert), Salomon went on to add another concert on June 6 and finished the season, according to the *Morning Herald*, with the "greatest éclat," the instrumental pieces by Haydn being received with an "extacy [sic] of admiration."

Fourteen important concerts consisting to a great extent of Haydn's own compositions seem a big program for one season, but by no means did they cover all his appearances in public. He conducted Salomon's benefit concert and those for his "brother in affection" the violinist Barthélemon, for the pianist Hässler, for Madame Mara, for the vocalists the sisters Abrams, and for many others. His creative activity was not confined to the music for the Salomon concerts and the opera. Other new works owed their origin to friendships that Haydn made in London. There was, for instance, Anne Hunter, who was married to John Hunter, the famous surgeon and anatomist. She showed him some of her poems, one of them set to music to the tune of an andante by Pleyel. This—as Marion Scott assumes[27]—may have stimulated Haydn to try his hand at these poems, the result being the charming *Six Original Canzonettas* published in 1794. Another time he heard of the financial worries of the Scottish violinist William Napier, who because of gout was unable to pursue his profession and was forced to support his numerous children as a music publisher. To help Napier, Haydn arranged Scottish folk songs for him, adding preludes and postludes, and an accompaniment of clavier, violin, and violoncello. The works brought both the publisher and arranger the benefits of an enormous success and greatly enhanced Haydn's popularity in the British Isles.

Finally there was a certain amount of teaching to be undertaken. Besides such nominal pupils as Mrs. Schröter and other ladies, there were the pianist Thomas Haigh; and the composer John Callcott, who really did study under the master.

How Haydn managed to get all this work done, and done so brilliantly, and at the same time to lead a very active social life; how, in spite of the tremendous forces

[27] Cf. *Music and Letters*, XXV/1 (1944).

released in his creative activity he was still able to muster the emotional capacity for love and friendship, is hard to understand. Several factors may have contributed to produce the rare phenomenon of a man of sixty with the creative power and zest for living of a person half his age. During the long, undisturbed years at Esterháza, when Haydn, in many respects, was not living to the utmost of his capacity, he stored tremendous reserves of energy for the years to come. (A lesser artist might have reacted differently, and probably would have aged prematurely in such an existence of unvarying routine.) Another important factor was Haydn's excellent physique. During the eighteen months he spent in England, in spite of the difference in climate, the unfamiliar food, frequent travels, and long hours, Haydn was generally in very good health. He once complained of "English rheumatism" (against which he wrapped himself from head to foot in flannel), and once he noted in his diary that he had had to be bled. But that was all. His discomforts from a polyp in the nose, inherited from his mother, were as old as Haydn himself. John Hunter almost used force to persuade Haydn to have an operation, but when the master was seized by Hunter's strong assistants to be tied to a chair, he screamed and struggled so vigorously with hands and feet that the surgeon had to give up.

When the concert season was over, the "worn-out" composer still used every available chance to see and enjoy interesting sights in England.

On June 4, 1792, he went to Vauxhall, where the birthday of the king was celebrated, and apparently liked it very much. "The place and its diversions have no equal in the world," he writes. "There are one hundred and fifty-five dining booths scattered about, all very neat, and each comfortably seating six persons. There are large alleys of trees, the branches meeting overhead in a splendid roof of foliage. Tea, coffee and milk with almonds cost nothing. You pay half a crown for admission. The music is fairly good." He also explored the country around Windsor and of Windsor itself he mentions in his notebook the "very old but splendid chapel" and the "divine view from the terrace." But while there are a few lines dealing with this subject, Haydn devotes more than six hundred words to a description of the races at Ascot Heath, which he attended on June 14. It must have warmed the hearts of his English friends to notice Haydn's eager interest in this national event. Here he saw eye to eye with them, just as he did in his passion for hunting and fishing. The following excerpt from Haydn's report shows what interested him most:

> In the first heat there were three riders who were compelled to go around the course twice without stopping. They did it in five minutes. No stranger would believe it unless he were convinced by observation. The second time there were seven riders and when they approached some fell back, but never more than about ten paces and when one thinks the one rider who is about to reach the goal will be the first, at which moment large bets are laid on him, another rushes past him with inconceivable force and reaches the winning post. The riders are very lightly clad in silk, each of a different color, to make it easier to recognize them and all lean as greyhounds. The horses are of the finest breeds, light, with very slender legs, the manes plaited into braids, the hoofs very neat. As soon as they hear the sound of the bell they dash off with the greatest force. Every leap of the horses is twenty-two feet long. These horses are very costly. A few years ago the Prince of Wales paid eight thousand pounds for one and sold it again for six thousand. But the first time he won fifty thousand pounds with it. I saw eight heats the first day, and in spite of a heavy rain there were two thousand vehicles, all full of people, and three times as many people were present on foot. Besides this there are all kinds of puppet plays, ciarlatanz [sic], conjurors, and buffoons performing during the races, and in a multitude of tents food and all kinds of wine and beer. . . .

The next day the indefatigable traveler went to Slough to meet William Herschel. Haydn was very much interested in this German musician who discovered the planet

Uranus in 1781 after working on astronomy as a hobby, and was now universally acclaimed as an astronomer. The main attraction for Haydn was of course Herschel's gigantic telescope. Before it was raised skyward Herschel's most prominent visitors were allowed to take a walk through the enormous tube. In 1787, King George III and his retinue did so and the monarch was delighted thus to be able to show the Archbishop of Canterbury "the way to Heaven."[28] Haydn had to content himself with gazing at the monster, the measurements of which he faithfully put down in his notebook. Apparently he was much impressed by Herschel's ability to "sit from five to six hours under the open sky in the severest cold."

Now the time for Haydn's departure was approaching, much to the distress of Mrs. Schröter, to whom "every moment of his company was more and more precious." Many other people also wanted to keep the master in England. Haydn, while quite willing to return to London, found it imperative to go home for the time being, so that he could put his affairs in order and straighten out matters with Prince Esterházy who had summoned him to Frankfort, where he was to attend the coronation of the Emperor Francis II.

So Haydn got his trunks ready and made various purchases for his Viennese friends, such as scissors, needles, knives, spectacles, and steel chains, the prices of which he carefully noted in his diary. He also took pains to jot down anecdotes that might amuse the people at home, such as the following: "An archbishop of London asked Parliament to silence a preacher of the Moravian creed who preached in public. The vice-president answered that it could easily be done: only make him a bishop, and he would keep silent all his life."

Until the last moment the round of social functions went on. On June 22, Haydn gave a dinner at Parsloes for the Musical Graduates' Society, and Salomon had to be invited as an interpreter, "Dr. Haydn having not made suffi-

[28] See Cecil Roberts, *And so to Bath* (London, 1940)

cient progress in the English language." Next day he attended a dinner for one hundred and eighty persons which the Duchess of York gave under a tent in her garden. After that it was time for him to take leave of his numerous friends, but he promised to return before long to the country that had received him so hospitably and had given him the most exciting time of his life.

CHAPTER 8

VIENNA OR LONDON?

1792–1795

No personal documents are available about Haydn's return journey from London. We know that he again stopped at Bonn, where he had spent such pleasant hours eighteen months previously. The Elector Maximilian had already left for the coronation at Frankfort, for which Haydn was also heading, but the elector's orchestra invited the master to a breakfast at Godesberg, that charming village overlooking the Rhine where the residents of Bonn still like to take their guests. On this occasion Haydn had a long talk with the young Beethoven, whom he may have met on his first visit to Bonn. The musician of twenty-two showed the master a cantata (possibly the cantata on the death of Emperor Joseph II) which Haydn praised greatly. Beethoven was planning to go to Vienna to study under Haydn, and it was arranged that he should do so as soon as he could get leave from the elector, who had undertaken to bear the expenses of his journey.

Haydn then proceeded to Frankfort, not without some misgivings as to his reception by his princely patron, as he had been forced to ignore Esterházy's earlier request for a speedy return. To his relief, however, the prince was so engrossed in the splendors of the coronation of Francis II that he merely remarked: "Oh, Haydn, you could have saved me forty thousand florins!"

The man who arrived in Vienna in one of the Esterházy carriages on July 29, 1792, was rather different from the Haydn who had left the imperial capital only nineteen months before. He had tasted both delirious success and freedom. A highly renowned university had awarded him the degree of Doctor of Music. The Prince of Wales and other members of the highest British nobility had shown him great respect and friendliness. The newspapers, though sometimes critical in their attitude, had dealt with him and his music as providing news of importance, and he had earned a considerable amount of money. Now he had returned to the city that had witnessed his rise from the humblest beginnings. How would Vienna receive the new Dr. Haydn?

The official circles of the capital proved most disappointing. No newspaper took the trouble to mention the master's return. No concerts were arranged in his honor. The Austrian court gave no sign of recognition to the composer who had contributed so immensely to the fame of Austrian music. In contemporary diaries, which Botstiber has searched carefully, Haydn's name hardly ever appears. What a contrast to the frenzied attention given to him in London! In private life things were of course different, for his old friends were delighted to welcome Haydn home. Still, one gap, never to be filled, greatly marred Haydn's joy in his Viennese circle. Mozart was dead. The news had reached Haydn in London, and at first he tried not to believe it, for rumors of that kind were not always trustworthy. (Haydn himself had been declared dead in 1778.) When he could doubt the fact no longer, it became, even for a man of Haydn's deeply religious feeling, a trial of faith to reconcile himself to the premature passing of this genius. In January 1792 he wrote to their mutual friend, Puchberg: "I was for some time quite beside myself about his death. I could not believe that Providence should so quickly have called an irreplaceable man into the other world. Have the kindness, dear friend, to send me a list of Mozart's works not yet known here, and I will do my utmost to push them in the interest of the widow. I wrote to the poor woman three weeks ago, telling her that when her dear son was old enough, I would teach him composition without payment as well as I could, so as to replace his father to some extent." Haydn was not able to interest the British public in Mozart; at that time very few cared for him (among them, characteristically, was the Prince of Wales, who even owned the autograph of *La clemenza di Tito*). We know, however, that when consulted by the music dealer Broderip in the presence of Dr. Burney regarding the purchase of a Mozart manuscript, Haydn exclaimed with the greatest emphasis: "Do buy it by all means. He was truly a great musician. Friends often flatter me that I have some genius, but he stood far above me." Truly, Haydn suffered deeply in losing this unique artistic friend, a loss that became still more evident to him amid the old, familiar surroundings. Even with the healing influence of time, the wound inflicted by Mozart's death did not cease to hurt. As late as 1807, when some friends mentioned the name of Mozart, Haydn burst into tears, exclaiming: "Forgive me, I must ever, ever weep when I hear the name of my Mozart."

On his return to a city that in a strange way seemed to have become different, Haydn felt more than ever the need of friends who really stood close to him. His wife, of course, was not among them. Time and distance had done nothing to soften the animosity between them. Frau Haydn's letters, in which she reported poisonous gossip against her husband by people dear to him (among them even Mozart), could not improve their relationship, nor did Haydn particularly care for her suggestion that he buy her a house in Vienna that she might use as a dower residence. The house itself, which Frau Haydn insisted on showing him, pleased the master well enough because of its "quiet and secluded location." As he could now afford to do so, he bought it in August 1793 after careful negotiations and had it repaired and a second story added, but he did not fulfill his wife's wishes to make her the owner of the property.[1]

No, it was not to Frau Haydn, but to Marianne von Genzinger that he turned again "for comfort." With her he felt at ease. In her home he was sure of never-failing,

[1] The house, situated in Vienna's sixth district, at 71 Untere Steingasse, now 19 Haydngasse, has been preserved by the city as a Haydn Museum.

sincere interest. To her he played his new works; to her he described what he had seen and heard in England. Only two short notes of the autumn of 1792 have been preserved, for there was now no need for correspondence. Then, all of a sudden, a catastrophe shook Haydn's existence. On January 26, 1793, Marianne died, at the age of thirty-eight, leaving five children. Through her death, Haydn lost the best friend he had. None of his other old acquaintances could replace her. The master, who had experienced the bliss of a really understanding and warmhearted friend only in his late years, now experienced a terrible loneliness that surrounded him like a wall. With Marianne's death, something never to be recaptured went out of Haydn's life. A certain sarcasm in his nature began to show, an asperity of which the diary of his second trip to London offers many instances.

The loneliness Haydn was suffering could not be dispelled even by the two interesting pupils who were then constantly in touch with the master. Young Pietro Polzelli came to stay with the Haydns, and the composer, besides teaching him, helped him to get well-paying students, and certainly enjoyed his company. His relation to the other pupil is not so easily described. Ludwig van Beethoven arrived in Vienna shortly after Haydn and started at once to take lessons, for which the master asked a nominal fee of eight groschen per hour. They met fairly frequently, and Beethoven's memorandum book contains such entries as "chocolate twenty-two x [kreutzer (farthings)] for Haydn and myself" and "coffee six x for Haydn and myself."

As early as 1787, Beethoven had paid a short visit to Vienna in order to meet Mozart. His great wish was to study with Mozart, but before his intention could be carried out he was recalled to his ailing mother in Bonn, and by the time he was ready to visit the Austrian capital again, Mozart had died. Thereupon Beethoven decided to study with Haydn instead, but it seems probable that he always regarded Haydn as a sort of understudy for Mozart. Such an attitude was also expressed by Count Waldstein, who wrote the following words of farewell in Beethoven's album on October 29, 1792, before the young musician's departure for Vienna:

> Dear Beethoven,
> You are traveling to Vienna in fulfillment of your long-cherished wish. The tutelary genius of Mozart is still weeping and bewailing the death of her favorite. With the inexhaustible Haydn she has found a refuge, but no occupation, and she is now waiting to associate herself with someone else. Labor assiduously and receive Mozart's spirit from the hands of Haydn.

Haydn, a very keen observer of men, may have realized the young man's true feelings. At all events, the deep sympathy and understanding that, in spite of very different temperaments, drew Mozart and Haydn irresistibly together, were entirely lacking in the relationship between Haydn and Beethoven. The difference in their ages was not the real barrier, for Haydn loved, and was loved by, young people. Nor, as has been sometimes assumed, were Beethoven's revolutionary tendencies in music abhorrent to Haydn. On the contrary, everything new interested Haydn and there are proofs enough in his last works that he was in complete sympathy with the newly rising romantic school. But Beethoven, headstrong and prone to suspicion, was not easy to get on with, and often irritated Haydn. His youthful arrogance was particularly hard to be borne by a man of Haydn's age, and the older master used to refer jokingly to Beethoven as "that Great Mogul." In addition to these tangible personal differences, dissatisfaction developed about the method of instruction that was shared by teacher and pupil. Beethoven wanted to study strict counterpoint as thoroughly as possible, for he felt that a complete mastery of the technical rules would entitle him to vary them in his compositions. Haydn therefore set him to work on the old textbook he himself had studied, Fux's *Gradus ad Parnassum*, but in the forty years since the master had pored over this manual it had naturally lost much of its significance for him. It is not surprising that

Haydn at the zenith of his fame and creative power found the correction of such elementary exercises rather tedious. Absorbed in his own thoughts and problems he did not give to the work of instruction the necessary attention, and he overlooked mistakes that Beethoven made. The pupil became suspicious of his teacher's competence, and complained of it to the renowned pianist, Abbé Gelinek, who introduced him to Johann Schenk, a composer of successful singspiels and a pedantic music teacher as well. Schenk was tremendously impressed by Beethoven's improvisations on the piano and went to call on the young genius the next day. "On his writing desk," he tells in his autobiography, "I found a few passages from his first lesson in counterpoint. A cursory glance disclosed the fact that, brief as it was, there were mistakes in every key. Joseph Haydn, who had returned to Vienna, was intent on utilizing his abilities in the composition of large masterpieces, and, thus laudably occupied, he could not well devote himself to the rules of grammar. I was now eagerly desirous to become the helper of the zealous student, but before beginning my tuition I made him understand that our cooperations must be kept a close secret. In view of this I recommended him to copy every exercise that I corrected, so that Haydn would not recognize the handwriting of a stranger when the exercise was submitted to him." And so it was done. Beethoven, for the sake of appearances, continued going to Haydn for instruction, but his real teacher at that time was Schenk. The young musician could not be blamed for his duplicity; he was eager to study counterpoint thoroughly, but could not risk offending Haydn. On the other hand, the older master's behavior is also understandable. As Schindler put it: "The eminent composer can be a good adviser on special cases, but he simply is not a teacher in the real sense of the word; that is, one who leads the student on with patience and devotion from easy to difficult problems." Nevertheless, Haydn and Beethoven kept on quite friendly terms.

An exchange of letters may throw some light on their relationship. Haydn went out of his way to intercede with the elector in Bonn on behalf of Beethoven and wrote him as follows on November 23, 1793:[2]

I venture to send to Your Serene Electoral Highness several pieces of music, namely, a quintet, an eight-part parthie, an oboe concerto, variations for the pianoforte, and a fugue, composed by Beethoven, my dear pupil, whose instruction has been graciously entrusted to me. I flatter myself that these will be graciously considered by Your Electoral Highness as good evidence for the industry displayed by him outside of his actual studies. Connoisseurs and non-connoisseurs will impartially infer from these works that Beethoven will eventually reach the position of one of Europe's greatest composers, and I will be proud to call myself his teacher. I only wish he could still remain for quite some time with me.

As I mentioned Beethoven, I trust Your Serene Electoral Highness will allow me to add a few words about his financial status. For the past year one hundred ducats have been granted to him. No doubt Your Electoral Highness is aware that this sum was not sufficient to even cover his living expenses; probably Your Highness had good reasons for sending him with so small a sum into the great world. Under this assumption and so as not to have him fall into the hands of usurers I have partly stood security for him, partly advanced him cash, and he owes me now five hundred florins, of which not a penny was spent unnecessarily, and I would ask you to send him this amount. And as the interest on borrowed money constantly increases, a situation results that is most irksome for an artist like Beethoven. I believe, in case Your Electoral Highness should grant him for next year one thousand florins, this would be the ultimate act of graciousness and relieve Beethoven of all worries. For the teachers that are essential to him and the outfit indispensable for his appearances among the highborn are so costly that from the one thousand

[2] Stephan Ley, *Beethoven* (Vienna, 1954), p. 60 f.

florins just enough for the bare necessities of life would be left. Regarding the extravagance which to a youth entering into the great world is often a grave temptation, I believe I may answer for that to Your Electoral Highness, for a hundred circumstances have proved to me that he is willing to sacrifice everything to his art. With so many tempting occasions presenting themselves, this is quite admirable and it gives Your Serene Electoral Highness the assurance that the favors granted to him will be refunded with interest. In the hope Your Serene Electoral Highness will see fit to fulfill my request henceforth to allow further help to my dear pupil Beethoven, I remain with the most profound respect,

Your Electoral Highness' most obedient
Joseph Haydn

The elector's reaction must have shocked Haydn, for, apart from refusing to increase Beethoven's allowance (which was stopped in March 1794), it stated in no uncertain terms that except for the fugue all the compositions submitted had been composed and performed in Bonn long before Beethoven left for Vienna. Apparently Beethoven had misinformed his teacher, thus putting him in a most awkward position. There apparently never was complete frankness between these two. Yet Haydn, deeply impressed by the young man's genius, put up with such shortcomings, and even though a few years later Gelinek divulged Schenk's secret after a disagreement with Beethoven, no outward break occurred in the relations of the two composers. Beethoven dedicated to Haydn his piano sonatas, Op. 2, for which, as for all other compositions by Beethoven, the old composer had the greatest praise. He found only Beethoven's trio, Op. 1, No. 3, in C minor too original and revolutionary to be understood by the great public, and therefore advised the young man to delay its publication until he had made a name for himself. In that advice the suspicious Beethoven saw proof that Haydn was not well disposed toward him and was even jealous, thus

totally misjudging his teacher's character. The idea of
envying a composer almost young enough to be his grand-
son would have seemed ridiculous to Haydn who, after
winning great triumphs in England, was at last receiving
proofs of unusual admiration at home. In 1793, to the
old man's tremendous gratification, Count Harrach erected
in the composer's birthplace a monument to this greatest
son of Rohrau, an honor hardly ever accorded to a composer in his lifetime.

No, Haydn was not jealous of the younger generation.
On the contrary, he got genuine satisfaction out of its
achievements and missed no opportunity to encourage its
members. A charming proof of this is offered by his letter
to the operatic composer Joseph Weigl, Jr., the son of his
old friend, the violoncellist of the Esterházy band, Joseph
Weigl:

Vienna, January 11, 1794

Dearest Godson,

When I took you in my arms shortly after your
birth, and had the pleasure of becoming your godfather, I implored omnipotent Providence to endow
you with the highest degree of musical talent. My
fervent prayer has been heard. It has been a long time
since I felt such enthusiasm for any music as for your
La principessa d'Amalfi yesterday: it is full of ideas,
noble, expressive, in short—a masterpiece. I felt the
warmest sympathy with the well-merited applause
bestowed on it. Persevere, my dear godson, in this
genuine style, that you may again show foreigners
what a German can accomplish. Keep a place in your
memory withal for an old boy like myself. I love you
cordially, and am, dearest Weigl,

Your sincere friend and servant,
JOSEPH HAYDN

When Haydn wrote this letter, he was in the midst of
his preparations for a second journey to London. According to a new agreement that had been concluded with
Salomon in the summer of 1793, Haydn was to conduct

six newly composed symphonies in the English capital. The financial terms are not known, but it seems certain that they were at least equal to those of the first contract. It is natural that Haydn should choose to revisit London, a city in which he had enjoyed so much success and appreciation. There was now very little to attract him in Vienna or in Eisenstadt, where he spent part of the time with Prince Esterházy, for the castle of Esterháza had been abandoned after the death of its creator, not to be used again for a century. But, although the prince had no real use for him and remunerated him insufficiently, he did not like to see his Kapellmeister go, and it was difficult for Haydn to get leave again. At last he succeeded, and the day of departure was fixed for January 19, 1794. This time he could not rely on Salomon's help on the journey. At first, he wanted one of his pupils, Polzelli or Beethoven, to accompany him, but after giving the matter more thought, he came to the conclusion that these young musicians would not have his welfare as much at heart as his trusted servant, Johann Elssler, so he wisely decided to take Johann to London with him. Young Elssler, another of Haydn's godsons, was the son of Prince Esterházy's music copyist, who helped Haydn with the first catalogue of his works (see p. 214). Born in 1769, Johann lived with Haydn during his youth and rendered him excellent service as a copyist, secretary, and general factotum. It speaks in favor of both master and servant that in spite of their being constantly together, Elssler's admiration for Haydn was boundless. There is even a report that the factotum, when he thought himself unobserved, censed Haydn's portrait as if before an altar. The lack of a woman's care in the aging master's life was, to a great extent, made up for by Elssler's constant devotion and thoughtfulness. To this excellent man, incidentally, a place of honor is due not only as the faithful servant, secretary, and copyist of Haydn, but as the father of the great dancer Fanny Elssler.[3]

[3] That Elssler—as Larsen proved (see *Haydn-Überlieferung*, p. 33)—made a collection of Haydn manuscripts during the composer's lifetime need not be interpreted as an act of dis-

On January 19, 1794, the two travelers set forth in a
coach provided by Baron van Swieten, director of the
Vienna court library, an ardent lover of music who was
later to play an important part in Haydn's life. About a
halt made at the well-known watering place, Wiesbaden,
Dies tells the following pleasant story. At the inn Haydn
heard the strains of the andante from his Surprise symphony issuing from another room. He followed the sound
and found a group of Prussian officers gathered around
the pianoforte, enjoying the beauties of this by then very
popular masterpiece. When Haydn introduced himself, the
Prussians could not believe that the composer of so youthful a tune was this aged man. They were at last convinced
when Haydn proudly took out of his trunk the letter bearing the signature of their own king, Friedrich Wilhelm II,
which had accompanied the diamond ring so highly treasured by the master.

About the journey no word from Haydn himself has
been preserved, and our information regarding this second
visit to England is altogether poor compared with that
about the first journey. It should not be inferred that less
happened to him or that his experiences did not seem so
interesting, but the incentive to describe his impressions
in letters had vanished with the loss of his most sympa-
thetic listener, Marianne. There was now really no single
person to whom he cared to write any detailed account
of his life in England. His notebook again confines itself
to the jotting down of facts interesting to him for one
reason or another, but no word of a more personal nature
has come down to us. Taken as a whole, the diary of this
second journey is more censorious in tone, and the comments on other artists are not very flattering.

Haydn's first appearance in London had been announced
for February 3. But again, to continue the old tradition,
the concert had to be postponed, as Haydn arrived on
February 4, and a soloist engaged by Salomon, the celebrated basso, Ludwig Fischer (who had sung Osmin in

---

honesty. It seems possible that the old and extremely forgetful
composer sometimes gave his faithful factotum a manuscript
without keeping the fact in mind.

the Vienna premiere of Mozart's *Die Entführung aus dem Serail*) also was late. The first concert therefore took place on February 10, and Haydn was received with the old enthusiasm and admiration, this time marred by no opposition whatever, as the Professional· Concerts had been given up in 1793. There was, however, a difference in the attitude of the London audience toward the master. Haydn was greeted like an old and highly treasured friend, but the element of sensation so characteristic of his first appearance was lacking. The reporter of the *Oracle* therefore, writing about Salomon's opening night, confined himself to this comment: "We must of necessity be brief. And after all it may be best, when the chef-d'oeuvre of the great Haydn is the subject. 'Come then, expressive Silence, muse his praise.' Viotti gave a concerto, simple and affecting, like his genius. Mara sang, *c'est assez dire*." But if Haydn did not supply as much material for the newspapers as he had three years before, the acclaim given to him was by no means less frenzied; indeed, if possible, it was even more so. A letter written on March 25 by the London correspondent of the *Journal des Luxus und der Moden* (Weimar) gives a lively description of the general reaction to Haydn's music:

But what would you now say to his new symphonies composed expressly for these concerts and directed by himself at the pianoforte? It is truly wonderful what sublime and august thoughts this master weaves into his works. Passages often occur that render it impossible to listen to them without becoming excited. We are altogether carried away by admiration and forced to applaud with hand and mouth. This is especially the case with Frenchmen, of whom we have so many here that all public places are filled with them. You know that they have great sensibility and cannot restrain their transports, so that in the midst of the finest passages in soft adagios they clap their hands in loud applause and thus mar the effect. In every symphony of Haydn the adagio or andante is sure to be repeated each time, after the most vehement encores. The worthy Haydn, whose personal acquaintance I highly value, conducts himself on these occasions in the most modest manner. He is indeed a goodhearted, candid, honest man, esteemed and beloved by all.

This love and esteem were felt also by the members of his orchestra, who enjoyed Haydn's sense of humor and friendly ways. On the other hand, they were not above playing little jokes on him. Young George Smart, for instance (the future Sir George, a friend of Beethoven, Weber, and Mendelssohn), liked to remember how he showed Haydn the "English way of playing the drums." At a rehearsal, when the drummer was absent, Smart, a violinist, volunteered to take his part, though he had never played the instrument before. Naturally he did not produce quite the desired effect. Haydn let it pass, but after the movement was finished, he went to Smart and remarked politely that in Germany the drumstick was used in such a way as not to check the vibration. Then, adopting his usual method of demonstrating his intentions on the instrument, he took the drumstick and showed himself, to the astonished orchestra, as an excellent drummer. Smart was quick to see where he had failed and exclaimed: "Oh, very well, if you like it better that way we can do it so in London too."

The Salomon series again gained added luster from the engagement of excellent soloists. The great violinist Viotti already has been mentioned. Very successful also was the blind glass harmonica virtuosa, Marianne Kirchgaessner, whom Mozart admired so much that he wrote for her an Adagio and Rondo for Harmonica and instruments, K. 617. (Incidentally it was in London that this unfortunate musician, who had been blind since her fourth year, was given an eye lotion that enabled her to distinguish the color and shape of objects.) Dussek again frequently appeared in the series, as did the popular singer Maria Hester Parke, who was also a good pianist. Madame Mara was engaged again, and Haydn continued to take an interest in her, though he did not always approve of her behavior, as is proved by a curious item in his notebook. It seems that the singer and her husband, Johann Mara, a talented but dissipated violoncellist, were not exactly in accord. As the oboist W. T. Parke expressed it in his *Musical Memoirs*: "Mr. Mara loved her and his bottle equally, and frequently broke the head of one and cracked the other." In writing about the singer's benefit concert on March 24, 1795, after mentioning the various artists, Haydn continued: "When the concert was over, Madame Mara gave a supper in the adjoining room. After midnight Mr. Mara stepped in quite boldly and asked for a glass of wine. Madame Mara, knowing what madness might result therefrom, appealed to her lawyer, who was sitting at the table, and this man said to Mr. Mara: 'You know our laws, you will be kind enough to leave this room, otherwise you'll have to pay two hundred pounds tomorrow.' The poor man left the party. Next day Madame Mara, his wife, traveled to Bath with her *cicisbeo*, but I think her obstinacy makes her ridiculous to the whole nation." It seems that in spite of the notorious faults of the husband, Haydn was definitely on his side.

While his feelings for the singer were of a mixed nature, Haydn wholeheartedly enjoyed the intimate friendship that during this second stay in England he established with Domenico Dragonetti, "Il Patriarca dei Contrabassi." Dragonetti's never-paralleled mastery of his instrument fascinated Haydn, as it did everyone else. The Italian virtuoso, playing on a double bass built by Gasparo da Salò, the teacher of Amati, apparently could express anything he wished on the unwieldy instrument. Haydn must have chuckled when Dragonetti told him how, by imitating a terrific thunderstorm on the double bass, he made all the monks in a Paduan monastery jump out of their beds one night. And the fact that Dragonetti collected dolls and operatic scores with the same fervor was something that Haydn, who loved puppets so much himself, could well understand.

The English composer William Shield also was among Haydn's new friends. They spent a few days together at Taplow, and Shield declared that on this occasion he had learned more about music than he had in years of study. This shows that if Haydn did not have to follow a text-book on counterpoint implicitly, he was a pretty good teacher.

Haydn again had some real pupils and received a fee of one guinea a lesson. Some remarks he made throw a sidelight on teaching conditions at that time: "If a singer, pianoforte or dancing master asks half a guinea for his lesson, he requests before the first lesson an entrance fee of six guineas. This is done because during the winter many Scottish and Irish people, out of pride, have their children taught by the best masters, and in the end find themselves unable to remunerate them. But the entrance fee is dispensed with if the master asks for a whole guinea. This however, has to be paid at every lesson.[4]

The name of Lord Abingdon frequently appears in Haydn's notebook. This musical enthusiast was among the first amateurs who had tried to bring the master to London. He now endeavored to direct Haydn's interest toward the composition of an oratorio, suggesting to him as a possible text a poem by Nedham used as an introduction to the English translation of John Selden's *Mare Clausum*. Haydn actually started working on it, but after composing a bass aria and a chorus, gave it up, feeling that he had too little knowledge of English to justify his composing an oratorio to a text in that language. Haydn and the aristo-cratic lover of music even collaborated in producing *Twelve Sentimental Catches and Glees*, which, according to the title page, were melodized by the Earl of Abingdon, while the accompaniments for the harp or pianoforte were written by "the celebrated Dr. Haydn." In the privacy of his notebook, however, Haydn could not help making fun of the earl's musical accomplishments. He quoted the fol-lowing epigram, which reads in an English translation:

King Solomon and David led merry, merry lives
With many, many lady friends and many, many wives.

[4] This is quoted by Griesinger in his biographical sketch in *Allgemeine Musikalische Zeitung* (1809) and probably was con-tained in the fourth diary of Haydn, which has disappeared.

> But when old age came creeping on, with many,
>   many qualms,
> King Solomon wrote the Proverbs and King David
>   wrote the Psalms.[5]

He added: "My Lord Abingdon sets it to music, but miserably. I do it a little better." Another story connected with his friend is set down by Haydn with evident enjoyment: "Lord Abingdon had an organ built in the church on his estate. When the bishop of the diocese heard of it, he reproved the nobleman in a letter for having done so without obtaining permission, which is not allowed in England. Whereupon he received the following answer: 'The Lord gave it—the Lord can take it away.' This is very ambiguous, but very good." Another of his hosts whose love of music was mentioned by Haydn was Lord Aston,[6] whom he visited at Preston, in the township of Hitchin, Hertfordshire.

Haydn, however, did not confine himself to intercourse with noblemen. How he became attached to a music dealer by the name of Howell is described by William Gardiner:

> One morning a neat little gentleman came into his [Howell's] shop and asked to look at some pianoforte music, and he laid before him some sonatas by Haydn which had just been published. The stranger turned them over and said: "No, I don't like these." Howell replied: "Do you see they are by Haydn, Sir?" "Well, Sir, I do, but I wish for something better." "Better,"

---

[5] The German version noted by Haydn is much more outspoken.

[6] This must have been Walter Aston (d. 1805), in early life a watchmaker, who claimed the title of Lord Aston of Forfar in the Scottish peerage. According to *The Complete Peerage,* there was some doubt whether, under the laws of succession, he and his immediate forebears were entitled to this peerage, and he was not allowed to vote in the election of Scottish peers in the House of Lords. However, in 1769, George III granted him a pension of three hundred pounds per annum under the title of Lord Aston of Forfar. The *Gentleman's Magazine* described him thus: "His Lordship, who had been in trade in the early part of his life, was an inoffensive man of a rather convivial turn."

cried Howell indignantly, "I am not anxious to serve a gentleman of your taste," and was turning away when the customer made it known that he was Haydn himself. Howell, in astonishment, embraced him and the composer was so flattered by the interview that a long and intimate friendship followed.[7]

Some of Haydn's friends were not connected with music at all. We read, for instance, in his diary: "Mr. March is at the same time dentist, coachbuilder, and wine merchant. He is eighty-four, keeps a young mistress, and has a daughter of nine who plays the piano quite well. I dined frequently with him. As a dentist he earns two thousand pounds a year; each carriage brings at least five hundred pounds; as a wine merchant he does not, I think, make so large an income."

But what about Mrs. Schröter? Did their friendship continue? There are no letters to help us get a clear answer to this question. It may be that at this time Haydn omitted to make copies or that they were included in his fourth notebook, which has not been preserved. Certainly the pleasant rooms Haydn occupied at this time, at 1 Bury Street, at the corner of King Street, opposite the St. James's Theatre, were near Mrs. Schröter's house. Pohl may be right in his assumption that they were chosen by the lady herself.

Furthermore, Haydn dedicated to her three of his finest piano trios (Hob. XV:24–26). The affinity of the second movement of the F sharp minor trio (No. 26) with that of symphony No. 102 may be owing to the fact that this symphonic movement was a favorite of Rebecca Schröter's.[8] Her name appears again in 1800 among the subscribers to *The Creation*. There is no reason to assume that the feelings of either had changed in the course of years. When we hear that Haydn left the scores of his last six symphonies "with a lady in England," it seems likely that the

[7] Gardiner does not give a date for this occurrence and it cannot be ascertained whether it happened during the first or second visit to England.

[8] See H. C. R. Landon, *The Symphonies of Joseph Haydn*, p. 565.

recipient of these treasures was his fervent admirer, Mrs. Schröter. Probably she again contributed much to making Haydn's stay in the British capital a happy one.

On his second visit Haydn was again most eager to get to know various aspects of life in England. When the concert season was over, this indefatigable man of sixty-two made frequent journeys and took an avid interest in all the new sights and facts that came his way. His notebook affords much information regarding different kinds of ships, chiefly in connection with a visit to Portsmouth. He visited the palace of Hampton Court, and the beautiful park there reminded him of Esterháza; he was conducted through the Bank of England, and later wrote a detailed report about it. When staying with Sir Charles Rich, whom he found a "rather good violoncellist," he examined the ruins of the famous abbey at Waverley and described his reaction in the following words: "I must confess that whenever I saw this beautiful wilderness, my heart felt oppressed at the thought that all this had once been subject to my own religion." He enjoyed trips to Cowes, Newport, Winchester (whose "beautiful Gothic cathedral" he praised), and Southampton. Mentioning the Isle of Wight in his diary, he extols the "most magnificent view of the sea" from the governor's green villa. The following remark in the diary also probably refers to this lovely island: "There is a story that Julius Caesar, on his flight, came by chance to the island and exclaimed: 'This is indeed the home of the Gods!'"

No such enthusiastic words were uttered by Haydn in connection with operatic conditions in London. Griesinger reports on the basis of the lost diary: "Dr. Arnold[9] composed an opera for Drury Lane Theatre. As the manager was afraid that the work might not be successful, Dr. Arnold agreed to have it performed three times at his own expense. He spent more than seven hundred pounds on it; the manager, however, paid a crowd of people to hiss the opera off each time. Finally Arnold handed the

[9] Dr. Samuel Arnold, composer, court organist, and conductor of the Academy of Ancient Music.

work to the manager, who had it performed, after a few alterations, with better costumes and decorations, and within a year earned twenty thousand pounds on it. The publisher alone netted five thousand pounds, but the poor composer lost seven hundred. Oh, rascals!" Haydn expressed himself in even stronger words after a visit to the Haymarket Theatre on July 29, 1794: "There they perform just as miserable trash as at Sadler's Wells. A fellow sang an aria so dreadfully and with such extravagant grimaces that I began to perspire all over my body. But he had to repeat the aria. *Oh, che bestia!*"

Any unpleasant memory of that evening was quickly dispelled by Haydn's visit to Bath, which took place only four days later and proved to be the most delightful experience of the summer. In this highly fashionable watering place lived many distinguished musicians who were eager to meet Haydn, the most desirous being the famous tenor Venanzio Rauzzini, about whom the composer Naumann said: "He sings like an angel and is also a remarkable actor." Haydn wrote a long description of the trip in his diary, part of which reads as follows:

On August 2, 1794, I left for Bath at five in the morning and arrived at 8 PM. I stayed with Mr. Rauzzini, a very famous musician who was one of the greatest singers of his time. He has been living there for nineteen years, supports himself with Subscription Concerts in the winter, and also gives lessons. He is a very good and hospitable man. His summer house, where I stayed, lies in a very lovely site on a hill that overlooks the whole city. Bath is one of the most beautiful towns in Europe, all the houses being made of stone. The stone is quarried in the nearby hills and it is so soft that it can be cut easily into all shapes, and is very white. The longer it is out of the earth, the harder it becomes. The whole town lies on a hill, and therefore there are few coaches, but there are plenty of chairs in which one can be carried a good distance for sixpence. There are many beautiful squares with the most excellent houses. I made the acquaintance of Miss Brown, an amiable, discreet person and a good pianist. Her mother is a very beautiful woman. . . .

The delight with which Haydn was received in the watering place is apparent from the welcome in the Bath *Herald and Register*: "Oh, had I Jubal's lyre, I would sweep the strings till Echo tired with repeating—Haydn treads upon Bathonian ground! Had this place, previous to his arrival, been the seat of discord, it must now be lulled into peace by the God of Harmony—while every individual who hath music in his soul must exclaim with enthusiasm: *Erit mihi magnus Apollo!*" At a later date the paper also published a French poem by a refugee in honor of the "immortal master."

Haydn had his own method of thanking his hosts for a charming reception. When Rauzzini showed him the tomb of his beloved dog Turk, in his garden, bearing the somewhat misanthropic inscription "Turk was a faithful dog and not a man," Haydn composed a four-part canon on these words, and the grateful recipient added it to the epitaph. For the renowned musician Dr. Henry Harington, founder of the Harmonic Society of Bath, Haydn composed the music to a poem, "What Art Expresses," which the doctor had written in the Austrian master's praise.[10] This collaboration between the two musicians caused Clementi to make the following rather involved statement: "The first doctor [Harington] having bestowed much praise on the second doctor [Haydn], the said second doctor, out of doctorial gratitude, returns the first doctor thanks for all favor received, and praises in his turn the said first doctor most handsomely."

After three delightful days, Haydn went on to Bristol,

[10] The composition has a rather strange form. The theme is first sung by a solo voice, then taken over by a mixed chorus, then follow variations for the piano. See the introduction to the Collected Edition of Haydn's songs, edited by M. Friedländer, p. xv.

which he also describes in his diary, praising the beautiful view from the hill, and remarking on the numerous churches, all in "the old Gothic style."

On returning to London in the autumn of 1794, Haydn began to make intensive preparations for the coming season. This time conditions were somewhat changed. Salomon suddenly decided not to continue his subscription series, probably because the war with France made it too difficult to secure first-class soloists. He therefore agreed to Haydn's being engaged for a new enterprise, the Opera Concerts, in which series he himself frequently appeared as a soloist. The new concerts were arranged on the largest scale known at that time. The performances took place every two weeks in the great new concert hall of the King's Theatre. Viotti was the artistic director, and Haydn shared the conductorship with Vincenzo Federici, who for three years had been accompanist at the Italian opera in London. The orchestra, led by the violinist William Cramer, was made up of no less than sixty players. The composers engaged, other than Haydn, were Muzio Clementi, Francesco Bianchi, and Vicente Martín y Soler (composer of the once successful opera *Una cosa rara* immortalized in the second act of Mozart's *Don Giovanni*). The soloists included the greatest artists available, among them Brigida Banti, who had come to London in 1794. This former street singer enjoyed a tremendous success, and the words of Lord Mount-Edgcumbe reflect the general attitude: "In her, genius supplied the place of science, and the most correct ear, with the most exquisite taste, enabled her to sing with more effect, more expression, and more apparent knowledge of her art, than many much better professors. Her voice had not a fault in any part of its unusually extensive compass." Haydn wrote an aria for her, which she performed at his benefit concert, but according to Griesinger, he noted in his diary (in English) that she "song [sic] very scanty," which again proves that at that time very few artists earned Haydn's full approval. He also found the oboist Giuseppe Ferlendis, who made his London debut in this benefit concert, "mediocre." But even if the master did not feel quite happy about the soloists, he could not help admitting that the benefit concert was a brilliant success. He remarked in his diary: "The hall was filled with a distinguished audience. The whole society was extremely pleased, and so was I. I netted four thousand florins on this evening. This one can make only in England." Altogether the Opera Concerts were received so enthusiastically that instead of the projected nine concerts, eleven had to be given. Among other works the tenth, eleventh, and twelfth of Haydn's London symphonies (Nos. 102–104) had their first performances in this series.

During this, his last London season, Haydn was in even closer touch with the court than in preceding years. It seems surprising that the master, in spite of his outstanding success, had never been introduced to the king, but George III was so passionately devoted to Handel's works that he took little interest in contemporary music. By now, however, Haydn had become so beloved in England that the monarch could no longer ignore his presence. The oboist William Thomas Parke tells about the first meeting in his *Memoirs*:

The Duke of York gave a grand concert of instrumental music at York House, at which Their Majesties and the princesses were present. Salomon led the band and Haydn presided at the pianoforte. At the end of the first part of the concert Haydn had the distinguished honor of being formally introduced to His Majesty, George III, by the Prince of Wales. My station at the time was so near to the king that I could not avoid hearing the whole of their conversation. Among other observations, His Majesty said: "Dr. Haydn, you have written a great deal." Haydn modestly replied: "Yes, Sire, a great deal more than is good." His Majesty neatly rejoined: "Oh, no, the world contradicts that." After his introduction, at the queen's desire, Haydn sat down at the pianoforte and, surrounded by Her Majesty and her daughters, sang and accompanied himself admirably in several of his canzonets.

From that day on, Haydn was frequently invited by the queen to her musicales at Buckingham House. He was treated most graciously, and the queen gave him the manuscript of Handel's oratorio in German *Der gemarterte und sterbende Jesus*. The Prince of Wales also continued to see and hear Haydn frequently. When he gave a brilliant concert and supper in honor of the king's first visit to Carlton House, the music consisted almost entirely of Haydn's works, with Haydn conducting from the clavier. According to Parke: "The magnificence of the scene on this occasion was truly fascinating. The splendor of the dresses and the elegance and beauty of the ladies all combined to strike the beholder with admiration and delight."

On April 8, 1795, the wedding of the Prince of Wales to the Princess Caroline Amalia Elisabeth of Brunswick took place. It was of course impossible for Haydn to take part in the ceremony, for it had to be entrusted to the official court musicians. He was asked only to help solve a certain problem arising from the participation of three different musicians, and he reports on it in his diary as follows:

On the twenty-first of January I dined with Dr. Parsons, and during dinner a dispute arose as to which of the three doctors, Parsons, Dupuis, or Arnold, should conduct Handel's anthem at the wedding of the Prince of Wales. Dr. Parsons is conductor of the king's band, the other two are organists of the royal chapel. In England the organist is, however, the head in all churches, and the singers are subordinate to him. Each of the three wanted to beat time. When I was forced to express my opinion, I said: "The younger organist should play the organ, the other conduct the singers, while Dr. Parsons should conduct the instrumental performers." This did not suit them, so I left the blockheads and went home.

In spite of the negative attitude of the three musicians

concerned, Haydn's advice was followed at the ceremony. Only three days later the master was invited by the newly married couple to a musical party, about which he remarks in his diary: "An old symphony of mine was given, which I accompanied on the piano; then a quartet; and later I had to sing German and English songs. The princess sang with me and played a concerto on the pianoforte quite well." (The description recalls the musical soirée at Oatlands arranged by the newly married Duke and Duchess of York four years previously, but how much warmer had been Haydn's praise of the "sweet little lady" then! Was this his preference for the daughter of the King of Prussia or was it just another symptom of the composer's general disillusionment?)

It seems that various members of the royal house made efforts to keep Haydn permanently in England. According to Griesinger, the queen offered him a residence at Windsor for the summer, adding, with a mischievous glance toward the king: "Then we can make music tête-à-tête." The king declared that he was not jealous of Haydn, a "good, honest German," and also extended a most cordial invitation to the composer. Nevertheless, Haydn refused, giving various reasons, among them even his attachment to his wife [sic], who, he said, would be unwilling to make so long a journey.

At first sight it does not seem easy to understand Haydn's attitude. England was giving him so much—much more indeed than Vienna ever had. He was the central figure of London's musical life; no other composer's works were performed so frequently or with greater applause. Respect and admiration were paid to him as the "God of musical science," while to the Viennese he was still nothing more than the court conductor of a Hungarian magnate. The income he made in England was most satisfactory too, a matter that was anything but unimportant to one who had actually known utter poverty. Personally, life in England suited him well enough, for he had a number of good friends there, probably not less than in Vienna, and many people seemed only too eager to make his stay in London enjoyable. If, in spite of all these advantages, he decided to return to Austria, he had good reasons for doing so.

Being the musical hero of London was gratifying, even fascinating, but also fatiguing. Haydn was living, as it were, under continuous high pressure. To produce that "electrical effect," as Burney terms it, on a large and exacting audience demanded the utmost concentration and vitality, and called for an effort that could not be maintained indefinitely. The constant demands for new works, even with their enthusiastic reception, which had inspired Haydn to his greatest achievements, would have drained him of his creative power in the long run. Haydn instinctively felt that now it would be better for him to stand in the limelight no longer. Age was beginning to tell, and though the man of sixty-three did not consider his creative work finished, he felt it imperative to economize his strength. A quiet life in England seemed out of the question; there was too much to do and see. Moreover, any real relaxation appeared impossible in a country where he still had a difficulty in understanding the language. The thought of his own little house in the quiet suburb of Gumpendorf drew him away; there at least he might be able to lead the secluded life, devoted mainly to his art, which he now craved.

There was yet another consideration influencing him. Prince Anton Esterházy had died a few days after Haydn's departure from Vienna. His successor, another Nicolaus, was following the tradition so gloriously established by his grandfather, Prince Nicolaus the Magnificent. He had written to Haydn that he planned to restore the former orchestra and asked the master to take over the leadership again. The composer consented, for after so many years of service for the family it was inconceivable to him that another should preside over the Esterházy orchestra. It would be wrong, however, to see Prince Esterházy's offer as the main attraction that drew Haydn back to Austria. At that time he had become independent enough in both character and financial status to choose the kind of life best suited for his art, and it will be seen that even as an employee of Prince Nicolaus Esterházy, he gave but a small part of his time and his interests to the service of his patron.

Leaving England, and this time he knew it was for good, was by no means easy, so Haydn lingered on and on. On May 4, 1795, his benefit concert took place; he directed two of his symphonies in concerts of artist friends on May 29, another one on June 8. After that he was free to go home, but he stayed on until August 15, eager to catch another and yet another glimpse of this English life that had become so dear to him.

His English admirers were not aware of Haydn's inner struggles; to them the matter wore a different aspect. The king had invited Haydn to take up his residence in England and the master had refused. The court was disappointed and rather offended, and, characteristically, no member of the royal family except the faithful Duchess of York appeared at Haydn's benefit concert. The newspapers ceased to mention his name, aware perhaps of the court's changed attitude, but his personal friends remained faithful to him. Anne Hunter, who had supplied the texts for Haydn's English canzonettas, wrote the poem "O Tuneful Voice," deploring that the composer's "accents which still vibrated in her heart" were to be heard no more. Haydn, pleased with his friend's tender words, did not hesitate to set to music the poem written in his own praise. He received various parting gifts, among them a talking parrot (which was auctioned off for fourteen hundred florins after Haydn's death), a beautiful cocoanut goblet from Clementi, and a silver goblet with a very respectful inscription from the Reverend W. D. Tattersall, to whose *Improved Psalmody* Haydn had contributed six melodies. The master's trunks were fairly bulging with musical compositions; according to his own list in the diary copied by Griesinger, he had written no less than seven hundred and sixty-eight pages of music during his two visits to England. Nor was the money he took home a mean amount. He had once more earned twelve hundred pounds for concerts, lessons, and symphonies, and to this was added the considerable income from other works, fees for appearances at Carlton House, and other sources. But the fruits of his stay in England cannot be expressed in figures alone. Haydn's mental outlook had been immensely widened, his self-confidence had tremendously increased, and if at the age of sixty-three he felt impelled to leave the country that had given him so much, it was not the quiet repose of old age to which he was looking forward. He now needed the seclusion necessary for starting on new artistic ventures.

CHAPTER 9

ON A NEW PATH

1795–1801

By the end of August 1795, Haydn was back in Vienna. This time things looked more promising for him than they had on his return from London three years previously. A new head of the Esterházy family was awaiting the Kapellmeister's return so that musical activities worthy of the traditions of Nicolaus the Magnificent could be arranged. Haydn had his hands full in reorganizing the orchestra and making all necessary preparations for a brilliant debut of the new *Kapelle*. The occasion was a grandiose performance on January 4, 1796, of the opera *Penelope* by Antonio Draghi. The audience was dazzled not only by excellent singers from the Vienna opera, but also by costly fireworks. The event took place in the prince's Viennese palace. Fortunately for Haydn, his new patron, Nicolaus II, was by no means enamored of the castle of Esterháza and much preferred spending the winter months in the imperial capital, the summer and autumn at Eisenstadt. In this respect the prince's wishes coincided fully with those of his conductor.

However this was nearly the only point on which the prince and Haydn saw eye-to-eye, and on the whole their relationship was not pleasant. Of the four Esterházy princes with whom Haydn was connected, the last, under whom the master served for fifteen years, was the hardest to satisfy. His predecessor had merely been uninterested in music, a state of affairs that Haydn really could not resent. With Nicolaus II, it was different. In many respects he, like his grandfather, was a passionate patron of the fine arts. He spent enormous sums in adding to his collections; he engaged well-known artists, such as the painter Franz Roesler and the sculptor Antonio Canova; he greatly embellished the castle and park of Eisenstadt; and he had excellent troupes of actors. He professed a love of music and showed himself generous to some composers. It is recorded, for instance, that on a visit to Paris he gave Cherubini a ring worth four thousand thalers. But he would not have dreamed of making such a gesture to Cherubini's idol, Joseph Haydn. The truth was that he did not really care for the old composer's works. His musical interest was concentrated almost exclusively on church music. One of his favorite composers was Haydn's former "teacher," K. G. Reutter, whose superficial, and at the same time entirely outmoded, compositions he could not hear too often. The prince also admired Michael Haydn because he had written some important church music and probably thought more highly of this minor composer than of the great master of instrumental music attached to his court. On the other hand, it was flattering to his vanity to have in his employ a composer whose services made Prince Esterházy the envy of many a potentate. Therefore, of course, he kept Haydn as his Kapellmeister. At first the prince paid the composer only the old salary of fourteen hundred florins (which Haydn had received from Prince Anton without doing any work). Nor did he strain himself in pretending an interest or sympathy for the master that he did not feel. Contemporaries describe the prince's nature as worthy of an "Asiatic despot." His lack of tact and feeling of superiority in his intercourse with composers are well revealed in his behavior toward Beethoven. At the prince's request, Beethoven wrote his first great work of sacred music in 1806–7, the Mass in C major, which ranks among the foremost works of the kind written in that period. After the performance the prince merely remarked to the composer, who had already proved his genius with the Eroica symphony, *Fidelio*, and other works: "But, my dear Beethoven, what is this that you have done here again?" Whereupon the outraged composer left the castle. Prince Nicolaus II seems not to have been aware of the new ideas released through the French Revolution. He was as complete an autocrat as his grandfather had been, but lacked the latter's charm and genuine understanding of music.

This placed Haydn in a difficult position. Willing as he had been to overlook the despotism of Nicolaus the Magnificent, who for all his shortcomings had been truly attached to the master, he felt much less inclined to put up with it from a man half his age, one who often did not understand what he was talking about. Once Haydn even went so far as to express this. When the prince uttered some unjustified criticism at a rehearsal, Haydn burst out with: "Your Highness, it is *my* job to decide this," whereupon Nicolaus indignantly went out of the room, leaving all the musicians "horror-stricken." Nor did Haydn lose any opportunity of impressing on his patron that he felt his salary to be inadequate. This is revealed in the following letter, which shows that the composer possessed a keen sense of business. Prince Esterházy had as a majordomo a certain Johann Alois Luegmayer, who had the good luck to be married to a niece of Haydn. The spendthrift nephew took ample advantage of this relationship, for he liked to contract debts in the name of his famous uncle, and he was so successful in these manipulations that, according to Haydn's own testimony, Luegmayer received from him in the course of years some six thousand florins. Eventually even Haydn, to whom the integrity of his family mattered greatly, lost patience. When informed by the prince's administration that his account was being charged with new debts of the majordomo, he not only refused to pay them, but also boldly changed from defensive to offensive tactics. This is the way he expressed himself in an undated letter, probably written in 1796:

To the Administrator of Prince Esterházy:

I see from the papers forwarded to me, and the enclosure from His Highness Prince Esterházy's economic administration that in consequence of Luegmayer's *inability* to pay his debt, I am condemned to do so. Pray, why? Because I am supposed to be *able*

to pay. Would to God this were the case. But I swear
by the Kyrie eleison, which I am at this moment composing for my fourth prince, that since the death of
my second prince of blessed memory I have fallen
into the same state of inability as Luegmayer himself,
only with this difference: he has descended from a
horse to the back of an ass, whereas I have remained
on the horse, but without saddle or bridle. I beg
therefore, gentlemen, you will at least have patience
till I have finished the "Dona nobis pacem," and till
the prince's majordomo Luegmayer, instead of receiving his salary from the poorly paid music director
Haydn (who spent thirty-six years in the princes'
service), shall begin to get the salary justly due to
him from his most gracious prince. For surely nothing
can be more sad or incongruous than that one servant
should pay another servant; that is, the Kapellmeister
pay the majordomo. If I should presently by my own
efforts (for flatter or beg I cannot) or by the volun-
tary impulse of my gracious prince be placed in a better position, I will not fail to comply with the above
demand.

Yours, etc. . . .

Usually, however, Haydn managed to restrain himself
and find a better method of reaching the prince's ear. On
such occasions he went to Princess Marie Hermenegild, the
wife of Nicolaus II, who liked and admired the master
greatly, and eventually she smoothed out matters for him.
For instance, he resented not being addressed with the
courtesy due a Doctor of Music of Oxford, and it was the
princess who saw to it that no one at court should speak
of the composer curtly as "Haydn" without a prefix, and
that official letters addressed to him were full of the flourishes accorded a person of distinction. In the course of
years the princess also obtained several increases of salary
for the composer, as well as other favors, such as the regular delivery of wine from the princely cellars.

Altogether, Haydn, although not enjoying the work for
his fourth prince, did not resent it too much because his

duties were not particularly heavy. His main obligation was that of regularly composing new Masses for his patron. This he did, and six masterworks were written for this purpose. Apart from that, Haydn's most important duty was to be on hand for festive occasions when the prince wanted to show off his famous conductor, as he did when the Archduke Joseph, Palatine of Hungary, visited Eisenstadt twice in 1797, and the emperor and empress once in 1800, events that were celebrated with the traditional Esterházian splendor. For the ordinary routine work there was a substitute, Johann Fuchs, a member of the orchestra, as Haydn himself felt entitled to give most of his time to occupations not connected with the service of his prince, occupations that were to assume paramount importance during the years to come.

The composer had returned to Vienna teeming with energy, and the work to be done for his narrow-minded patron was but a poor outlet. While still in London, Haydn is said to have declared: "I want to write a work that will give permanent fame to my name in the world." The unforgettable experience of the Handel Commemoration in Westminster Abbey had convinced the composer that an oratorio was best suited to link his name indissolubly to the future. In addition to this consideration, Haydn's constant urge to experiment with new ways of expression drove him toward the oratorio. After writing the London symphonies, he felt that he had reached a summit never to be surpassed by him in this type of music. Orchestral composition offered no further attractions to him, and though he was in his middle sixties, he felt eager to measure his strength against a new genre, one in which he had not as yet proved his mastery.

That Haydn chose the Creation for a subject is again because of England. There are various reports about it. It seems that Salomon gave the master a libretto that a man by the name of Lidley[1] had compiled for Handel from

---

[1] Tovey (*Essays in Musical Analysis*, V, 119) suggests that Lidley might be a misprint for Linley, father of the well-known violinist Thomas Linley and the singer Elizabeth Ann Linley (Mrs. Sheridan).

Milton's *Paradise Lost*. On the other hand, according to Purday,[2] the violinist Barthélemon, one of Haydn's great friends, when asked to suggest a suitable subject for an oratorio, pointed to the Bible and exclaimed: "There! Take that, and begin at the beginning." It does not seem impossible that both stories are true. Haydn, influenced by Barthélemon, may have mentioned his intention to Salomon, who then procured the libretto, which Haydn took with him to Vienna. This book was in English and the composer, who was determined to compose a German text, needed a translator. Chance helped him to find the right man.

Vienna had among its musical amateurs of noble birth, a baron of Dutch origin whose hobby was the oratorio, especially the works of Handel. This was Gottfried van Swieten, prefect of the Vienna court library and president of the educational commission. His father, Gerhard van Swieten, had played an important part at court as the favorite physician of the Empress Maria Theresia. The son chose a diplomatic career, and from 1771 to 1777 was ambassador to the court of Frederick the Great of Prussia, where he became acquainted with north-German music. There for the first time he heard the name of Johann Sebastian Bach, and his curiosity was stirred to such an extent that he traveled to visit Bach's son, Philipp Emanuel, in Hamburg and bought from him several manuscripts and copies of works by the cantor of the Thomasschule, together with some music by Emanuel himself. When he returned to Vienna, he was probably the only person in the city who owned a copy of *The Well-Tempered Clavier*. On the other hand, in 1769 the baron visited England, where he became an ardent admirer of Handel. He took home the scores of some of Handel's greatest oratorios, and thenceforth considered it his mission to propagate the music of Handel and Bach in the Sunday morning musicales that he arranged in the magnificent baroque hall of the court library. As no organ was available, the baron made one of the regular guests, Wolfgang Amadeus Mo-

[2] This information was given to C. F. Pohl by Sir George Grove, who had it from Purday's son.

zart, reorchestrate various Handel oratorios by substituting wind instruments for the organ. Swieten also induced the young composer to arrange some Bach fugues for string trio or quartet with the addition of introductory adagios, and by drawing Mozart's attention to baroque music, exercised an important influence on the composer's artistic development. Beethoven too was patronized by the baron and repaid him by dedicating his first symphony to him. Swieten was a composer himself, and though his orchestral works were "as stiff as their composer" (Griesinger), his symphony in E flat enjoyed the undeserved privilege of being attributed to Haydn for a long time. Altogether the baron was not what one would call a lovable person. He was obstinate, despotic, and, despite his considerable wealth, decidedly closefisted. It was he who, when approached on Mozart's death by the destitute widow, advised Constanze to bury the master in a pauper's grave so as to save expense. Culturally his influence was sometimes anything but beneficial, and, according to Riemann, the Vienna court library suffered under his leadership greater damage than from wars or fires. He gave orders for the removal of everything that "merely gratified the imagination or was a scholastic luxury," and by so doing he had many priceless incunabula destroyed.

Nevertheless, in spite of his faults, Gottfried van Swieten was the right man for Haydn. He was much more than a mere translator, and in the chapter dealing with Haydn's last period of composition, his share in Haydn's oratorios will be pointed out. What concerns us here is·the fact that van Swieten, through his influential position, gave the works the best possible start. In those times composers as a rule did not write an important work unless it was commissioned. Even Haydn, in spite of his enormous fame and secure financial position, probably would have been reluctant to do so. Had he stayed in England he might have written such an oratorio for Salomon or Gallini. To whom could he turn in Vienna, where businesslike concert enterprises in the English manner were hardly known? At this point van Swieten stepped in. He got together a group of twelve music-loving noblemen and each guaranteed a contribution of fifty ducats to defray the expenses of performance and pay an honorarium to the composer. Thus Haydn had firm ground under his feet, and started on the composition of *The Creation*, to which he devoted most of his time and energy during the following years. The work progressed slowly, for, as Haydn remarked, he spent much time over it, because he intended it to last a long time.

These years devoted to the composition of *The Creation* were among the richest and happiest in Haydn's life. He was fully absorbed by a task in which, perhaps better than ever before, he could express the innermost forces of his nature. Haydn had always been deeply religious and free from doubt and skepticism; he was really sincere when he wrote the words *Laus Deo* at the end of each of his compositions. In spite of life's darker sides, which were well known to Haydn, who had led an unsheltered life from earliest childhood, the world seemed a very good and beautiful place. To some slight extent, each of his works was a Creation, expressing praise and thankfulness to the Heavenly Father. Now he could do so on a much larger scale and with a freedom he never had had in the composition of a Mass; at the same time he had a chance to depict in sounds the beauties of nature, which delighted this passionate hunter and fisherman so much. Here he could—as was always his aim—"depict Divinity through love and goodness" and express in his own idiom the harmonious view of life, the serene affirmative spirit that filled his soul. When he worked on this oratorio, Haydn felt uplifted and in close communion with his Creator. "Never was I so devout," he said, "as when composing *The Creation*. I knelt down every day and prayed to God to strengthen me for my work." He remarked to Carpani that when he felt his inspiration flagging, he "rose from the pianoforte and began to say his rosary." He "never found this method to fail."

The effect that Haydn wanted to achieve with this work cannot be better expressed than in the words that Princess Eleonore Liechtenstein used in a letter to her daughter about *The Creation*: "One has to shed tender tears about

the greatness, the majesty, the goodness of God. The soul
is uplifted. One cannot but love and admire."[3]

April 29 and 30, 1798, were exciting days for the Viennese. Although only invited guests were admitted to these
first performances of *The Creation* at the palace of Prince
Schwarzenberg, a tremendous crowd of onlookers gathered
outside the building. The market stalls on the Neuer Markt
(formerly the Mehlmarkt), where the palace (demolished
in 1893) was situated, had to be removed, and twelve
policemen and eighteen mounted guards were stationed to
keep order in the approaches to the house. The privileged
who were allowed to enter consisted mostly of the nobility,
among them, as Princess Liechtenstein records, "all the
elegant Polish, English, and Viennese ladies." Carpani also
relates: "I was present, and I can assure you I never witnessed such a scene. The flower of the literary and musical
society of Vienna was assembled in the room, which was
well adapted to the purpose. The most profound silence,
the most scrupulous attention, a sentiment, I might almost
say, of religious respect prevailed when the first stroke of
the bow was given." On this occasion the master was not
his usual placid self. "One moment," he said later, "I was
cold as ice, the next I seemed on fire. More than once I was
afraid I should have a stroke." The musicians were of the
first rank. Haydn himself conducted in the modern way
with a baton, as was customary for choral performances.
At the piano sat the court composer, Salieri. The soprano
part was sung by Christine Gerardi, whom a contemporary critic described as follows: "Flexibility and beauty of
voice, a lovely figure, expressive features, and lustrous eyes
give vigor to each of her words and grace to every sound
rising from her throat."[4] The male soloists were Ignaz Saal,
bass of the court opera, and Mathias Rathmayer, professor
of the Theresian Academy, whose beautiful tenor voice
Princess Liechtenstein praised. Success was overwhelming
and far beyond expectation. Most of the listeners may have
felt like the Viennese correspondent of the *Neuer teutscher Merkur*, who wrote: "Three days have gone since

[3] See Pohl and Botstiber, *Joseph Haydn*, III, 130.
[4] In the *Neuer teutscher Merkur*, (May 3, 1798).

that enrapturing evening, and still the music sounds in my
ears and in my heart; still the mere memory of all the flood
of emotions then experienced constricts my chest."

Furthermore, Haydn had good reason to be well satisfied
with the material success. Not only did his aristocratic
patrons pay him the agreed honorarium, but in addition
they presented him with the entire receipts from the admission fees. But this was only the beginning. For years
The Creation was to prove so unfailing an attraction that
the proceeds from it, mostly given to charitable institutions,
by far surpassed even the receipts from the London benefit
concerts that had once seemed so extraordinary to Haydn.

As early as May 7 and 8 of the same year, the work was
again played at the Schwarzenberg Palace. Suddenly, however, the exertion of these last years made itself felt: Haydn
broke down and had to spend some time in bed. Though
his absorption in the congenial task of composing *The
Creation* brought him the greatest happiness, it also imposed a tremendous strain. On many occasions physical
weaknesses checked the flow of his inspiration and caused
Haydn to despair, and when he had recovered and could
go on with his work, a certain lack of confidence in what he
was doing taxed his strength as the writing of symphonies
or string quartets never had. A letter that he addressed to
Breitkopf and Härtel on June 12, 1799, is very significant
in this respect. Although written one year after the memorable first performance of *The Creation*, it vividly reflects
the strain of the past years of composition and shows that
Haydn was not certain even then how the more conservative critics would receive the work that was now to be
circulated in print throughout the musical world:

My business unhappily expands with my advancing
years. The world daily pays me many compliments,
even on the fervor of my latest works; but no one can
believe the strain and effort it costs me to produce

them, inasmuch as time after time my feeble memory
and the unstrung state of my nerves so completely
crush me to earth that I fall into the most melancholy
condition. For days afterward I am incapable of for-
mulating one single idea, till at length my heart is
revived by Providence, and I seat myself at the piano
and begin once more to hammer away at it. Then all
goes well again, God be praised! . . . I only wish and
hope that the critics may not handle my *Creation* with
too great severity and be too hard on it. They may
possibly find the musical orthography faulty in various
passages and perhaps other things also, which for so
many years I have been accustomed to consider as
minor points, but the genuine connoisseur will see the
real cause as readily as I do, and willingly ignore such
stumbling blocks. *Nulla Regola s[enza] e[ccezione].*

Writing a full-sized oratorio with such painstaking care
would be a heavy task for any artist in his late sixties, but
Haydn by no means confined himself to this work. During
these same years he wrote two large Masses, a vocal arrangement of *The Seven Last Words*, a concerto for keyed
trumpet, some of his very best string quartets, three trios
with piano, and his own favorite, the national hymn "Gott
erhalte," which more than anything else enhanced his
popularity in his own country. The impulse to compose the
Austrian hymn came from England. Noticing the deep
impression produced in London whenever "God Save the
King" was played, Haydn felt that in the distressed times
of the Napoleonic Wars Austria also needed a patriotic
song. Here, too, van Swieten proved of service in the reali-
zation of the master's idea. He discussed it with the imperial chancellor, Count Saurau, who gladly took up the
project and commissioned a poet by the name of Leopold
Haschka to write a suitably patriotic text. In January 1797,
Haydn set it to music and on February 12, on the birthday
of the emperor, the hymn was sung in all the theaters
of Vienna and the Austrian provinces. The enthusiasm
aroused by the new hymn was tremendous, and the following little story throws a sidelight on its fast-growing

popularity. A wealthy Englishman, who seemed to have stepped out of a fairy tale, offered to provide trousseaux for twenty-four engaged couples in Vienna who did not have enough money to be married, and thus make their marriages possible. The fortunate young people all were married simultaneously at St. Stephen's and then liberally entertained at Jahn's, the court caterer. Music was provided by a military band which, upon urgent request, had to play three times in succession the national hymn introduced to the Viennese only two days earlier.

Haydn received from the emperor a gold box with the monarch's portrait and a substantial gratuity. The composer would have considered a decoration an appropriate gesture of thanks for this national hymn that so greatly built up the public morale at a time when it was sorely needed. But even though the Emperor Franz and his second wife, another Maria Theresia, felt much more friendly toward the master than their predecessors on the Habsburg throne, the grant of such an honor simply did not occur to them. In spite of the innumerable tributes of admiration that Haydn received in his old age, the award of a decoration from court was not among them.

But other honors were bestowed on him. One came from Sweden, when the Austrian composer was made a member of the Royal Music Academy. Another one, awarded in Vienna, had a symbolic significance, as it annulled an injustice under which Haydn had long smarted. The Viennese Tonkünstlersocietät coolly had rejected Haydn's application in 1778, but now offered him membership as "perpetual assessor" with exemption from any admission fees. This was a very unusual procedure, as the Societät, whose main function was to insure musicians and their families, naturally was dependent on the payments of its members. The musicians, however, felt it imperative to make an exception in the case of Haydn, in order to obliterate their former shortsightedness. In doing so they not only gave great pleasure to the old master, but also brought important material benefits to the institute. From that time on Haydn showed himself most generous to the Societät. Shortly after his election he gave them the music to his new vocal version of *The Seven Last Words* and himself conducted two brilliant performances, thus assuring unusually high receipts. How little Haydn spared himself when there was a chance of helping the Societät is revealed in his calendar for March 1799. This month was devoted mainly to rehearsals of *The Creation*, which was to be performed for the first time in a theater open to the general public on March 19. In addition to this task, the burden being increased by two performances of the oratorio on March 2 and 4 at the Schwarzenberg Palace, Haydn conducted performances of *The Seven Last Words* for the Societät on March 17 and 18, the two days immediately preceding the great event. Nevertheless, on March 19 he showed no signs of fatigue, and the first public performance of the oratorio brought him sensational success. Indeed, so thrilled were the Viennese about the event (it drew the greatest crowd ever seen in the Burgtheater) that they hardly seemed to notice the Russian army under Suvarov that was passing through the capital on the same day. The correspondent of the Leipzig *Allgemeine Musikalische Zeitung* wrote as follows:

> On the nineteenth I heard Haydn's "Creation." Not to report to you about this good fortune (for this is what it was) would reveal either too little feeling for art or for friendship. The crowd was immense and the receipts amounted to 4088 fl. 30 kr., a sum never before collected by a Viennese theater. Moreover, the nobility paid for all the not inconsiderable expenses of production. One can hardly imagine with what quiet and reverence the whole oratorio was received, only gently interrupted by soft exclamations at the most striking passages, and what enthusiastic applause sounded at the end of each piece.

The soprano singer was the seventeen-year-old Therese Saal, whose father, Ignaz Saal, performed the bass solos. One critic wrote of her performance: "The part of Eve in Haydn's *Creation* will hardly ever be sung again with such warmth, delicacy, and devout simplicity."

As a Christmas present for the Societät, Haydn conducted two performances of *The Creation* on December 22 and 23, 1799, and thereby again greatly improved the institute's financial status. On this occasion a critic of the *Allgemeine Musikalische Zeitung* wrote: "Haydn's gestures were most interesting to me. With their aid he conveyed to the numerous executants the spirit in which his work was composed and should be performed. In all his motions, though anything but exaggerated, one saw very clearly what he thought and felt at each passage." From that time forward it became the custom for Haydn to let the Societät perform his great oratorio, usually under his own direction. In a letter that the publisher George Thomson wrote to Haydn's friend Mrs. Hunter, he remarked: "Haydn wrote me lately that in three years forty thousand florins had been raised for the poor families of musicians by the performances of *The Creation* and *The Seasons* at Vienna."

One year after the first public performance in Vienna, the oratorio was heard in London, and in this event the rivalry between competing impresarios played an important part. This time it was a race between Salomon and Ashley,[5] both having ordered the score from Haydn. The unlucky Salomon decidedly came out second. Not only did he have to pay the outrageous sum of £30.16.0 for postage, whereas Ashley's expenses for delivery through the courier of the British Legation amounted to only £2.12.6, but also, what was worse, Ashley was far quicker in presenting the oratorio. *The Creation* was performed by him in Covent Garden on March 28, only six days after receipt of the score, while Salomon followed on April 21. The amazing speed of this production was owing mainly to the excellent organization of the copyist, Thomas Goodwin, who had to get one hundred and twenty parts copied out in so short a time. When praised for his efficiency, Goodwin remarked: "Sir, we have humbly emulated a great example; it is not the first time that the Creation has been completed in six days." In spite of all his ill luck, Salomon's performance united, as a critic

[5] Ashley directed the Lent oratorios at Covent Garden inaugurated by Handel. He began directing them in 1795.

remarked, "in the overcrowded hall all of London's most distinguished friends of music." In the same year a performance of *The Creation* took place at the Three Choirs' Festival in Worcester.

Paris followed London's example a few months later. Interest in Haydn's compositions had been steadily increasing there, and the French friends of music desired that the composer himself conduct his oratorio. This attitude was rather remarkable in view of the almost continual state of war in those years between France and Austria. However, if the French were magnanimous enough to forget political controversies for the sake of good music, the Austrian police definitely did not adopt this attitude. When Pleyel, who had settled in Paris and become a French citizen, was sent to Vienna by the Opéra in the summer of 1800 to present in person the French invitation to Haydn, and possibly carry him off as Salomon had done ten years previously, the Austrian authorities did not allow the musician, lest he might be a spy, to cross the border from Germany. All the endeavors of Haydn and the publishing house of Artaria proved of no avail, and Pleyel had to return to Paris without having accomplished his mission. At first Haydn felt greatly tempted to go to Paris, for he had not forgotten how delightful it was to travel in a foreign country. In the end, however, he decided against it, and the Paris performance took place on December 24, 1800, under Steibelt's direction. Unfortunately the attention of the audience was greatly distracted by the news that Bonaparte, then First Consul, who was attending the concert, had just escaped a bomb attempt on his life in the rue Nicaise. In spite of this drawback the musicians were so enthusiastic about *The Creation* that they had a large gold medal engraved in commemoration of the event. This medal, designed by Gatteaux, was presented to Haydn one year later and gave him immense pleasure.

Although Haydn would certainly have enjoyed a visit to Paris, he was wise not to yield to the temptation. His physical strength might have been unequal to the exertion, for since the spring of 1800 his health had not been satisfactory. Early in April he had been seized by a "rheumatic

head fever" that kept him in bed and at first looked so
serious that, according to Straton's letter to Thomson, the
Viennese "were not altogether devoid of alarm in regard
to his recovery." Although Haydn was allowed to get up
by the end of April, his convalescence proceeded very
slowly. Throughout the summer at Eisenstadt he was tired
and dispirited and it was not until August 2 that he was
able to write to Luigia Polzelli that he was feeling better.

This breakdown, far worse than the one two years before, was not surprising. Indeed it is rather to be wondered
at that it had not occurred earlier. Haydn had been absorbed in too many activities. He had even, for the first
time, tried his hand in business by being his own publisher.
In so doing he apparently followed the advice of van
Swieten, who considered the publication of *The Creation*
through a business firm "not honorable." Haydn collected
the subscriptions for the score of the oratorio himself and,
with his characteristic politeness, in many cases took pains
to write detailed answers. The subscribers' list to be found
in this first edition of the oratorio is illuminating in many
respects. That both Austria and England claimed Haydn
for their own is shown by the illustrious names heading the
list: the Austrian Empress and various archdukes of the
House of Habsburg, the King and Queen of England, the
Prince and Princess of Wales, the Duchess of York, and
the Princesses Augusta, Elisabeth, Maria, Sophia, and
Amalia. About half the remaining subscriptions came from
England. Among them were the names of many persons
who had become Haydn's friends during his stay in the
British capital: Bartolozzi, Barthélemon, Salomon, Mrs.
Schröter, the Misses Abrams, Sir Patrick Blake, Lady Rich,
and Haydn's colleagues in the Doctorate of Oxford, Dr.
Arnold, Dr. Aylwood, and Dr. Ayrton. In addition there
was a surprisingly large number of members of the British
nobility; characteristically, many of the subscribers were
women. Apparently the memory of Haydn's earlier social
success still was very much alive. Among the Austrian subscribers we also find many aristocratic music lovers, names
like those of the Princes Lichnowsky, Kinsky, and Liechtenstein, all familiar to us from Beethoven's dedications, Ger-

many too was represented by various princes and duchesses. Looking over this imposing list, the son of the modest wheelwright must have felt great satisfaction. But when the preparatory work was done and the score of the oratorio securely launched, Haydn entrusted the firm of Artaria with the distribution of the work, recognizing that his time might be spent in a more congenial way.

The constant awareness of "so much to be done" drove the old master on inexorably, heedless of his diminishing physical strength. He was now almost exclusively absorbed in creative work. An interesting document preserved in the Mozarteum at Salzburg and entitled *Daily Schedule of the late Herr v[on] Haydn*[6] (possibly written by Elssler) gives some details of the composer's way of life. It reads as follows:

In the summertime he rose at 6:30 AM. First he shaved, which he did for himself up to his seventy-third year, and then he completed dressing. If a pupil was present, he had to play his lesson on the piano to Herr von Haydn, while the master dressed. All mistakes were promptly corrected and a new task was then set. This occupied an hour and a half. At eight o'clock sharp, breakfast had to be on the table, and immediately after breakfast Haydn sat down at the piano, improvising and drafting sketches of some composition. From eight to eleven-thirty his time was taken up in this way. At eleven-thirty calls were received or made, or he went for a walk until one-thirty. The hour from two to three was reserved for dinner, after which Haydn immediately did some little work in the house or resumed his musical occupations. He scored the morning's sketches, devoting three or four hours to this. At 8:00 PM Haydn usually went out, and at nine he came home and sat down to write a score or he took a book and read until 10:00

[6] It was customary in the Austrian Empire to employ the word "von" (abbreviated "v.") in addressing every person of good standing, although it was rightfully confined to the nobility.

PM. At that time he had supper, which consisted of bread and wine. Haydn made a rule of eating nothing but bread and wine at night and infringed it only on sundry occasions when he was invited to supper. He liked gay conversation and some merry entertainment at the table. At eleven-thirty he went to bed, in his old age even later. Wintertime made no difference to the schedule, except that Haydn got up half an hour later.

Griesinger amplifies this schedule by telling us that every evening Haydn carefully went through the household accounts in order to keep his servants in bounds. On the other hand, he liked to play cards with them in winter evenings, and got much amusement from seeing their delight when they won a few pence from him. Haydn, fully absorbed in creative work, probably enjoyed intercourse with such simple people as a relaxation. On the whole, this way of life left but little scope for close relationships of any kind, and indeed there is not much to relate about Haydn's personal activities during these years. From 1797 he lived in his own house, doubly enjoyable because his wife was hardly ever there. Frau Haydn, who was suffering from severe rheumatism, spent most of her declining years at the sulfur springs of the little town of Baden, where she died on March 20, 1800. The event probably meant little to her husband, for he had become used to a sort of bachelor existence and was well looked after by Elssler and the cook, Anna Kremnitzer. There was one person, however, who was sent into a flurry of excitement by the news of Frau Haydn's death. Luigia Polzelli again was living in Vienna, although not in the service of Prince Esterházy, for Haydn apparently did not attempt to obtain an engagement for her. Luigia lost no time in reminding Haydn of his former promise to marry her when he was free. The old composer did not like the idea at all; he felt too settled in his ways for any further matrimonial experiments. All that mattered to him was to pass the remainder of his life in a smoothly ordered routine that would be instrumental in conserving his creative powers. When Luigia found it was impossible to change his attitude, she made him sign the following document:

> I, the undersigned, promise Signora Luigia Polzelli, in case I should marry again, to take nobody else for wife other than the above-mentioned Luigia Polzelli; and if I remain a widower, I promise to leave the above-mentioned Luigia Polzelli after my death a pension of three hundred florins in Vienna currency for so long as she lives. Valid before any judge, I sign

> JOSEPH HAYDN
> *Maestro di Cappella to his Highness*
> *the Prince Esterházy*

Vienna, May 23, 1800

Luigia, on her side, did not promise anything. Thus, with Haydn's pledge safely in her pocket, she saw no reason for remaining single. She therefore married an Italian singer, Luigi Franchi, and they went to Italy. The old master, while not feeling jealous, did not like to be imposed upon, and therefore in his will he reduced the promised pension to half the amount.

So Luigia Polzelli gradually faded from Haydn's life, and no other woman appeared to take her place or that of Marianne von Genzinger. As the above-mentioned *Daily Schedule* testifies, Haydn still had some pupils. He had lost the one to whom he had been particularly attached. Pietro Polzelli, Luigia's eldest son, died in 1796, at the early age of nineteen. His place was taken to some extent by Sigismund Neukomm, who worked for seven years under Haydn and became attached to him. In 1799 Anna Milder (the first to sing the part of Leonore in Beethoven's *Fidelio*) also became a sort of pupil. Haydn found that the girl of fourteen had a voice "as big as a house" and handed her over for instruction to Neukomm. Haydn probably took an active interest in the singer's development. When she won her first laurels in 1803, Griesinger wrote: "Her voice sounds like pure metal and as her teacher Neukomm is schooled by Haydn, she produces long vigorous notes without flourishes and exaggerated ornaments."

The name of Griesinger frequently has been mentioned in this book. From 1799 he was in close contact with Haydn, and his letters and his *Biographical Notes on Joseph Haydn*, based on direct information from the composer (who was quite aware of his friend's intention to use this material in a book), are among the most valuable sources of information for the Haydn biographer. Georg August Griesinger, after studying theology, went to Vienna in 1799 as tutor to the children of the Saxon ambassador, Count Schönfeld. In 1804 he became secretary of the Saxon Legation, and in 1806 its councilor. Griesinger was known to Gottfried Härtel, the head of the publishing house of Breitkopf and Härtel, Leipzig. The publisher was most eager to establish business contacts with Haydn, but having found out that the master, overburdened with work, was slow in answering letters, he hoped for better results through an intermediary and asked Griesinger to undertake the task. Härtel's idea proved excellent and fruitful. Griesinger was delighted to have an opportunity of meeting the world-famous composer, whom he described after his first visit as "a cheerful and still well-preserved man, and to all his colleagues a model of modesty and simplicity." Haydn immediately took a fancy to the young man, who understood how to humor him and thus obtained important contracts for the Leipzig publisher. (On the other hand, presents from Breitkopf and Härtel, such as a diamond ring, Indian-silk handkerchiefs, waistcoats of English cashmere, and colored silk hose pleased the old man immensely.)

Another publisher who also used a personal emissary was George Thomson of Edinburgh, who asked Mr. Straton and subsequently Mr. Stuart, both of the British Legation, to negotiate with Haydn for arrangements of Scottish folk songs to be published by him. Haydn approved the suggestion and in the course of years adapted some two hundred and fifty airs for Thomson, for which, according to the publisher's statement, he received £291.18.0. No friendship, however, developed between Haydn and Straton, who apparently did not have much use for musicians. The following passage in a letter from Straton to Thomson reveals a feeling of superiority that made impossible a closer relationship with the composer:

> Haydn called here yesterday and mentioned that he had already written to you and also begun the composition of the accompanyments to the Scotch airs (fifteen in number) that you had sent him through me. He seemed desirous of having rather more than two Ducats for each air, but did not precisely insist upon this point, which I therefore left undecided exhorting him to proceed with his composition as speedily as its nature as well as that of his other occupations will admit of. This he solemnly promised but said that he could not possibly determine a period for finishing the airs in question. Upon the whole he appears to be a rational animal, whereas all that can be said of the other, I mean Koz[eluch],[7] is that he is a Bipede without feathers.

Similar work was done by Haydn for the publisher William Whyte of Edinburgh, the Viennese firm of Artaria serving as intermediary. Whyte published sixty-five arrangements of Scottish folk songs, paying Haydn twenty florins for each. This undemanding task, in which Haydn may have received help from his pupils, seems to have given him satisfaction and also provided pleasant additional income.

In 1800, Haydn met two English people of great renown. Early in the fall, Admiral Nelson and Lady Hamilton paid a visit to the Esterházys at Eisenstadt. Haydn asked his publisher Artaria to send him a copy of his cantata *Arianna a Naxos* because Lady Hamilton wanted to sing it. Griesinger reports about the event to Breitkopf: "In Lady Hamilton, Haydn found a great admirer. She visited the Esterházy estate in Hungary, but paid little attention to its splendors, and for two days did not budge

[7] Leopold Anton Koželuch, serving as Viennese court composer, also arranged Scottish airs for Thomson.

from Haydn's side." There is also an unconfirmed story that Nelson asked for Haydn's pen and in exchange gave the master his valuable gold watch.

In the same year the Bach biographer and musicologist Johann N. Forkel visited the composer and brought him a poem that the famous poet Christoph Martin Wieland had written on hearing *The Creation.*

Haydn was happy to be reminded of the years in London by visits from his good friends Domenico Dragonetti, the double-bass virtuoso, and the young Johann Baptist Cramer. Michael Haydn's short visit to Vienna also gave both brothers much enjoyment. To Michael, who had lived in Salzburg since 1762, a trip to the capital was about as exciting and important as the London visits had been to his brother. He kept a diary of all he saw and did, and after the lapse of a year he tried to revive the memory of all those delightful experiences by rereading his notebook.[8]

Although Joseph enjoyed such pleasant episodes, his main interest always lay in composition. The year of the first performance of *The Creation,* 1798, also saw the completion of the *Nelson Mass;* 1799, that of the *Theresia Mass.* During these same years Haydn composed two string quartets, Op. 77, for Prince Lobkowitz, and some small vocal works such as the thirteen vocal duos, trios, and quartets, written, according to the composer's words, "*con amore* in happy hours, without being commissioned." All this happened, as it were, on the fringe of his creative life, the center of which was fully occupied after the completion of *The Creation* by another oratorio, *The Seasons.* The impulse for the composition of this oratorio came from van Swieten, who, after winning so many laurels with Haydn, was eager to continue on this path. He translated James Thomson's *The Seasons* and adapted it as a libretto for an oratorio, giving Haydn minute instructions as to the sequence of the arias and recitatives. Haydn, though he

[8] This is mentioned in a letter from Michael to Joseph Eybler, dated November 5, 1799. See Pohl and Botstiber, III, 133. Joseph Eybler was an intimate associate of both Haydn and Mozart and studied under Albrechtsberger.

considered the guidance of the composer by the poet to be quite in order, did not feel so happy as when he had composed *The Creation*. The somewhat verbose and philistine text did not inspire him as strongly as van Swieten's earlier libretto. When he had to compose the words in praise of Industry, he observed that though he had always been very industrious himself it had never occurred to him to set Industry to music. In particular he felt doubtful about van Swieten's advice to insert tone pictures wherever possible. The imitation of natural sounds and voices, such as the song of birds and the roll of thunder, which had long been familiar in music, gradually had become unacceptable to certain aesthetic circles. Their rejection of such devices made the old master uncertain of his work in composing music to a libretto that seemed urgently to call for them. Haydn naturally blamed van Swieten for any passages in his score that seemed to savor of such devices, and there are records about various disparaging remarks that he made about the libretto. When correcting the proofs of the pianoforte adaptation of the work, he wrote against No. 22: "This whole passage imitating a frog has not flowed from my pen. I was forced to write down this Frenchified trash. With the whole orchestra the miserable idea easily disappears, but it cannot be so treated in the piano score." Unfortunately, through an indiscretion, the German critic Johann Gottlieb Spazier got hold of Haydn's own comments and used them in his review as an argument against van Swieten's text. The baron was furious and promised to rub this remark into Haydn with "salt and pepper." Two weeks later, however, Griesinger was able to report to Breitkopf and Härtel that the storm had passed. After all, van Swieten was too happy basking in the sunshine of Haydn's triumphs to sever so important a connection.

In point of fact, *The Seasons* achieved a triumph. Amazingly enough, the completed work, in its freshness of inspiration, revealed no trace of the physical handicaps and difficulties that the composer had suffered while writing it. Haydn won the battle, but the price he had to pay was tremendous. His health was now definitely shattered, for as he said himself, "*The Seasons* has finished me off." Still, stubborn like so many of his forefathers, Haydn doggedly continued doing what he felt to be essential, and the very months before the first performance of the work show him trying to continue his active life in the face of increasing physical failings. In January 1801, when war was again ravaging unhappy Austria, Haydn helped to raise money for the wounded. A performance of *The Creation* conducted, according to Rosenbaum,[9] by the composer "with youthful fire," netted 7183 florins for the good cause, and a concert in which Haydn and Beethoven cooperated with Christine Gerardi, who first sang the part of Eve, brought in as much as 9000 florins. But in February 1801 Haydn was again laid up with "rheumatic head fever." This kept him inactive until the middle of March. Still, on March 29 and 30 he again conducted *The Seven Last Words* for the Societät, and, above all, he was burdened with the exacting preparations for the production of *The Seasons*. Again, Prince Schwarzenberg had the privilege of being host for this important event, which took place on April 24, 1801; the oratorio was repeated on April 27 and May 1. The soloists were the same as for the first public performance of *The Creation* and again produced a great effect. As for the reaction of the listeners, the correspondent of the *Allgemeine Musikalische Zeitung* described it with these words: "Silent reverence, amazement, and loud enthusiasm alternated for the powerful appearance of colossal visions, the immeasurable abundance of splendid ideas surprised and overwhelmed the boldest expectations."

Shortly afterward, the Empress Maria Theresia insisted on having a performance of *The Seasons* at court, to be followed the next day by *The Creation*. In both oratorios the empress sang the soprano solos "with much taste and expression, but a small voice," according to Haydn. These events occurred on May 24 and 25, and four days later the first public production of *The Seasons* took place in the

---

[9] J. C. Rosenbaum, official in the service of Prince Esterházy, kept a diary that affords much interesting information about Haydn after his return from London. (Cf. p. 208.) Rosenbaum was married to Haydn's godchild, a singer at the Vienna opera, Therese Gassmann.

Redoutensaal. Haydn had reason to be well satisfied with the financial result for, in addition to the receipts of 3209 florins, he was presented with an honorarium of six hundred ducats by a group of aristocrats who also paid all the expenses. But it is doubtful whether the composer was much impressed by this fact, though as a rule he showed an increasing eagerness to earn large sums of money in his old age. He was now too weary, too exhausted from the unending struggle between his urge to create and his worn-out body. His thoughts were moving more and more toward the ultimate goal, and on June 5, 1801, Griesinger wrote to Leipzig: "Haydn has just drafted his last will."

CHAPTER 10

RETIRING FROM LIFE

1801–1809

Haydn's last will, which he worked on from June to December 1801, is an interesting document, for it throws light on his character. It is the testament of a man of means, for when Haydn died he left bonds to the value of 14,800 florins; property that, when auctioned off, brought 23,163 florins; and a house that was sold for 17,100 florins —a total equivalent to 27,000 dollars, which of course meant much more at that time than the same amount would today. But the man who had risen so high in the world did not forget his humble origin. Although he had left his father's house at the age of five, and never since had been more than an occasional visitor to it, he retained a deep-rooted attachment to his widely branched family. For a man who hardly knew what it was like to grow up in the midst of brothers and sisters, such an existence was imbued with a certain nostalgic fascination. Possibly he felt close to his relatives because he had never been obliged to live with them, had never suffered the fate of other growing artists, that of being hampered by a family's narrow-mindedness and lack of understanding. He always had relied on himself alone. Throughout his life he hardly ever received a favor from any relative, though he had assisted dozens of them materially. In many villages near Eisenstadt and Esterháza there dwelt nephews and nieces of Haydn who had settled in the neighborhood mainly because of their generous uncle. Haydn loved visiting them, and again and again became the godfather of their children and helped one or another of them to set up business or get good training in a trade. A charming instance of Haydn's family sentiments is recorded by Carpani.[1] Once a year Haydn invited all his relatives of the neighboring villages to the little town of Bruck an der Leitha, where he gave them a feast in the best inn, presented each with a small sum of money, and on parting embraced each and extended a cordial invitation for the next year. "Haydn called this family gathering his day of grandeur and went to it happily and proudly." While writing his testament, he saw himself as if again presiding over such a family gathering and made the greatest effort to remember everyone and to distribute his riches fairly. So the last will of the world-famous composer provided, for the most part, legacies to hardworking artisans. A shoemaker, a blacksmith, a silversmith, two seamstresses, a saddler's widow, and two lacemakers were among the legatees.

On the other hand, various bequests to women not related to him point to the master's interest in the fair sex. It is much to be regretted that it seems hardly possible to follow up these interesting clues. The only legatee whom we know even a little about is the singer "Babett," or Barbara, Pilhofer, first soprano at the Esterházy court. But there are also legacies to Mesdemoiselles Anna and Josepha Dillin, to the blind daughter of the choirmaster at Eisenstadt, to the four daughters of the wigmaker Sommerfeld of Pressburg, to the daughter of the bookkeeper Kandler, and others. Most tantalizing is the provision of a thousand florins for Mademoiselle Catharine Czech, waiting woman to Princess Grassalkovics. The princess was the daughter of Prince Nicolaus the Magnificent, and it seems possible that she employed a girl from her father's estate as a waiting woman who might have known Haydn well. (Was she the predecessor of Luigia Polzelli?) The entry, however, was subsequently crossed out by Haydn, just as he canceled the bequest to his first love, the sister of his late wife (see p. 42). Whether Haydn acted thus because he believed these women to be dead is not known. In the case of his sister-in-law, Josephine Keller, he would have

[1] *Le Haydine* (Milan, 1812), p. 15.

committed an error, for she died ten years after Haydn, at the age of eighty-six. The legacy to Luigia Polzelli has been mentioned. Haydn left her an annuity of one hundred and fifty florins and remarked: "I hereby revoke the obligation in Italian, signed by me, which may be produced by Madame Polzelli, otherwise so many of my poor relations with greater claims would receive too little."

Other important legacies were left to the master's faithful servant, Johann Elssler, to the cook, and to the housekeeper. But it was to Haydn's two brothers, Michael and Johann, that the two largest sums of four thousand florins each were bequeathed. Of these brothers Johann was probably nearer to the composer's heart because it had fallen to Haydn to look after him since after the death of their father Johann had joined his brother in Eisenstadt. Although trained as a wheelwright, Johann became a tenor singer in the church choir, but his musical accomplishments seem to have been very modest, for in spite of his brother's influence, he never rose from this inferior position during forty years of service. As his salary was very small, he was mainly dependent on Joseph, and his distinguished brother helped him continually, found pupils for him, and for twenty-five years sent him every summer to the sulfur springs of Baden near Vienna, where Johann had to take the cure.

Thus to set his house in order was no sad task for Haydn. Rather it afforded him satisfaction, for his heart was warmed by the thought of how much his financial assistance would mean to some of these humble people. His health improved while he was engaged in the task; indeed, it seemed in those summer days of 1801 as if he had recovered from the "terrible worry and torture" of composing *The Seasons*. He went again to Eisenstadt and was industriously working on a new composition for his prince, the so-called *Creation Mass*. On September 11 he wrote to Thaddäus Weigl, son of the cellist: "Poor old boy that I am, I have just come to the end of my new Mass which is to be produced the day after tomorrow." Again this splendid work reveals no signs of fatigue, and in addition to its composition Haydn continued to deliver Scottish songs to Thomson.

His contented state of mind also was owing to various proofs of worldwide recognition that reached him during this year. From Amsterdam came a letter announcing that the Society Felix Meritis had made him an honorary member. From Paris arrived Gatteaux's beautiful medal. Haydn cherished it immensely and told his prince that he would bequeath the medal to him, provided he could be assured that it would be kept in the Esterházy treasury. Nor was this the only tribute that the master received from France in 1801. In December he was elected an *associé étranger* to the class of fine arts of the Institut de France, and this time a medal was engraved by Dumarest. This great honor caused some disappointment and bitter remarks in England, for Sheridan had been an unsuccessful candidate for membership. It would be wrong, however, to deduce from outbursts of indignation in some parts of the press, a changed attitude among British music lovers toward Haydn. When, at about the same time, the sculptor Grassi made busts of the composer in two different sizes, five of each size were immediately ordered from England.

While the entire world was paying homage to Haydn, there were still fellow countrymen who did not even know him by name. This is revealed by a rather absurd episode that happened in July 1801. The little town of St. Johann in Bohemia wanted to hear *The Creation*. Rehearsals were started under the auspices of the music-loving pastor, who applied to the Prague consistory for permission to perform the oratorio in an old unused church. Strangely enough the reply was negative. The indignant citizens then tried to build an improvised concert hall, but when this plan proved to be impracticable, they decided to have the performance in the old church in spite of the prohibition issued by the authorities. The good pastor was abducted in a carriage, so he would not be held responsible for the violation of the decree from Prague, and the citizens duly had their performance of *The Creation*. Another pastor, hearing about the matter, delivered a fulminating tirade against the desecration of the church by the performance of the work of a "heathen" (the German word for "heathen" having the same sound as the name of the composer). Naturally the pastor of St. Johann became worried about the reaction in Prague and appealed to Haydn. The master, in a reply[2] written to the pastor, said that the whole strange story "did no credit to the head and heart of those responsible," and continued: "At all times the story of the Creation has been considered the loftiest, most awe-inspiring one for mankind. To accompany this great work with suitable music could certainly have only the effect of increasing the holy emotions in man's heart and making him more sensible to the goodness and power of the Creator. How could this stirring of divine emotions be a desecration of the church?" Finally Haydn promised to intercede, if necessary, with the emperor, who had always listened to the oratorio with the deepest emotion. We do not know the outcome of this storm in a teacup, but it is to be assumed that the persons responsible for it did not persist in their ridiculous persecution.

The report of a *Creation* performance in another little circle was likely to make Haydn forget the annoying incident. In the small German town of Bergen on the North Sea island of Rügen, enthusiastic music lovers got together and performed Haydn's oratorio with a very modest number of players. So great was their delight and gratitude that they felt bound to express them to the composer. Coming from the heart, this expression moved Haydn deeply, and he answered with one of the most charming letters of thanks he ever conceived:

Vienna, September 22, 1802

Gentlemen:

It was indeed a most pleasant surprise to receive such a flattering letter from a place where I could have no idea that the fruits of my poor talents were known. When now, however, I see that not only is my name familiar to you, but that my compositions are performed by you with approval and satisfaction,

[2] The letter is dated "Eisenstadt, July 24, 1801." See *Deutsche Zeitung* (Doc. 23, 1873).

the warmest wishes of my heart are fulfilled: to be considered by every nation into which my works penetrate as a not wholly unworthy priest of this sacred art. You reassure me on the point so far as regards your fatherland and, still further, you give me the pleasant conviction (which cannot fail to be a most welcome consolation of my declining years) that I am often the enviable source from which you, and so many families susceptible of true feeling, derive pleasure and enjoyment in domestic life. What happiness does this thought cause me! Often, when contending with obstacles of every sort that interfered with my work, often when my powers both of body and mind were failing and I felt it a hard matter to persevere in the course I had entered on, a secret feeling within me whispered, "There are but few contented and happy men here below; everywhere grief and care prevail; perhaps your labors may one day be the source from which the weary and worn, or the man burdened with affairs, may derive a few moments' rest and refreshment." What a powerful motive for pressing onward! And this is why I look back with heartfelt and cheerful satisfaction on the work to which I have devoted so long a succession of years and such persevering efforts and exertions. And now in the fullness of my heart I thank you for your kindly thoughts of me, and beg you to forgive the delay of my answer. Feeble health, the inseparable companion of the gray-haired man of seventy, and likewise pressing business, have until now deprived me of this pleasure. Perhaps nature may yet accord me the gratification of composing a little memorial for you from which you may gather the feelings of a gradually dying old man who would fain, even after death, survive in the charming circle of which you draw so pleasing a picture. I have the honor to be, with the highest consideration,

Your obedient servant,
JOSEPH HAYDN

The references in this letter to declining years, feeble health, and death are very significant. At that time Haydn was already prone to stress these points, a tendency that was to increase in the years to come. While up to the time of his return from England the composer had felt younger than his actual age, the opposite was becoming his state of mind now. He did not let any opportunity go by to refer to his advanced age (he occasionally pretended to be older than he was). It is also significant that on receiving letters he did not care to answer, he merely sent the respective person his musical visiting card bearing his name and above it a quotation from his four-part song "Der Greis" which reads, in English translation: "Gone forever is my strength, old and weak am I." Yet he did not stop working. Indeed, the summer of 1802 saw him "laboring very wearily" (as he termed it) on his last Mass. In addition, he was engaged on the quartet Op. 77, No. 3, and supplied Scottish folk songs to Whyte of Edinburgh. Official duties kept him busy as well, and documents in the Esterházy archives contain various reports by him on engagements of new musicians, on dismissals, and on the examinations of singers. But old age was beginning to bear heavily on this man who had led so extremely industrious a life. He was not really ill, except for the discomfort caused by his old enemy, a nasal polyp which, according to Griesinger, made him "grumpy and uncomfortable." (Now he probably regretted having refused so vehemently the help offered him by the celebrated surgeon John Hunter in London.) But he grew increasingly weary, and fits of dizziness often prevented his working at the piano. The prince, aware of the state of affairs, began to look for an adequate substitute, and as he was mainly interested in church music, he sought an expert in this kind of composition. His choice fell at last on Michael Haydn who, after the occupation of Salzburg by the French in 1800, had been robbed of all the valuables and cash in his possession and appeared willing to leave his old post. Brother Joseph thereupon lent a helping hand, sent him a golden watch to replace the silver one Michael had lost, promised him money as soon as the interests on his savings were due, and, on Michael's visit to Vienna in 1801, seems to have been instrumental in the negotiations with Prince Esterházy. Michael was offered a yearly salary of fifteen hundred florins, more than twice the stipend he received in Salzburg. The prince apparently counted on Michael's arrival, but the musician, after long hesitation, felt more inclined to remain in Salzburg and to work there under its new ruler, Grand Duke Ferdinand III of Tuscany. A draft of Joseph's answer to his brother's notification has been preserved,[3] and is noteworthy because it throws light on Joseph's opinion of his patron:

> Your action regarding His Royal Highness the Archduke and my Prince was carefully considered and courageous. Though I and the whole world must regret it, neither side can reproach you in any way. Both patrons are great, but the Grand Duke's love for and understanding of music surpass that of my Prince. Your heart and mind must decide whom to give the preference. Meanwhile I wish you happiness for whatever position you choose and hope to hear as quickly as possible about your final decision.

Michael remained in Salzburg and Prince Esterházy had to find another man. Abandoning his search for the moment, he appointed Johann Fuchs, who really had done the work for the past years, as vice-conductor, while Tomasini was to be responsible for the chamber music in Haydn's absence. At last, in 1804, at Haydn's recommendation, he engaged as concertmaster and composer Johann Nepomuk Hummel, Mozart's pupil, who had also received some instruction in organ-playing from Haydn, and it was Hummel who actually took over the master's duties. Moreover, since 1807 Haydn's pupil Antonio Polzelli served as "substitute concertmaster and director." Even after Haydn had ceased working with the Esterházy musicians, they maintained their loyalty to their fatherly friend. That they honored him on his name day is revealed in a charming

[3] It is dated January 22, 1803. See H. Jančik, *Michael Haydn* (Vienna, 1952), p. 244.

letter to Antonio Polzelli which Haydn dictated and signed on March 20, 1808:

The true filial feelings expressed by you and all the members of the princely Esterházy band on the occasion of my name day have made me shed scalding tears. Deeply moved I thank you and the others with all my heart and ask you to tell all members on my behalf that I regard them all as my dear children whom I ask to show patience and forbearance with their old, infirm father. Tell them that I am attached to them with fatherly love and that there is nothing I wish more than to have strength enough to experience once more the harmony at the side of these worthy men, who made the fulfillment of my duties so pleasant. Report to them that my heart will never stop remembering them and that it is my greatest pride to stand—thanks to the grace of my serene Prince—at the head of great artists who are noble and grateful human beings as well.

The release from official duties after 1802 caused Haydn's physical condition to remain for a while comparatively stationary, with occasional periods of well-being. In June 1803 he started on his last quartet. However, only two movements were ever completed.

In the same year the master made his last appearance as a conductor when he performed *The Seven Last Words* for the benefit of the civic Hospital of St. Marx, a charitable institution in which he took a great interest. From then on he was more and more confined to his house and hardly ever was seen in public. Even when special homage was to be paid to him on his seventy-third birthday (in 1805), he could not attend the celebration. The scene was the first appearance in public of Wolfgang Mozart *fils*, who was to perform among other works a cantata he had composed to words by Griesinger in honor of Haydn's birthday. It was planned that Haydn should introduce the young musician to the audience, but finally the project had to be abandoned: it was feared the excitement would be too much for the invalid master.

Short walks, which were all Haydn could manage with his badly swollen legs, were taken in his own little garden, supported and almost carried by the faithful Elssler. Once the actor August Wilhelm Iffland saw Haydn returning from a stroll in his garden with flowers in his hands, and the old man, who "clearly took comfort in their fragrance," remarked to his guest that "he had attended to his devotions in nature."

Now that the composer definitely felt that the period of his creative work was over, he liked to look back on his former achievements and was eager to see a catalogue of his life's work prepared. With the help of earlier lists, the thematic catalogue intended to embrace all the works composed by Haydn in the last fifty-five years was compiled in 1805 and written out by Elssler.

Haydn spent his last years in increasing bodily discomfort, and they cannot be called happy ones. They differed too completely from his former way of life to satisfy him, and forced inactivity weighed heavily on him. For instance, Carpani describes his mood as a "habitual state of sadness" and an "absorption in the melancholy sentiment that life was escaping him." Still, there were brilliant patches even in this shadowy existence. Haydn was fortunately spared the tragic fate of other aging masters who were forgotten in their own lifetimes. On the contrary, evidence of his outstanding reputation again and again broke the dreary monotony of an invalid's life. He even experienced the strange sensation of reading obituary notices about himself. In 1805 the rumor spread over Europe that Haydn had died. In England the *Gentleman's Magazine* announced the master's death (at ninety-seven years of age!) and the publisher Thomson wrote a letter of condolence to the Viennese bankers, Fries and Company, who had handled his business with Haydn. In Paris the greatest consternation prevailed. Cherubini wrote a cantata on Haydn's death and Kreutzer composed a violin concerto based on themes from Haydn's works. A special memorial concert with these works and Mozart's *Requiem* was planned for February 1805, but good news from Vienna put a stop to the undertaking.

Haydn was rather amused by the whole matter. He signed a letter to Thomson "to prove that he was still of this base world," and when he heard about the plans in Paris, he remarked: "The good gentlemen! I am greatly indebted to them for the unusual honor. Had I only known of it in time, I would have traveled to Paris to conduct the *Requiem* myself."

High tribute was projected to be paid to the dead composer, nor was this surprising. After all, it has always been so. It is far more rare to see a living composer as greatly honored as Haydn was. In 1803 he had been awarded the gold Salvator Medal by the city of Vienna, and one year later the city named him an honorary citizen. The French, in spite of the honors previously awarded, still felt that they had not done enough for so great a master. In 1805 a diploma of membership was handed him from the Paris Conservatory, another in 1807 from the Société Académique des Enfants d'Apollon, both accompanied by gold medals. In the following year the Philharmonic Society of St. Petersburg followed the example of Paris. It is not surprising that the old master, when he was feeling particularly low and depressed, should have taken out the box holding his medals, drawing encouragement from these visible signs of his success.

Of course, he derived an even greater pleasure from displaying them to his guests, and this was usually part of the ceremonial observed with visiting strangers whom the name of Haydn had drawn to the little house in the quiet Viennese suburb. These visits meant much to the invalid, and although they sometimes tired him greatly, he would not have missed them for anything. He was always ready to receive anyone who might drop in unannounced. He once remarked to Dies: "You seem to be surprised that I am fully dressed, though I am ailing and weak and cannot go out. My parents trained me strictly as a child to be clean and orderly, and these two qualities have become second nature to me." But the simple wheelwright and Count Harrach's cook would never, in their wildest dreams, have thought of seeing their Sepperl attired on an ordinary working day in the manner that the Czech musician Johann Wenzel Tomaschek describes: "Haydn sat in an armchair, very much dressed up. A powdered wig with sidelocks, a white neckband with a gold buckle, a white, richly embroidered waistcoat of heavy silk, in the midst of which shone a splendid jabot, a dress coat of fine coffee-colored cloth with embroidered cuffs, black silk breeches, white silk hose, shoes with large silver buckles curved over the instep, and on the little table next to him a pair of white kid gloves made up his attire."[4]

The year 1805 was particularly rich in interesting visitors. The pianist Marie Bigot (to whom Beethoven gave the autograph of his Sonata Appassionata) delighted Haydn so much with her interpretation of his own works that he exclaimed: "My dear child, you have not only played this, you have composed it." The visit of the violinist Pierre Baillot may have left a less pleasant memory, for when the friendly host opened his arms, the impetuous Frenchman embraced him with such violence that he almost knocked out the old master's last two teeth. Another visitor from France was Haydn's former pupil and later competitor, Ignaz Pleyel, now a successful publisher. He had greatly pleased the master by his model edition of Haydn's complete string quartets. Pleyel was accompanied by his son, Camille, who described the visit as follows in a letter to his family dated June 16, 1805:

> We found him very weak; the face, it is true, has hardly changed, but he can scarcely walk, and when he speaks for some length of time, he completely loses his breath. He told us that he was only seventy-four years old [as a matter of fact, Haydn was seventy-three], and looks as if he were eighty, so weak is he. We found him holding a rosary in his hands, and I believe he passes almost the whole day in prayer. He says always that his end is near, that he is too old, and that he is useless in this world. We did not stay long because we saw he wished to pray. I embraced him and kissed his hand, which gave him great pleasure. He has a very pretty and well-fur-

4 See Libussa, *Jahrbuch für 1846*, p. 330.

nished house, but it seems that he does not see anyone. [Here Camille was definitely mistaken.]

The most welcome of all his guests from France proved to
be Luigi Cherubini, who took the opportunity of calling
on his beloved "Father" when he was invited to produce
his operas in Vienna. They spent many happy hours together. Haydn found Cherubini a "handsome little man
full of distinction" and gave him the autograph of his
symphony No. 103 (with the Drum Roll). He wrote under
his name 'Giuseppe Haydn' the words: *Padre del Celebre
Cherubini ai 24to di Febr. 806.*

Viennese friends of course continued to visit Haydn,
above all Griesinger, who, as he wrote to Breitkopf, could
not bear to give up these visits, though the old man was
growing weaker from day to day. He tried to get whatever information he could from the composer for his proposed book, and the same was done by a new friend, the
painter Albert Christoph Dies, who paid thirty calls and
set down the contents of his conversations in his *Biographische Nachrichten von Joseph Haydn,* published in 1810.
Haydn did not object to the inquisitiveness of his friends.
He lived more in the past than in the present and evidently
enjoyed looking back on the struggles of his childhood and
youth.

Another welcome visitor was Magdalena von Kurzböck,
an excellent pianist, to whom Haydn's last piano sonata
(Hob. XV:52) and his last piano trio (Hob. XVI:31),
both in E flat, are dedicated.

Sometimes Haydn had the pleasure of seeing his dear
Princess Esterházy in his house. It was she, for instance,
who brought the deeply moved master the sad news of the
death of his brother Johann in May 1805. She was, as
Haydn said, like a good angel to him, and thanks to her
influence, her husband now showed himself much more
gracious to the invalid composer and increased his salary
in 1806 to twenty-three hundred florins. Moreover the
prince offered him the use of his carriage and paid the accounts of his doctor and apothecary, all of which Haydn
greatly appreciated.

On no other occasion did the love and respect shown to the composer become more apparent than at the remarkable performance of *The Creation* in Italian on March 27, 1808. The concert was planned in celebration of Haydn's approaching seventy-sixth birthday. The master was formally invited, and in view of the mild weather, his physician allowed him to leave the house. Prince Esterházy was prevented from attending the performance because of important business, but he sent his carriage, and Haydn rode slowly to the university with Magdalena von Kurzböck. A huge crowd, which had to be kept in order by military guards, had gathered in front. Members of the high nobility, as well as distinguished musicians—among them Beethoven, Salieri, Hummel, and Gyrowetz—received the master, who was carried in an armchair into the beautiful lecture hall. On his appearance, a flourish of trumpets and drums was sounded, mingled with jubilant exclamations: "Long live Haydn!" The master was seated with the highest aristocracy, next to Princess Esterházy, who wrapped the old man in her own shawl when she noticed him shivering a little. Many other ladies followed her example, and soon Haydn was covered with the costliest of garments. The French ambassador, noticing with pleasure that Haydn was wearing the gold medal from the Concerts des Amateurs on his coat, exclaimed: "This medal is not enough; you should receive all the medals that are distributed in the whole of France." Poems in German and Italian were written for the occasion and were handed to the master by his friends Magdalena von Kurzböck and the Baroness Spielmann. The conductor was Salieri; at the leader's desk sat the famous virtuoso Franz Clement, who thus repaid the master for having conducted the benefit concert for the boy of eleven in London. The audience was in an unusually receptive state of mind. When thunderous applause followed the words "Let there be light—and there was light," Haydn lifted his hands upward and exclaimed: "Not from me, from thence comes everything." The reception given to him and his work moved the master indescribably. Indeed, he was so shaken that it was thought advisable not to let him stay on after the interval.

Everybody present realized that the days on earth of the frail old man were numbered. The people thronged around him with tears in their eyes, shaking his hands and embracing him. Beethoven at this moment behaved not at all like a "Great Mogul," for he knelt down before Haydn and kissed the hands and forehead of his old teacher. Only in broken sentences could Haydn express his thanks and good wishes, but before he was carried out, he lifted his hand as if to bless the whole assembly.

Princess Esterházy had the scene painted by Balthasar Wigand and mounted on a costly box which she gave to the delighted master. It contained a sumptuous album with the most cordial inscriptions from the princely family and was furnished with elegant writing equipment and all kinds of useful instruments in fine English steel and gold. After Haydn's death the princess acquired the box again for the sum of four hundred florins, and later gave it to Franz Liszt. Eventually it became the property of the Museum of the City of Vienna. During the turbulent events of 1945 the relic was destroyed, however, and only a few tiny parts of it have been rescued.[5]

Although the admiration of the Viennese for Haydn had reached its greatest intensity, it never succeeded in pervading the official court circles. Right after the memorable performance of *The Creation* Count Chotek, minister of state, wrote to the emperor:

> I have just come from the University Hall, from Haydn's triumph with *The Creation*, heard with solemn, holy emotions in his presence among the irrepressible acclaims of a gathering of the first of Your Empire and the most august friends of music. On this occasion, the most blissful feelings, which only Virtue and Religion call forth, and which Haydn so powerfully and ardently depicted in this and his other immortal works, took hold of all hearts and were expressed so loudly in thanks for the composer that he, conscious of his infirmity, felt obliged to leave the

[5] See L. Nowak, *Joseph Haydn,* 2d. ed. (Vienna, 1959), p. 454.

circle of his admirers. At this occasion soft wishes were uttered to me that this ever righteous and greatly respected man, who wrote works inspiring us to goodness, works—one might say—that are holy, should before his demise be honored by his gracious monarch through the conferment of the Leopold order.

This letter, dated March 28, 1808, reached the monarch only on November 26, 1814, when Haydn was no longer on this earth. The file contains a remark that the delay was insignificant as the Leopold order was intended only for excellent service in church, state, or military matters, as well as for outstanding patriotic merits in connection with charitable activities, and therefore could not have been conferred on the composer of *The Creation*. (The fact that Haydn had composed the Austrian national anthem was not thought worthy of mention.) The emperor confirmed his agreement with this attitude by signing the act.

Haydn, who had heard of the minister's suggestion, is reported to have been "as happy as a child" about it and to have prepared what to reply in an audience with the emperor. It is good to know that he never became aware of the court's attitude.

The performance of *The Creation* at the university proved to be Haydn's last public appearance. Before long, political conditions made festivities of the kind impossible, as Austria again became the scene of a devastating war. Decisive battles were fought in the spring of 1809, and the French army came nearer and nearer to Vienna. These were indeed dark days for the invalid master. His greatest concern was in the revision and alteration of his last will. In the years that had passed since he first drafted it, Haydn's two brothers, Johann and Michael, had died (in 1805 and 1806 respectively). The master, while leaving most of the legacies unaltered, made his only surviving nephew, Mathias Frölich, his principal heir. Mathias, who had been trained as a blacksmith at Haydn's expense, lived in the village of Fischamend, near Vienna. One year after his uncle's death he settled down in Rohrau, where he stayed for the rest of his life and had the pleasure of witnessing, in 1841, the first Haydn Commemoration, which took place in the master's native village. Whether Mathias was worthy of his uncle's inheritance is open to doubt. Schmid's information that he kept a piano owned by his uncle in a loft and used it as a flour bin does not impress us favorably. Be that as it may, Mathias did not derive from his uncle's rich bequest the benefit that Haydn fondly imagined. Owing to the inflation following the Napoleonic Wars, the money that Mathias inherited lost its value almost entirely and the principal heir of the wealthy composer died a poor man.

Six weeks before his death, Haydn called his servants and his grandniece, Ernestine Juliane Loder, who was looking after him, into his room and read them his will, for he wished to know whether they were satisfied with its provisions. Ernestine was especially favored as, apart from one thousand florins, she was bequeathed furniture to equip a room. All of them heartily thanked him with tears in their eyes. By the beginning of May the French had captured some of the western suburbs of Vienna and made the castle of Schönbrunn their headquarters. Haydn's house was perilously near the enemy and Magdalena von Kurzböck entreated him to move to her house in the center of the city. Haydn refused, for he felt unequal to coping with any change in his life. On May 12 the great bombardment of the city started, and a cannon ball fell with a tremendous noise quite near Haydn's house. The house shook as in an earthquake and the members of Haydn's entourage were scared out of their wits. Not so the old invalid, who exclaimed above the uproar: "Children, don't be frightened; where Haydn is, nothing can happen to you." (Marion Scott very aptly called this "sublime illogicality" the "Nelson touch in Haydn.") For twenty-four hours the bombardment went on, shattering the poor man's nervous system. When Vienna capitulated and quiet was restored, the invalid, at whose doorstep Napoleon had placed a guard of honor, was unable to recover. He suffered no pain, but his strength was ebbing away. On May 26 kind fate allowed him one great joy. A French officer of hussars, by the name of Clément Sulemy, called and after conversing with the master about his *Creation,* sang to him the aria "In native worth." According to a letter from Andreas Streicher[6] (who got the report from Elssler), he sang in "so manly, so sublime a style, and with so much truth of expression and real musical sentiment that Haydn could hardly restrain his tears of joy and assured the singer as well as the people in his house that he had never before heard the aria sung in so masterly a manner. After half an hour's visit the officer mounted his horse in order to go against the enemy." (Schnerich asserts that Sulemy fell soon afterward in the battle of Aspern.) On the same day, Haydn called his people to the piano and played for the last time his favorite, the Austrian hymn. In those days of Austria's collapse, the act had an unusual significance. Haydn, playing it three times in succession, put into the immortal tune all that he felt for his unhappy country, and although his strength nearly failed him, he achieved an "expressiveness that surprised even himself."[7] But on the next day he could rise no more. A second doctor was called in for consultation, but was unable to suggest anything to combat the quickly progressing exhaustion. The master seemed to be quite happy, and when asked how he was feeling, whispered: "Children, be comforted, I am well." Nevertheless the periods of unconsciousness increased and on May 31, 1809, shortly after midnight, he went "blissfully and gently" to sleep, to wake no more.

Austria, in the throes of a deadly struggle, could not pay the departed the honors that unquestionably would have been extended to him in normal circumstances. Indeed, there was so great an upheaval in the town that the news of Haydn's death was hardly circulated before the funeral. Thus the obsequies, which took place to the sound of Michael Haydn's *Requiem,* were of the simplest kind. Carl Rosenbaum, ex-secretary of Prince Esterházy, commented on the event as follows in his diary: "Haydn lay in his large room, dressed in black, not disfigured at all. At his feet were placed the seven medals from Paris, Russia,

[6] Streicher's letter to Griesinger is dated July 2, 1809.
[7] Elssler's letter to Griesinger, dated June 30, 1809.

Sweden, and Vienna. After five o'clock he was borne in an oak coffin to the Gumpendorf Church, carried around it three times, blessed, and carried to the Hundsturm Cemetery. Not a single Viennese conductor accompanied him." However, Rosenbaum could not deny that the official obsequies, which took place on June 15, were "very solemn and worthy of Haydn." Members of the French army alternated with grenadiers of the municipal militia to form a line around the catafalque. The medals were placed in front of it and among them the little ivory tablet with Haydn's name which had been handed to the master as a free pass to the London concerts.[8] High-ranking French generals, officials, and officers, as well as the whole cultured world of Vienna, were present. The music was chosen very fittingly for the occasion, for it was the *Requiem* by his beloved Mozart that Vienna's musicians played on taking leave of Joseph Haydn.

[8] According to Griesinger, Haydn was particularly impressed by this courtesy and laid stress on the fact that nothing of the kind had ever been shown him in Vienna.

CHAPTER 11

AN INCONGRUOUS POSTLUDE

In the year of Haydn's death Prince Esterházy applied for permission to have the body exhumed and moved to Eisenstadt. But presently the whole matter slipped his memory, and though he received the permission, no action was taken. Haydn's tomb remained neglected until in 1814 the master's devoted pupil, Sigismund Neukomm, on returning to Vienna from France, had a simple marble tablet erected bearing as an inscription Haydn's favorite quotation from Horace, *non omnis moriar*, set as a five-part riddle canon. The prince continued to ignore the question of Haydn's last resting place until in 1820 he was reminded of his obligations by Adolphus Frederick, Duke of Cambridge. This distinguished visitor observed, after attending a gala performance of *The Creation* given in his honor at Eisenstadt: "How fortunate was the man who employed this Haydn in his lifetime and now possesses his mortal remains." Prince Esterházy did not care to contradict his guest's assumption, but he gave orders immediately for the body to be brought to Eisenstadt for burial in the Bergkirche, where Haydn so often had performed his own Masses. When the coffin was opened for identification, the horrified officials found no head on the body, but only the wig. Inquiries soon brought an explanation of the mystery. Two students of Gall's and Spurtzheim's work on phrenology, namely Haydn's friend Carl Rosenbaum, former secretary of Prince Esterházy, and Johann N. Peter, the administrator of a penitentiary, had bribed the gravedigger and stolen Haydn's head a few days after the funeral in order to "protect it from desecration." Peter had a black wooden box made with glass windows and decorated with a golden lyre in which the skull was placed on a white silk cushion trimmed with black. When Haydn's body arrived in Eisenstadt without the head, the prince was furious and sent the police to Peter, who said that he had given the skull to Rosenbaum. A search in the latter's house did not yield any result, as Rosenbaum's wife, the singer Therese Gassmann, hid the skull in her straw mattress and lay down on the bed. The prince now tried bribery, and his emissary promised Rosenbaum a large sum if he would deliver the skull, whereupon the skull of an old man was handed to the prince and buried with Haydn's body. Not unnaturally, Prince Esterházy did not keep his promise of a reward, but neither had the wary ex-secretary acted honestly, as he had not delivered the right skull. On his deathbed Rosenbaum gave Haydn's skull to Peter and made him promise to leave it in his will to the museum of the Society of Friends of Music in Vienna, the owner of a great number of valuable Haydn relics. There the skull had its resting place from 1895 on.[1] In 1932, Prince Paul Esterházy had a Haydn mausoleum erected in the Bergkirche with a marble sarcophagus surrounded by four stone figures representing the seasons. But twenty-two years had to elapse before the skull was united with the other remains. Since 1954 Haydn has been buried in the little town of the Burgenland which played so important a role in his artistic growth.

[1] The authenticity of the skull of the Society of Friends of Music was proved beyond any doubt by Joseph Tandler in "Über den Schädel Haydns," *Mitteilungen der anthropologischen Gesellschaft* (Vienna, 1909).

PART TWO

WORKS

THE SOURCES

The student who undertakes the compilation of a work dealing with the music of Joseph Haydn is faced with difficulties that it would be hard to overestimate. Collected editions have been published of the works of Bach and Handel, Mozart and Beethoven, Schubert and Schumann, Mendelssohn and Chopin, Berlioz and Brahms. Even the compositions of the less familiar old masters, Josquin des Prés, Palestrina, Orlando di Lasso, Monteverdi, Lully, and others have been painstakingly collected and printed. No such edition, however, exists for the creator of the Clock and Surprise symphonies. A definitive Collected Edition of Haydn's works was begun in 1907: Eusebius Mandyczewski presented a thematic list of one hundred and four symphonies, and gradually the first forty-nine works of the kind, as well as the piano sonatas and songs, *The Creation* and *The Seasons*, were offered in this series published by Breitkopf and Härtel, Leipzig. However, the work progressed very slowly, and in the 1930s it came to a complete stop. Thanks to the initiative of H. C. R. Landon, a new enterprise was started in 1950 in Boston by a group of Haydn enthusiasts under the leadership of J. P. Larsen. The Haydn Society issued the symphonies Nos. 50–57 and 82–92 as well as four Masses, whereupon it was forced to relinquish the plan. Ultimately the Joseph Haydn Institute of Cologne took over this task, with F. Blume as president and J. P. Larsen serving as general editor up to 1960, when this position was assumed by G. Feder. Every thing points to full success for this venture, which is being carried out with scholarly thoroughness. Yet so far only a fraction of Haydn's works is available in the new Collected Edition published by G. Henle Verlag, Munich.[1]

Better, though not completely satisfactory, is the situation with regard to a thematic catalogue of Haydn's works. Around 1765, the composer himself started on a thematic list of his works, the *Entwurfkatalog* (draft catalogue), which is of great significance, especially for the time up to 1777. Much more extensive is the *Verzeichniss aller derjenigen Compositionen welche ich mich beyläufig erinnere von meinem 18ten bis in das 73ste Jahr verfertiget zu haben* (list of all those compositions that, as nearly as I can remember, I composed from my eighteenth to the seventy-third year), a compilation made by Haydn's faithful amanuensis, Johann Elssler, in collaboration with the composer. This catalogue, preserved in the Budapest National Library, contains many hundreds of themes of Haydn's works entered on one hundred and twenty-three pages; it is indeed an important document and at first sight it creates the impression of real completeness. Unfortunately, however, the memory of the man of seventy-three left much to be desired, and all the friends who visited him in 1805, the year of the completion of this catalogue, agreed that Haydn's recollections were far from trustworthy. He and Elssler used the best sources at their disposal for this work, the above-mentioned *Entwurfkatalog*, autographs and other manuscripts from Haydn's collection, and reliable printed editions authorized by himself. But in spite of their great efforts this catalogue is far from being satisfactory. While it affords scarcely any evidence that Haydn included works by other composers, it nevertheless contains many mistakes. Among the operas, for instance, a work called *L'infedeltà fedele* (Faithful Unfaithfulness) is listed. Actually Haydn never wrote any opera by that

[1] A significant supplement is offered by the publication of all the symphonies and of numerous other hitherto unpublished instrumental and vocal works which H. C. R. Landon edited for Universal Edition and Doblinger Publishing Houses, Vienna.

name, and the title should not have been included.[2] Similarly, among the Masses the so-called *Little Organ Solo Mass* is quoted twice: once with measures three and four of its beginning, as *Mass No. 4*, and then with measures one and two, as *Mass No. 13*. In the list of symphonies, Haydn and Elssler quote as No. 17 the first movement and as No. 91 the second movement of the same symphony (No. 34 of the Collected Edition). Similarly they note as No. 32 the slow introduction and as No. 100 the following presto of one symphony (No. 54 of the Collected Edition). Worse than these mistakes is the fact that many of the works listed in the catalogue are not to be found in any library; probably they were lost during one of the fires that ravaged both Esterháza and Eisenstadt. On the other hand, a number of Haydn's compositions of which the authenticity cannot be doubted are missing from the Haydn-Elssler catalogue. Especially for the period before 1765 and for such occasional compositions as the little pieces for musical clocks or the lira concertos, the 1805 list is not a reliable source.

In the second half of the nineteenth century, the Haydn biographer C. F. Pohl made extensive research toward a thematic Haydn catalogue, but he presented only a fraction of his material as an appendix to the second volume of his book.[3] Shortly before the outbreak of the Second World War, J. P. Larsen offered a highly significant contribution by investigating carefully all of the source material and publishing both the draft catalogue and the Haydn-Elssler list of 1805 in facsimile.[4] Larsen's work also includes the "Kees catalogue," a list of Haydn's symphonies that belonged to the composer's friend Hofrat von Kees and constituted the basis for the enumeration of the symphonies in the Haydn-Elssler list. All this extensive material

---

[2] Bartha-Somfai, *Haydn als Opernkapellmeister* (Budapest, 1960), p. 95, points out that the libretto of Cimarosa's opera *L'infedeltà fedele* was used as a model for Haydn's *La fedeltà premiata*, a work listed among the operas in the catalogue.

[3] C. F. Pohl, *Joseph Haydn* (Berlin, 1875 and 1882).

[4] J. P. Larsen, *Die Haydn-Überlieferung* (Copenhagen, 1939). *Drei Haydn Kataloge in Faksimile* (Copenhagen, 1941)

was built by Anthony van Hoboken into a monumental thematic catalogue,[5] the first volume of which, dealing with the instrumental music, appeared in 1957. Apart from compiling the material, the scholar, thanks to research carried out in the important European and American libraries, was in a position to present a considerable number of new results.

Highly gratifying though this contribution is, it offers but a partial solution to the Haydn problem. The second volume dealing with the vocal output is still missing.[6] Moreover, within the instrumental volume a chronological order of the compositions and answers to questions of authenticity were not always attempted. The Haydn student is thus faced with the difficulty that an insufficient number of the composer's works is available in reliable new editions and that the full extent of Haydn's output has not been made clear. There is certainly no lack of Haydn scores in the various libraries, but the problem which of them are to be considered authentic has yet to be solved fully.

The reason for this situation is no less fantastic than the situation itself. It can be expressed in a brief sentence: Haydn was too famous. During the last part of the eighteenth century and the beginning of the nineteenth there was a continual demand from amateurs and professional organizations all over the world for new compositions by Haydn. The master did all in his power to satisfy these urgent calls, but his creative output was never able to keep pace with the unending stream of orders. Haydn often sold the same work both to private persons or organizations and to publishers of different countries. The Paris symphonies, for instance, were sent to Paris for perform-

[5] A. van Hoboken, *Joseph Haydn: thematisch-bibliographisches Werkverzeichnis* (Band I. Mainz, 1957). Henceforth instrumental works by Haydn will be quoted in this book with the number appearing in Hoboken's catalogue, preceded by the abbreviation Hob.

[6] Here the lists offered by Marion Scott in *Grove's Dictionary of Music and Musicians*, 5th ed. (London, 1954), and by J. P. Larsen and H. C. R. Landon in *Die Musik in Geschichte und Gegenwart*, V, prove helpful.

ances in the Concerts de la Loge Olympique and were sold later to the publishers Imbault in Paris, Artaria in Vienna, and Forster in London. Somewhat different is the case of the symphonies written for Prince Ernst of Öttingen-Wallerstein. In 1787 this ardent music lover asked Haydn for three symphonies that "besides himself nobody else must own." When the music was delivered, the delighted prince sent the master a heavy gold snuffbox filled with fifty ducats. Soon after, however, these same symphonies mysteriously found their way to different publishers, such as Hummel in Amsterdam, André in Offenbach, Le Duc in Paris, and Forster in London. We cannot avoid the suspicion that Haydn secretly connived at these publications. If so, he was but following a custom usual in the eighteenth century. One of the most puzzling problems created by the enormous demand for Haydn's music is that of the piano trio in C major (Hob. XV:3). The composer sold this work to Forster in London in 1784, and it was also printed by Artaria in Vienna. Nevertheless, in 1803 the master rather surprisingly informed Breitkopf and Härtel that this trio was not his own work but a composition by his brother, Michael. This is a case of Haydn versus Haydn, and it seems not unlikely that the composer, hard pressed for new compositions, sent the publishers a work by his younger brother.

But with all his shrewdness, and even with the use of petty devices, Haydn was never able to satisfy all the publishers. Soon these disappointed men found an easy way out of their difficulties. They produced their own Haydn compositions. The number of works by other composers published during Haydn's lifetime under his name is excessive. Jens Peter Larsen points out that the so-called Haydn symphonies in his Op. 9, 12, and 13, printed in Paris, contain sixteen works of which only three are authentic Haydn compositions. The case of his string quartets is even worse. Op. 18, 21, and 28 contain eighteen pieces, of which not one is genuine. It is known that Forster in London, though a personal friend of Haydn, printed authentic and spurious Haydn symphonies indiscriminately. The Czech composer Gyrowetz tells us in his autobiogra-

phy that when he arrived in Paris in 1789 he was surprised
to find his own symphony in G major printed under Joseph
Haydn's name (see p. 87). In this case the publishers
excused themselves by saying that they had bought the
symphony from the violinist Tost, a member of the orchestra at Esterháza. Probably they acted in good faith, as
they knew of Tost's connection with Haydn's orchestra
and the violinist had sold them genuine symphonies together with the counterfeit one.

It is not easy to determine in every case who was really
responsible for the fraudulent use of Haydn's name. Very
often the publishers were the culprits; sometimes, however, the copyists in Vienna, or even members of Haydn's
orchestra, were approached, and these men were often
more interested in gaining substantial fees than in scrupulously observing the truth. It was much easier to take a
composition by Vanhal, Dittersdorf, Gyrowetz, or Michael Haydn and change the name on the title page than
to obtain a new work from Haydn himself, who had the
inconvenient habit of disposing of every composition even
before it was put on paper.

Neither the dubious nor the outright false compositions
of Haydn were always printed. Before 1780 in particular,
music was often produced by professional copyists. How
important this form of reproduction was is shown by the
fact that between 1760 and 1787 the publishing house of
Breitkopf and Härtel issued no less than twenty-five thematic catalogues of "musical works that have not been
made public through printing" and were "now to be
had in correct manuscript copies." The name of Haydn
appears frequently in these catalogues, but they are a
source of both information and of confusion, for again
only part of the compositions listed under the master's
name were really written by him. Haydn, however, may
have felt a certain consolation in the fact that he was by
no means the only composer whose name was falsely used.
In his article on Sammartini,[7] Georges de St. Foix proved
that of the four symphonies listed under the name of Sam-

[7] In *Sammelbände der Internationalen Musikgesellschaft*
(1914).

martini in the Breitkopf catalogue of 1762 only two were by the composer himself, the third and fourth being by Martinelli and Pergolesi respectively.

The nineteenth and twentieth centuries made their contributions to the confusion. Adolf Sandberger, known for his important work in various fields of Haydn research, startled scholars in 1932 by declaring that Mandyczewski's list of Haydn's symphonies omitted at least seventy-eight works. According to Sandberger, a number of the symphonies that Mandyczewski considered dubious or false clearly are genuine, whereas other authentic Haydn symphonies were not even known to Mandyczewski. One of the foundations of Haydn research, erected slowly and painstakingly by Pohl and Mandyczewski, seemed about to collapse. Nobody, therefore, was much surprised when, in 1938, under the auspices of the eminent Sir Donald Tovey, a "rediscovered" symphony was printed under the name of Joseph Haydn, though an autograph score clearly proved that all movements but one were by Michael Haydn.[8]

Another case of mistaken identity took a rather surprising turn. In 1936, Ernst Fritz Schmid edited the Göttweig sonatas, which he considered to be unknown pianoforte sonatas by Joseph Haydn; but in the very next year he had to confess that instead of Haydn, one of his lesser contemporaries, the publisher Franz Anton Hoffmeister, was the real author of these compositions. Also, the *Requiem* edited by Schmid under Haydn's name turned out to be the work of a minor composer.

Thus it is certainly not easy to form a correct idea of what Haydn actually wrote; yet some sources are above suspicion. Among the best are Haydn's autographs. If a work is in the master's own script, written with his characteristic thin, energetic notes on a sheet of paper showing one of the familiar watermarks, there is hardly any room for doubt. This is especially so if one finds written at the beginning the typical *Di me Giuseppe Haydn*, together

[8] See Marion M. Scott, "Mi-Jo Haydn," *Monthly Musical Record* (March–April 1939).

with the date of the composition, and at the end *Finis. Laus Deo* (The End. Praise the Lord).

Altogether, perhaps two hundred autographs of Haydn are accessible, a not inconsiderable quantity, though woefully small compared with the composer's whole output. The majority of these autographs are to be found in the National Library, Budapest, which took them over from the archives of Prince Esterházy. The large collection of Haydniana that was built up through the composer's long service for the princely family was vastly increased by the purchase of autographs after his death. A smaller, though still important amount of Haydniana is to be found in the three German libraries that hold possessions of the former Prussian State Library—the German State Library, Berlin, the West German Library, Marburg, and the University Library, Tübingen. Also highly significant are the collections of the Austrian National Library and the Society of Friends of Music, Vienna; the Conservatory Library and the National Library, Paris; the British Museum, London; and the Library of Congress, Washington, D. C. All these contain not only autographs, but also a vast amount of contemporary prints and copies of Haydn's works. They are supplemented by the libraries of monasteries and aristocratic families that maintained contact with Haydn. Research in these archives, located in the territory of the former Austro-Hungarian monarchy, is proving eminently fruitful.

Authentic contemporary editions also furnish important sources of information about Haydn's music. Not all the publishers and copyists were pirating Haydn. Many of them were authorized by the master himself, and in some cases we know that he personally supervised the publication of the music. Early editions of this type must certainly be considered fully reliable. Among these authentic prints the editions of the Viennese publishers Artaria and Company are of special importance. Between 1780 and 1790 one hundred and fifty-seven works by Haydn, both original compositions and arrangements, were published by Artaria. Of equal rank are the editions of the Paris symphonies by Imbault, Paris, for which Haydn furnished the autographs.

After Haydn visited England, business connections with London publishers predominated. He worked with William Forster, Longman and Broderip, John Bland, William Napier, George Thomson, and others. At the beginning of the nineteenth century a German firm printed the greatest amount of Haydn's work. From 1800 to 1806, Breitkopf and Härtel in Leipzig published twelve installments of the so-called *Oeuvres complettes*. The master at first did not answer the publishers' written inquiry as to whether or not he would agree to the publication of such an edition. But when Griesinger offered his services as an intermediary and called on the old composer, Haydn gladly gave his consent. The *Oeuvres complettes* were, of course, not a collected edition in the modern sense. They contained only compositions for piano alone or works with piano, such as songs and piano trios, and even these types of composition were by no means complete.

Haydn's former pupil Ignaz Pleyel supplemented these Breitkopf editions by publishing simultaneously in Paris a *Collection complette des Quatuors d'Haydn*. This was an excellent edition of all the string quartets and became the basis of most of the later printings.

A last source of information on the extent of Haydn's work is the authentic manuscript copies of his compositions. If the work of a copyist is supplemented by Haydn's own writing—for instance in his corrections or signature—there can be no doubt that the master approved of it.[9] The same may be said of those manuscripts that display the familiar handwriting of the master's copyists such as Joseph and Johann Elssler or Radnitzky. Even if the identity of the writer is unknown, the mere fact that an eighteenth-century manuscript can be traced back to Haydn's own library or that of Prince Esterházy makes its authenticity appear highly probable.

This book makes no attempt to deal with all the works of Haydn. Such an endeavor would be of little practical

[9] Thus the Haydn House at Eisenstadt possesses a score of Haydn's opera *Armida* written by a copyist but containing many annotations and corrections by Haydn himself.

significance as long as the composer's complete works are not available in reliable modern editions. It tries, however, to include those authentic compositions that are important for the outlining of Haydn's artistic personality.

CHAPTER 12

YOUTH

The First Period: 1750–1760

Like the work of other great masters, the creative output of Joseph Haydn can be divided into several periods clearly distinguished from each other. As lines of demarcation we may consider the end of the decades constituting the second half of the eighteenth century. Thus the youth would reach from 1750 to 1760, the preparatory period from 1761 to 1770, the middle period from 1771 to 1780, the full maturity from 1781 to 1790, and the period of supreme mastery from 1791 to 1803.[1]

There is nothing sensational about Haydn's early compositions. Unlike the precocious geniuses of the eighteenth century—a Pergolesi or a Mozart—who died at an early age, or the masters of the romantic period, who wrote some of their best works at the beginning of their careers, Haydn developed with the utmost slowness. If an accident had caused his death when he was thirty-one, the age at which Schubert died, he would not have written a single work capable of bringing him lasting fame. Like Handel and Verdi, Haydn composed his greatest masterpieces during the latter part of his life. He was nearly sixty when he wrote his first London symphony and close to seventy when the two great oratorios, *The Creation* and *The Seasons*, were completed.

Hardly any of the young musician's first attempts

[1] J. P. Larsen divided Haydn's creative output into eight periods instead of the author's five periods. See "Zu Haydns künstlerischer Entwicklung" in *Festschrift Wilhelm Fischer*, (Innsbruck, 1956), p. 123. He also considers the years 1750, 1760, and 1790 significant turning points.

pointed to future greatness. His first period is characterized by youthful immaturity and dependence on the models of other composers. It starts approximately at his eighteenth year, when, according to the testimony of the Elssler catalogue, he began to compose. To the first years belong the earliest string quartets, Masses, and symphonies. In these works Haydn adopted the tenets of the "preclassical" school, creating light, playful, gay compositions. He was just one of the many exponents of the *style galant*, and by no means the most important.

In order to understand the position of the young composer, it is necessary to look back at the general evolution of music during the second quarter of the eighteenth century.

Even before Johann Sebastian Bach wrote his most important works, a strong reaction had set in against the style of the great old master of baroque music. "The essence of the new artistic creed was," as Paul Henry Lang[2] points out, "an urge for liberty; liberation from the rules that had become stereotyped, from the stylistic conventions that had become rigid, from the artistic forms that had become immutable." The new rococo period tried to supplant majestic splendor with graceful delicacy. Whereas baroque art had striven toward a powerful unity of form, the younger generation preferred looseness and variety. Music had changed the buskins of pomposity for the dancing slippers of the *style galant*.

This revolutionary movement originated mainly with Italians, Austrians, and Bohemians born during the first quarter of the eighteenth century. The "preclassical" composers, as they frequently are called, stood midway between the baroque and the classical masters. They were from fifteen to thirty years younger than Bach and from fifteen to thirty years older than Haydn. This "preclassical" school disliked every type of polyphonic writing. Strict counterpoint was practically eliminated and so were the forms of the Italian *sonata da chiesa* and the French

[2] *Music in Western Civilization* (New York, 1941), p. 533.

ouverture, which as a rule included a fugue. On the other hand the *sinfonia,* the artless curtain-raiser of the Italian opera, consisting of a fast, a slow, and another fast movement, now came into frequent use as a separate instrumental piece. Its popularity was matched only by the suite, a set of pieces of dance character. Both these forms exhibit the easy gaiety and the colorful variety so dear to the rococo period.

Soon the sinfonia and suite began to attract and influence each other. A great number of hybrid forms resulted from the combination, one of which was to become of outstanding importance. About 1740 the Viennese composer Georg Matthias Monn wrote a sinfonia consisting of an allegro, a slow aria, and a final allegro; between the last two movements he inserted a minuet taken from the suite of dances. But the possibilities of the newly created form were not realized immediately, at least in Vienna. Monn and his contemporary, Georg Christoph Wagenseil, still preferred the sinfonia in three movements to the cycle of four movements.

Even more important than the shaping of the new instrumental form was the development of its first movement into the so-called sonata form. The beginning of this process was to be observed as far back as the baroque period and was not completed until about the year 1770. The aim of this evolution was to create, as an analogy to the three movements of the sinfonia, three sections in its first movement. An "exposition" displayed the themes, a "development" treated them in a varied way and modulated to distant keys, and a "recapitulation" brought a restatement of the first section. Even the exposition itself was in three parts, for between the main theme at the beginning and the concluding theme, a subsidiary theme was inserted. These transformations were made with a view to giving greater solidity and poise to the levity of the sinfonia form. For no sooner had the massive grandeur of the baroque style been overcome than a new process of complication set in, and it is significant of the German mentality that German composers took the lead in this movement. Joseph Haydn's work carried the development to a climax, but he was only continuing a process begun by the preceding generation.

This leads to the question, who were Haydn's immediate predecessors? It seems almost as difficult to determine the origin of Haydn's orchestral style as it is to ascertain the origin of his family. Hugo Riemann[3] tried to prove that Haydn was a disciple of such Bohemian and Austrian composers as Franz Xaver Richter (b. 1709), Ignaz Holzbauer (b. 1711), and Johann Stamitz (b. 1717), living at Mannheim in southwestern Germany. Fausto Torrefranca[4] and Robert Sondheimer,[5] on the other hand, considered that certain Italian composers, especially Giovanni Battista Sammartini (b. 1701), exercised a decisive influence in the development of the classical style. But it is hardly to be doubted that Guido Adler and Wilhelm Fischer[6] were correct when they stated that Haydn carried on from where such Viennese composers as the younger Georg Reutter (b. 1708), Georg Christoph Wagenseil (b. 1715), and Georg Matthias Monn (b. 1717) left off. Haydn may have known of the Mannheim group and of various Italian composers, but as their style differed so little from that of the Viennese masters, he had no need to draw from foreign sources what he was able to find at home. It is true that young Haydn used the Mannheim *walze* (road roller), a melody rising by steps with a simultaneous crescendo and the accompaniment of a pedal point; he liked sudden changes from forte to piano, from strong sections in unison to soft harmonized sections. He employed subsidiary themes in the minor with their characteristic imitations, and the "rocket" themes that suddenly rise from a low to a high range. But all these devices

[3] See *Handbuch der Musikgeschichte* (Leipzig, 1922), II, 3, and Prefaces to *Denkmäler deutscher Tonkunst in Bayern*, second series, III:1, VII:2, VIII:2.

[4] "Le origini della Sinfonia," *Rivista Musicale Italiana* (1913).

[5] "G. B. Sammartini," *Zeitschrift für Musikwissenschaft*, III (1920–21).

[6] See Adler's and Fischer's works in the Bibliography.

were the general property of the time and Haydn had no need to go to Mannheim or Milan to become acquainted with them; he found them right on his doorstep, in the city where he grew up. In those few cases, however, in which Viennese "preclassical" composers differed from their contemporaries, Haydn always tended to identify himself with the Austrian tradition. Like Monn and Wagenseil, the young master in turn wrote symphonies in three and in four movements; like those Austrian composers, he used recapitulations that brought in a complete restatement of the material of the exposition. On the other hand, Haydn did not follow Stamitz and other early symphonists in their penchant for incomplete recapitulations.

While in his orchestral music young Haydn favored the sinfonia form with slight influences from the suite, his works for pianoforte and his chamber music were based on the suite form with slight influences from the sinfonia. The composer employed here the divertimento, the partita, or the cassazione, sets of pieces in which the use of the same key and dance character prevailed, with one or more movements displaying simple sonata form. In these pieces Haydn closely followed the "preclassical" style. His minuets, for instance, with their typical motion in triplets and formalistic cadences, clearly show the rococo spirit.

In discussing the works in such an order as to begin with the compositions written for small ensembles and gradually proceeding to those written for bigger groups of instruments, we must first deal with the sonatas for keyboard instruments. It should be emphasized here that in his youth Haydn probably employed the predecessors of the piano, the harpsichord, and the clavichord. This soon changed, and the harpsichord remained in use mainly as a solo instrument in concertos. On the other hand, from sonata No. 6 on, the pianoforte seems to have been in Haydn's mind for this type of composition. The words *per il cembalo* or *pour le clavecin* on some of the old manuscripts or printed editions must not lead us to believe that the composer actually wrote these compositions for the harpsichord. *Pour le clavecin ou fortepiano* was a standard indication on clavier compositions of the period and is found even on a number of Beethoven's piano sonatas.[7] However, Haydn's pianoforte should not be imagined as the instrument used in the nineteenth century. The piano of the romantic period, with its cast-iron frame, repeating action, and heavy strings, was very different from the lighter, smaller Haydn clavier with its weak tone, thin strings, and small hammerheads producing transparent, clear sounds.

* * *

Haydn wrote piano sonatas from early youth to old age. The fifty odd works that he contributed to the form cover a period of about four decades. To the first period belong in all likelihood Nos. 1, 2,[8] and 4 of the Collected Edition (we are using the order of this collection edited by Karl Päsler, whose numbers were also adopted by van Hoboken to list the clavier sonatas in group XVI of his catalogue). The first sonata shows the composer completely absorbed in the Austrian art of Georg Christoph Wagenseil. The use of the same tonality in all three movements, the name *partita*, the inclusion of a minuet with a trio in the minor key, the Alberti basses, the occurrence of melodies that seem to have been conceived first for the violin and later arranged for the pianoforte, and the clear separation of the three themes in the exposition of the first movement are typical of the Viennese piano style of the rococo period. On the other hand, the second sonata shows some marks of the influence of Philipp Emanuel Bach, which was to assume much larger proportions in the years to come. The syncopations and unison passages, the passionate and quite personal character of the largo,

[7] The fact that during the last years of his life Haydn owned a precious English harpsichord made by Burkat Shudi and John Broadwood has no connection with his clavier compositions. From this harpsichord the master may have conducted symphonies or other large ensemble works, but it was not used as a solo instrument for his sonatas.

[8] The authenticity of Nos. 1 and 2 could not be definitely established, but it seems likely that these two works are genuine.

with its sudden contrasts of mood, are unmistakably of north-German origin. But there is no doubt that at this early age Haydn's art grew primarily out of the soil of his native country. Although in the fourth sonata some technical details, such as the division of passages between the two hands, still remind us of Bach, the predominantly Austrian character, especially conspicuous in the minuet and trio, shows the true origin of the work.[9]

* * *

No other type of Haydn's chamber music equals in importance his compositions for strings alone. The author has attempted to prove[10] that the origin of the string quartet is to be found in the four-part instrumental compositions by Austrian and German composers of the early seventeenth century, such as works by Peuerl, Posch, Schein, Hausmann, Franck, and Staden. These compositions are definitely intended for performance by string instruments; the thematic material is evenly distributed among the four parts, the thematic invention is simple, almost like that of a folk song, and the technique of composing variations is expertly handled. Not much imagination is needed to see in these pieces early precursors of the classical string quartet. But this type of composition came to an end around 1620 because of the degeneration of the tenor part, which was assigned to the viola. The quartet was thus transformed into a trio sonata consisting of two violins and figured bass, the latter to be executed by a violoncello and a keyboard instrument that improvised chords to fill the gap between the two treble instruments and the bass. (This trio sonata was, therefore, in reality a sort of keyboard quartet.) For a hundred years the trio sonata prevailed as the main form of chamber music and all the great masters of baroque music, Corelli, Purcell, Handel, and Bach, wrote pieces for this ensemble. Nevertheless,

[9] The early compositions for a keyboard instrument accompanied by a violin and cello will be discussed in the following chapter (see p. 245).

[10] In a paper read in New York at a meeting of the American Musicological Society in 1943 (see also Karl Geiringer, "Paul Peuerl" in *Studien zur Musikwissenschaft*, Vol. XVI).

during the first half of the eighteenth century it was gradually pushed into the background. Alessandro Scarlatti's
sonate a quattro which, according to Edward J.
Dent, were written between 1715 and 1725, were again real
string quartets, reinstating the former viola part in sub-
stitution for the part filled by the keyboard instrument.
The new string quartet of the eighteenth century soon
became very popular, especially in Germany, as compositions by Franz Xaver Richter, Johann Zach, Joseph Starzer,
and others prove. But in all these works, and in the quartets of young Haydn as well, the viola part was still dependent on that of the violoncello, which frequently was
figured, thus implying that the addition of a keyboard
instrument was optional. The close relationship to the old
trio sonata thus was established. Haydn followed the general trend of his time. He wrote trio sonatas before attempting the string quartet, as it never occurred to the
young composer to deviate from established conventions.

Haydn's trios for two violins and violoncello, which are
apparently based on the baroque form of the trio sonata,
belong to the composer's earliest attempts in the field of
chamber music. Hob. V, its list based on that in the Haydn-
Elssler catalogue, enumerates twenty-one pieces, of which
Nos. 15–20 appear as early as 1766 in a Breitkopf and Härtel catalogue and probably were written around 1750.[11]
The rather thin texture of the compositions and the occasional crossing of the part of the first violin with the
bass (noticeable even in one of the later trios) indicate
that a keyboard instrument, doubling the bass of the violoncello in the lower octave and filling the gaps between
the middle parts, is to join the ensemble, changing the
string trio into a keyboard quartet. These compositions,
with their rather trivial melodies built on the triad, display
the simple, gay character of the *style galant*.

More important than the trios are Haydn's string quartets for two violins, viola, and violoncello. Whenever the
master's music is mentioned, we like to think of his quartets, and there is every reason for doing so. Although

[11] No. 15 can also be found in the Austrian monastery of
Göttweig in a written copy dated 1762.

Haydn wrote a great many of them, all are interesting, and at least half are unquestioned masterpieces; they were declared unequaled by Goethe, who was not even particularly interested in Haydn.

There is still another reason why the string quartet plays so important a role in Haydn's musical evolution. The composer was in his early twenties when he wrote his first quartet, and he had passed his seventieth birthday before he began to work on his last, which proved to be the last significant composition he was ever to write. No other form of music occupied the composer for an equal length of time.

We do not know the exact number of Haydn's string quartets. Eighty-three are enumerated in the Haydn-Elssler catalogue of 1805, which in turn was based on the thematic list presented in 1801–2 by I. Pleyel in his collected edition of the string quartets (cf. p. 221). These quartets include the adaptation of an early symphony in three movements, as well as seven arrangements of Haydn's highly successful composition *The Seven Last Words of Our Saviour on the Cross* (see p. 325). Thus the eighty-three compositions actually include only seventy-five quartets, and even this figure is not quite reliable. The authenticity of certain quartets has been doubted (*cf.* p. 249); on the other hand the composer omitted at least one work written in his youth, the quartet in E flat major, "No. 0" (Hob. II:6), which was erroneously listed among the *Divertimenti auf verschiedene Instrumenten*.[12]

[12] Early editions of Haydn's six string quartets forming Op. 1, such as those printed by J. J. Hummel, Amsterdam, Longman and Broderip, London, and Bremner, London, include this quartet "No. 0" together with the quartets Hob. III:1–4, and 6. Later editions, however, such as that of La Chevardière, Paris, omitted the quartet in E flat major, replacing it with the aforementioned adaptation of an early symphony in three movements (Hob. III:5), which was designated as quartet, Op. 1, No. 5. The score of the orchestral version, including oboes and horns, was edited by H. C. R. Landon as an appendix to his work *The Symphonies of Joseph Haydn* (London, 1955). Score and parts of quartet "No. 0" were edited in 1932 by Marion Scott for Oxford University Press (London) and independently from it by K. Geiringer for Nagel's *Musikarchiv* (Hanover).

Just as uncertain as the exact number of the early quartets are the dates of their composition. Haydn's friend
Griesinger contends that the master's first quartet was written in 1750. Pohl, the great Haydn scholar, considers this
too early and assumes that the quartets Hob. III:1–18
(known as Op. 1, Nos. 1–6; Op. 2, Nos. 1–6; and Op. 3,
Nos. 1–6) were written about five years later. While this
does not seem wholly acceptable, there is no doubt that
the twelve quartets of Op. 1 and 2, as well as the quartet
"No. 0," reflect the earliest phase of Haydn's contributions
in this field. They will accordingly be discussed in this
chapter.

The *quadri* and *cassazioni*, as the Breitkopf catalogue
calls the earliest quartets, quite clearly show the influence of the suite. They are always in the major key and
contain five movements, two of them minuets. The order
of the movements is well balanced and symmetrical: allegro, minuet, adagio, minuet, presto (or allegro molto).
Slight variations of this scheme are to be found in Op. 1,
No. 3, and Op. 2, No. 6, in which the first and third movements change places. The majority of the movements in
each quartet preserve the same key except that for the trios
of the minuets, in compliance with the Viennese tradition, the tonic minor is preferred, while the slow movements are written in the subdominant, the dominant, or
again in the tonic minor. Within this rigid scheme, however, Haydn displays a surprising variety of details, indicating both the richness of his imagination and the rather
immature state of his technical knowledge. The treatment
of the sonata form differs in practically all of the first
movements, sometimes two, sometimes three, or even four
themes being introduced. A genuine development of
themes, in the manner of Haydn's mature style, is not to
be found in any of these early compositions. But the composer conscientiously tried to make a choice of themes
for the second parts of his sonata forms, usually giving
preference to the second or third melody over the main
theme. An interesting experiment in form is shown in the
quartet, Op. 2, No. 3,[13] in which the trio of the second

[13] This quartet, as well as Op. 2, No. 5, was also written by

minuet consists of a theme with three rather free variations.

These early string quartets need not necessarily be performed by four players only; the execution by a small orchestra of stringed instruments is correct, as the difference between chamber and orchestral music is not manifest in this first period. Nevertheless, the first signs of a genuine string quartet style already are to be noticed. It is true that the viola frequently uses the same rhythm as the violoncello, and even plays in octaves with that instrument; the composer occasionally concentrates the whole of the melodic life in the first violin part, so that the adagio of Op. 2, No. 2, for example, with its six-four chord for the cadenza near the end, resembles a concerto rather than a quartet. There are also many dialogues between the two violins, reminding us of the technique of the old trio sonatas. At the same time the crossing of the parts of the second violin and viola, such as we find in the second trio of Op. 2, No. 5, and the transparent style of the third movement of Op. 1, No. 3—in which all four instruments are granted an equal share of the thematic material —give a fair promise of future achievements.

The contents of the quartets are simple and gay, with a preference for melodies resembling folk songs of Austrian character. An exception is found only in the adagio of Op. 2, No. 4, the passionate ardor of which reminds us of the north-German art of Philipp Emanuel Bach, with which Haydn had just become acquainted. A movement of similar character is the above-mentioned largo of the second piano sonata, which was probably written about the same time.

In the 1750s, Haydn also wrote a quintet for strings in G major (Hob. II:2). Although this work exists in different versions, the *a cinque* of Haydn's own catalogue (No. 2 of the *Divertimenti auf verschiedene Instrumenten*) indicates that the quintet is an original one and also set-

Haydn as a sextet for two violins, viola, bass, and two horns (Hob. II:21, 22), but as the horn parts have little significance, they can easily be omitted.

tles the old argument as to whether or not Haydn ever
wrote a quintet. The six movements of the composition
again show the character of the suite. Most of the movements are in the same key, simple in form, and of a light
and graceful character.[14]

*   *   *

A transitional phase, coming between the works in
three to five parts, and the symphonies, is represented by
the six scherzandi for flute, two oboes, two horns, two
violins, and bass (Hob. II:33–38).[15] They are little pieces
in four short movements (allegro, minuet, andante or
adagio, presto) that probably would not have been attributed to Haydn if the master himself had not listed one
of them (the scherzando in A major) on the first page of
his draft catalogue.

Of a more brilliant character is a nonet for two oboes,
two horns, two violins, two violas, and bass (Hob. II:20)
probably written before 1757. This composition has the
same arrangement of its five movements as the early string
quartets. In an old manuscript the work is called *concertante*, as the composer shows a marked tendency to let
each of the nine instruments have an interesting and independent part; the oboes particularly have attractive passages.[16]

A transitional character can also be noticed in Haydn's
concertos of this period, which are written mainly for keyboard instruments and small orchestra. In his own catalogue Haydn listed four concertos for the clavier (or organ), but according to subsequent research he probably
wrote a much larger number of such compositions.[17]

[14] There is also a string sextet or double trio called Echo
(Hob. II:39) which is attributed to Haydn, but does not seem
to deserve his name.

[15] The scherzandi were edited by H. C. R. Landon (Vienna,
1961).

[16] Works of a related character composed at the turn from
the first to the second period will be discussed in the next chapter (see p. 251).

[17] See Hans Engel, *Die Entwicklung des deutschen Klavierkonzertes* (Leipzig, 1927). Hob. XVIII lists eleven authentic

Whereas the early string quartets occasionally assume the character of concertos, the first concertos for keyboard instruments show a definite leaning toward chamber music. The musical form is remarkably well developed, but nowhere is there any display of technical brilliance. The origin of the keyboard concerto from the violin concerto, so clearly shown in Bach's compositions, is also noticeable in Haydn's works. As a rule, the left hand of the solo instrument doubles the bass, and only the right hand is melodically independent. Sometimes both hands participate in brilliant scale runs or triad passages. The Organ Concerto in C major (Hob. XVIII:1) of 1756 is typical of these early works. The composer lists it in his draft catalogue as *per il clavicembalo* while it is headed in the autograph as *Concerto per l'Organo*. Here the baroque ambiguity in the use of the term clavier is evident; one is reminded of Bach's nomenclature *Clavierübung* applied to music for both the organ and stringed keyboard instruments. However, in Haydn's concerto the fast runs seem to be much better suited for a harpsichord than for the serious church instrument. In this concerto the importance of the solo instrument still is diminished by a comparatively large orchestra (strings, two oboes, two trumpets); the composition is much more like a piece of ensemble music than a real concerto.

Similar in character is another C major organ concerto (Hob. XVIII:8). Although its accompanying orchestra dispenses with oboes, it entrusts significant tasks to the brass instruments (two trumpets or two horns). The work, the authenticity of which is not certain, may have originated somewhat later than the first organ concerto.

A concerto in F major for clavier and violin solo with

---

and six spurious concertos. Closely related to these works are some of the divertimenti for clavier and strings, such as Hob. XIV:3, 4, and 11—Hob. XVIII:1 was edited by M. Schneider (Wiesbaden, 1953); Hob. XVIII:6 by H. Schultz (Leipzig, 1937); Hob. XVIII:5 by H. Heussner (Kassel, 1959); Hob. XIV:11 by H. C. R. Landon (Vienna, 1960); Hob. XVIII:8 by H. C. R. Landon (Vienna, 1962).

strings (Hob. XVIII:6) also belongs to Haydn's early works in this field. It points to the origin of such compositions in the baroque double concerto for two violins. The thematic material is distributed between solo violin and keyboard instrument, the clavierist's right hand assuming leadership, while the left, in the manner of a continuo instrument, strengthens the bass and supplies filling notes. Technical virtuosity is not aimed at in any of these three concertos.

Closely related to these early concertos are several divertimenti for keyboard instrument and strings (Hob. XIV:1–13) mostly written in the fifties or early sixties. These pieces, which appear in old manuscripts under varying designations and, as is customary in Haydn's early works, in different instrumentations, stand on the borderline between concerto and chamber music. A good example is supplied by the little C major concertino in three movements (Hob. XIV:11). The short, simple work, which Haydn composed in 1760, is scored for cembalo, two violins, and bass, without viola and wind instruments, and assumes the character of a quartet with obbligato clavier rather than that of a concerto.

* * *

In discussing Haydn's symphonies we can use as a basis the excellent list of one hundred and four works provided by Eusebius Mandyczewski in 1907 and printed in the symphony volumes of the Collected Edition.[18] In spite of many attempts to make the list seem unreliable, no conclusive evidence against it has been found. It is true that Mandyczewski did not always have access to the best sources for his edition, so that the musical text of the symphonies is not authentic in every detail; still, the list of works, which was the basis of his edition, stands up remarkably well even in the light of the most recent research. The catalogue of Haydn's symphonies in Hob. I

[18] Up to 1961 the following symphonies had been printed in the Collected Edition: Hob. I:1–40 (Mandyczewski), Nos. 41–49 (Schultz), Nos. 50–57 (Schultz and Landon), Nos. 82–92 (Landon).

still uses the Mandyczewski numbers, adding, however, four works, the concertante symphony of 1792 (I:105), the orchestral version of the string quartet Op. 1, No. 5 in B flat (I:107), the so-called "partita" in B flat (I:108), and a symphony in D lost today (I:106). The main corrections needed in the old list concern the chronological order: Mandyczewski entered in the wrong places some works, whose dated autographs he did not know. Thus, symphony No. 40, according to the original manuscript, was written in 1763 and therefore belongs to symphonies Nos. 13 and 14 from the same year. No. 49 was composed in 1768 and ought to be placed between Nos. 38 and 39. No. 72 should for stylistic reasons be assigned to the first half of the 1760s, possibly after No. 20; the Paris symphonies Nos. 83 and 87 were written in 1785, and accordingly should be inserted between Nos. 81 and 82.

It is not quite clear how many of Haydn's symphonies were created before the composer entered the service of Prince Esterházy. In the symphonies Nos. 1 and 2, which may be considered representative of this early group, Haydn certainly did not establish himself as a great innovator. Both works are in three movements without minuet. No. 1 begins with the fashionable "roller" Haydn borrowed from a symphony by Stamitz, and introduces a subsidiary theme in the minor key with imitations, typical of the Viennese "preclassical" composers. The wind instruments (two oboes and two horns) are employed mainly to increase the sonority of the full orchestra; no use is made of them in the piano passages or in the slow middle movements. A continuo instrument, such as a harpsichord, is essential for filling the occasional gaps between the melody and the bass. This is particularly noticeable in the andante of No. 2; as only the melody and the bass are written out, the cooperation of a harpsichord is necessary. Two works of a somewhat related character will be discussed in the next chapter.

* * *

In his works for the stage, Haydn began his career as a close adherent to the Viennese tradition, and Joseph Felix

Kurz-Bernardon, the Viennese actor and author of farces, became his librettist when the composer was only nineteen. A truly Austrian book, filled with merry gaiety and coarse realism, delightfully ridiculing the stilted style of the serious opera, was used by the composer in his first work for the stage, a Singspiel entitled *Der krumme Teufel* (based on Lesage's *Le Diable boiteux*). Haydn's music to this comedy is lost. In an interesting study, Robert Haas suggests[19] that Haydn was attracted by the subject and in 1758 worked on a new version of the same libretto called *Der neue krumme Teufel*; this composition, however, also seems to be lost. On the other hand, Haas assumes that young Haydn kept up the connection with Kurz-Bernardon during the intervening years, occasionally writing music to other comedies by the poet-actor. If these theories are correct, it may be presumed that a collection of *Teutsche Comedie Arien* in the Vienna National Library, containing texts by Kurz-Bernardon from the years 1754 to 1758 and set to music by anonymous composers, contains pieces by Haydn. Volume 33 of the *Denkmäler der Tonkunst in Oesterreich* offers a valuable selection from this collection. The arias, duets, trios, and quartets of this volume are imbued with a healthy earthiness and keen wit, displaying a surprising sense of musical form, so that it does not seem altogether impossible that young Haydn contributed his share to the collection.

* * *

Another of Haydn's earliest dated compositions, besides the organ concerto in C major, is his first *Salve Regina* in E major. Both these works, according to their autographs, were composed in 1756. The *Salve Regina* is scored for soprano solo and four-part chorus, two violins, organ, and bass. It is a short piece in three movements, showing in its typically Italian melodies and coloraturas for the soloist the influence that Haydn's new teacher, Porpora, exercised on the responsive mind of the young composer. On the other hand, the choral numbers are simple and forceful,

---

[19] "Die Musik in der Wiener deutschen Stegreifkomödie," *Studien zur Musikwissenschaft* (1925).

and the insertion of the solo part is very skillfully handled.

In his settings of the Mass, Haydn naturally followed models that he had studied as a choirboy at St. Stephen's. They were by such composers as the two Reutters, father and son, Antonio Caldara, and Johann Joseph Fux, the great master of counterpoint; possibly also by older musicians like Johann Stadlmayr and Christoph Strauss. The style of these composers had its roots in Italy. The solid texture and the tendency to assemble solo voices, vocal tutti, and orchestral instruments in individual choirs used alternately, point to the styles of Venice and Rome. The display of arias and duets with brilliant coloratura and the use of operatic effects, however, show the influence of Neapolitan music, but these devices of south-Italian art had been used in Austria for over a century, with the result that by Haydn's time their origin was all but forgotten.

The little Mass in F major written at the beginning of the 1750s is one of the most important works of Haydn's early youth. It is a so-called *missa brevis*, a concise composition of the Mass text, using a very small accompanying orchestra. This work is written for two solo sopranos, a four-part chorus, two violins, organ, and bass (an ensemble very similar to that used for the *Salve Regina*). The words are crowded together as much as possible, and in order to abbreviate the composition, occasionally the four voices simultaneously sing different sections of the liturgical text. Only in the Benedictus given to the two solo sopranos is the melodic impulse allowed to develop freely. This little duet and the coloratura of the solo voices display the influence of the Neapolitan school. Remarkable is the composition of the Kyrie, which, as in later Masses by Haydn and in Beethoven's first Mass, is also used for the "Dona nobis pacem." The words of the Kyrie eleison (Lord have mercy on us) were set to a melody with a folk song character (Ex. 1), the music showing so carefree and gay

Allegro

(f) Ky- ri- e · e- lei- son, e- lei- son

an attitude that it hardly seems appropriate to the solemn words of the prayer(This brings us to an important feature of Haydn's church music, which must be understood in order to appreciate the master's sacred works. Haydn's "attitude toward religion was not gloomy and repentant, but gay, reconciled, and trustful, and this character is also to be found in his compositions for the church" (Griesinger). To Haydn's pious optimism a prayer for mercy seemed to involve a grant of this request, and he felt justified in beginning and ending his Mass in a spirit of gay confidence. Haydn made hardly any distinction between sacred and secular music. As a painter of the Renaissance period did not hesitate to give to the Madonna the features of some girl he knew personally, so Haydn applied the principles of instrumental music to his Mass by starting and ending with an allegro. As Alfred Schnerich, the champion of Haydn's church music, explains,[20] this can also be defended from a liturgical point of view, since on a festive day the congregation ought to be received as well as dismissed in a spirit of joyousness.

Haydn himself was always fond of this work of his early youth, and as an old man he took it up again, having wind instruments (flute, two each of clarinets, bassoons, and trumpets, as well as timpani) added to the modest score.[21] "What I like particularly in this little work," he confessed to the painter Dies, "is its tunefulness and a certain youthful fire." No modern critic can be so sophisticated as not to acknowledge these merits in the unpretentious composition.

At about the same time originated the Mass in G major *Rorate coeli desuper.* Its title derived from Isaiah 45:8 is to be found in the Introit for the Fourth Sunday in Advent, and a part of this Gregorian chant is used in the

[20] See his *Messe und Requiem seit Haydn und Mozart* (Vienna, 1909).

[21] This arrangement was probably merely supervised by Haydn. The manuscript of the later version in the Esterházy library shows the parts of the original composition written by Haydn's copyist Elssler, and those for the wind instruments inserted by his pupil, Polzelli.

Kyrie. The work,[22] written for four-part chorus, two violins, organ, and bass, is again a typical *missa brevis*, allotting not more than thirteen measures to the Kyrie, eleven to the Sanctus, and only nine to the Cloria.

[22] The Mass was edited in 1957 by H. C. R. Landon. Although it is mentioned in both Haydn's draft catalogue and the list of 1805, its authenticity has been doubted, since it is to be found in eighteenth-century copies under the names of other composers, such as Georg Reutter, Jr., and F. P. F. Arbesser. Moreover, the entry in the draft catalogue was made in the nineties when Haydn's memory was possibly no longer so reliable.

CHAPTER 13

A PHASE OF TRANSITION

The Second Period: 1761–1770

It is a new Haydn that we meet after the composer becomes conductor for the Princes Esterházy. No longer is he the poor and unimportant musician making a scanty living by teaching youngsters or playing in third-rate bands. The Haydn of the 1760s is a successful man occupying an important post and held in high esteem by both his superiors and his subordinates.

Now Haydn could work regularly with a group of well-trained singers and players. He could study at the closest range the possibilities of each instrument and the human voice. He could hear each of his compositions almost before the ink of the manuscript was dry, a state of matters that should appear enviable to young composers of our time, who almost despair of ever hearing their symphonies performed.

Slowly, gropingly, Haydn was now finding a way toward the expression of his true self. During the first ten years of his appointment as conductor for Prince Esterházy he made it his object, with that infinite slowness and carefulness so characteristic of all his actions, to master the overpowering influence of the past. He was no longer satisfied to be just one among a large number of insignificant composers. We watch his first timid attempts not to be influenced by others, but to be himself. There was, to be sure, no deliberate effort to shelve the past. But while on the whole preserving the musical language of the "preclassical" composers, Haydn became increasingly able to imbue it with his own personality. The playful grace of the *style galant* was frequently replaced by a leaning toward serious baroque means of expression, and at the end of the decade an increasing number of stylistic features pointed to the passionate subjectivity of the "storm and stress" period. The sixties of the eighteenth century were for Haydn essentially a phase of transition. Old and new elements were more closely interwoven than in any other period of his artistic evolution; and while the man of thirty was discovering himself, the world was slowly becoming aware that a genius was living and maturing in the remoteness of the Hungarian plains.

*   *   *

In his sonatas for the pianoforte of the second period (Hob. XVI:3, 5–15, 18, 19, 44–47), the influence of the past at first seems particularly strong.[1] Up to No. 15 the character of the suite is predominant: the minuet is never missing, and in most sonatas the same tonality is preserved in all movements.[2]

Undoubtedly Haydn's early piano sonatas are influenced by his ensemble music. Many sections seem really meant for violin and figured bass, and it is not at all surprising that some of these sonatas were also printed "with the accompaniment" of a violin or a violin and violoncello. Some passages are definitely inspired by the technique of the violin, and the frequent changes from high to low registers suggest arrangement for pianoforte of an orchestral composition. As a matter of fact, the above-mentioned No. 15 is a clavier arrangement of three movements from Haydn's cassation for woodwind and string instruments (Hob. II:11).

---

[1] There are good reasons to doubt the authenticity of Nos. 16 and 17. Cf. R. Steglich, "Eine Klaviersonate J. G. Schwanbergs in der J. Haydn-Gesamtausgabe" in *Zeitschrift f. Musikwissenschaft*, XV, p. 77 ff. Also uncertain is whether the piano version of No. 15 was done by Haydn himself.

[2] The air with variations in No. 15 is a typical suite movement, and the brief first allegro with its gay 6/8 subject displays divertimento character. Very fittingly, in the old manuscripts most of these sonatas bear the designation *divertimento*, which well expresses their stylistic features.

At the same time, these sonatas do not lack indications of future trends. In addition to violinistic features, one finds here freely modulating passages, especially in the development sections, exhibit a definitely pianistic character (see the first movement of No. 5). Still more important is the fact that Haydn was already striving toward the unity and concentration of form so characteristic of the best among his mature compositions. In the first movement of No. 3, the continuous use of triplets, sometimes in the bass and sometimes in the treble, gives the work considerable uniformity. (As such a homogeneous construction is inconceivable in the composer's first period, it seems likely that No. 3 is a later composition than the less mature No. 4.) In No. 10 the second subject is closely related to the first, and it remains for the third to bring in new melodic material, a procedure that was to become important in Beethoven's compositions.

The closer we come to Haydn's third period, the clearer become the indications of the influence of Philipp Emanuel Bach. No. 46, of 1765–68, contains a wide-contoured adagio in D flat major, testifying, with its pathos and sudden changes of mood, to the impact of the north-German master's music on Prince Esterházy's conductor. No. 19, of 1767, was even considered by an English periodical[3] to be a parody of the style of the Hamburg master. According to the author of the article, Haydn wanted thus to revenge himself for the unfriendly attitude that Bach had assumed toward him. A refutation of this statement was made by Bach himself when he declared most emphatically in an article for a Hamburg paper[4] that he and Haydn were the best of friends and that all assertions to the contrary were to be considered mere lies. But it cannot be denied that a certain similarity exists between Haydn's sonata No. 19 and Emanuel Bach's piano compositions. The transparency of the two-part writing in the work of the younger composer, the accompaniment of melodies in high register by low-pitched basses resting on accented beats of the measure, the dramatic development in the

[3] *The European Magazine* (London, October 6, 1784).
[4] *Hamburger Unpartheiische Correspondenz,* No. 150 (1785).

first movement, the broad baritone melody of the subsidiary theme in the second movement, and most of all, the unrelenting intensity of feeling permeating the whole work all show Haydn as a diligent disciple of Johann Sebastian's great son.

Unlike Mozart, Haydn showed little interest in music for piano duet. A piece of this kind, probably written in the sixties, seems to make fun of the educational aims that as a rule were responsible for the composition of such works. *Il maestro e lo scolare* (Hob. XVIIa:1) consists mainly of an andante with seven variations. The instructor plays a short phrase, and the pupil immediately repeats it two octaves higher. This simple game is continued throughout the set of variations, eventually becoming tiresome. A simple *tempo di menuetto*, fortunately without imitation, serves as a coda.[5]

*   *   *

Haydn's trios for piano, violin, and violoncello belong, in a way, to his piano music. The keyboard instrument is completely dominant, while the use of the violin, and especially of the violoncello, seems more or less optional. Hob. XV:1, 2, and 33–41 belong to Haydn's earliest contributions in this field.[6] In these trios the character of the suite is clearly expressed. No. 2 in F major is in three movements, all in the same key; the second is a minuet, the third an adagio with variations. The violoncello part is practically identical with that of the bass of the piano, and its sole function is to increase the volume. The writing for the keyboard instrument is not lacking in purely pianistic effects, such as the crossing of hands in the development section of the first movement. The violin—though retaining a certain amount of independence—exhibits none of the technical brilliance to be found in the first violin parts of

[5] The little partita in F major (Hob. XVIIa:2) attributed to Haydn is of doubtful authenticity.

[6] No. 34 in E major, edited by H. C. R. Landon (Vienna, 1959), seems in its melodic idiom somewhat to adhere to baroque conceptions and represents in all likelihood an initial phase within Haydn's output.

Haydn's string quartets of the same period. Rather similar is No. 1 in G minor. But, as is customary in compositions in the minor mode, the character of the suite is not so clearly revealed. The finale (presto) brings us an attractive example of the contrasts between forte passages in unison and harmonized piano passages which were so dear to both Haydn and Mozart. (Compare the beginning of the Jupiter symphony.)

Among the trios for two violins and violoncello, Hob. V:1–4, 8, 10, and 12 belong to the second period. They are musically far more attractive than the earlier works of this type and show clearly that Haydn wrote them after he had entered the service of Prince Esterházy. The first violin parts, which ascend nearly up to c♯ and frequently introduce double stops, indicate that Haydn had the brilliant violinist Tomasini in mind when he wrote these movements. But the substance of the trios also has changed. The pastoral character of the deeply felt adagio in No. 2, the ardent passion in the adagio in B minor in No. 3 (Ex. 2) and the frequent daring modulations all show that

Divertimento for 2 Vlns. and Bass, B minor
1 Vln. (*Adagio*)

Haydn had begun to outgrow the superficiality of the rococo style.

These trios for two violins and violoncello were succeeded by trios for baryton, viola, and violoncello, which Haydn wrote for Prince Nicolaus Esterházy, enthusiastic devotee of the baryton. This unusual stringed instrument is a relative of the bass viola da gamba. As a rule, six or seven gut strings extend over its fingerboard, and about twice as many metallic strings are stretched behind the neck, and consequently cannot be reached by the bow. These metallic strings can be plucked by the thumb of the left hand, the neck of the instrument being open in the back. Pizzicato and arco notes are at times sounded simultaneously, which makes any performance on the instrument rather difficult. In consequence the baryton never attained great popularity, and its use was always confined to a small circle.

Contemporary sources vary in their estimates of the merits of the instrument. Friedrich August Weber, a physician who was one of the most spirited musical writers of the time, praised it, saying, "One seems to hear the gamba and the harp at the same time," and confessed that he was "moved to tears" by its sounds.[7] Dr. Burney, discussing the performance of the baryton virtuoso Andreas Lidl, who had been in the service of Prince Esterházy before going to London, writes: "Mr. Lidl, indeed, played with exquisite taste and expression upon this ungrateful instrument with the additional embarrassment of base [sic] strings at the back of the neck with which he accompanied himself, an admirable expedient in a desert, or even in a house, where there is but one musician; but to be at the trouble of accompanying yourself in a great concert; surrounded by idle performers who could take the trouble off your hands, and leave them more at liberty to execute, express, and embellish the principle melody, seemed at best a work of supererogation."[8]

Haydn wrote more than one hundred and sixty baryton pieces for his patron. About one tenth of these compositions seem to be lost.[9] Among the others, the one hundred and twenty-six baryton trios form the largest and most important group.[10] The earliest of these pieces were created in 1762 when Nicolaus the Magnificent became the ruling prince, but Haydn seems at first to have displayed a rather lukewarm attitude toward this form. When, however, he received in 1765 his patron's energetic command to apply

[7] *Musikalische Zeitung* (1788).

[8] See Burney, *A General History of Music* (1789), Vol. II, p. 1020 (Harcourt, Brace & Co., New York, 1935).

[9] This fact ought to be stressed, for in 1904 William Henry Hadow wrote in the *Oxford History of Music* (V, 41) about Haydn's baryton compositions: "This vast mass of music has wholly disappeared, except for three divertimenti and a few inconsiderable fragments."

[10] The trios Hob. XI:25–96 were presented in the Collected Edition of Haydn's works, Series XIV, Vols. 2–4, edited by H. Unverricht (Munich, 1958, and 1960).

himself to composition of pieces playable on the baryton of which but few had been supplied so far (see p. 64), he acted accordingly: through the following decade a steady flow of new works for the baryton may be observed. Only around 1775 did the prince's interest in the instrument wane when he became engrossed in operatic productions that kept his conductor more than busy.

The first ninety-six trios were originally entered in four volumes, each of which contains twenty-four works. There is good reason to assume that Hob. XI:1–48 were composed between 1762 and 1767, Nos. 49–72 in 1767 and 1768, Nos. 73–96 between 1769 and 1771, and Nos. 97–126 between 1771 and 1775.

The form of the baryton trios shows a certain resemblance to that of the trios for two violins and violoncello. The pieces for baryton, viola, and violoncello are mostly in three movements, with a minuet in the middle or at the end, and the second movement usually in a key closely related to that of the other movements. A number of fine specimens is to be found in this collection, showing that Haydn gave of his best even when he did not expect his compositions to be heard outside the court of his prince. Nearly every trio has an interesting little detail, such as the charming melody for baryton in the adagio of No. 1, the attractive changes of dynamics in the minuet of No. 34, and the pretty variations in No. 38.[11] The humorous minuet *alla zoppa* (limping minuet) in No. 52,[12] the remarkable changes between plucked and bowed baryton passages, with an occasional combination of the two effects in the adagio of No. 56, and the pizzicato of the baryton in the trio of the minuet No. 61 are additional examples. The august baryton player also will have enjoyed the quotations from operas Haydn inserted, such as the tune of the aria "Che farò senza Euridice" from Gluck's *Orfeo ed Euridice* in No. 5, or a melody from Haydn's own comic opera *La canterina* in No. 29. Although the

[11] The theme of these variations appears also in the piano duet *Il maestro e lo scolare*.
[12] This piece and the ensuing trio also appear in Haydn's symphony No. 58.

best baryton trios were written during Haydn's third period, these earlier pieces certainly do not lack charm.

* * *

Haydn's string quartets of the 1760s are probably the
only compositions of this period that still enjoy a certain
amount of popularity, at least with ambitious amateurs.

Rather different from his Op. 1 and 2 are the quartets of
Op. 3 (Hob. III:13–18). The fact that these six pieces were
not mentioned in Haydn's draft catalogue and were only
published in 1777 (by Bailleux, Paris, a firm known to have
issued spurious Haydn works) casts doubt on their authenticity. The suite-like pieces of the Op. 3 certainly differ from
the rest of Haydn's early quartets. No. 2 consists of a slow
set of variations, a minuet with trio and a presto finale. In
No. 4 there is no minuet, and the central adagio has shrunk
to a few measures so that the piece consists basically of two
fast movements only. Other stylistic deviations may likewise
be observed, and it was even suggested that not Haydn but
the Bavarian monk Hofstetter was the author of the Op. 3.[13]
On the other hand, these six quartets are included in the
thematic list of the Pleyel edition approved by the composer
and subsequently incorporated into the Haydn-Elssler catalogue of 1805. It seems hard to imagine that neither of these
three men should have noticed a foreign body in the carefully assembled list of the quartets.

Certainly the set is not lacking in attractive details. The
first quartet is distinguished by interesting sound effects in
the trio of the minuet, and a melody of touching fervor in
the following andantino grazioso. Most attractive is also its
rondo finale. The last entry of the theme reaches a climax
by the simple expedient of putting the melody in octaves to
be played by the viola and the first violin, whereas previously the first violin had played it alone. In No. 2 the set of
variations is the most remarkable movement. Here the bass
of the theme is retained throughout the whole piece thus

[13] Cf. L. Somfai in *Haydn Emlékére. Zenetudományi Tanulmányok*, VIII (Budapest, 1960); A. Tyson and H. C. R. Landon
in *Musical Times*, July 1964.

endowing it with basic consistency. Likewise the first movement of No. 3 adheres strictly to a single permanently recurring motive. In the finale of No. 4 the composer proves to be an expert in the style of the Italian comic opera. In two places, short adagio sections are followed by lively presto passages. Pergolesi's immortal Serpina, who interrupts her outbursts of hypocritical sadness with expressions of merry insolence,[14] seems here to be peeping over the author's shoulder, while the famous serenade of the same quartet, a counterpart to the slow movement in No. 1, reveals a simplicity, innocence and ardor that make the great popularity of the movement easily understandable.

The following series of six quartets (Hob. III:19–24), known as Op. 9, was composed before 1769. In this cycle, four movements, with a minuet as the second one, have become the rule. In the movements in sonata form, the development section assumes increasing importance. Whereas in the first movement of Op. 3, No. 4, the exposition is nearly three times as long as the development, the two sections of Op. 9, No. 2, are almost equal in length. At the

String Quartet, Op. 9 No. 2

[14] *La serva padrona*, Intermezzo II, aria "A Serpina penserete."

same time, the developments begin to outgrow the traditional sequences and modulations; they show—for example, in the first movement of Op. 9, No. 4—a subtle sense of discrimination between ideas more and less suitable for elaboration. Moreover, the composer now tries to express greater intensity of feeling. The fervent ardor that seemed like an episode in the adagio of Op. 2, No. 4, attains increasing importance in the quartets of Op. 9. There can be no doubt that these works foreshadow the master's storm-and-stress period. Some aspects of this may be found in the first movement of No. 1, with its use of the minor key and of syncopations in the subsidiary group of themes and with the surprising hold over the six-five chord. These tendencies are still more obvious in the impassioned introduction to the slow movement of No. 2 (Ex. 3), where they create a mood of tension and pathos to be resolved in the ensuing poignant cantabile.

This applies also to the first movement of the dramatic quartet No. 4 in D minor; the chromaticism, syncopations, and pauses seem like a challenge to the levity of the rococo period. In the ardent minuet of this quartet, the grand pause on the first beat of the third measure is easily recognizable as one of Philipp Emanuel Bach's favorite means of expression. But the antithesis of this mood, uncontrollable mirth, also is beginning to gain in importance. The same D minor quartet contains in its finale certain sections that foreshadow Beethoven's scherzos.

A peculiarity of this cycle, as well as of the next six quartets, is the brilliant character of the first violin part, with its difficult runs and double stops and its predilection for the highest registers. An explanation for this tendency is easily found in the fact that Haydn then had at his disposal a player of unusual technical gifts, Luigi Tomasini, first violinist of the prince's orchestra. It must not be overlooked, however, that the personal and somewhat rhapsodical character of the music really calls for a certain display of virtuosity. Looking at the problem from this angle, it would seem that Tomasini was the ideal interpreter rather than the instigator of the brilliant parts for the first violin.

The next group comprises a number of smaller works for

either string and wind instruments or wind instruments alone. Of particular significance are the so-called *Feldparthien*,[15] small compositions that Haydn wrote up to 1765, first for the wind band of Count Morzin in Lukaveč, later for the musicians of Prince Esterházy. They were primarily scored for two oboes, two horns, and two bassoons, but clarinets, trumpets, and English horns made their appearance in some of the later pieces. These compositions, as well as some chamber music works for both string and wind instruments, mark the transition toward symphonic music. Haydn listed them in the catalogue of 1805 as *Divertimenti auf verschiedene Instrumenten*.

Characteristic of the compositions in this class is an inexhaustible interest in sound effects; musical color is so important for the composer that for a short time it even obscures his interest in form. These divertimenti provided Haydn with a training field for the use of orchestral instruments, particularly the winds. At first, however, his experiments produced scanty results; for example, in the version of the string quartet, Op. 2, No. 3, with two French horns (Hob. II:21), the horns are used mainly as ripieno instruments. In the adagio, as in Haydn's first symphonies, they are omitted altogether. A change is noticeable in the little *Feldparthie* in F major for two oboes, two bassoons, and two horns (Hob. II:15), written in 1760. In it, significant roles are given to the horns both in the adagio and in the presto finale. Similarly, in the divertimento in F major scored for the same instrumental combination and written before 1765 (Hob. II:23) the musical ideas seem to grow out of the technical potentialities of the horn. This tendency is stronger still in the divertimento for horn, violin, and violoncello dating from 1767 (Hob. IV:5). In its theme and variations, the horn has some really interesting technical problems to master, and occasionally the instrument's role as the ardent singer of German romanticism is foreshadowed.

[15] A number of *Feldparthien* were edited by H. C. R. Landon (Vienna, 1959–60), who presented also other divertimenti, among them Hob. II:11 (Vienna, 1961) and IV:5 (Vienna, 1957). Hubert Steppan edited Hob. II:17 (Vienna, 1960).

As for the woodwind instruments, the octet for two horns, two English horns, two violins, and two bassoons of 1760 (Hob. II:16) exploits with rare skill the colorful quality of the gentle, melancholy English horn. Sound effects of great beauty are realized, particularly in the adagio of this piece (Ex. 4).

Divertimento in F for 2 Engl.Horns, 2 Bsns., 2 Hns. & 2 Vlns.

While these divertimenti display a decisive preference for the five-movement form with two minuets, deviations from this pattern are not rare. The horn trio (Hob. IV:5) consists of two movements only, while the cassation in C for two oboes, two horns, two violins, two violas, and bass (Hob. II:17), composed before 1766, is made up of no less than nine movements, among them a spirited march and an expressive recitative.

The favorite form of these divertimenti is the variation. In each variation, Haydn entrusts a different instrument with the melodic line. A good example of this procedure may be found in the popular cassazione called *Der Geburtstag* (The Birthday), with the andante "Mann und Weib" (Husband and Wife), which was probably composed around 1760 and is scored for flute, oboe, two violins, violoncello, and bass (Hob. II:11). The finale gives the lead to the first violin in the theme, to the violoncello in the first variation, to the flute in the second, to the second violin in the third, to the oboe in the fourth, and again to the first violin in the fifth; however, in the last three variations the instruments more or less blend together, with no one entirely taking the lead.

Such an employment of the instruments brings elements of the concerto into the divertimento. This is revealed with particular clarity in the cassazione for flute, oboe, two violins, violoncello, and bass written at the beginning of the sixties (Hob. II:1). It frequently shows, as in a concerto grosso, a real concertino of flute, oboe, and first violin, to which a proper cadenza is entrusted in the slow movement.

The lack of technical brilliance noticeable in the keyboard concertos of Haydn's youth is to be observed in this period too. Thus the concerto (divertimento) in C major of 1764 (Hob. XIV:4), written for clavier, two violins, and bass, is really a keyboard sonata with doubling and accompanying string parts. In early English editions[16] it was published as a "Lesson for the harpsichord," omitting the insignificant parts for the other instruments. Close to the spirit of a real concerto comes Hob. XVIII:3 in F major, composed around 1765. This cembalo concerto is, however, rather conventional in musical language and old-fashioned in its technique, thus revealing the composer's moderate interest in the form.

Among the violin concertos,[17] the G major (Hob.

[16] Forster (London, 1783–84); Cooper (London, after 1800). The original version was edited only recently by G. Wertheim (London, 1955).

[17] The concertos Hob. VIIa:4 and 1 were edited by W. Davisson (Leipzig, 1909), and Hob. VIIa:3 by H. C. R. Landon (Salzburg, 1952).

VIIa:4), listed in the Breitkopf catalogue of 1769, probably is an earlier work. The concentration of the thematic life in the parts of the accompanying orchestra and the small share accorded to the solo instrument in the development of the main ideas seem to prove this. More significant still is the very simple technical equipment of the violin part, which hardly ever oversteps the first three positions, and a certain austerity in the melodic idiom, combined with a predilection for subsidiary themes in the minor. Quite different are the two concertos in C major (Hob. VIIa:1) and A major (Hob. VIIa:3), one written around 1765, the other before 1770, and both apparently intended for Haydn's favorite violinist, Luigi Tomasini. In these the violin competes with the orchestra in the elaboration of the themes; and double stops, big skips, fast runs, and melodies in the highest register offer a more gratifying task for the skill of the soloist. Tomasini seems to have given good advice to the composer as far as violinistic technique is concerned. Moreover, the concertos are imbued with a warmth of expression rarely to be found in Haydn's early concertos.

In Haydn's concerto for the French horn of 1762 (Hob. VIId:3), the technical problem of writing a concerto for a brass instrument that was not yet equipped with valves seems to have inspired the master. The many gaps between the notes of the horn are barely noticeable; the melodies are adapted to the possibilities of the instrument, and the expressive music displays all shades of emotion, from powerful energy to tender longing.[18]

❊　❊　❊

While it seems hardly possible to determine which of Haydn's early symphonies were written before 1761, it is certain that the symphonies Nos. 1–41, 49, 107, and 108 were created before 1771. In all likelihood, more sympho-

[18] A flute concerto in D major mentioned in the draft catalogue (Hob. VIIf:1) seems to be lost. A second flute concerto attributed to Haydn (Hob. VIIf:D1) is the work of Leopold Hoffmann. An oboe concerto in C major (Hob. VIIg:C1), edited by A. Wunderer (Leipzig, 1926), is spurious.

nies were composed by Haydn in the sixties than in any other decade of his life.

Haydn's third symphony (before 1762) belongs to the earliest works displaying a subsidiary theme in the dominant major. In this work the light rococo spirit of previous compositions is replaced by a rather rigid and polyphonic style. The first movement shows a strong contrapuntal tendency; the minuet—the great innovation of the symphonies belonging to the second period—furnishes canonic imitations, and the finale shows a real double fugue. Similarly No. 40 has a fugue as its final movement; and No. 26, "Lamentatione," displays the *canto fermo* technique in both its first and second movements. Haydn may have been stimulated to produce these works by a desire to display technical skill to his superior, Kapellmeister Gregorius J. Werner, a master of contrapuntal technique.

Altogether, this period marks the beginning of a new phase in Haydn's symphonic output. For the first time, No. 5 (before 1762) uses the wind instruments in the slow movement; they are even entrusted with short solo passages. Still more important are Haydn's attempts to enrich the rather brilliant and impersonal character of his early symphonies by the introduction of elements of the concerto and of the suite. The most remarkable products of this experiment are the symphonies Nos. 6–8 known as "Le Matin," "Le Midi," and "Le Soir," dating from 1761. In "Le Midi" the presence of two slow movements following each other in immediate succession appears to be most unusual. But a closer examination reveals the true meaning of this arrangement: the first slow movement is a sort of dramatic accompanied recitative, the second a beautiful aria of lyric character. In both pieces (as in Spohr's violin concerto No. 8, *in modo d'una scena cantante*) a solo violin is used for the declamation as well as for the aria. In a truly romantic way Haydn introduces the form of the vocal aria into his symphony, giving the part of the singer to a violinist. "Le Matin," "Le Midi," and "Le Soir" are based on a poetical program that Hermann Kretzschmar attempted to interpret. Such clearly defined pieces as the sunrise in the introductory adagio of "Le Matin," the amus-

ing parody of a solmization class in the slow middle movement of the same work, and the effective thunderstorm,
la tempestà, in "Le Soir" facilitated his task.

Solo instruments are widely distributed through these
three symphonies. In its slow middle movement, "Le Matin" uses a solo violin; in the trio of the minuet, a solo bassoon and a solo violoncello; and in its finale, a solo flute, violin, and violoncello. In "Le Midi" and "Le Soir" the genuine
concertino of two violins and violoncello used by Corelli
and Handel alternates with the ripieno instruments. In
later symphonies of this period the influence of the concerto also is noticeable; a solo flute is used in the slow
movements of Nos. 24 and 30, a solo violin and solo violoncello appear in the slow movement of No. 36. A good
example of the graceful art of orchestration acquired by
Haydn in the 1760s is provided by the adagio of No. 31,

Auf dem Anstand—mit dem Hornsignal (On the lookout—with the horn signal), of 1765, with its delightful combination of the tones of the horns and the solo violin (Ex. 5). In this work Haydn used four rather than the traditional two horns. Two instruments are in the key of D, two in the key of G, so that their notes may supplement each other. (This expedient had to be used because valves for the brass instruments were unknown.) The symphony No. 31, an interesting precursor of Haydn's famous "La Chasse," contains many attractive passages for the wind instruments and it seems hardly surprising that a theme with variations, the favorite form in the suite, is used as its finale. In other symphonies too, strongly idiomatic use of the wind instruments may be observed. In particular the trios of the minuets employ them to best advantage, conjuring up sounds of exquisite charm and folk-songlike simplicity (see Nos. 22 and 40).

Haydn's tendency to unify certain movements of his works, so obvious in most types of his instrumental output, is developed with particular strength in his symphonies. Apart from the predilection for contrapuntal forms mentioned before, occasionally—as in the first movements of No. 28—a whole movement in sonata form grows out of a single motive. The tendency of the mature Haydn to develop the subsidiary theme out of the main idea already is noticeable; in the first movement of No. 39, for instance, the contrasting idea appears only in the epilogue. The principle of the 1780s, providing each musical instrument with a fair share of the thematic development of the musical material, is foreshadowed in the beginning of symphony No. 37. In the finale of No. 36, Haydn was so eager to give thematic material even to the accompanying parts that his exposition assumed certain aspects of a development; accordingly, the real development seems all but superfluous and is six bars in length. Johannes Brahms, who was a great admirer of Haydn and followed his example in many respects, used a similar device in the last movement of his first symphony. It brings so many elements of the development into the exposition as to make possible the omission of the sonata form's middle part.

The subject matter of the symphonies is at first merry and carefree, with a rather robust popular note in some of the minuets. The pleasure in little surprises, in sudden unexpected changes of a slightly humorous character already is evident. At the same time a quality of grave seriousness is by no means absent. It is indicated in No. 3, and is even more clearly expressed in the first movement of No. 22 (The Philosopher). Here the grave notes of the *canto fermo* intoned by horns and English horns (replacing the oboes) create an atmosphere foreshadowing the solemn passages of Mozart's *Magic Flute*. There are also early signs of the *Empfindsamkeit* (sensibility) of the storm-and-stress period. No. 16 has as a main theme a sequence of wailing "sighs," prepared dissonances introduced on the strong beat and resolved by stepwise progression downward on the weak beat. To emphasize the unusual character of these "sighs," Haydn introduces them in the bass. The tragic symphony No. 26 in D minor probably was written around 1768. From the stirring syncopation of the beginning to the passionate lament of the minuet (Ex. 6),

Symph. No. 26 *Menuett*

this work strikes a note of suffering and despair. The title "Lamentatione" under which the work usually is known, seems fully justified; this all the more as the *canti fermi* used show a definite resemblance to the Gregorian chants sung during Holy Week. The symphony No. 39 in G minor also was written before 1770, and in its first movement anticipates the mood of suffering and grief in Mozart's string quintet in the same key. The climax of these efforts to give greater depth of feeling to the symphonies is reached in No. 49 of the year 1768, with the characteristic name of "La Passione." This work displays, particularly in its second movement in F minor, a feverish fierceness of expression that few musical or poetical works of the eighteenth century surpassed.

But intensity does not prevail only in the expression of dark moods. The lighter colors also assume greater brilliance, and thus the second movement of No. 34, composed before 1766, creates an atmosphere of turbulent gaiety.

These symphonies of the 1760s reveal Haydn's tenacity in keeping to territory previously occupied. Even where he makes progress, he tries not to relinquish completely the area in which he started. Thus, among the symphonies of this era of transition occur features reminiscent of Haydn's early attempts. No. 27, probably composed in 1764, is in three movements without a minuet; No. 33, written in all likelihood in the middle 1760s, uses wind instruments merely for tutti reinforcement and omits them in the slow movements, and the trio of the minuet in No. 39, composed around 1768, offers an andante in two parts that cannot dispense with a filling continuo part. This stubborn clinging to acquired possessions, inherited from his peasant and artisan forebears, mingled as it was with a keen interest in novel experiments, constitutes one of the salient features of Haydn's personality.

❊   ❊   ❊

Although the string quartets and symphonies of the second period offer, in spite of their indisputable beauties, more promise than real achievement, Haydn's operas of the second period are equal, if not superior, to his later output.

Very little can be said about the Italian comedy *La marchesa Nepola*, written in 1762 for festivities in honor of Prince Nicolaus when he became reigning head of the family, for only part of the score (five complete and two incomplete arias) has survived.[19]

More interesting is the Italian *Acide* (*festa teatrale*), written in the same year for the festivities accompanying the wedding of the prince's eldest son. Part of this score also has been lost; nevertheless, enough remains to give a good idea of the character of a work that is concerned with a subject treated by Handel some forty years earlier. Haydn's work gives a rather long-winded account of the love story of Acis and Galatea and the murder of the handsome shepherd by the giant Polyphemus. The intervention of the traditional deus ex machina, in this case the sea-goddess Thetis, makes possible the happy ending that an eighteenth-century audience expected. The hero, Acis, after being murdered, returns to life as a fountain and—as a fountain—joins vigorously in the final quartet, the only ensemble in the whole opera. The music closely follows the style of the Italian *opera seria*, containing numerous secco recitatives and isolated recitatives with orchestral accompaniment. It keeps pedantically to the *da capo* aria trimmed with ornate coloratura, never attempting to reach more dramatic expression. The overture in three movements conforms to the shallow type of the symphony of the Italian opera. The melodies are merry, gay, and rather trivial. This overture is nothing but a glorified signal to indicate the beginning of the performance, a piece that might easily be replaced on the modern stage by the ringing of a bell. As this overture has no connection whatever with the opera, there is no objection to its being performed as a separate instrumental piece without any reference to the stage work. In fact, this often has been done; conversely, the eighteenth century did not hesitate to use as

---

[19] Cf. Bartha-Somfai, op. cit., p. 379.

overtures to vocal compositions symphonies composed as separate instrumental pieces.

The unnatural character of the *opera seria* ultimately provoked in Italy a reaction that led to the composition of gay and popular works. Haydn also felt the attraction of this type, and his opera *La canterina* (The Songstress), composed in 1766, is no mythological drama, but a lively farce taken from everyday life. It is an intermezzo, similar in character to Pergolesi's *La serva padrona*. It has no overture, and its two parts are meant to be performed in the intermissions of a three-act serious opera. *La canterina* is the first of Haydn's operas of which a nearly complete score has been preserved.[20] It is the earliest of Haydn's dramatic compositions that can be enjoyed without reserve in our day.

No one could uphold the morality of the plot, for the young vocalist Gasparina sees no impropriety in encouraging two lovers at the same time. Her double-dealing is discovered, and this places her in a very embarrassing position, but she is clever enough to know the well-worn trick of threatening to commit suicide and pretending to faint, whereupon the fury of her lovers gives way to compassion. They repent of their anger and once more shower gifts upon her. The music is simple and graceful, following, like the libretto, the tradition of the Italian intermezzo. The composer replaces the schematic construction of the *opera seria* with a freer, more lively dramatic spirit. The undramatic *da capo* aria is avoided; instead, there is a preference for Logroscino's trick of introducing recitatives into the aria. The very first aria of the work is interrupted and concluded by a recitative. Accents of tragedy are used only for the purpose of burlesquing the pathos of the *opera seria*. Gasparina's aria in the second act, intended to move the heart of her infuriated lover, assumes—

[20] In the finale of the second act a short solo and the beginning of the concluding tutti are missing. A piano score of the opera with English text (*The Songstress*) was edited by K. Geiringer (New York, 1947). The full score edited by D. Bartha appeared in the Collected Edition of Haydn's works, Series XXV, Vol. II (Munich, 1959).

by the use of the somber English horns, the key of C minor, the tremolo of the strings, the "sighs," and augmented intervals of the melody—a mood of exaggerated grief, easily recognized as a parody. The fits of despair of the lovers, produced by Gasparina's fainting, are of a similar nature. Such agitated syncopations and wild runs were used in the *opera seria* in moments that decided life and death for its heroes. In the quartet that concludes the first act Haydn attempted what Mozart was to accomplish in his great masterpieces: the expression of the personality of each of his characters, without violation of the musical beauty of the whole. The fury of the singing teacher, the cowardice of the second lover, the despair of Gasparina, and the impudence of the duenna all find expression in this charming piece of music. In spite, or perhaps because, of its great simplicity, *La canterina* is a really effective stage work. At its first performance, which took place at Pressburg during the carnival of 1767, the effect on the audience must have been particularly hilarious, as the part of the young male lover was sung by a female soprano, while the part of the duenna, originally intended for a soprano, was entrusted to a male tenor.[21]

Lo speziale (The Apothecary), written in 1768, carries on the tendencies of *La canterina*. In this opera in three acts, based on a libretto by Goldoni, as many as three suitors compete to win the love of pretty Grilletta. Sempronio, an old apothecary, who is thinking too much of distant countries and not enough of his business, wishes to marry his ward Grilletta; Mengone, a serious young man, is inspired by his love for the young girl to enter the apothecary's shop as a clerk; and the bold and frivolous Volpino tries to win Grilletta's love by pert little improvisations. Sempronio and Mengone are tenors; the part of Volpino, like that of Don Ettore in *La canterina* and Cherubino in Mozart's *Figaro*, is for a soprano, to be sung not by a man, but by a disguised woman. Among these four characters, two sopranos and two tenors, the comedy is enacted, and eventually the faithful Mengone wins Grilletta's hand.

[21] Cf. D. Bartha, Collected Edition preface.

Haydn succeeded in making *Lo speziale* a true musical comedy. The conceit of narrow-minded Sempronio, whose knowledge is based mainly on newspaper reports, is beautifully described in his very first aria. Mengone's aria in A major paints the sufferings of indigestion and the soothing effect of rhubarb with a daring realism that makes the piece hardly suitable for a refined audience. Very different is the attitude of the young man in the trio at the end of the first act. Here Grilletta and Mengone whisper tender words of love while the old man meditates on war in the Far East (a conflict that seemed fantastic and improbable in Haydn's time), but as soon as the apothecary leaves the room, the flame of suppressed passion starts to blaze. The bold impudence of Volpino is well expressed in his second-act aria in E major. An interesting detail in this number deserves special attention. When Volpino mentions Grilletta's lovers, he sings a tune that reappears in the quartet finale of the act as soon as the names of the apothecary and the two young men are uttered. It is probably the first, though by no means the only, time that Haydn used the technique of the "leading motive." In this finale, Sempronio dictates to the two suitors, disguised as lawyers, his marriage contract with Grilletta. While pretending to repeat the words, they really burlesque them, changing every sentence to their own purposes. A tender melody of the oboe accompanies the main part of this scene. Repeated changes of tempo and the introduction of roguish, but also affectionate, mirth make this piece one of the most attractive numbers of ensemble music in the pre-Mozart *opera buffa.*

Unfortunately, a small part of this score also has been lost. The arrangement of the opera by Robert Hirschfeld that ordinarily is used in modern performances[22] condenses the three acts of the original into a single act and interpolates in lieu of missing numbers a duet from Haydn's *Orlando paladino.* Unfortunately the arranger did

[22] It was first presented in Dresden in 1895 and published in Vienna in 1909. The score of the opera, edited by H. Wirth, appeared in the Collected Edition, Series XXV, Vol. III (Munich, 1959).

not know of the existence of the overture, missing in the autograph, but found since; moreover he replaced the tenor Sempronio with a baritone.

* * *

Haydn's early cantatas are closely related to his early operas. The Esterházy cantatas written for Prince Paul Anton's nuptials, for Prince Nicolaus' name day, and in honor of the patron's return from Paris follow Neapolitan models, and the same is true of the *Applausus* performed in 1768 to celebrate the fiftieth anniversary of the Abbot's profession in an Austrian monastery. These works consist of a succession of *da capo* arias introduced by recitatives and only rarely interrupted by ensemble numbers or choruses. In the *Applausus,* the text of which is written in Latin, the conversation conducted by the four Cardinal Virtues and Theology about the merits of life in the seclusion of a monastery is of such a dry and abstract quality that the composer found it extremely difficult to get inspiration from the words. A happier choice of subjects was provided in the earlier works, which assume a heroic note in their glorification of Haydn's patron. Here the composer was more in sympathy with his theme. Consequently, the D minor aria, "Quanti il mar," in the cantata *Destatevi o miei fidi* of 1763, has the quality of inspired passion. The accompaniment in fast-moving sixteenth notes describes the roaring of the ocean and at the same time reflects a deep emotion; the wide intervals of the melody display unusual fervor (Ex. 7).

Arias of an equally impressive character are, however, not very frequent in these works. It is true that the instrumentation offers some variety; very attractive use is made, for instance, of the solo harpsichord, and occasionally in the *Applausus* Haydn employs a solo violin, muted strings, and divided violas. Yet it must be admitted that the composer's approach to his subject was slightly mechanical. Here Haydn followed a certain tendency of Neapolitan art to manufacture rather than to create music.

The composer was unable to be present at the first performance of *Applausus* and therefore accompanied the score with a memorandum enumerating his wishes about its production. The following are the main features of the ten points on which he laid most stress in this remarkable document:

1. The composer asks that his indications of tempo be carefully observed and that, in accord with the festive character of the text, the allegros be taken a little faster than usual.

2. As an overture, the allegro and andante of any symphony may be used; its finale is to be replaced by the first ritornello of the cantata.

3. In the recitatives, the instrumentalists should come in immediately after the vocalist has finished, but on no account is the vocalist to be interrupted, even if such a procedure were prescribed in the score.

4. The composer requires that the dynamic signs be strictly observed and points out that there is a great difference between piano and pianissimo, forte and fortissimo, crescendo and sforzando.

5. He professes to have been annoyed often by musicians who neglected slurs and warns the violinists to avoid such an "unpleasant and faulty" way of playing.

6. He wishes the viola part to be performed by two musicians, "as the middle parts are sometimes more important than the melody," and adds the interesting remark: "It can be seen in all my compositions that the viola rarely doubles the bass."

7. He advises the copyist to write out the parts in such a way as not to have all the violinists turn the pages at the same time, as that reduces the volume of sound in a small ensemble.

8. He requests good slow diction of the soloists, so that every syllable may be understood.

9. He hopes that at least three or four rehearsals will be given to his composition.

10. He recommends the addition of a bassoon to the violoncello and double bass, as this makes the bass of the composition more distinct than in a work scored only for string basses. He asks the musicians to work hard on the production in their own interest and his, and concludes: "If I have failed to guess your taste, it must not be taken amiss, as I did not know the performers or the locality. My ignorance of these matters really has made the work hard for me."

This document is of unusual importance. Not only does it show what a good music director Haydn was—many of his wishes still are expressed by twentieth-century conductors—but it indicates his progressive attitude as a musician. His request for strict observance of the dynamic indications, the emphasis on the importance of the middle parts, the desire for a lively tempo: all these show that Haydn was eager to fight the obsolete traditions of the past.

*   *   *

Among Haydn's smaller church compositions two offertories that adapt music from the Esterházy cantatas to liturgical texts in Latin should be mentioned: "Accurite hunc mortales" and "Plausus honores date." From the *Applausus* five numbers were used, the result being the offertories "Dictamina mea," "Concertantes jugiter per calamitatem," and "Christus coeli atria" (with preceding recitative "Quae admiranda res"), the bass aria "Resonant tympana," and the motet "O Jesu te invocamus."[23] The method employed here may be explained through two examples. For the Latin offertory "Plausus honores date," two pieces with an Italian secular text were used. As instrumental prelude, a condensed version of the introduction to the recitative "Da quel gioia improvisa" is em-

---

[23] See K. Geiringer, "Joseph Haydn als Kirchenmusiker," in *Kirchenmusikalisches Jahrbuch* (1960).

ployed. The recitative itself is omitted and the music to
the chorus "Sembra in questo giorno" follows straight
away. Apart from minor deviations, the contrast between
soli and tutti is newly introduced into the offertory; moreover, the melody played in the cantata by the cembalist's
right hand is now entrusted to the solo violin, the harpsichord's sound apparently being considered unsuitable for
church music. A different procedure was adopted for the
offertory "Dictamina mea." As the original employed Latin
words with an allegoric meaning, comparatively few
changes had to be made in the text. On the other hand,
the *da capo* form of the duet in the *Applausus* was not
preserved in the offertory, which omitted the repeat of
the first section. To round off the work, Haydn added a
short "Alleluja" for soprano and alto solo with mixed chorus
and strings. This graceful, brisk finale, not to be found in
the cantata, has been preserved in Haydn's hand,[24] and
supplies evidence that Haydn himself was responsible for
adaptations of this kind. The first part of the duet is in
C major and the middle section ends in the dominant G.
As there is no *da capo*, the Alleluja is in G major. Thus
an offertory starting in C major ends in G major, a bold
feature rarely found in eighteenth-century music.

An independent composition is the first *Te Deum* in
C major, written before 1765. The relating of the first
chorus "Te Deum laudamus" to the following tenor solo
"Tu Rex Gloriae" by means of the same impetuously rising motive in thirty-second notes shows the hand of a
master. The transition from a trio of solo voices to the
full chorus at "Per singulos dies" anticipates the contrast
between solo and tutti that Haydn was to use so effectively
in his later church compositions. A very poetical thought
is expressed at the end of the work, where the music to
"Non confundar in aeternum" is immediately added to
the motive of "In te Domine speravi" as a sort of counterpoint. Haydn's attitude in religious questions is shown by
this little detail: to put one's hope in the Almighty is identical with the certainty of salvation.

[24] The autograph was the property of S. Wolf, Eisenstadt,
and was later incorporated into the town's Haydn Museum.

The *Stabat Mater* of 1767 points in various ways to the idiom of the "storm-and-stress" that was to sway Haydn decisively within a few years. Chromatic runs, "sighs," and syncopations combined with sudden dynamic changes create an atmosphere of restlessness and suffering superbly matching that of the text. Especially stirring is the solo quartet with chorus "Virgo virginum praeclara." Here the soloists have the leadership, while the chorus, in somber responses, merely enunciates brief passages and frequently only single words. Most impressive are the moments when to the soloists' passionate utterance "Passionis fac consortem—fac ut portem Christi mortem—fac me plagis vulnerari," the chorus again and again adds the word "fac," like an urgent prayer. In the manner of Haydn's youthful cantatas, the *Stabat Mater* employs Neapolitan formal principles, and it is not surprising that the work was given particular praise by Hasse.[25] The text is divided into individual numbers, those for soloists taking up twice as much room as those for chorus. It is interesting to observe the way in which the Neapolitan predilection for coloratura is combined here with Haydn's zest for intense expression (Ex. 8). Despite the text's lack of contrasts and

the tendency toward large lyrical structures, Haydn succeeded in creating a work displaying dramatic vigor and stirring diversity.[26]

Two exquisite pieces for a single vocalist and instruments exist with both Latin and German texts. In the

[25] See Haydn's autobiographical sketch and his letter to Anton Scheffstoss, dated March 20, 1768 (p. 69).
[26] Three litanies in C major also are attributed to Haydn. They are to be found in the Esterházy castle at Eisenstadt, the Vienna National Library, and the West German Library, Marburg. The one preserved in Eisenstadt was considered a true Haydn work (see Larsen, *Drei Haydn Kataloge*, and Geiringer, *Musical Quarterly*, 1959), but doubts recently have been cast on its authenticity. See H. C. R. Landon's edition (Vienna, 1960).

accompanying orchestra of the *aria de venerabilis* for contralto, "Lauda Sion Salvatorem," the composer employs flutes (rarely to be found in his early church works) so as to create a mood of gentle exaltation. Deeply felt is "Ein' Magd, ein' Dienerin,"[27] a *cantilena pro Adventu* for soprano, two oboes, two horns, strings, and organ, built in the form of a *da capo* aria. This song in praise of the Virgin combines fervor of expression with vocal brilliance in a manner significant for Haydn's works of this period.

Just as in Haydn's operas, cantatas, and smaller church works of the 1760s, so in his settings of the Mass the influence of the Neapolitan style is strong. The *Great Organ Mass*[28] of 1766 is a brilliant *missa solemnis* differing in style from the modest short Masses of the first period. It calls for a four-part chorus, four solo singers, string instruments, an obbligato organ part, two English horns, bassoon, and two horns. The parts of the vocal soloists are enriched with coloratura like arias in a Neapolitan opera, and the organ part also is embellished with brilliant ornaments and runs (especially in the Kyrie and the Benedictus). Some numbers of the Mass, such as the beautiful "Qui tollis" (Ex. 9) exhibit a distinct tendency to express the meaning of the words in sounds, but on the whole

[27] Edited by H. C. R. Landon (London, 1957).
[28] Edited by C. M. Brand in Collected Edition, Series XXIII, Vol. I (Boston, 1951).

Haydn was more interested in the musical possibilities offered by a composition on so large a scale than in the interpretation of the mysteries of the Mass text. This is clearly shown in the "Dona nobis pacem," a presto in 6/8 time introducing in the organ part a playful motive in triplets which seems better suited to an instrumental finale than to a Mass, a detail criticized even by one of Haydn's earliest biographers.[29]

[29] Carpani, in *Le Haydine* (Milan, 1812), p. 159.

CHAPTER 14

STORM AND STRESS

The Third Period: 1771–1780

The author of a short article on Haydn printed in 1766[1] called the master's music "charming, ingratiating, engaging, naturally humorous and enticing." If the man who wrote these words had read them again a few years later, he would have found them surprisingly inadequate, for by then Haydn's music had lost most of the characteristics he had mentioned. The composer had grown tired of the charm and gracefulness of rococo music, so dear to him in his earlier days. To express personal feelings and strong emotion now seemed one of the main aims of Haydn's art, and his creative activity experienced what the great French Mozart scholar Theodor de Wyzewa called "a romantic crisis."

As was said earlier, the impulse to such a change came to Haydn from the outside. The slogan "back to nature," which implied a return to sincerity of feeling, originated with Jean-Jacques Rousseau, and German literature and music accepted it eagerly. In the early seventies of the eighteenth century Goethe wrote his *Sorrows of Young Werther*, and all over the world its unrestrained emotionalism moved people to bitter tears, even to suicide. At about the same time, Mozart wrote his first G minor symphony (K. 183, not to be mistaken for the great symphony K. 550 of 1788), a surprisingly deep and moving work for a youth in his teens.

[1] *Wiener Diarium* No. 84, Anhang *"Gelehrte Nachrichten,"* XXXVI. *Stück.*

No musician felt the importance of the new movement more keenly than Joseph Haydn, for it opened his eyes to qualities that had been lacking in his own music. It is true that even during the sixties the composer's work exhibited several attempts to introduce a more emotional musical language, but this tendency broke forth with full power only after 1770. The composer of Esterháza found himself in complete accord with the artistic tendencies of his time and there was no longer any reason for him to suppress his passionate feelings.

As always in outbreaks of a revolutionary character, the reaction against the past went beyond the mark. Haydn's *Sturm und Drang* (storm-and-stress)—as the movement was frequently called in Germany—reached its climax in 1772, a year in which works of a strangely exaggerated character were created. Thereafter, Haydn's compositions gradually assumed a more normal aspect, though the aftereffects of the "romantic crisis" were destined to be felt all through the seventies. Just as the French Revolution, despite its aberrations, made an essential contribution toward the formation of human society, so the crisis of the storm-and-stress period through which Haydn passed played a vital part in his development and in the attainment of his full maturity. It was indispensable to him as an antidote against the excessive lightness of the rococo style.

The movement toward subjectivity and sentimentality brought Haydn closer and closer to the *Empfindsamkeit* that Philipp Emanuel Bach had revealed in his compositions more than twenty years previously. But Haydn really did not copy Bach. The relation between the two masters was not so much that of teacher and pupil as that of two artists who for a short time were pursuing the same artistic goal. The study of Bach's compositions helped Haydn overcome a deficiency in his own compositions, and as soon as he had succeeded in doing so, he freed himself from the overpowering influence of the older master.

⁂

The pianoforte sonata Hob. XVI:20 of 1771 shows Haydn in the midst of his "romantic crisis." In this composition, the master's only piano sonata in C minor, all the formal restraints of the *style galant* are broken, and passion and subjective feeling triumph. The finale of the C minor sonata is no longer a carefree affair destined solely to dismiss the listener in a gay mood; it becomes the climax of the whole work and is imbued with dramatic tension. In the first movement the beginning of the development exhibits Haydn's art as constituting a link between the music of P. E. Bach and that of Beethoven. The contrapuntal style used in the elaboration of the main theme, the daring modulation to B flat minor, the sudden change from tragic feeling to a completely lighthearted mood points both to the past and to the future.

The next six sonatas (Nos. 21–26), written in 1773, were rather different from the work composed two years earlier. As a reaction against the previous subjectivism, Haydn's style was, at least temporarily, becoming less personal. No strong expression of feeling is noticeable here. These six sonatas contain only two real adagios, and in No. 26 the slow movement is replaced by a minuet. The insignificant finale of the same sonata certainly is different from the remarkable last movement of No. 20. At the same time a tendency may be noticed to make the form of the sonata increasingly compact. In No. 24 the adagio leads straight into the finale, and in No. 30, composed between 1774 and 1776, the dividing lines between the movements are omitted altogether. As the last two movements of this sonata are rhythmically related to each other, the connection is particularly strong. Within individual movements, too, the subjects are intimately linked and often grow out of the germ cells of a few basic motives. The first movement of No. 21, for instance, is based entirely on a dotted march rhythm and a motive in sextuplets; its subsidiary theme is derived from the main subject. A fairly frequent use now is being made of polyphonic devices. In No. 25 the finale is a canon. In No. 26 the minuet and trio are composed *al rovescio*, each being designed to be played forward, the way it is written, then backward, as a "crab canon."[2]

The piano sonatas Nos. 27–39, written after 1773, again display the "sensibility" of the storm-and-stress period, though not with the intensity of the C minor sonata. Three sonatas of this time were written in the minor key. The development section of the finale of No. 32 in B minor, introduces a remarkable contrapuntal elaboration of the theme. Moreover, the unexpected rumbling unison of the coda furnishes a good example of Haydn's sense of humor. At the beginning of sonata No. 34 in E minor, written before 1778, bass and melody answer each other in a rather original way. (Beethoven attempted a similar device in the first movement of his string quartet Op. 18, No. 5.) The very first theme of the sonata No. 36 in C sharp minor, written before 1780, displays an unconventional contrast of moods between the fragments of the main subject, and the development is characterized by rich modulations. The second movement of this sonata is a gay scherzando in two-four time, the finale a minuet in C sharp minor with a trio in C sharp major. Although the use of a minuet as the last movement of a sonata reminds one of the old suite form, the inversion of the traditional key relation (minuet in the minor, trio in the major) and the personal expression of this movement, with its now vigorous, now tender melodies, offer a striking contrast to the *style galant* of the previous period.

Particularly charming are the sets of variations that Haydn often introduced as finales to his sonatas. He was continually experimenting with fresh possibilities. In both No. 27 and No. 28 a passage in the minor key is suddenly inserted into a set of variations in the major; in No. 29 the minor passage is used to separate the theme from its variations; in No. 33 a theme in major and a theme in minor are varied in turn. The technique of the variation is also applied occasionally to the rondo form. Haydn now wrote rondos in which, as in the works of Philipp Emanuel Bach, each entrance of the main theme displays new figu-

[2] The minuet *al rovescio* of No. 26 also occurs as the third movement of symphony No. 47, composed in 1772.

rations, and even episodes are variations of the main theme. It is interesting to note that the second movement of No. 36 and the first movement of No. 39 grow out of the same theme. In an *avertimento* preceding the publication of the sonatas through Artaria and Company in Vienna in 1780, the master himself stated: "Among these sonatas are two movements that begin with the same theme. . . . The composer explains in advance that he has done this on purpose, modifying the continuation of the movement in each case." Haydn obviously was interested in the problem of developing two different movements from a single theme. The movement in A major displays a light, frisking gaiety, whereas that in G major, in spite of its buoyancy, distinguishes itself by a vigorous and expressive introduction.

❀ ❀ ❀

The six sonatas for violin and viola (Hob. VI:1–6) probably were written during the first half of the seventies or perhaps already in the late sixties. Here Haydn revived the old style of solo sonata with *basso continuo*. The whole melodic life is concentrated in the violin part, the viola providing the basis for the harmonic support. The violin displays the inventive power and brilliant conception to be expected in a composition of the seventies, and were it not for the poor treatment accorded the viola part, these sonatas would have to be counted among Haydn's representative compositions of this period. It might be worthwhile to use this viola part as the bass for a newly made piano accompaniment; a set of rather interesting violin sonatas thus could be produced; they might easily take the place of the inferior arrangements for violin and piano published under Haydn's name (see p. 341).[3]

The most interesting of Haydn's trios for baryton, viola, and violoncello were composed during his third period. The erudite "Canone in Diapente" in the minuet of Hob. XI:94 (composed about 1771), the attractive variations

[3] The publishers of the earliest editions, Bailleux (1775) and Campbell (1782), seem to have had a similar idea: they edited the works as *Sonates à violon seul avec la Basse.*

in No. 95 and No. 111 (composed about 1771 and 1772, respectively), and the unusual intensity of expression of the largo of No. 96 (about 1771) are examples of the many beauties to be found among these charming pieces. Of the few surviving autographs, that of No. 109[4] (about 1772) deserves special mention. Haydn marked at the beginning *fatto a posta* and *nihil sine causa* (done on purpose—nothing without reason) evidently implying that the piece was written for a very special occasion.[5]

Haydn wrote twelve string quartets during his third period of composition. The six quartets Op. 17 (Hob. III:25–30) were finished in 1771; in the following year originated the six "Sun" quartets Op. 20 (Nos. 31–36), so called because of the lovely symbol of the rising sun in an old edition.[6]

The quartets of Op. 17 show how closely Haydn approached the art of P. E. Bach during this period. Like the middle movement of the north-German master's first Prussian sonata, the adagio of No. 5 includes a dramatic scene with recitatives and ariosos. The austere sternness in the beginning of the adagio of No. 1 and, still more, the bold harmonies in the slow movement of No. 3 also show the north-German influence. In the first movement of No. 5, Haydn wrote a development longer than the exposition. He carried on with tendencies noticeable at an earlier period; at the same time, these tendencies harmonized with Emanuel Bach's aim to give greater solidity

[4] Preserved in the National Library, Budapest.

[5] Most baryton trios also were arranged for violin, viola, and cello so as to be performed on the usual string instruments. As a rule, modern editions publish the works in this version. Nos. 109 and 113 were edited by C. Döbereiner (Mainz, 1939), Nos. 108, 114, and 124 without editor's name (New York, 1943).

[6] Dated autographs of the two collections are preserved in the library of the Society of Friends of Music in Vienna. That of the Sun quartets was bequeathed by Johannes Brahms, who was a great admirer of Haydn's quartets and owned miniature scores of the complete "eighty-three." Brahms carefully compared the printed with the written editions and marked in the miniature scores all deviations from the originals.

and concentration to his works. The unexpected pianissimo ending of the finale of No. 2 is true Haydn, but it also reminds us of the pleasure Bach took in such sudden surprises.

These quartets are full of interesting effects of timbre. In the adagio of No. 2, Haydn introduced a theme first on the two highest strings, and then repeated it immediately on the G string. In the trio of the minuet of No. 3, the second violin was given the melody while the first accompanied. Haydn apparently took into consideration the fact that the player who usually performed a part of minor importance assumed in the long run a quality of tone different from that of the leader of the ensemble.

Rousseau's "back to nature" movement resulted in a general reawakening of interest in national folk music. Haydn showed himself in complete sympathy with this tendency. In the minuet of No. 1, for instance, lively skips of an octave and a tenth exhibit the character of the lighter type of Austrian popular music; the last subject of the finale of No. 6 shows clear traces of the Hungarian atmosphere in which Haydn had lived since he was twenty-eight years old.

In the Sun quartets, Op. 20, all the features of the quartets of Op. 17 are intensified. The designation *affettuoso* found twice in the directions for the tempo of slow movements can be applied to the whole opus. Here an artist is aiming at intensification and deepening of expression, and it is not surprising that Beethoven felt induced to make a copy of the first work in this superb set. To emphasize his rejection of rococo lightness, Haydn reverted to baroque features, adopting contrapuntal devices that also approach the ideal of emotional concentration. Thus he introduced the architectural form of the fugue into the finales of three of the six quartets in this series. In a naïve way he boasted of his scholarly achievements. The fugues were inscribed *a due, a tre,* and *a quattro soggetti;* the canon cancrizans ("crab canon") was marked *al roverscio* (sic), and the stretto, *in canone.* Such remarks seem to indicate that he considered the contrapuntal idiom not quite a natural form for expressing his feelings. Yet it should be pointed out that Haydn's string quartets with fugues were by no means isolated in this period. In 1773, Florian Leopold Gassmann, the composer of the opera *La contessina*, wrote six quartets, each of which contained two fugues; in the same year Mozart (influenced by Haydn) finished six quartets, twice using fugues as finales. The use of the fugue is not the only instance of Haydn's return to baroque devices. The adagio of No. 2, with the unusual name *capriccio*, has an introduction of four bars, and its weighty unison is reminiscent of the ritornello in a concerto of the Bach-Handel period.

Haydn's markings now were far more explicit than before. We find such directions as *allegro di molto e scherzando* and *mancando* (dying away).

The Haydn of the storm-and-stress period was more daring in the choice of keys than most composers of his time. The use of C sharp minor and C sharp major in the piano sonata No. 36 certainly was a proof of boldness, and accordingly, it seems hardly surprising that the Sun quartets should display a predilection for the minor mode. No. 3 is in G minor, No. 5 in the then unusual key of F minor, and modulations into the minor are frequent in the other works. Except for the first violin, the violoncello becomes the melody instrument in these quartets; in the beginning of No. 2 and in the fourth variation of No. 4, a role of unexpected importance is entrusted to it. The national element again is conspicuous in these pieces, and Haydn openly confessed his predilection for the music of the Hungarian gypsies in the *menuetto alla zingarese* and the following *presto e scherzando* of No. 4. This finale is certainly one of the most fiery and, at the same time, one of the most amusing pieces that Haydn ever wrote.

The composer liked to reveal his sense of humor in still another way. At the end of the fugue that forms the finale to No. 2, he wrote: *Laus omnip. Deo. Sic fugit amicus amicum* (Praise to the Almighty Lord. Thus one friend runs away from the other). This is certainly an apt description of the fugue, in which the themes appear repeatedly in the different voices as if fleeing from each other.

* * *

Haydn's six *divertissements à huit parties concertantes* (for flute, two horns, string quartet, and bass) probably were written in 1775 as ensemble pieces with baryton. In order to make these compositions available to a wider circle, Haydn replaced the baryton with a flute, transposing the part up an octave when necessary. In this form the six octets (Hob. X:12 and 1–5) were published by Artaria in 1781 as Op. 31.[7] Haydn's earlier divertimenti consisted of as many as five movements, but these pieces have no more than three. However, a diversity of forms is to be found in them. They contain sets of variations in which the theme is repeated after each variation and a little coda is attached at the end. The result is one of the many different mixtures of the rondo with variation forms that Haydn liked. Moreover, some minuets have two trios, a form not very frequent in Haydn's time. The subject matter of these pieces reveals their origin in the composer's storm-and-stress period. They are imbued with severe dignity, passionate fervor, and dramatic intensity. Particularly expressive are also the adagios of Nos. 1 and 12.[8] In the development section of the opening movement of No. 12 the thematic material is allotted impartially to all the instruments (Ex. 10 on facing page), a feature heralding Haydn's period of maturity.

Even though it appears very difficult at times in Haydn's first two periods to distinguish between clavier concertos and divertimenti with a clavier obbligato, the third period at last produced concertos worthy of this name. In the G major concerto (Hob. XVIII:4)[9] the increased impetus

[7] Hob. X:1–5 are listed in the Haydn-Elssler catalog. No. 12 is missing in this list, but in view of its stylistic similarity to the other pieces of the set, we may assume that it likewise originated from an octet with baryton.

[8] The second and third movements of No. 12 were edited by K. Geiringer (London, 1940), the complete No. 12 as well as No. 4 by E. F. Schmid (Kassel, 1952).

[9] Edited by K. Schubert (Hanover, 1932).

of the passages and the occasional use of full chords show
Haydn's effort to endow the part of the soloist with at
least a moderate amount of brilliance. The expression of
heroic defiance in the first movement proves this work to
be a product of the storm-and-stress period. The final rondo
brings the entrances of the tutti-ritornello on different de-

Divertissement à 8 parties concertantes, in G.

grees of the scale, thus displaying a certain similarity to
the form of the Vivaldi concerto, and it surprises us both
by its bold modulations and by the inexhaustible imagination that continually finds new ideas for the retransitions to
the main theme.

As Haydn's second concerto for the French horn (Hob. VIId:4)[10] first was announced by Breitkopf and Härtel in 1781, it also was probably the work of the third period. Although no conclusive proof for the authenticity of this composition can be furnished, its close relationship to the first concerto for horn makes Haydn's authorship almost certain. It is a more mature and musically more interesting composition, and preference is justly given to the later work. If it is played in the right chamber music style, this unusual concerto is bound to interest any audience.

*   *   *

Like most other types of Haydn's instrumental music, the symphonies show a decrease in number and an increase in quality during the seventies. Against some forty symphonies written before 1771, we find only about twenty-five in the third period. A similar reduction in number is evident in later decades too.

In the 1770s, Haydn's symphonic style was determined by a striving for truth and strength of expression. The composer wrote works that almost remind us of Beethoven, so obvious is their emphatic diction. The powerful unison at the beginnings of Nos. 46 and 53 and the first and last movements of No. 44 express the unbending energy characteristic of this period. This symphony No. 44, known as "Trauer-Symphonie" (Symphony of Mourning), laments the death of a hero. Haydn wanted its beautiful adagio in E major, in which the dramatic impetus of the first and last movements is replaced by a gentle expression of grief, to be played at his own funeral service.

The changed feeling in this period made Haydn eager to find new means of expression. Particularly daring is his choice of keys. One symphony is in C minor (No. 52), another in E minor (No. 44), a third in F sharp minor (No. 45), and a fourth even in B major (No. 46). In the finale of No. 46, Haydn introduced a little reminiscence of the preceding movement (a minuet) just before the beginning of the coda. This seems to foreshadow the cyclical form so important in the nineteenth century.

[10] Edited by H. H. Stevens (London, 1954).

The most unorthodox of these symphonies is in all likelihood also the most important. This is the famous "Farewell" symphony[11] No. 45 of 1772. In this work, "back to nature" results in a process of simplification. The orchestra of strings, two oboes, and two horns[12] is no larger than that of Haydn's first symphony. The initial movement has only about thirty measures of real development; the exposition is more than twice as long. This short development ends dramatically on a general pause, and a new melody of heavenly calm, not used in the exposition, is then presented. At the end of this lovely section, which equals the development in length, the recapitulation begins. In an earlier symphony (No. 42, composed in 1771) Haydn corrected a few measures of the original manuscript and remarked: "Dieses war vor gar zu gelehrte Ohren" (This was for too scholarly an ear). In the Farewell symphony too, Haydn meant to avoid making too learned an impression. He wanted (like Beethoven) to write music "coming from the heart, to go to the heart." An adagio in A major and a minuet in the unusual key of F sharp major are followed by a presto finale. As a coda this presto has an adagio resuming the tempo and key of the slow second movement. According to the poetical program, one instrument after another falls silent in this long, drawn-out coda. By the end, only one first and one second violin are left, and they finish the movement pianissimo on a sixth chord. From an artistic point of view this adagio ending of a symphony in several movements was even bolder than Haydn's attempt to teach his inconsiderate prince a lesson.

It is interesting to note that in the symphonies of the early seventies also a certain display of contrapuntal techniques may be observed. No. 44 has a canon in its minuet; in No. 47 the minuet and trio are *al rovescio*. The second movement of No. 47 is constructed in double counterpoint

[11] A fine facsimile edition of the autograph owned by the National Library in Budapest was edited by L. Somfai (Budapest, 1959).

[12] Bassoons may have been used to reinforce the violoncellos and basses, but they have only a few independent bars in the last movement.

at the octave. Here we have the same combination of such contrasting elements as free expression of personal feeling and polyphonic severity that we found in the quartets of this period.

Haydn's innate pleasure in the use of unexpected ideas, noticeable in the Farewell symphony, may also be observed in other orchestral works. In the first movements of Nos. 43 and 55, the main theme appears in the tonic soon after the beginning of the development. But this apparent recapitulation turns out to be merely a deception; presently the merry game of the development starts all over again with increased intensity. Even the famous "Surprise," to which Haydn owed so much of his popularity in England, had made an earlier appearance. After a diminuendo, the first movement of No. 60 brings a sudden loud tutti, in which the timpani greatly contribute to the intensity. The same work, a sort of suite based on Haydn's incidental music to the comedy *Il distratto* (performed in 1775 at Esterháza), contains in its adagio a sudden fanfare, and its affinity to a program is obvious. The symphony embodies in its finale a joke that was certain to amuse any audience in the eighteenth century. After a grand pause of the whole orchestra Haydn required the violinists to retune their instruments. The E, A, and D strings proved to be correct. But when they tried the G string, they found to their dismay that its pitch was no longer G, but had gone down to F. Disregarding the listening audience, the players raised the lowest string again to G; whereupon they continued as though nothing at all had happened. To play wrong notes purposely is one of the oldest and most effective comic devices. Haydn did this in the second movement of "Le Matin," Mozart in "Ein musikalischer Spass" (K. 522).

The symphony "Il distratto" probably was written in 1774 or 1775. By that time the climax of the storm-and-stress movement had been passed and Haydn gradually returned to his former path, though he had almost been lured away by the "romantic crisis." Problems of musical form and color regained much of their previous interest for him. In the first movement of No. 54, of 1774, for instance, he connected the slow introduction thematically with the following *allegro quasi presto*. He again showed a preference for the highly artistic form of the variation with frequent changes of major and minor within the same set. In No. 55, "Der Schulmeister" (The Schoolmaster), also of 1774, Haydn even used two sets of variations, one in the slow movement, the other in the finale. Particularly interesting is the "Laudon" symphony, No. 69, composed in 1778–79 and named in honor of the great Austrian field marshal Gideon Ernst von Laudon. Its first theme is practically identical with the first theme of the symphony "Maria Theresia," No. 48, written a few years earlier (Ex. 11).

At about the same time Haydn did something similar in his compositions for the pianoforte (cf. 275). He wanted to show that the main problem in a composition was how to deal with a theme, not how to invent one; it is an idea that Beethoven brought to full development.

Haydn now also showed greater interest in the wind instruments. In No. 54 the main theme of the allegro was given to bassoons and horns. The effects that Haydn produced by entrusting the violins with the melody and accompanying them in the lower octave by bassoons are interesting (cf. the third movements in Nos. 54 and 66). A particularly wide field of activity was offered to the woodwind and the brass sections in the numerous movements in variation form.

Many features in the symphonies written between 1774 and 1780 prove that even in later years the storm-and-stress movement did not lose its significance completely for Haydn. Thus, the first movement of No. 67, composed around 1778–79, introduces, like the "Farewell," a new idea in the development section; moreover, its finale is so crammed with musical themes as to replace sonata form by three-part form, the middle part introducing a new idea, new tempo, and new rhythm. The second movement of this remarkable symphony contains, near the end in the string parts, the surprising direction *col legno del arco*. Instead of the hair, the wooden part of the bow is to be used to give an insubstantial and ghostlike quality to the tone.

* * *

During the seventies the majority of Haydn's works for the stage had their premieres at Esterháza, and it may be more than a mere coincidence that the largest number of dramatic works were written in a period characterized by loosening of emotional expression. The eight extant stage compositions of this decade are:

Le pescatrici (The Fishermaids), 1770 (composed 1769), libretto by Goldoni;

L'infedeltà delusa (Unfaithfulness Deluded), 1773, librettist unknown;

Philemon und Baucis, 1773, text based on the play by C. G. Pfeffel;

L'incontro improvviso (The Chance Meeting), 1775, text arranged after the French book of Dancourt by Karl Frieberth;

Die Feuersbrunst oder Das abgebrannte Haus (The Conflagration or The Burned House), 1776–78, librettist unknown;

Il mondo della luna (The World of the Moon), 1777, libretto by Goldoni;

La vera costanza (True Constancy), 1776–79, libretto by F. Puttini and P. Travaglia;

L'isola disabitata (The Deserted Island), 1779, libretto by Metastasio.[13]

[13] *L'infedeltà delusa* and *Philemon und Baucis* were edited by H. C. R. Landon (Vienna, 1960, and Kassel, 1962, respectively); *L'incontro improvviso* by H. Schultz (Leipzig, 1937); *Il mondo della luna* by M. Lothar (Berlin, 1932) and again by Swarowsky-Füssl-Landon (Kassel, 1959); *L'isola disabitata*

Philemon und Baucis originally was conceived as a German puppet opera and performed in celebration of the Empress Maria Theresia's visit to Esterháza (see p. 66). On this occasion it was preceded by a prologue "Der Götterrat ober Jupiters Reise auf die Erde" (The Deliberations of the Gods or Jupiter's Journey to Earth). Apart from the libretto and a few fragments of music, this version with the prologue is lost, but a later arrangement of the work as a German Singspiel has survived. Similar in character is the German buffoon-comedy *Die Feuersbrunst,* which likewise was intended for marionettes.[14] *L'isola disabitata,* on the other hand, is an Italian opera of more serious character bearing the rather neutral designation *azione teatrale.* The remaining six works are classified as *burletta* or *dramma giocoso* and are Italian comic operas.[15] It is interesting to note that Haydn used in *Philemon und Baucis* and *L'incontro improvviso,* as well as later in *Armida* and *Orfeo e Euridice,* topics earlier employed by

was published in Vienna in 1909; *La vera costanza* (*List und Liebe;* with German text only) by G. Schwalbe and W. Zimmer (Berlin, 1960).

[14] The score of the Singspiel version of *Philemon und Baucis* was found by J. P. Larsen in the Bibliothèque du Conservatoire, Paris; that of *Die Feuersbrunst* by H. C. R. Landon at the Music Library of Yale University, New Haven, Connecticut. The librettos of three other marionette operas have been preserved: *Didone abbandonata* (reprint of 1778), *Genovevens vierter Theil* (1777), and *Die bestrafte Rachbegierde* (1779).

[15] It appears doubtful that Haydn is really the author of the music to *King Lear* (Hob. Ia:9 and XXX:5), which is ascribed to him by some scholars. The old parts of the work in the Esterházy collection do not mention Haydn's name, and in the Schwerin Library it appears as a composition by W. G. Stegmann. I was at first inclined to adopt the verdict of Mandyczewski, who considered the work authentic, and I therefore made the interesting composition, consisting of a French overture, several intermezzi ("The Hatred against Ingratitude," "The Thunderstorm," "The Pity," "The Battle"), and a funeral march, available for performances. In view of Larsen's research (*Die Haydn-Überlieferung,* p. 271), I now consider the authenticity of the work doubtful. (See also R. Heger, "Die Musik zum Trauerspiel König Lear," in *Österreichische Kunst,* 1932). Hob. does not attempt a definite solution of the problem.

Gluck (*Orfeo ed Euridice*, 1762; *La rencontre imprévue*, 1764; *Bauci e Filemone*, 1769; *Armide*, 1777).

The comic operas of the seventies are different from similar works that Haydn had written in the preceding decade. They are more ambitious, and decided prominence is given to the music. It is not surprising that in the long run the farcical character of *La canterina*, which offered no scope for deeper musical expression, was no longer able to satisfy the artistic leanings of a Haydn than was the shallow pathos of the *opera seria*. The composer now tried to combine comic and serious elements; the beginning of such tendencies could be noticed in *Lo speziale* (The Apothecary). In the seventies, Haydn's comic operas increasingly were permeated with warmth and tenderness, his gay characters more and more contrasted with serious and dignified figures, and thereby a type of seriocomic or mixed opera was created, a type that Mozart was to develop to perfection. It was no mere accident that Goldoni, the Venetian playwright mainly responsible for the division into *parte serie* and *parte buffe* (serious and comic characters), should have supplied the libretto for three of Haydn's operas.

A similar distinction is clear in the music. The language of the serious characters is practically that of the great *opera seria* of Naples. Preference is given to big arias in three-part form, with rich coloratura and frequent repetitions of the text. The recitative accompanied by the orchestra is used in moments of dramatic tension. The *parte buffe*, however, employ two-part song or strophic form, simple melodies with folk-song tendencies and free from flourishes and coloratura.

Haydn's tendency to attach increased importance to the music may be seen in his growing use of ensembles. At Esterháza he had no chorus at his disposal; therefore he combined his soloists into quartets, quintets, and occasionally even septets and octets. Of special importance are the finales, which show the composer at the height of his dramatic mastery. The tempo, the rhythm, the key, and the number of singers are constantly varied, but the musical unity always is maintained. In each finale a great climax is reached after several interruptions. In some of

these operas Haydn included purely instrumental numbers of an illustrative or "programmatic" character, and also
some ballets.

It is interesting to analyze Haydn's arias of the seventies.
At first they show, like the arias of Hasse, a great similarity
to the forms of instrumental music. In two-part arias in
the major, the first part modulates to the dominant; in
two-part arias in the minor, to the relative major. The
second part begins like a *da capo* and keeps the tonic up
to the end. In arias in three-part form, the first part assumes the function of an exposition, the third part that of
a recapitulation; the middle part rarely brings in any contrasting new idea, but consists as a rule of a sort of development of the text and music of the outside parts.

Toward the end of this period, Haydn occasionally dis-
carded this principle. Arias in three, four, and five different parts, sometimes interspersed with recitatives, now
were used. The form of these arias was dictated by the
exigencies of the libretto rather than by musical considerations. Haydn began to realize the deep truth of Gluck's
axiom, that in the opera, music always has to serve the
drama and never to dominate it.

The first of these mixed operas, *Le pescatrici*, introduces
one serious couple, Prince Lindoro and his bride, Eurilda,
and two lively pairs: the fishermen Burlotto and Frisellino
and their sweethearts, Nerina and Lesbina. The contrast
between the couples likewise is shown in the choice of
voices. The prince is a bass, Eurilda a contralto, whereas
the merry couples consist of sopranos and tenors. The first
act of the work is an excellent example of the pleasure
Haydn took in ridiculing the stiffness of the *opera seria*.
In a solemn manner, Lesbina praises her own beauty, and
this part of her aria in B flat major would be quite in place
in any of the great Neapolitan operas. But suddenly her
roguish temperament gets the better of her, and in conformity with the best traditions of the *opera buffa*, she
calls her rivals all sorts of names. It is interesting to note
that in Pergolesi's lovely intermezzo *La serva padrona*, an
aria of Serpina displaying a similar character is in the same
key, B flat major. Haydn apparently knew the work of the

great Neapolitan composer well. Also full of humor is Frisellino's F major aria, in which a bassoon conjures up the sounds of a bagpipe. On the other hand, scenes of a more contemplative character are not missing, and the orchestral sound assumes a more lyrical quality through the occasional use of English horns.

Besides effective arias, a considerable amount of ensemble music is used in this work. The first act has two quartets, a sextet, and a septet. *La canterina* and *Lo speziale* employed four vocalists, but now even seven were not enough for Haydn; in the introduction to the third act he used several choristers besides the regular cast.

L'infedeltà delusa of 1773 was performed during the Empress Maria Theresia's visit to Esterháza. Its rather weak libretto deals with the triumph of true love over all obstacles; the number of ensembles is small and most pieces are arias, though of a rich variety of expression. True dramatic passion as in the arias of the serious heroine, Sandrina, and of her lover Nanni, is replaced by insolent mirth in those of the gay and energetic Vespina. Altogether, the portrayal of human characters in music is particularly successful in this work. An interesting feature in the bass aria of Nanni is the introduction of the violoncello obbligato. (Such association of a solo instrument and a voice of the same range is often seen in compositions of J. S. Bach.) The aria "Come piglia si bene la mira" deals with a favorite subject of the rococo period, describing how Cupid, in spite of the bandage over his eyes, does not fail to pierce the heart of his victims. Although the piece abounds in coloratura, the expression is warm and deeply felt.

In *L'incontro improvviso*, Haydn treated a Turkish subject as Mozart was to do in 1781 in his *Abduction from the Seraglio*. In Haydn's opera, Calandro, a real *basso buffo*, and his servant Osmin are comic parts; the noble Rezia and the Sultan of Egypt are completely serious characters. It is interesting that, according to the fashion of the time, the clergy is ridiculed in the person of the roguish monk Calandro. The score is full of charming details. Ali, for instance, sought by the Egyptian soldiers, disguises himself as a painter. He shows the officers a number of pictures and describes their subjects to them, the orchestra offering exquisite portrayals. His aria in D major illustrates a magnificent Italian banquet, a sweetly murmuring little brook, and an appalling battle scene with the discharge of muskets and guns. Delightful effects of tone color are attained in the trio "Mi sembra un sogno" for three sopranos, accompanied by muted strings, English horns, and French horns. Another remarkable number is an orchestral interlude in the third act, in which such conventional Turkish instruments as the triangle and tambourine are used to evoke the atmosphere of an oriental fairy tale. The opera has three important finales, the most interesting being that of the second act which consists of three sections contrasting in tempo and rhythm. It is preceded by a duet in E major, which together with this finale forms a sort of larger unit.

Il mondo della luna (1777) is based on a libretto by Goldoni and is related in its content to Lo speziale, the first Goldoni opera composed by Haydn. The apothecary Sempronio in the earlier work is crazy about geography, and Buonafede in The World of the Moon is all too fond of astronomy. His excessive interest in it is destined to become his undoing. Thinking that he lives on that distant satellite, he permits his daughters to marry suitors whom he would never have approved on earth. This rather amusing farce was very popular in the eighteenth century, and composers such as Piccinni, Gassmann, and Paisiello successively set it to music. Il mondo della luna includes an unusually large number of instrumental movements. In the first act a short orchestral piece leads us into the world of the moon, and three times the trusting Buonafede looks through a telescope prepared by a fraudulent astronomer, Ecclitico. On each occasion the same instrumental piece is played, only to be interrupted by a recitativo secco and an arietta in which Buonafede explains what he sees. The orchestration changes after each observation; for its original appearance Haydn used strings in the instrumental piece and oboes, horns, and strings in the arietta. At the first repetition in both pieces flutes are added. Buonafede's last observation is particularly unpleasant, which induced Haydn to add bassoons to his orchestra and to change the key of the piece from D to E flat. The prelude to the second act, with its dotted rhythms and the use of timpani, describes the pompous entry of the sovereign of the moon. At the beginning of the first finale the sensations of flying are painted with realism by the orchestra. Haydn was obviously following the tradition of Gluck's reform operas composed for Vienna, in which descriptive orchestral preludes and ballets were of great importance. Strangely enough, in this opera Haydn also uses a male alto. The relatively unimportant part of the cavaliere Ernesto was sung in the first performance by the castrato Pietro Gherardi, who was in Prince Esterházy's service from 1776 to 1778. This is one of the rare instances of Haydn's composing for a castrato. The overture to the opera, which is in one movement only, has no direct connection with the work. According to the custom of the time, Haydn used it also for other purposes. Without the extensive coda employed in the opera, and with a somewhat smaller orchestra, it appears as the first movement of the symphony No. 63, "La Roxolane."

The opera *La vera costanza* was composed for Vienna and shows an interesting relationship to a work by Mozart. By an odd coincidence, the heroine, who rises from humble beginnings to the position of countess, bears the name Rosina, and like the Countess Rosina in Mozart's *Le nozze di Figaro*, she is devoted in deep love and faithfulness to her husband, though the count, despite his own gallant adventures, torments her with his unfounded jealousy. The tender, sensitive Rosina has as a counterpart the merry Villotto, who tries to win her love. *La vera costanza* is perhaps the most mature of Haydn's comic operas, for the new and dramatic form of its arias is indeed remarkable. The count's aria in the first act is introduced by an accompanied recitative in preparation for the tempestuous atmosphere of the first part of the aria; the second section, with an abrupt change of mood, is a tender adagio, inspired by the thought of his beloved. Irritated by a motion of his clumsy rival, the count suddenly starts; another recitative accompanied by the orchestra leads to the third part of the aria, bringing in new thematic material. The count's overwrought state of mind could not be better expressed than by the free form of this passionate piece, and a similar feeling is portrayed in the count's solo in the second act. An accompanied recitative built on the thematic material of the first part of the aria is followed by an intricate vocal number consisting of as many as five sections. These contrast in tempo, rhythm, and character and are interspersed with occasional recitatives. In these two numbers Haydn succeeds in presenting a vivid picture of the weak, unstable character of the count. The finales, too, reveal the hand of the mature artist: the first consists of seven contrasting parts in different keys related to each other; the number of singers gradually increases from three to seven; and in the second finale nine sections can be distinguished. At the beginning one singer and one sleeping person are on the stage, but at the end all the seven characters take part. The composer gives a great amount of variety to these finales without ever endangering the continuity of the plot and the musical unity. When he was composing this work Haydn obviously had the rich resources of the opera in the imperial capital in mind.

La vera costanza showed Haydn's growing interest in the serious opera, but he took a more important step in the same direction in L'isola disabitata. This is a real opera seria, based on a simple, short drama of Metastasio, previously set to music by composers like Bonno, Holzbauer, Jommelli, and Traetta. Costanza, separated by pirates from her husband Ernesto, lives with her sister Silvia on a deserted island until, after many years, she finds her beloved spouse. The work shows that the composer knew Gluck's operas and allowed himself to be influenced by them. It is hardly mere chance that Haydn called L'isola disabitata an "azione teatrale," the designation Gluck had used for his Orfeo ed Euridice. The recitativo secco accompanied by harpsichord only is banished from Haydn's opera, as it was from Gluck's work. It is replaced by a carefully designed recitative accompanied by the orchestra and fills the greatest part of the score. Unity among the scenes is achieved through the use of simple, constantly recurring motives. The recitative is sometimes transformed into a real arioso; the arias themselves are unaffected and powerful, without excessive development of the musical element. To some extent, however, Haydn deviated from this rule in the arias of Silvia, which he wrote for Luigia Polzelli. In these lovely pieces he attained a tenderness of expression reminiscent of Mozart. It is a pity that he included only a single ensemble number, the final quartet, in the score; the fire that shortly before had ravaged the theater at Esterháza may have been responsible for such economy. As Haydn did not have a real stage at his disposal, he had to be satisfied with four singers only and to abstain from ballets and changes of scenery. There is only one instrumental number in this opera, the overture in G minor (Hob. Ia:13), the slow introduction of which uses the same main idea as the following allegro. The fast movement gains unity from the prevailing accompaniment in eighth notes. After a short contrasting allegretto in G major, the first allegro returns as a kind of coda. In the restless allegros Haydn meant to describe the terrible existence on the desolate island; the allegretto voiced the hope of the eventual union of the loving couple.

Different in character from the Italian operas are the two German works. The spirit of sensibility is clearly noticeable in the German Singspiel *Philemon und Baucis*. In this work not only is the dialogue spoken, but also the gods Jupiter and Mercury are entrusted with purely spoken parts so as to stress their difference from mortal beings. The overture consists of only two movements because by the custom of the period the introduction to the first vocal number was used instead of a finale. Both movements have passages full of tenderness, illustrating the moving idyl enacted by the loving couple. To deepen the picture of conjugal affection the work introduces the couple's son Aret and his bride Narcissa, who were felled on their wedding day by lightning. Philemon's canzonet "Ein Tag der allen Freude bringt" voices his grief over these events. All shades of emotion are expressed here, and sad resignation ultimately is called forth in this simple piece, which dies away pianissimo. Revived upon Jupiter's command, the young people voice in moving terms their affection for each other. A gem of the score is Aret's aria, which with its delicate oboe solo stirringly conveys the feeling of bewildered happiness experienced by a man returned to earth from another world. It is supplemented by Narcissa's aria portraying with the help of a delicate orchestra accompaniment the young girl's tender sweetness and charm. Significantly enough, Haydn again used this exquisite piece—offering a highly rewarding task for the singer—with different words, in his opera *Il mondo della luna*. As the reference to the empress' visit at the end of the original marionette opera (see p. 66) had to be omitted from the Singspiel, it concluded with a ballet taken from Gluck's opera *Paride ed Elena* (1769). This insertion seemed altogether fitting, as Haydn's score reveals in many aspects affinities to Gluck's idiom.[16]

Unlike *Philemon und Baucis, Die Feuersbrunst oder Das abgebrannte Haus* is a typical Austrian popular comedy, introducing *Hanswurst*, the clown of the Viennese stage, a mischievous hostler, a fierce dragon, and a pathetic ghost. Very coarse language and at times a thick Viennese dialect are sported by some of the characters, and the traditional disguises (*Hanswurst* appears in both male and female attire) add to the fun. The music is light, gay, and uncomplicated. It consists mainly of simple arias, but duets, choruses, and descriptive instrumental numbers enrich the tonal picture. Colorature are avoided in the vocal pieces, as the composer aims at maximum clarity of the text while matching the popular nature of the libretto. Yet the individual characters are subtly portrayed with the help of melodic and orchestral devices. Unfortunately, the only score of the work thus far known does not contain the text

[16] Landon ("Haydn's Marionette Operas" in *Haydn Yearbook*, 1962, p. 150) points out that the poignant little minuet accompanying the revival of the young couple appears also in Ordoñez' marionette opera *Alceste*, performed in Esterháza in 1775. The scholar assumes that Haydn borrowed the number from Ordoñez. Might it not seem more likely that the lesser known composer felt inclined to pay homage to the Kapellmeister by including one of Haydn's pieces in his score?

of the spoken dialogue connecting the individual numbers, and no libretto is known, so that an authentic revival of the comedy is impossible.

*   *   *

Haydn composed no cantatas during his third period of composition, but in the years 1774–75 he wrote an even bigger work. It was his first oratorio, *Il ritorno di Tobia* (The Return of Tobias), based on a book by Giovanni Gastone Boccherini. This work still adheres to the Neapolitan vocal style. Even a cursory glance at the many arias with abundant coloratura discloses the influence of Italian art. At the same time the intricacy of the musical craftsmanship and the close connection between words and music give this oratorio a character all its own. The libretto differs favorably from the typical Neapolitan oratorio text; instead of the traditional feeble allegories, a definite plot is established, a plot by no means lacking dramatic episodes, such as his parents' meeting with Tobias, whom they thought dead; the miraculous healing of old Tobit's blindness; the revelation of the archangel's identity, and his return to heaven. This oratorio, written for Vienna, follows the best musical traditions of the Austrian capital. The Habsburgs always preferred a more severe musical style, and, accordingly, oratorios in Vienna were kept free from the aberrations of Neapolitan music. In his storm-and-stress period, Haydn himself was striving for an expressive musical language; now he was emotionally qualified to write a work in accord with the exacting tradition of Viennese art. The remarkable overture to the work consists of a largo in C minor, the lofty character of which reminds us of Gluck, and an *allegro di molto* in C major in sonata form. The slow introduction is thematically related to the first chorus, "Pietà d'un infelice," and a spiritual affinity exists between the allegro of the overture and the final chorus of the work. In this overture, Haydn deals with the main idea of the oratorio: out of sorrow and darkness a way is leading to happiness and light. The basic idea of Beethoven's C minor symphony is not very different.

The arias frequently renounce the stereotyped *da capo*

form. They show the same strong influences of sonata form that were to be noticed in the opera arias. There are two contrasting ideas in the first part of the aria. The middle section brings development of feeling and action, and the last part once more recapitulates it. Dramatic and musical points of view are in complete accord here. Haydn by no means dispenses with the antitheses so important for the dramatic impact of an aria, but introduces such contrasts between the first and second ideas of the main section. In her first aria, for instance, the mother of Tobias deplores the weakness of her husband. In the initial section, the achievements of the warrior and peasant are glorified and then, after a modulation to the dominant, the passivity of the husband is lamented. In the second (development) section in the minor, the passionate reproaches increase. Anna cannot help remembering once more (recapitulation) the gallant warrior and the diligent peasant, both of them so sadly contrasting with her husband.

The recitatives too are most carefully treated. The shy, delicate portrait of Tobias' young wife in No. 8 of the first part and the healing of blind Tobit in No. 7 of the second part are strikingly depicted, surpassing by far the average recitatives of the period.

The most important numbers of the score, however, are the choruses. At first the work contained only three choruses, one each at the beginning and end of the first part and one as the finale of the second part. For a performance in 1784, Haydn added two more choruses, one in each part. Most effective in the first number are the combination of solo voices and chorus and the use of the instruments to which the melody is frequently entrusted while the chorus provides a harmonic basis. The last number is in a sort of rondo form. Again and again the chorus repeats its moving supplication, "Rendi a Tobit la luce, o della luce autor" (Return the light to Tobit, Creator of the light), interrupted only by the five soloists, who send their individual prayers to the heavenly Father. Particularly dramatic is the moment when the humble wailing of "mira le calde lacrime" (notice our scalding tears) suddenly changes into the passionate outcry "odi le nostre voci" (listen to our voices). Perhaps the most important of the ensemble numbers is the "Storm Chorus," which Haydn wrote in 1784 for the second part. The effective contrast between pictures of darkest horror and of heavenly peace makes this piece equal to the best creations of the mature Haydn. In this oratorio, Haydn bestowed particular care on the instrumentation. He did not content himself with clothing almost every number in its own coloristic garb; he also achieved superb clarity and transparency of texture. A passage for wind instruments like the following (Ex. 12) anticipates the orchestral technique of the London symphonies.

Ritorno di Tobia, 2nd Part, Aria No. 2 (Sara)

Three years before Haydn's death his pupil Sigismund Neukomm arranged *Il ritorno di Tobia* on behalf of the composer. Some of the unnecessary repetitions of the text and excessive coloratura were eliminated, which is all to the good. Neukomm's changes and enlargements of the orchestration, however, might well have been avoided, for they coarsened some charming details of Haydn's original instrumentation. Even if the pupil acted in full conformity with Haydn's own wishes, it is doubtful that the composer himself, after the passing of more than thirty years, was able to conjure up the atmosphere of the original work in order to judge the merits of this "improvement."

✿   ✿   ✿

Haydn's church compositions of this period start with a *Salve Regina* in G minor written for four solo voices, mixed chorus, solo organ, and strings. At the beginning of the work, the keyboard instrument is entrusted with an extensive solo; subsequently its cantilena attractively alternates with the singers' utterances. In accord with the organization of the text, Haydn wrote a composition in three movements in an effective tempo sequence. The fastest section is in the middle, whereas an adagio forms the beginning and an allegretto with an introductory largo concludes it. It is an attractive composition, clearly showing the characteristic Viennese version of the Italian style that Haydn used in this period for sacred compositions and oratorios.

The end of the autograph of the *Salve Regina* contains two prayers to the Holy Virgin imploring Her to help the composer. Each of them has the form of a chronogram whose capitals express the year of composition (1771):

oro te o pla et DULCIs VIrgo Vt assIstas CoMposItorI

pla DULCIsqVe VIrgo assIste CoMposItorI.[17]

Of Haydn's Offertory *Animae Deo gratae* (also known under the title *Agite properate*) for a solo tercet of two sopranos and tenor, mixed chorus, two oboes, two trumpets, strings, and organ, parts in the Göttweig monastery dated 1776 prove that this brilliantly festive piece in the key of C major originated at the latest in that year.

The monumental G major chorus in *da capo* form *Ens aeternum*, using for accompaniment strings, oboes, bassoon, trumpets, timpani, and organ, is a solemn, powerful piece whose bass incipit is listed in the Haydn-Elssler catalogue. The technical mastery and elegance of formal structure here displayed point to its origin at the threshold of Haydn's maturity.

A place of its own is occupied by the *Offertorio in Stillo a Capella* (as the draft catalogue lists it), *Non nobis Domine*, set merely for four vocalists and a figured bass.[18] The composition starts with an impressive fugato, which leads to a homophonic section. This imposing work of the seventies, related to baroque motets, testifies to the importance the preclassical idiom held for Haydn at this time,

[17] It is not quite clear who wrote these chronograms. Possibly the person who did even changed the date on the first page, which gives every indication of having been tampered with. There is another chronogram on the final page whose meaning has not yet been cleared up. The autograph is preserved in the University Library, Tübingen.

[18] Edited by K. Geiringer (St. Louis, 1960) with Latin and English text.

an attitude noticeable also in the fugues of the Sun quartets.

The *Motetto de Sancta Thecla: Quis Stellae*,[19] for soprano solo, mixed chorus, strings, and organ probably dates from the early seventies. It starts with a secco recitative for soprano, followed by an attractive *da capo* aria, whereupon a gay, simple hymn for mixed chorus brings the work to a close. The melodic material of this amiable little piece displays a certain affinity to Austrian folk songs.

Three Masses also belong to this period. The Mass of St. Cecilia written between 1769 and 1773,[20] is the longest work of its kind composed by Haydn and also the one most nearly approaching the style of the Neapolitan cantata. The seven parts of the Gloria, for instance, consist of more than eight hundred measures, several choruses interrupted by solo episodes, a coloratura aria for soprano, and a trio for alto, tenor, and bass. Like J. S. Bach's B minor Mass,[21] this work, which probably was written for the feast of St. Cecilia, was not intended for regular liturgical use. The connection between text and music is fairly loose. The old printed edition of the Mass, published by Breitkopf and Härtel, omits whole movements of the composition, and the surplus text is used as well as possible for the remaining music. Thus, for example, in the shortened edition the words "Domine Deus, rex coelestis, Deus Pater omnipotens" are set to music originally composed to the words "et in terra pax hominibus bonae voluntatis," but the change of text does not seem bad, as in this section the music happens to be uncharacteristic. In other parts of his score, Haydn shows, however, real understanding of the dramatic possibilities of the text of the Mass, one instance being the striking contrast used for "iudicare vivos—et mortuos" (to

[19] Parts of it written by a copyist were found in the Eisenstadt Pfarrkirche, their authenticity being proved by Haydn's signature in the bass part.

[20] Scores of this Mass and the *Missa Sti. Nicolai* were edited by C. M. Brand in the Collected Edition of Haydn's works, Series XXIII, Vol. 1 (Boston, 1951). The score of the *Missa Sti. Joannis* was edited by Landon and Füssl in Series XXIII, Vol. 2, of the Collected Edition (Munich, 1958).

[21] Haydn owned a manuscript score of Bach's B minor Mass.

judge the quick and the dead). Also the repetition of the word "credo" after each section of the profession of faith, and the use of the orchestral recitative in "et incarnatus est," anticipating Beethoven, show that Haydn was not satisfied merely to copy the Neapolitan models. In the employment of the strings, in the emphasis on oboes and trumpets among the wind instruments, and, above all, in the work's expressive impact, there is a notable return to the baroque idiom, resulting in a composition imbued with vigor and grandeur.

The form of the cantata Mass not really suited for liturgical purposes did not wholly satisfy Haydn, and he never again produced a composition of this kind. However, the *Missa Sti. Nicolai,* probably written for the name day of Prince Nicolaus the Magnificent, is a *missa brevis* conceived on an unusually large scale. Two oboes and two horns are added to the orchestra, and the soloists have an uncommonly important task. This Mass is one of the most lyrical and tender of Haydn's church compositions. The Kyrie, which is quoted in the "Dona nobis pacem," has the character of a pastorale in six-quarter time, the Gratias is a soprano solo, the Benedictus a solo quartet of winning gracefulness. The modern critic finds it somewhat disconcerting that in the Credo different sections of the text are sung simultaneously; however, similar devices to save time were used not only by Haydn, but also by other composers of the period. The sensibility of the storm-and-stress period perhaps is not so strongly expressed in this Mass as in other compositions of 1772. But the frequent sforzandi in the Kyrie, the mournful repetition of the words "et homo factus est" after the menacing Crucifixus, and the moving accents of the Agnus Dei show that Haydn was well aware of the supreme drama unfolding in the text of the Mass.

It was probably around 1775 that Haydn created the little organ solo Mass in B flat to which he gave the title *Missa brevis Sti. Joannis de Deo.* Saint John of God was the founder of the order of the Brothers of Mercy, for whose Eisenstadt church the Mass apparently was destined. In this case the necessity of a concise structure made impossible a strong participation by the soloists. Only in the more broadly treated Benedictus does a solo soprano compete with the concertizing organ. All the other movements are entrusted to the chorus and the small instrumental apparatus of two violins and bass. The trend toward deepened expression characteristic for the works of the seventies also is noticeable in this short Mass. Deeply felt is the Crucifixus. At the dramatic climax of the text, the beginning of "et resurrexit" after the end of the Crucifixion, Haydn quotes the music of the Gloria. Better than a date on the manuscript, the expression-mark *perdendosi* used at the end of the "Dona nobis pacem" indicates the period in which this work was written. The pianissimo at the end of the prayer for peace certainly conforms to the idea of the text, though it deviates from the traditional musical construction.[22]

[22] In Haydn's original manuscript of the Mass, the notes of the bass and the organ parts were written about twice as large as those of the rest. Apparently the organist—probably Haydn himself—intended to play from the full score.

CHAPTER 15

MATURITY

The Fourth Period: 1781–1790

With the year 1781 Haydn entered upon his classical period of composition. Both the frills of the rococo period and the exaggerated emotionalism of the storm-and-stress period were overcome, though they left their imprint on the master's work. Out of the combination of features in the second and third periods of composition there grew the classical style of his full maturity, in which the principle of "thematic elaboration" found its widest use.

The term "classical" can hardly be better explained than by the words "well balanced." In classical music one finds a perfect blend of the work of the mind and the work of the heart; inspiration is as important as the action of the intellect. Cheerfulness and seriousness, the tragic and the comic spirit all are called upon to make their contributions. Classical works seem to be born out of the fundamental qualities of the instruments or voices for which they were written. All technical problems are completely solved, and the compositions are neither too long nor too short. The musical ideas fit the musical form to perfection. Those works that deserve to be termed "classical" exhibit a beauty and composure comparable to those of the best architecture and sculpture of ancient Greece.

Although Haydn had undergone an artistic development that seemed to lead him inevitably toward classicism, his work would hardly have reached the full height of perfection had he not associated artistically with Mozart, who moved to Vienna in 1781. It has been shown in the first section of this book that the friendship between the two masters resulted in an amazing musical relationship. Not only did Haydn influence Mozart (this is not particularly surprising, as he was twenty-four years older and by far the more successful of the two), but he also allowed himself to be influenced by the young genius. It was a perfect example of mutual give-and-take, equally beneficial to Mozart and Haydn, for in helping one another, each of the two masters reached in the eighties the consummation of his classical style and with it his full artistic maturity.

* * *

It is evident that even before the first meeting of the two composers, Haydn had studied Mozart's work, for some of his pianoforte sonatas published before the date of that meeting show clear signs of Mozart's influence. For instance, the melodic invention in the second movement of sonata Hob. XVI:35 and the striking separation of the subsidiary subject from the main subject in the first movement of sonata No. 37 (both sonatas having been published in 1780) show a certain similarity to Mozart's works, as does the connection of the end of the exposition with the beginning of the development in the first movements of Nos. 41 and 49, two sonatas composed after the musicians first met. In the adagio of No. 49, too, the melodic character appears to be inspired by Mozart to some extent.

However, pianoforte sonatas certainly are not among the most representative works of Haydn's classical period. In 1784, three sonatas (Nos. 40–42) were published and dedicated to Princess Marie Esterházy. Each sonata has only two movements, and the influence of the divertimento seems to be particularly strong (especially so in No. 40). A comparison of the brilliant finale of No. 39 with the tame *allegretto innocente* at the beginning of No. 40 reveals a striking difference of character. Obviously the princess was not in favor of bold innovations, and the finales of Nos. 41 and 42 show that a display of strict counterpoint was more to her taste. These sonatas denote a decided lack of deeper interest in the form, and in the following years Haydn completely neglected the piano sonata.[1] Chamber

[1] Nos. 44–47, published in 1788–89, are earlier works, probably composed between 1765 and 1768.

and orchestral music in which "thematic elaboration" could be displayed to best advantage occupied his mind to such an extent that other forms receded into the background. Only at the end of the eighties did he revert to the piano sonata. First, as a kind of preparation, he wrote the rather insignificant No. 48, in two movements, which was followed in 1789–90 by a real masterpiece, the large sonata No. 49 in E flat major, intended for Marianne von Genzinger. For once Haydn completely forgot the educational purpose of his piano music and followed only his inspiration. In the exposition of the first movement, the subsidiary and concluding subjects, though derived from the main idea, show an independent character of their own; the retransition to the recapitulation is full of dramatic tension, and the important coda seems to be a sort of second development. The solemn adagio, with its dramatic episode in B flat minor, is reminiscent of Mozart. Haydn himself considered this movement the climax of the whole work, as his letter to Marianne von Genzinger shows (see p. 96). The finale is very different from this middle movement. In its gay, energetic character it supplies a cheerful solution of the conflict. Thus Haydn's interest in the piano sonata got a fresh impetus from his devotion to Marianne von Genzinger, for everything connected with her had to be perfect. It is significant that the composer could not even bear the thought of his friend playing the sonata on her old, inferior piano. He was not satisfied until he had persuaded his prince to present Frau von Genzinger with a new instrument, he himself giving elaborate advice as to the final choice.[2]

[2] Although Haydn wrote to Marianne von Genzinger: "This Sonata . . . is quite new and eternally intended for Your Honor," the autograph of the work bears in Haydn's hand the dedication "Composta per la stimatissima Signora Anna de Jerlischek." This lady, a friend of Marianne and housekeeper at the Esterházy court, later married Johann Tost, to whom Haydn dedicated several string quartets (see p. 312). As we learn from Haydn's letters to Marianne, while he was composing this sonata for her, Fräulein de Jerlischek commissioned him to write a piano sonata meant as a gift for Frau von Genzinger. Haydn complied and dedicated the work to the housekeeper,

Two smaller piano compositions of Haydn, the capriccio in G major (Hob. XVII:1) and the fantasia in C major (Hob. XVII:4), were published in 1788–89 by Artaria, but only the latter was composed at that time, whereas the autograph of the former is dated 1765. We know from Griesinger that Haydn loved to lose himself in improvisations on the piano. "I sat down at the clavier," he remarked to his friend, "and began improvising in a sad or happy mood, according to what I just felt. When I had caught an idea, my aim was to carry it out and sustain it according to the rules." The capriccio is written as a sort of rondo; the fantasia approaches sonata form. Haydn had a high opinion of the fantasia, which he offered to Artaria with the following words: "In a humorous mood I have composed an entirely new capriccio for the piano; its good taste, singularity, and elaborate finish are sure to please both experts and amateurs. It is in a single movement, rather long, but not particularly difficult." The fantasia shows, better even than the sonatas, the colorful character of Haydn's piano-playing. We seem to hear in this piece the tone of violins and double basses, of horns and flutes; moreover the rapid crossing of the hands, the arpeggios, and the distribution of passages between the hands exhibit the composer's concern for purely pianistic devices. The effect that Haydn achieved by holding notes in the bass until they die away (*tenuto intanto finchè no si sente più il sono*) is rather notable. This fantasia was written by a master who exploited the possibilities of piano technique in transcribing ideas of an essentially orchestral nature.

* * *

During the 1780s, Haydn composed eleven piano trios (Hob. XV:3–13). On the whole these compositions resemble the earlier trios, though divertimento features become

---

who paid for it, but as he was obliged to "be very careful not to lose her favor," he concealed the fact that he had meant to write a sonata for Marianne in any case. It seems likely that when the manuscript finally reached the Viennese lady, it was inscribed to her. Van Hoboken, loc. cit., p. 773, remarks that the dedication to Fräulein Jerlischek in the autograph apparently had been pasted over.

rarer and the influence of Mozart is occasionally to be observed. The piano parts still contain runs and passages given to both hands, and also occasional cadenzas. The violin is limited to the first three positions, and it is entirely subordinate to the keyboard instrument; the violoncello as a rule merely duplicates the bass of the piano part. The first movement of No. 9 (1785), in which violin and violoncello are used in conjunction and opposed to the piano, is certainly an exception.

In 1784, Haydn sent to England his six divertimenti for first violin or flute, second violin, and violoncello (Hob. IV:6–11), which were published by William Forster in London as Op. 38. According to Haydn's receipt for the honorarium, which accompanied the manuscripts, these trios may also be performed by two flutes and violoncello. They are pleasant pieces of no great consequence, largely arranged from baryton trios, works for the stage, etc.

* * *

Haydn's string quartets, Op. 33, of 1781 (Hob. III:37–42), were dedicated to the Grand Duke Paul of Russia, and therefore are known as the "Russian" quartets. The six pieces are also called both *Gli scherzi,* as in this series the composer gave the name of scherzo to his minuet movements, and the *Jungfernquartette,* from the title page of an old edition. Since the composition of the preceding series of string quartets, Op. 20, of 1772, no less than nine years had elapsed, during which Haydn had composed several operas, the oratorio *Il ritorno di Tobia,* and many symphonies. The string quartet had been abandoned temporarily, probably because Haydn felt that further progress along the lines established in his Op. 20 was impossible. In the fugue movements of the Sun quartets, a strong concentration of both form and content had been attained, but in time this sort of solution seemed too radical to him and not in conformity with the spirit of the string quartet. The progressive Haydn was not satisfied to use an antiquated contrapuntal form of the baroque period in the young string quartet. He wanted unification and concentration, but not knowing how to achieve them adequately, he renounced the composition of string quartets for the time being and it was not until nine years later that he found a solution of his problem.

The Russian quartets, which, according to Haydn himself, were written "in an entirely new and particular manner," raised the principle of "thematic elaboration" to the status of a main stylistic feature. Haydn had used thematic development—a method of dissecting the subjects of the exposition and then developing and reassembling the resulting fragments in an unexpected manner—in his earlier works, but never with such logic and determination. Henceforth this device, combined with modulations, ruled the development sections of the sonata form. Each of the six Russian quartets provides examples of this technique. Thus, for instance, in the first movement of No. 5, part of the main subject (Ex. 13a on following page) grows into the succeeding intricate texture (Ex. 13b on following page). Thematic elaboration is by no means confined to the development sections. Even the transition from the first to the second subject in the exposition might make use of an elaboration of the main theme, and occasionally new developing episodes can be found in the recapitulation. The quartets Op. 20, with their fugues, already had done away with the predominance of the first violin. In the Russian quartets, all instruments as a matter of course were given equal shares in the melodic work. Even the accompanying and purely filling parts were based on motives taken from the main subjects.

Haydn exercised wise economy in using the sonata form only in the first movements of the Russian quartets. The slow movements are mainly in three-part (romanza) form, with a contrasting middle part instead of a development, whereas in the finales there is a return to the rondo form. Only in his last period was Haydn to give to the rondo the characteristic features of sonata form, thus creating at the end of the cycle a counterpart to its beginning. The most apparent innovation of the Russian quartets, the use of a scherzo instead of the traditional minuet, should not be taken too seriously. An analysis of these pieces shows that the change is limited to the name of the movement and

does not affect its character. Only the scherzo of No. 5
foreshadows the piquant flavor and fire of Beethoven's
movements of the same title.

(13a)

The synthesis of the homophonic rococo style with the
contrapuntal idiom noticeable in the form of these quartets
also may be discerned in their contents. Without avoiding
the earlier grace and liveliness, they reveal greater depth
of feeling. The last traces of *galant* superficiality have disappeared, and the music breathes quiet serenity and classical nobility. Still, an experience of the importance of the
"romantic crisis" necessarily left its imprint on the master's
work. The augmented octavos in the introduction of No. 1,

and the last movement of No. 2, with its adagio episode, its grand pauses of increasing length, and the unusual pianissimo ending bear witness to it. However, these para- phernalia of tragedy are employed to achieve a purely comical effect. This finale rightly bears the nickname "The Joke." It seems to be a pleasant, though not particularly amusing, rondo with two episodes. The real fun comes in the coda, for after a solemn adagio episode, the eight measures of the main subject are repeated in an odd man- ner. Each phrase of two measures is followed by a rest of two. When the whole subject is played, Haydn doubles his rest and starts all over with the first measures of the mel- ody, and before anybody in the audience has a chance of voicing a protest, the end has come, leaving the listener puzzled and amused. Perhaps the most charming work of the set is No. 3, "The Bird." Both the grace notes in the main subject of the first movement, and the trio of the scherzando, an unusually charming duet between first and second violin, are responsible for the nickname of the work.

The next quartet, Op. 42 (Hob. III:43) is a sort of for- eign body within the whole set of string quartets. The very terse construction of its four movements induced Pohl and Sandberger to classify this composition as one of Haydn's earlier works. Some details, however, such as the dramatic development of the first movement, the pianis- simo endings of the first and last movements, and the use of contrapuntal devices in the finale, prove Op. 42 to be the product of a later period. Additional evidence is pro- vided by the autograph in the West German Library, Mar- burg, which bears the date 1785. The work must certainly be considered a composition of Haydn's maturity which— for unknown reasons—was conceived in a particularly un- assuming manner.

In 1787, six new quartets (Hob. III:44–49) were pub- lished by Artaria in Vienna as Op. 50 and dedicated to King Friedrich Wilhelm II of Prussia. In these pieces the thematic elaboration employed in Op. 33 is continued. The four stringed instruments again are treated individually, but cooperate on a single task: to discuss each subject thoroughly so as to cast full light upon all its potentialities.

It is most significant that Haydn, who increasingly exploited the possibilities of the transformation of themes, often rejected the use of a contrasting subsidiary subject. He was eager to concentrate his compositions not only by using thematic elaboration, but also by letting a whole movement unfold from a single germ. The complete expression of his straightforward and undivided personality is to be found in movements that seem hewn from a single block. Thus, the finale of No. 1 shows a monothematic construction. The main subject stated in the first two measures is treated either as a whole or in halves all through the movement. In No. 2, the second section of the minuet (the name scherzo vanishes again in this set of quartets, though the character of Beethoven's scherzo occasionally is intimated) is a development of the first section, not a new idea, thus again emphasizing the idea of unity. Similar tendencies prevail in the first movement of No. 4, in F sharp minor, probably the most interesting of the entire set. Although the main subject is in the minor mode and the subsidiary subject in the major, this subsidiary subject obviously is derived from the first idea. The impassioned, subjective character of this movement, together with the fugue of the finale, seems to indicate that No. 4 originated during the early seventies, but a very important detail shows that the quartet can belong only to a later period: both the transition to the subsidiary subject and the subject itself display the spirit of Mozart. In the andante of this quartet, the main theme in the major mode is followed by a contrasting melody in the minor, and there is one variation each on the major and minor sections, followed by a second variation of the main theme which brings the movement to an end. Similar combinations of the variation form with that of the rondo were of the greatest importance in Haydn's later compositions. In No. 5, the slow movement, which has some elaborate solo passages for the violin, is known as "A Dream." In the third movement, both the minuet and its trio are governed by the same grace note motive, showing that the idea of unity seemed to Haydn more important than the traditional contrast between minuet and trio. In this rather serious and thoughtful series there is one quartet imbued with Haydn's particular sense of humor. It is No. 6, "The Frog," and its finale is filled with gay croaking sounds produced by playing the same notes alternately on two neighboring strings. Brahms has made a good use of this same effect in some of his chamber music.

Between the quartets Op. 50 and those of Op. 54, the arrangement of Haydn's *Seven Last Words* for string quartet is inserted in some editions as Op. 51 (Hob. III:50–56). This work is discussed on page 325.

In the years 1789–90, the quartets of Op. 54, Nos. 1–3, and Op. 55, Nos. 1–3 (Hob. III:57–62), were published. In 1790, Haydn composed six additional quartets that were published in the same or the following year and are known as Op. 64, Nos. 1–6 (Hob. III:63–68). The quartets of Op. 64 were dedicated to Johann Tost, and the same is probably true of the six earlier quartets.[3] The boldness and variety of invention in these works and their well-balanced musical form show Haydn at the summit of his quartet production.

A characteristic of these quartets is again the basing of a whole movement upon a single subject. The adagio in Op. 55, No. 1, grows out of one idea only; so do the finale of Op. 64, No. 2, and the first movement of Op. 64, No. 1, both in sonata form. In each of these two compositions the subsidiary subject is developed out of the first subject and the composer revealed his desire for unity by using in the recapitulation the main subject itself rather than its trans-

---

[3] There seems to be some doubt about the personality of this man. Pohl (II, 373) mentions a violinist of this name who was a member of the Esterházy orchestra from 1783 to 1789. In 1789 he went to Paris, where he carried out dubious transactions with some of Haydn's symphonies and string quartets. About the later fate of this man nothing is known. However, in 1790 a second Johann Tost, a wealthy cloth-merchant who was also a violinist, made his appearance in Haydn's biography (Pohl, II, 229). It is possible that the quartets of Op. 54 and 55 were destined for Prince Esterházy's violinist, the Op. 64 for the merchant, but the assumption seems more likely that there was only one Johann Tost active at first as violinist and subsequently as businessman. (Besides Pohl, loc. cit., see Larsen, op. cit., p. 154–55, and Hob. I:414.)

formation. Occasionally Haydn employed contrasting ideas but postponed their entrance as long as possible so that they became epilogues rather than subsidiary subjects (see the first movements of Op. 54, No. 1, and Op. 64, No. 1). Mozart's type of construction, in which the subsidiary idea is a countermelody of sweet and tender character, is not often found in these works (the finale of Op. 64, No. 4, provides one of the infrequent examples), and it is significant of the difference in character between the two masters that the older composer stressed unity, the younger contrast.

The "Tost" quartets are full of attractive little surprises. Haydn liked to introduce into his rondos and the developments of his sonata forms interesting fugato sections, as in the finales of Op. 55, No. 1, Op. 64, No. 2, and Op. 64, No. 5, and the second movement of Op. 55, No. 2. Harmony and modulation sometimes seem to foreshadow the romantic period. The delicately veiled episode of the second subject in the allegretto of Op. 54, No. 1, introduces tender modulations of a hazy, elusive character. With the help of hardly noticeable chromatic progressions and enharmonic changes Haydn modulates from G major over C, B flat, and E flat to D flat, and back to the initial key. We seem to be lifted by some magic in a fantastic flight through the air, eventually to be deposited at the spot from which we started. Similarly the harsh dissonances in the trio of the minuet of Op. 54, No. 2, contradict all sentimental conceptions of good old "Papa" Haydn. The same quartet has a rather striking adagio finale that in all likelihood was originally meant merely as the slow introduction to a presto. It assumed such proportions, however, that it developed into the main section of the movement while the short presto was reduced to a mere episode losing its significance through the re-entry of the adagio, which brings the movement to an end. The arrangement of the voices in this movement is also most unusual; the first violin carries the melody while the violoncello keeps crossing the middle parts, passing again and again into the treble register. The quartet in F minor, Op. 55, No. 2, is known as the "Razor" quartet. In this work the first two movements change places. It begins with a set of variations in slow time, alternately in minor and major, but the second movement is an allegro in sonata form of peculiar charm, with sudden half-tone progressions. A forte cadence in F minor is followed, after a grand pause, by a delicate piano passage beginning in G flat major; later a cadence in A flat is succeeded in the same way by a passage beginning in A major. Similar devices were used by Philipp Emanuel Bach, for instance, in the big "Heilig" published by Breitkopf and Härtel in 1779. Op. 64, No. 1, exhibits in the development section of its finale an excellent example of Haydn's strong sense of humor. The drumming main subject is used here for a little fugato, the constant note repetitions of which make an irresistibly droll impression. Op. 64, No. 2, in B minor, is filled with passionate energy. Although the exposition of the first movement has a subsidiary subject in the relative major, the recapitulation reintroduces it, surprisingly enough, in the tonic minor, and only the following simple, sweet *adagio ma non troppo* in B major brings a harmonious solution. The trio of the minuet, taking the first violin up to the highest positions, shows what great demands Haydn made at that time on the technical abilities of his players. It should not be assumed, however, that the master's reason for inserting this trio was to give the player of the first violin a chance to show off his technical ability. Haydn's motives were purely artistic, for after the ponderous heaviness of the minuet the silvery lightness of the high registers was needed to achieve a perfect balance. The finale brings yet another example of Haydn's sense of humor in the entertaining interplay between piano passages as the seeming bearers of timid and faltering questions and replies to them in the form of brusque, loudly declaimed unisons. Here again the technique of the comic opera is employed in a work of chamber music. The slow movement of Op. 64, No. 4, has in its parts for the second violin and viola an accompaniment that is surprisingly pianistic in its whole conception. Haydn, like other eighteenth-century composers, sometimes wrote pianoforte parts that showed the influence of stringed instruments, but he occasionally inverted this relationship.

The lovely first movement of Op. 64, No. 5, is responsible for the name, "The Lark," given to the quartet. From the earthbound accompaniment of the lower parts, the first violin soars up to heavenly heights. The finale of this quartet, with its unrelenting motion in sixteenths, forms a sort of *perpetuum mobile.* The trio of the minuet in Op. 64, No. 6, a counterpart of the same movement in Op. 55, No. 1, again presents technical difficulties that almost equal those of a violin concerto. The second violin carries the subject while the first violin accompanies like a tenuous chime, with notes ascending to more than four octaves above middle C (see Ex. 14):

String Quartet Op. 64 No. 6, Trio

*　*　*

In the years 1782–84, Breitkopf and Härtel's catalogues listed "VI Divertimenti da Giuseppe Haydn," three of which were scored for two oboes, two clarinets, two horns, and two bassoons, the other three for two oboes, two horns, three bassoons, and a serpent, an obsolete bass cornet in the form of a snake. These divertimenti (Hob. II:41–46), which are similar in character to Haydn's early *Feldparthien* (see page 252), probably were intended for the

wind band of Prince Esterházy.[4] Some of the slow movements have titles, like *La Vierge Marie*, reminiscent of
similar tendencies in the French suites of the seventeenth
and eighteenth centuries. The most important of these
partitas is the one in B flat major (Hob. II:46). In 1870,
Haydn's biographer Pohl showed a copy of it to his friend
Johannes Brahms, who immediately copied the second
movement in his notebook. Fascinated by the "Chorale St.
Antoni," the old Austrian pilgrims' song upon which this
movement was based, Brahms used it as the theme for his
variations on a theme by Joseph Haydn, Op. 56, which
he wrote during the summer of 1873. This partita[5] is in
four movements, all of which exhibit a close melodic relationship; in fact, it may be said that the first movement,
the minuet, and the finale are in a way variations of the
"Chorale St. Antoni," introduced in the second movement.
The old German variation suite of the seventeenth century,
in which the different dances of a suite are made up of
variations of a main dance, is here revived, and the cyclical
form so dear to the composers of the nineteenth century is
foreshadowed.

Like the partita in B flat major, the other pieces of this
set are in four movements. The simple construction of each
work, the use of the same key for all movements of the
short suites, the insertion of marches and little character
pieces, all show that the composer had no intention of
discouraging the members of the band by setting complicated music before them.

The "Toy" symphony or "Sinfonia Berchtolsgadensis"
(Hob. II:47), for seven toy instruments and strings, is
traditionally considered to be a work of Joseph Haydn,
though in recent years it has been assigned to various
other composers, among them Michael Haydn and Leopold
Mozart. It is a charming piece in three brief movements
displaying an amiable sense of fun and deep understanding
of the world of children.

[4] Their authenticity has, however, not been proved. *Grove's
Dictionary*, 5th ed., IV, 177, ascribes them to Pleyel.
[5] It was first edited by K. Geiringer (Leipzig, 1932). Hob.
II:41 was edited by K. Geiringer (Vienna, 1931).

Closely related to Haydn's divertimenti are also the five concertos for two lire organizzate (Hob. VIIh:1–5) composed in 1786.[6] This instrument was a sort of hurdy-gurdy and looked like a big guitar. A wooden wheel turned by a crank pressed on the strings from below and set them vibrating. Some of these strings were mere drones that could be connected or disconnected at will; two of them were meant for the performance of the melody and tuned in unison. These melody strings were shortened with the aid of wooden bridges or tangents, which in turn were operated by a system of keys. A little organ attachment was built into the instrument, and the keys, besides shortening the strings, admitted air to the tiny pipes sounding two octaves higher than the strings. The wheel had the double function of serving as a bow and of working the bellows if the player chose to include the little organ attachment.[7] It seems rather surprising that Haydn, who was not particularly interested in the concerto form, should have written so large a number of pieces for this strange instrument. It has been mentioned before that they were composed at the order of the King of Naples, who delighted in playing duets for lire organizzate with his teacher, the Austrian minister, Norbert Hadrava. To stimulate the august pupil's interest, Hadrava commissioned original compositions for the lira from Haydn, Gyrowetz, Pleyel, and Sterkel. A close examination of Haydn's works will show that they are not so much concertos as divertimenti in which the various partners, in the manner of chamber music, compete with each other. The technical possibilities of the clumsy lira were less than modest: as a rule the keys of C, F, and G had to be used, and its range scarcely reached two octaves. Haydn wrote these pieces as a sort of ensemble music for nine or ten instruments: two violins, two violas, violoncello (possibly reinforced by double bass),

[6] No. 3 was edited by K. Geiringer (Berlin, 1932), Nos. 1–4 by H. C. R. Landon (Vienna, 1959–60).

[7] See K. Geiringer, *Musical Instruments: Their History in Western Culture from the Stone Age to the Present* (New York, 1945), and H. R. Edwall, "Ferdinand IV and Haydn's Concertos for the Lira Organizzata," *Musical Quarterly* (April 1962).

two horns, and two lire. A very modest amount of prominence is accorded to the solo instruments. As their parts
resemble those of woodwinds, it is possible to replace them
in modern performances by oboe, flute, or even recorder.
The high-spirited, gay compositions, including several
dances and even a hunting scene (finale of No. 2), display
classic balance in the distribution of the thematic material.
Accordingly the composer was in a position to use two
movements of the fifth lira concerto for his symphony No.
89, written in 1787. The allegretto of the symphony No.
100 ("Military") also shows a certain relationship to that
of the third concerto.

The lira concertos pleased the King of Naples so much
that he also commissioned eight notturni for two lire organizzate, two clarinets, two horns, two violas, and bass
(Hob. II:25–32).[8] In order to make wider use of these
charming works the composer himself later changed their
instrumentation by replacing the lire with flute and oboe
or two flutes, the clarinets with violins. It is interesting that
in making these alterations Haydn did not modify a single
note in his scores.

The notturni are graceful pieces, but in them Haydn's
fantasy is somewhat restrained by the soft tone and technical limitations of the two principal instruments. It is characteristic of his fine feeling for orchestral coloration that he
divided the parts of the violas so as to balance the delicate
tone of the two lire better. For the most part, the works
display the traditional three movements and again are in
either C, F, or G major. A movement like the spirited fugue
in the last movement of No. 5 in C major is an exception.
Although meant for a small group of players only, they
frequently are imbued with the symphonic spirit.

Haydn's two most famous solo concertos were written
during the eighties. The authenticity of the violoncello
concerto in D major (Hob. VIIb:2) has been doubted; it

[8] Nos. 4 and 5 were edited by K. Geiringer (Vienna, 1931–
32); Nos. 2, 7, and 8 by E. F. Schmid (Karlsbad, 1932, and
Leipzig, 1936); No. 3 by A. Sandberger (Munich, 1936); No. 6
by E. Fendler (New York, 1946); No. 1 by H. C. R. Landon
(Vienna, 1961).

has been suggested that Anton Kraft, a cellist of the Esterházy orchestra and pupil of Haydn, was its author, though
the first edition, published by André Offenbach in Haydn's
lifetime, bore the inscription "Edition d'après le manuscrit
original de l'auteur," and Köchel, the great Mozart scholar,
testified to having seen this autograph. Fortunately it was
rediscovered in Vienna by the middle of this century, and
all doubts of Haydn's authorship thus were removed. In
this work, composed in 1783, the part for the solo instrument not only is brilliant, but also has been made the center of the composition: all the other instruments look to it
for leadership. The concerto is often performed with an
enlarged orchestral accompaniment that was provided by
François-Auguste Gevaert in 1890. The original version,
using only two oboes and two horns now is also available,[9]
and is certainly preferable because of its more intimate
character.

In 1784, another D major concerto, written for piano
and orchestra, was published. This work (Hob. XVIII:11)
not only has an attractive solo part, probably intended for
the new pianoforte instead of the harpsichord, but also has
a very effective accompaniment by the orchestra. The
middle movement grows out of the thematic material of
the first eight measures of the tutti; and a simple motive,
in which the same note is repeated six times, is expanded
into an important dialogue between solo instrument and
orchestra. The most interesting movement of the concerto
is the final *rondo all'ungarese*. It contains two episodes in
the minor, the impassioned strength of the second reminding us of nineteenth-century romantic music (see Ex. 15):

Piano Concerto in D Major, "Hungarian Rondo"
Allegro assai

Piano, R.H.

[9] Edited by K. Soldau (Leipzig, 1934).

Haydn's symphonies[10] use the same guiding principles of construction as his string quartets and also show the increasing influence of Mozart's compositions. Haydn renounced the contrapuntal constructions so important during the seventies and replaced them with the free, unconventional polyphony evolved from the principle of thematic elaboration, using motives taken from the main melodies to weave a rich thematic texture of accompanying voices. The finale of the symphony No. 73, "La Chasse"—the famous hunting movement making extensive use not only of horns and oboes, but also of trumpets and timpani—was written in 1780 as a prelude to the third act of Haydn's opera *La fedeltà premiata*. To make this piece available to a larger audience, in the following year the composer added three movements, one of which, an andante in G major, also is connected with a vocal work, as it appears in condensed form in the song "Gegenliebe,"[11] likewise written in 1781. The other two movements are independent pieces, however, and the opening allegro in particular displays in its harmonic language and structure a brilliance and technical mastery heralding the beginning of Haydn's maturity.

No. 74, composed at about the same time, is one of the earliest symphonic works to show the influence of Mozart. The opening movement (which is also distinguished by an exceptional development section) has a subsidiary subject in clear contrast to the first one; the main idea of the second movement has all the ingratiating qualities of Mozart's melodies.

No. 75, written not later than 1781, affords a delightful contrast between a melancholy set of variations on a song-like theme and an extremely gay minuet and finale. The

[10] Symphony No. 73 was edited by F. Wüllner (Leipzig, 1876); No. 76 without editor's name (Offenbach, 1895); No. 77 ditto (Leipzig, 1868); No. 78 ditto (Leipzig, 1873); No. 80 edited by A. Einstein (Vienna, 1937); No. 81 without editor's name (Offenbach, 1860); Nos. 82–87 by H. C. R. Landon, Collected Edition Series I:9 (Boston, 1950); Nos. 88–92, ditto, Series I:10 (Boston, 1951).

[11] Edited by Paul Mies, Collected Edition, Series XXIX, Vol. 1, p. 20.

work was performed by Haydn in England, and the composer noted in his diary that an English clergyman thought that he heard the prediction of his imminent death in the slow movement, and actually died shortly afterward.

The symphonies Nos. 76–78 were composed in 1782. No. 76 is perhaps the least distinguished of the set, but it contains a fine slow movement whose dark sections in the minor mode foreshadow trends in the romantic period. The middle section in the first movement of No. 77 has a kind of *stretto maestrale*, a short-range imitation of the first bar of the main subject in which all the string and woodwind instruments join (Ex. 16):

The symphonies Nos. 79–81 were written in or about 1784. Again the first work of the group is not equal in importance to the other two. From a formal point of view, however, the first movement of No. 79 deserves special attention, as it resumes the work of development even in the recapitulation. No. 80 in D minor starts with a passionate *allegro spirituoso*, and the following adagio also contains an episode imbued with strong emotion. Here the broad cantilena of flute and first violin accompanied by the Alberti bass played by the second violin once more testifies to the artistic friendship between Haydn and Mozart. Similarly No. 81, with an unusual and exciting pedal point at the beginning of the first movement, uses a subsidiary subject that appears like a cordial greeting to the newly won friend.

The symphonies Nos. 82–92 were composed between 1785 and 1788, largely for performances and publishers in Paris. In 1784 the board of directors of the Concerts de la Loge Olympique asked Haydn to compose six symphonies for them, which he did during the two following years. These works (Nos. 82–87) are usually referred to as the Paris symphonies.

No. 82, the so-called "First Paris" symphony, was, according to the testimonial of the autograph, written in 1786, one year after the Paris symphonies No. 2 and No. 6. Its name, "L'Ours," is derived from the last movement, the famous bear—or rather bagpipe—dance. In its transparent and richly colored setting, this finale is certainly one of Haydn's most attractive compositions for orchestra. And the first movement, in which the thematic development is so abundant that even the transition from the first to the second subject is imbued with it, and the charming allegretto, with a theme in the major mode separated from each of its two repetitions by a rather threatening passage in the minor, are worthy of this finale.

No. 83, the second of the Paris symphonies, got its name "La Poule" from the subsidiary subject of the first movement, in which the oboe peevishly repeats the same note while the first violin offers a piquant melody adorned with many grace notes. On the whole this movement in

G minor shows a surprisingly serious character; the dramatic quality of the following andante is equally unusual. A stubborn minuet and a charming finale in the style of a siciliano contribute a peculiar charm to this work.

No. 84, the third of the Paris symphonies, has a first movement that almost completely grows out of the main idea. Haydn postpones the entrance of the contrasting subject so long that it assumes the role of an epilogue instead of a subsidiary subject. The second movement, an andante with variations, separates the theme in the major from its first variation by a rather dramatic passage in the minor. The finale is gay and carefree; its sudden changes from the pianissimo of a few instruments to the forte of the whole orchestra anticipate the famous "surprise" of symphony No. 94.

No. 85, "La Reine," was perhaps a favorite of Marie Antoinette. The slow movement of the symphony provides a set of variations on the French romance "La gentille et jeune Lisette," which are full of coloristic effects while the melody and harmony of the theme undergo but little change. Of equal charm is the following minuet, in which the trio presents a typical Austrian *Ländler*. Like most of Haydn's finales from this period the concluding presto grows out of a single germ-subject.

The formal construction becomes more and more artistic, but Haydn does not fail to counterbalance it occasionally with movements of a looser structure. The slow movement of No. 86, the fifth of the Paris symphonies, shows an affinity with both the sonata and the rondo forms, but without adopting either. Haydn called this interesting and surprisingly serious movement a capriccio. The *allegro spiritoso* of the first movement and the final *allegro con spirito* certainly deserve the designation "spirited," as they are full of life and wit. They contribute to make this work one of the greatest of the Paris symphonies.

It is characteristic of the lighter and more charming character of No. 87, the sixth of the series, that among its most valuable sections is the minuet, especially the lovely oboe solo of its trio. The slow movement also is delightfully orchestrated, but the work as a whole belongs among the less significant of Haydn's mature symphonies.

The symphonies Nos. 88 and 89 probably were composed in 1787. Haydn gave them to Johann Tost, who sold them to the publisher Sieber in Paris. No. 88, in G major, is one of the finest works of this period; all four of its movements are of equal importance. The main subject of the first movement is accompanied by a counterpoint at its first forte entrance, and this counterpoint also appears in the transition to the second subject. The subsidiary subject is so completely embedded in material taken from the main subject that the listener hardly notices the break in the homogeneous texture of the movement. The solemn largo introduces a theme with variations, and its beautiful tune has since been used for the hymn "Praise God from Whom All Blessings Flow." A characteristic of Haydn's newly acquired unconventional treatment of instruments is the use of horns and timpani in the minuet. In the composer's early works, such instruments were employed as the typical reinforcements of the tutti; now, however, he presents them in mysterious piano and pianissimo passages as an accompaniment of the main subject. The *allegro con spirito* of the last movement is a rondo of unusual charm, good humor, and brilliance.

In No. 89, Haydn used for the second and fourth movements material from the fifth concerto for lire organizzate. The newly composed first and third movements are treated in a somewhat perfunctory manner. Apparently the composer for some reason had to provide a symphony quickly and did so without taking much interest in the task.

In 1788–89, Haydn wrote three symphonies (Nos. 90–92) which probably had been commissioned by the Comte d'Ogny, a French nobleman with whom he had been in contact for some time.[12]

No. 90 is again worthy of Haydn's maturity. Its andante uses variations on a theme in the major and one in the minor mode, a form that became increasingly interesting to Haydn at that time. In the last movement the fortissimo

[12] The same works were sold the following year to Prince Öttingen-Wallerstein.

ending in C major is remarkable, for it is followed, after a grand pause, by a timid pianissimo of the strings and a single bassoon in D flat major. (Haydn used a similar device in the second movement of his "Razor" quartet.)

Sudden upward progressions are also to be found in the first movement of No. 91, with an unusual chromatic main subject. Here Haydn rises in an almost modern way from D flat major over E flat minor to F minor. The second movement of this symphony has an andante with variations, with a contrasting minor passage between the first and second variations (cf. symphony No. 84). Near the end, the finale introduces a stretto of the main subject in the second violins and basses accompanied in eighth notes by the first violin. Haydn seems to have thought very highly of this symphony, for in his letters from London to Frau von Genzinger he again and again asked his friend to send him the score from Vienna.

The "Oxford" symphony, No. 92, will be discussed in the next chapter, together with the London symphonies, for it is related to them in both style and content.

*   *   *

Hardly any other of Haydn's works has so interesting a history as *The Seven Last Words of Our Saviour on the Cross*. In 1785, he received the invitation to write an instrumental composition based on *The Seven Last Words*, to be performed in Cádiz during Lent. He accordingly wrote, as he explained in a letter dated April 8, 1787, to the English publisher William Forster, a "work consisting merely of instrumental music, divided into seven sonatas, each lasting from seven to eight minutes, as well as an introduction and ultimately a *terremoto* or earthquake. These sonatas," he added, "are so conceived as to fit the words Christ Our Saviour uttered on the cross. . . . The whole work requires a little over an hour, but after each sonata there is a pause to ponder the ensuing text in advance." Haydn's orchestra consisted of two flutes, two oboes, two bassoons, four horns, two trumpets, two timpani, and strings. In this version the parts were published in 1787 by Artaria, Vienna. In the same year an arrangement of the work appeared for string quartet. This was made by the composer, who also transcribed *The Seven Last Words* for piano.

Haydn himself said of this work: "It was no easy matter to compose seven adagios lasting ten minutes each and following one after the other without fatiguing the listener." The warm reception given everywhere to *The Seven Last Words* proved that he had succeeded completely in this task. This is all the more admirable as throughout the work Haydn employs a homophonic idiom and makes hardly any use of thematic elaboration. He wished to keep his composition readily understandable in order to be sure of the effect "from the heart to the heart" which he was most eager to achieve. Just this economy of style enabled Haydn to rouse the listener's emotions. A *maestoso ed adagio* in a single movement serves as an introduction. With its baroque dotted rhythms, frequent changes between forte and piano, and repeated sforzandi, this brief piece in D minor unfolds a dramatic, deeply moving picture of the crucifixion. Haydn is not satisfied, however, merely to describe suffering and torment. In the middle section and in the coda, ending pianissimo, Jesus' divine mercy and love are expressed. The second "sonata," based on the words "Verily I say unto thee, today shalt thou be with me in paradise," is developed entirely out of a single idea. It appears timidly at first in the key of C minor, as if the poor malefactor did not dare to believe in his own good fortune. Gradually, however, the knowledge of God's mercy enters the heart of the tormented man; the main idea is now transposed to E flat major as a noble cantilena full of sweet happiness. In the development section the shadows of death seem to obscure the mind of the dying man, but the return of the cantilena, this time in C major, again conjures up all the wonders of paradise. The art of developing, as it were, out of a single germ cell ideas of wholly different emotional substance shows that this work is a product of Haydn's maturity. The third "sonata" is based on the words "Woman, behold thy son!" and "Behold thy mother!" Jesus brings his beloved disciple and his mother together. Accordingly, the beginning of the piece is imbued with beauty and love, but at the same time the drama of Golgotha is not forgotten, and the subsidiary theme that grows out of the main idea leads us to its anguish and suffering. The original motive, played here by the basses, now seems like a nightmare. It is of interest that No. 5, "I thirst," is based on the same motive as No. 3. Here Haydn resumed the idea originally used to describe the love of a mother for her son. In his agony the Saviour becomes a child again, asking his mother for help. This can also explain the idyllic character of No. 5. Later, however, when vinegar mingled with gall is given to Jesus, the distress of extreme misery breaks through with elemental force.

In his *Seven Last Words*, Haydn successfully avoids the danger of monotony presented by the text. From the stirring introduction to the forceful earthquake, new musical pictures are presented again and again, illustrating the drama not only of the Passion but also of the miracle of salvation that grows out of the sacrifice on the cross.

Another version of *The Seven Last Words* made by Haydn in the 1790s will be discussed in the next chapter.

* * *

For the classicists the song did not have the importance that was attributed to it in the romantic period. To Haydn, Mozart, and even Beethoven it was a form of little consequence, too unimportant to be given much attention. It is well known that in spite of this attitude a few real masterworks were created; but the courage of Schubert, who had a single song ("The Erlking") printed as his Op. 1, was inconceivable in the eighteenth century. Only in his maturity did Haydn become interested in the song. His first collection of twelve lieder was published in 1781, a second set in 1784, both through Artaria and Company in Vienna.[13] These lieder clearly show their derivation from the rhythmically and harmonically simple songs of the

[13] Haydn's songs were edited by M. Friedländer in the Collected Edition, Series XX, Vol. 1 (Leipzig, 1932). They were re-edited in revised form by P. Mics in Series XXIX, Vol. 1, of the Collected Edition (Munich, 1960).

German Singspiel (a type of opera using simple melodies of folk-song character and spoken dialogue). Italian influences may be found in the graceful melodic lines; the mastery of instrumental composition is revealed in important preludes, interludes, and postludes. In the selection of texts, Haydn was helped by his friend Hofrat Greiner. Nevertheless, or perhaps because of such help, their poetical value sometimes is doubtful.

In a letter to Artaria dated July 20, 1781, Haydn pointed out that three of his songs had previously been set to music by the Viennese Kapellmeister, Leopold Hoffmann, and added: "Just because this braggart thinks himself on an equal with Mount Parnassus and at every opportunity tries to belittle me in the eyes of certain circles of society, I have composed these same three songs to show these circles the difference—*sed hoc inter nos.*" In the same letter he says: "I particularly request you not to allow anyone to copy or sing these songs at present or spoil them in any way whatever, for when they are finished I intend to sing them myself to critical audiences. A composer must maintain his rights by his presence to ensure the proper execution of his works. They are indeed merely songs but not 'street songs' like those of Hoffmann, devoid of ideas, of expression, and, above all, of melody."

The twenty-four songs are printed on two staves only. A separate line for the voice is not necessary, as its melody is identical with that of the top line of the piano part. Haydn frequently used the form of the strophic song (stanza form). The influence of music for the stage is shown in the employment of chromatic progressions, little coloratura phrases, and melodies of a more cantabile character. In the serious or sentimental songs Haydn approached the character of the aria. "Die Verlassene" (The Deserted Woman), for instance, is filled with the pathos of dramatic grief. If the *opera seria* is godmother here, the charmingly humorous "Lob der Faulheit" (Praise of Laziness) certainly owes much to the *opera buffa.*

During the eighties, Haydn wrote a sizable number of arias to be inserted, according to the custom of the period, into the works of other composers. As the majority of these arias originated at a time when the onerous duties as opera director prevented him from writing full-size dramatic works regularly, these short pieces composed during Haydn's maturity are of great interest to the Haydn student.[14] Gay and light is the bass aria "Dice benissimo," written in 1780 for Salieri's *Scuola de' gelosi*, in which men are warned against the fetters of matrimony. Its counterpart is formed by the graceful soprano aria of 1785(?), "Dica pure," destined for Anfossi's *Il geloso in cimento*, in which women's qualities are extolled and men's evil nature condemned. Somewhat similar are the soprano aria of Giannina, "La moglie quando e buona," composed in 1790 for Cimarosa's *Giannina e Bernardone*, in which the perils of jealousy are pointed out, and the soprano aria of Donna Stella, "D'una sposa meschinella," composed in 1777 for Paisiello's *La frascatana*. This latter starts with a tender, fervent adagio featuring an oboe solo and a pizzicato accompaniment by the basses and rises to a brilliantly virtuoso presto section. A delightfully graceful and whimsical soprano aria, "Son pietosa, son bonina," was provided by Haydn for the pasticcio *La Circe, ossia l'isola incantata*, which he manufactured in 1789, also using material from two other operas (*Ipocondriaco* by Naumann and *La Circe*, whose composer has not yet been ascertained). The same pasticcio contains a dramatic scene for Pedrillo (tenor), an extended *accompagnato* recitative in which Haydn displays a number of amusing tone-paintings.

Several arias are intended for the composer's lady friend, the mezzo-soprano Luigia Polzelli. These pieces ("Signor, voi sapete," for Anfossi's *Il matrimonio per inganno*, 1785; "Chi vive amante," for Bianchi's *Allessandro nell'Indie*, 1787; "Il meglio mio carattere," for Cimarosa's *L'impresario in angustie*, 1790; etc.) have a certain affinity in character. Andante seems to be the favorite tempo indica-

[14] The aria for soprano and orchestra "Chi vive amante" was edited by A. Orel (Leipzig, 1937); fourteen additional arias for soprano and orchestra and the cantata *Miseri noi* were edited by H. C. R. Landon (Vienna, 1959–61); the scena of Pedrillo for tenor and orchestra by D. Bartha and L. Somfai as a supplement to their work *"Haydn als Opernkapellmeister"* (Budapest, 1960).

tion. The arias use simple, tender melodies; they display a gentle, graceful, and somewhat impish nature and avoid excessive technical difficulties. Haydn, while deeply in love with the attractive singer, certainly had no illusions about her technical abilities.

A serious tenor aria, "Ah tu non senti amico," was contributed by Haydn in 1786 to Traetta's *Ifigenia in Tauride*. With its dramatic *accompagnato* recitative, which leads to an F minor aria full of pathos, it fits admirably into the grand, tragic opera of the time. Deeply stirring in its outbursts of passionate grief is the soprano aria of Beatrice, "Infelice sventurata," written in 1789 for Cimarosa's *I due supposti conti*.

Similar to the insertion arias, though conceived on a larger scale, are the independent scenes Haydn composed for the concert hall. Only the voice part is left of the solo cantata *Deutschlands Klage auf den Tod Friedrich des Grossen*, for voice and baryton, which Haydn wrote around 1786 for the baryton-player Karl Franz, a former member of the Esterházy orchestra. Another solo cantata, *Ah cuome il cor mi palpita nel seno*, published 1782–83, is preserved, however. It begins with a recitative intoned by horn and flute that expresses a longing for a beloved person who has died, and its melody is used again in the slow part of the succeeding aria, thus giving greater unity to the composition. Related in character is the solo cantata *Miseri noi, misera patria*, for soprano and orchestra, which may have originated around 1790, and apparently was taken by Haydn to England. (At present it is preserved in the Library of Congress in Washington, D. C.) This is a heroic work with a brilliant and rather difficult solo part consisting of an extensive orchestral recitative and an aria abounding in virtuoso coloratura.

Haydn was particularly successful with the Italian cantata *Arianna a Naxos*, for mezzo-soprano with piano accompaniment, which he composed in 1789. The aria, in which Haydn challenges comparison with no less a composer than Claudio Monteverdi, was a favorite of the master. He called it his "dear Arianna" and accompanied it personally at a most successful London performance (one of the two recitals in which he appeared as pianist in the English capital). Although the work has only a piano accompaniment, this part seems like the reduction of an orchestral score, and the various instrumentations that have been made of the cantata certainly are defensible. The relation to the opera is also quite obvious here. As in a dramatic scena of Gluck, not the aria but the recitative forms the main part of the piece, and this recitative not only precedes, but also interrupts, the aria. The music is completely dependent on the dramatic spirit of the text. *Arianna a Naxos* is enriched by many striking passages, such as the interlude before the denouement, with its chromatic progressions describing Ariadne's climbing up the rock and at the same time her utter despair.

* * *

Only three complete works for the stage by Haydn had their premieres during his fourth period. The dramma giocoso *La fedeltà premiata* (Faithfulness Rewarded) was first performed in February 1781, after the opera house at Esterháza, destroyed by fire in 1779, had been rebuilt. It is interesting that Haydn in this opera reversed the traditional distribution of serious and comical characters. Instead of highborn persons, a pair of shepherds are treated as *parti serie*, whereas the antics of a count are meant to amuse the audience. Haydn's music was written to a weak and confusing libretto, and it is therefore not surprising that one of the best numbers of the score is a purely instrumental piece, the above-mentioned overture to the third act, later used by Haydn as the finale for his symphony No. 73, "La Chasse." Some of the vocal pieces of this opera were adapted by Haydn's pupil Fritz von Weber, the stepbrother of Carl Maria von Weber. In 1789, Fritz performed a German pasticcio, *Der Freibrief von Josef Haydn*, at Meiningen and used the music of four numbers from *La fedeltà premiata*. Music by Mozart was adapted for most of the remaining pieces, and Carl Maria von Weber contributed an aria and a duet. The fact that Haydn apparently did not object to this arrangement seems to prove that he did not feel too much concern for the original work.

Haydn's next opera, the dramma eroicomico *Orlando paladino*, was based on a libretto by Nunziato Porta, who was in the service of Prince Esterházy. It was first performed in 1782 and deals with a subject repeatedly treated before. Bojardo wrote his *Orlando inamorato* in 1495; Ariosto his *Orlando furioso* from 1516 to 1532. Handel, who composed an *Orlando* in 1733, considered the subject as completely serious. However, Lope de Vega already had written various comedies on this topic, and Guglielmi's *Le pazzie d'Orlando* of 1771 is partly humorous.[15] Haydn too conceived his work as an opera in the mixed genre. But, unlike *La fedeltà premiata*, this last of the partly serious and partly comical operas is one of the composer's great masterpieces. At Esterháza it was performed thirty times during the seasons of 1782–84. During the composer's lifetime, thirty-three opera houses in Germany and Austria—among them those at Prague, Budapest, Frankfort, Cologne, Nuremberg, Berlin, Bremen, Leipzig, Munich, Königsberg, Hamburg, Breslau, and Dresden—performed it, no other stage work by Haydn being so frequently produced.[16] *Orlando paladino* contains striking ensemble numbers, finales full of dramatic fire. Above all, the treatment of the individual characters and the emphasis on comical elements were responsible for the opera's success. At first glance it appears that six serious characters in the cast are faced by merely two comical ones. However, parodistic features may be noticed even in the heroic numbers. The exaggerated outbursts of savagery from Rodomonte, King of the Barbarians, whom H. Wirth rightly describes as a "saber-rattling bumpkin squire," the crazy passion of Orlando, who attempts to impose his love on a completely unresponsive girl, the pitiful weakness of

[15] Cf. Helmut Wirth, in Joseph Haydn, *Orfeo ed Euridice*, analytical notes to the recording of the Haydn Society, p. 38. (Boston, 1951).

[16] A critical revision of the score of *Orlando paladino*, to be published in the Collected Edition of Haydn's works, and an edition for performance purposes are being prepared by the author of this book.

the flute-playing swain Medoro, and the magic tricks of the
sorceress Alcina—all these portrayals are made, as it were,
with tongue in cheek and at times approach real farce.
Funniest of all is the character of Orlando's servant, Pasquale, a boastful swaggerer rivaling his seventeenth-cen-
tury brother, Cervantes' Sancho Panza. The patter song
listing his travels to all parts of the world (reminding us
slightly of the "catalogue aria" in *Don Giovanni*, written
five years later), the charming aria demonstrating the performance practice and musical ornaments of the period,
and the cavatina in which Pasquale, on horseback and
heralded by trumpets and horns, boasts of his feats of
valor, rank among the best numbers that the comic opera
of the eighteenth century produced.

In 1784 the dramma eroico *Armida*, based on Tasso's
Gerusalemme liberata was performed at Esterháza. This
work represents the beginning of a new phase in Haydn's
output for the stage. Between 1769 and 1782, he had
written no less than seven mixed operas, the last being
in many respects the most significant. He felt that he had
exhausted the potentialities of this genre, and he turned
accordingly to *opera seria*, which he had cultivated only
in an early work and one more recent composition in which
he had labored under specific restrictions. *Armida* displays a completely homogeneous character renouncing
all contrasting elements, and thus conforms to the attitude of the mature Haydn, who was increasingly eager
to unify his instrumental music. In its dignity and un-
relieved seriousness it appears like a secular counterpart
to *The Seven Last Words*, written in the following year.
Armida is an imposing work full of dramatic power, but
it lacks some of the greatest assets of Haydn's art: charm,
naturalness, simplicity, and humor. The libretto is based
on a subject familiar to students of Gluck's works, and in
the music too Haydn adopts an important tenet of the
older composer. Gluck said of his overture to *Alceste*: "My
idea was that the overture ought to indicate the subject
and prepare the spectators for the character of the piece
they are about to see." The same might have been said
of the prelude to Haydn's *Armida*. Whereas in the older

Italian operas the overture was independent of the work to follow, in this case Haydn has produced a sort of tone poem covering the whole plot of Rinaldo's sinful passion for the lovely sorceress Armida, and his eventual return to duty. In its first four measures, the opening theme of the overture[17] depicts Rinaldo's carefree life of knighthood and in its second half his youthful longing for love. The energetic second subject portrays the hero's attachment to his military duties, but the development of the movement introduces a serious conflict. Abruptly a yearning allegretto is heard, and this corresponds to that part of the opera in Act III in which the hero arrives at Armida's paradise. At last Rinaldo breaks away from the arms of the sorceress. The return of the first part of the prelude then reveals the victory of duty over love, and the overture closes with the Rinaldo theme, but without the love motive of its second half. This interesting prelude resembles in its form Mozart's overture to *Die Entführung aus dem Serail*, performed two years before Haydn's *Armida*.

In the opera itself, Haydn unfortunately does not follow Gluck's method to the same extent. The old *recitativo secco* of the Italian opera takes up whole scenes, but the number of ensemble pieces is very small (one duet in the first act, one trio in the second, and a sextet at the end of the opera). The lovely finales of the earlier operas are completely absent. The best numbers of the score are the big solo scenes, such as the aria describing Rinaldo's attempts to escape from the bondage of Armida. The accompanied recitative, in which the orchestra follows each fluctuation of Rinaldo's expression, the aria growing organically out of this recitative, and the final presto bringing the tragic episode to its climax—all these display such strong dramatic vigor that they counterbalance the formal coloratura arias in other parts of the score. Of almost equal importance is the big monologue of despair by the deserted Armida; and particularly attractive, in spite of the use of conventional means of expression, is a scene in the third act in which Armida displays her witchcraft.

[17] The overture was edited by Hans Gál (London, 1939).

With *Armida*, Haydn's operatic output reached a crisis. Apparently he felt unable to give of his best in a purely serious work; yet the mixed genre no longer interested him. Thus he may not have regretted too much that his arduous duties as opera director made it impossible for him to write more works for the stage at Esterháza.

* * *

During his fourth period of composition, Haydn wrote only a single Mass, the *Missa Celensis* (Mass of Mariazell, in Styria) in C major, composed in 1782.[18] The inscription on the autograph, "Fatta per il Signor Liebe de Kreutzner," gives the name of the person who commissioned the work. C. F. Pohl[19] assumes that Herr Liebe meant the Mass to be played in the famous pilgrims' church of Mariazell in thanksgiving for his elevation to nobility. The *Missa Celensis* shows a decrease in the number of solo arias; on the other hand, Haydn begins to employ the quartet of solo voices that was to become extremely important in the Masses of his last period. The quartet offers the same possibilities for drama and color as do the voices in separate solos, but without their excessive display of virtuosity.

In this work, both elements of a purely musical style and a style inspired by the content of the text are to be found. The Kyrie is given the shape of an instrumental movement in sonata-allegro form, and the Gratias, an aria for soprano, includes some real coloratura. The Resurrexit uses the superficial technique of the earlier *missae breves*, bringing simultaneously in each of its voices a different section of the text, so that while the soprano sings "et resurrexit," the alto has the words "et in spiritum sanctum," the tenor "et iterum venturus," and the bass "qui cum patre." The Benedictus uses an aria originally written for the comic opera *Il mondo della luna*; yet the poignant

[18] The work was edited by H. C. R. Landon, K. H. Füssl, and C. Landon in the Collected Edition, Series XXIII, Vol. 2 (Munich, 1958).

[19] *Joseph Haydn*, II, p. 197.

piece, with its powerful baroque beginning and the effective changes between chorus and solo quartet, by no means disgraces the score. Many passages in this Mass show a deep understanding of the true meaning of the text. An excellent example is provided by the aria for tenor, "Et incarnatus est." Beginning in A minor, it modulates to C major at the words "homo factus est" and reaches the melancholy C minor when the catastrophe of the Crucifixus approaches. This Crucifixus, sung by the chorus and gradually rising from the low bass register, is most impressive.

Thus the style of the *Missa Celensis* is far from homogeneous. As in the opera, Haydn had reached a crisis in this field. He may not have resented it when, in 1783, the Emperor Joseph II passed a decree that practically banned the more complicated forms of instrumental music from the church. Haydn accordingly stopped composing Masses, and when he resumed fourteen years later, after most of the confining regulations had been revoked by the emperor's successors, his style had changed greatly.

CHAPTER 16

CONSUMMATE MASTERY

The Fifth Period: 1791–1803

Haydn reached the summit of his artistic achievements in his fifth period of composition. As Kapellmeister for Prince Esterházy he had done outstanding work and attracted the attention of the whole musical world, but after thirty years of life in a remote castle, toiling mostly with the same artists and for the same narrowly restricted audience, he found that Esterháza was becoming less and less a challenge to his genius. Some of his very best works of the eighties, such as the Paris symphonies and *The Seven Last Words*, were not written for Haydn's prince. It is therefore not surprising that the composer accepted the invitation to go to London without a moment's hesitation.

The trip provided a complete change of atmosphere: a new landscape, new people with a new culture, a strange language, and the experience of living in the largest city in the world. Of still greater importance was the change in social standing, combined with a change in working conditions. The esteem accorded to Haydn at Esterháza never allowed him to forget that he was living there as a servant, dependent on every whim of his employer. In England he was free to do what he liked, free to go where he pleased, and responsible to no one but himself. He felt like a man who had escaped from a golden cage. Furthermore Haydn was now in a position to conduct an excellently trained large orchestra and his compositions were to be played to a most exacting and fastidious audience of a size he had seldom encountered.

The effect of these favorable conditions on Haydn's creative output was amazing. Even though he was nearly sixty years old, he started to write compositions surpassing in both accomplishment and daring enterprise anything he previously had attempted. The beautiful balance of the classical style was noticeable in these works, their quality surpassing even that of his best achievements in the eighties. Practically every work of this latest period was a masterpiece, belonging among those compositions for which Haydn still is admired.

Even after Haydn had returned from London to settle down in Vienna, the influence of his English journeys remained alive. He composed more slowly than in any of the earlier periods, often relying on preliminary sketches, and the quality of his creative products was permanently on the highest possible level.

The most remarkable feature of these compositions written in the nineties is that they occasionally present a somewhat problematical and experimental character. They show a definite tendency toward trying out new devices, even at the sacrifice of the poise of former years. Fundamentally, Haydn remained a classical composer, but again and again episodes are to be found in his music in which expressiveness and passionate feeling break through classical composure. Under the influence of the new experience of freedom, Haydn's musical style lost some of its former restraint. He seemed to revive characteristic features of his storm-and-stress period. But we shall be nearer the truth if we consider the little irregularities in his later music to be the first indications of a movement that was shortly to exercise a profound influence over the whole artistic world: romanticism.

It is significant that at the age of sixty-three Haydn, in his love for experiments, abandoned the symphony, which had brought him such overwhelming successes, in order to devote his powers to vocal composition. And it is of symbolic importance that his first great achievement of this sort, *The Creation*, begins with a piece that in its whole conception unmistakably heralds the great romantic revolution of the future.

❋ ❋ ❋

Only three sonatas for the pianoforte (Hob. XVI:50–52) were written during Haydn's fifth period. All three were composed in 1794–95 for the pianist Theresa Jansen, who married the engraver Gaetano Bartolozzi in May 1795 (Haydn being one of the witnesses at the wedding). According to Strunk,[1] the sonata in E flat major (No. 52) is the first of the set, No. 51 in D major the second, and No. 50 in C major the third, the last composition written by Haydn for the piano alone. While No. 49, the sonata composed for Marianne von Genzinger, displays the full maturity of the classical style, these last works aim to employ a more personal and expressive musical language. No. 52 uses in its first movement all the devices of Philipp Emanuel Bach's style. At the same time the second movement, an adagio in the unexpected key of E major, introduces ornaments that may almost be compared to those of Chopin. The relationship between Haydn's third and fifth periods of composition here is emphasized once more. The loose construction in the first movement of No. 51 and its charming second subject presage Schubert; the powerful energy and mysterious character disclosed in the first movement of No. 50 occasionally foreshadow Beethoven (Ex. 17):

Piano Sonata No. 50

Among the smaller compositions for piano, the variations in F minor (Hob. XVII:6), composed in 1793 and published in 1799, are of special importance. They belong to the type of variations with two themes in which Haydn proved particularly successful. The main theme is in the style of a funeral march and is followed by a trio in the major mode. Both are varied twice, and a most imaginative coda ends the composition. The harmonic and coloristic

[1] Oliver Strunk, "Notes on a Haydn Autograph," *Musical Quarterly* (1934).

idiom of this important work anticipates certain aspects of the romantic style. Landon[2] may be justified in assuming that the work originated under the impact of Marianne von Genzinger's sudden death.

Haydn's compositions for musical clocks are related to his smaller works for the piano. Pater Primitivus Niemecz, Prince Esterházy's librarian, was an expert in constructing tiny organs equipped with flute pipes and played mechanically. So great was his reputation that the clocks provided with his organs were exported even to England. We know he constructed a clock for Prince Liechtenstein in 1792 and another the following year for Prince Esterházy; he probably made a third clock, which originated around 1789.[3] All three instruments have a light, gay, very clear tone; their repertoire consists mainly of music by Niemecz' friend and teacher, Joseph Haydn. E. F. Schmid, who edited these pieces for the first time,[4] has compiled thirty-two compositions, partly from autographs of Haydn and old manuscripts, partly from notes written down while the tunes were played by the instruments. He adapted them for the piano by making slight alterations and thus presented some short and unpretentious though very attractive pieces. The sixteen numbers of the clock of 1789 (Hob. XIX:1–16) contain one piece with a charming middle part in F minor, all'ungarese (No. 2), a Russian dance (No. 4), and a fuga (No. 16), the pseudo-erudition of which sounds particularly amusing on the toylike instrument. The Russian dance is based on a composition by the violinist Giornovichi; this same piece later was used by Beethoven as a theme for his twelve variations in A major. Owing to the character of its accompaniment, the piece was nicknamed "The Bagpipe" by the clock's original owners. Similarly, No. 8 was named "The Call of the Quail," No. 6 "Gossip at the Coffee Table." The minuet No. 9 was used in slightly changed form for the minuet in Haydn's string quartet Op. 54, No. 2.

[2] Op. cit., p. 559.
[3] Cf. Die Musikforschung, Vol. 13 (1960), p. 63.
[4] Hanover, 1931. Cf. also E. F. Schmid, "Joseph Haydn und die Flötenuhr" in Zeitschrift f. Musikwissenschaft, XIV, No. 4.

The 1792 clock, with its sweet, weak tone, plays twelve pieces, one each hour. Twelve numbers also form the repertoire of the 1793 clock, which Haydn gave to Prince Esterházy before leaving on his second trip to England. Of the twenty-four numbers performed by the two instruments, ten (Hob. XIX:7–16) also appear on the 1789 clock. The remaining fourteen numbers belong partly to the eighties, partly to the nineties. No. 20 shows a certain relationship to the trio of the minuet from symphony No. 85, "La Reine." No. 25, a march in D major, is also in the repertoire of a musical clock constructed in the beginning of the nineteenth century. This instrument plays it together with a grenadier march by Beethoven, a fact responsible for the erroneous attribution of the D major march to the younger composer. No. 28 is a simplified version of the finale of the string quartet Op. 71, No. 2 (composed in 1793). No. 29 is a minuet that was used the following year in symphony No. 101 ("The Clock"), and No. 30 is a sort of piano arrangement of the *perpetuum mobile* from the quartet Op. 64, No. 5 (composed in 1790). Two pieces (Nos. 31 and 32) are preserved in Haydn's original manuscript, but none of the clocks known so far plays them. No. 32 is a sketch for the finale of symphony No. 99 of 1793. All together, these tiny pieces, in spite of their unassuming garb, are not entirely lacking in importance. They point to Beethoven's bagatelles, Schubert's *moments musicaux*, and all those short pianoforte pieces that were instrumental in building up nineteenth-century keyboard music.

❋   ❋   ❋

Haydn's violin sonatas are not really duets for a bowed and a keyboard instrument, as are the contemporary sonatas of Mozart; they are written as pieces for piano solo accompanied by an optional violin part. The string instrument moves in unison or in thirds with the upper part of the piano score; it accompanies or performs little imitations, but even when short melodic fragments are entrusted to it, they may be omitted without really endangering the effect of the composition. No true cooperation between the two instruments is attempted, as the violin part is always considered *ad libitum*, and it seems quite possible that no one of the so-called violin sonatas originally was conceived for this combination.[5] Haydn may not even have taken part in the transcription. In the well-known collection of eight violin sonatas published by Peters, Nos. 2–4 are ordinary piano sonatas (Nos. 24–26), to which Burney had added a violin part.[6] Likewise, No. 5 is a transcription of the piano sonata No. 43, No. 6 an arrangement of the piano sonata No. 15, which in turn is based on the divertimento in C major for strings, flute, and oboe (Hob. II:11). The original was more extensive than the arrangement, and in an apparent reflection of the ideas Haydn eventually developed of matrimony, the latter version eliminates the andante "Mann und Weib," which was supposed to describe the harmonious cooperation of husband and wife. The violin sonatas Nos. 7 and 8 are arrangements of the string quartets Op. 77, Nos. 1 and 2, eliminating in each case the minuet and trio of the original composition. The only violin sonata independent of piano sonatas and string quartets therefore seems to be No. 1 of the Peters edition, an unpretentious piece in two movements. And even with this work the possibility cannot be excluded that it was originally conceived as a trio for piano, violin, and cello (Hob. XV:32). In spite of attractive episodes to be found in almost any of the eight compositions, this type of violin sonata, in which the bowed instrument always serves and accompanies the keyboard instrument, is of only historical interest today. As long as only weak and fragile pianos were built, with tonal volumes hardly equaling those of the violins, such an arrangement was well designed, but with the arrival of heavier and stronger pianofortes, violin sonatas were developed that gave full equality to the two instruments. It is noteworthy that Mozart's later sonatas for violin and piano already displayed such a progressive attitude.

*   *   *

[5] See Hoboken, op. cit., p. 727 and 753.

[6] The scholar manufactured violin parts to no less than eighteen of Haydn's piano sonatas (Nos. 20–32, 35–39).

During the 1790s, the piano trio changed from a type of composition treated in an offhand manner to a carefully elaborated form. Haydn composed no less than nineteen trios (Hob. XV:14–32) within six years. They are larger compositions than the earlier trios, and their contents are of greater importance. The wealth of modulations in these last trios is remarkable. In the first movement of No. 26, in F sharp minor, the development, with the help of enharmonic changes, reaches the key of E flat minor; gently sliding passages of the kind used by Mozart lead back to the tonic. In a similar way the first movement of No. 28, in E major, introduces in the development a section in A flat major, and No. 14 has a first movement in A flat major followed by an adagio in E major. This adagio ends in D sharp major, which is enharmonically identical with E flat major, the dominant of the main key. Such well-planned modulations are symptomatic of the new importance that the piano trio now assumed for Haydn. Characteristic pieces, such as the lovely theme and variations in the first movement of No. 25, in G major, the simple and fervent prayer in E major of its second movement, and the high-spirited *rondo all'ungarese* of the finale would never have been written by the earlier Haydn in the form of a piano trio. Remarkable also is the middle movement of No. 28. Its unrelenting ground bass in eighth notes, on which the whole piece is based, makes it appear as a sort of passacaglia, reminding us of Johann Sebastian Bach, whose works Haydn heard in Baron van Swieten's home. The finale of Haydn's Trio No. 30 of 1795, a presto with some traits of Beethoven's scherzos, abandons completely the old idea of the piano sonata accompanied by violin and violoncello. Here the parts of the two bowed instruments are organically linked together while the accompanying clavier supports their melody (Ex. 18 on following page). A new type of piano trio in which all three members share responsibility is breaking through, a type that was to gain increasing importance in the future.

The three little trios and the single movement in G major for two flutes and cello[7] (Hob. IV:1–4) which Haydn

[7] Edited by Leo Balet (Hanover, 1931).

wrote in London in 1794 are short pieces without any claim to importance. Haydn obviously did not spend much time on these compositions; nevertheless, the middle movement of the first trio exists in two versions, a sign of the

Piano Trio, No. 30, Finale.

greater care he was bestowing in this period even on compositions of lesser consequence.

* * *

Haydn produced fifteen string quartets during his last period of composition; among them are some of the greatest works he has given to this form. According to the autographs, Haydn composed six string quartets in 1793. They were printed as Op. 71, Nos. 1–3, and Op. 74, Nos. 1–3 (Hob. III:69–74), and were dedicated to Count Apponyi. He wrote them at a time when he was strongly interested in orchestral composition, and they accordingly display a certain symphonic character. An innovation in these quartets is the use of introductions to the first movements, a feature so important in Haydn's symphonies. In Op. 71, Nos. 1 and 3, and Op. 74, No. 1, this introduction consists only of chords of the full ensemble; in Op. 71, No. 2, however, it is a real adagio of four bars. Op. 74, Nos. 2 and 3, have as the preliminary sections unison passages of eight measures, of great significance in the following movement. Particularly in Op. 74, No. 3, the connection between introduction and exposition is so intimate that the listener is surprised when he finds the main idea, and not the unison of the introduction, which he had been led to expect, at the beginning of the recapitulation. In the first movement of Op. 71, No. 2, the defiant downward octave leaps given to all four instruments are completely alien to the intimacy of chamber music and approach the realm of symphonic composition. The first violin introduces whirling passages in sixteenths, and the other instruments come in gradually to carry the melody to a climax. When, at the end, the violoncello joins the general uproar, the feeling is produced that the contrabass should accompany in the lower octave in order to give the necessary foundation to this imposing structure. In the first movement of Op. 71, No. 3, the viola part goes below the violoncello part (measures 21–23 of the development), thus causing undesired six-four chords. While writing this passage, Haydn may have been under the illusion that contrabasses doubling the violoncello part in the lower octave would take care of the situation.

The dawn of romanticism is noticeable in the string quartets of Op. 74. Haydn resumes his experiments with the sonata form, and the first and last movements of No. 1 contain development work in the recapitulation. The A major trio of its minuet in C major introduces a softly rocking melody with roots in Austrian folk song and contains passages that make us think of Schubert. The lovely quartet No. 2 goes even further in the key relations between its minuet and trio. Here the former is in F major and the latter stands a major third lower, in D flat major. This daring combination certainly would not have been attempted by the younger Haydn. In the first movement of the "Reiterquartett," No. 3, the main subject following the powerful introduction is of less significance than the subsidiary idea accompanied by the triplets of the transitional section. Innumerable romantic compositions of the nineteenth century show this phenomenon, assigning more importance to the second subject than to the first (cf. Schubert's "Unfinished" symphony). This quartet in G minor uses as a slow movement a *largo assai* in E major. A climax is reached in the brilliant finale, with its first and second themes in the Hungarian and Austrian folk vein, introducing some charmingly gay passages in the development.

In 1797, six string quartets (Hob. III:75–80) were written and published as Op. 76, with a dedication to Count Erdödy. If an appropriate motto were sought for this series, the word Excelsior should have the first choice. Everything here is condensed and intensified, the expression more personal and more direct. It is characteristic of Haydn that he now repeatedly increases the tempo in the course of a movement, as in Nos. 5 and 6, in which the initial allegretto is transformed into allegro; the concluding *allegro ma non troppo* of No. 4 twice increases its speed. In these quartets, the minuet has lost completely the character of a graceful allegretto. In Nos. 1 and 6, Haydn's tempo marks are presto, and an approach to Beethoven's scherzo is also evident in the spirit of the compositions. The same quartet No. 1, in G major, has a finale beginning in G minor. It would seem that Haydn wanted to change the mood of the composition, but the opposite is true: he desired merely to introduce a retardation before the definite solution; the finale, in its second half, passes quite regularly from minor to major so that the beginning and end of the quartet conform. A similar situation may be found in No. 3.[8] As the quartets of Op. 76 are contemporary with Haydn's *Creation,* it is not surprising that the last move-

[8] Sir Donald Tovey points out that Brahms's Third symphony shows quite similar tendencies. This is by no means the only point the two composers have in common, and as Brahms was a most diligent student of Haydn's scores, the resemblance does not seem to be accidental.

ments of two of them should be based on the idea expressed in the great passage from minor to major at the words "Let there be light."

No. 2 of this set is known as the "Quintenquartett" because of the use of fifths in its main subject. A strange piece is its *Hexen-Menuett* (Witches Minuet), a canon in which the two violins play the melody in octaves while viola and violoncello (also in octaves) perform the imitation. No. 3, in C major, is a surprisingly uninspired quartet that hardly would deserve its place among Haydn's last works of this type were it not for its *poco adagio cantabile*. Like Schubert in his quartet "Death and the Maiden" and in his "Trout" quintet, in this slow movement Haydn presents variations on one of his own songs, the Austrian national anthem, "Gotte erhalte Franz den Kaiser." There are only four variations, and in each a different member of the quartet is entrusted with the melody. It is a work of great simplicity and dignity, fully deserving the great popularity that it enjoys. No. 4 is known as the "Sunrise"; its main subject beautifully expresses the feeling of growth and expansion that we experience on an early summer morning. No. 5, based on a single melody, presents in its first movement a greatly simplified sonata form. As Haydn liked to use two movements of the same form within a single work, the succeeding famous largo in F sharp major (the first movement being in D major!) is similarly constructed. It is a piece full of luxuriant beauty, just as romantic in its whole conception as the variations on the Austrian hymn in the preceding quartet were classical. The first movement of No. 6 introduces a set of variations on an allegretto theme. The last of these variations reveals traces of serious polyphonic construction. Like many nineteenth-century composers, Haydn concludes his set of variations with a display of counterpoint. The following fantasia moves from B major through the keys of E, G, B flat, B, A flat, and finally back to the tonic. This unconventional piece, rich in enharmonic changes, at first has no key signature at all. As in works of Philipp Emanuel Bach, and of some twentieth century composers, the accidentals are written separately for each note. The trio (*alternativo*) of the minuet of this quartet uses as a theme the scale of E flat. It runs through all parts, sometimes ascending and sometimes descending, while Haydn constantly invents new counterpoints to it. Beethoven may have remembered this humorous piece when composing his canon on the words "I beg you, write down the E flat scale for me." In 1799 the composer wrote two string quartets (Hob. III:81–82) that were printed as Op. 77, with a dedication to Prince Lobkowitz. More than ever, Haydn delighted at this time in little experiments in form. For instance, in the recapitulation of the first movement of No. 1, the subsidiary subject has been omitted because he thought that it had been sufficiently used in the development section. In the second quartet, the minuet is in F major, the trio in D flat major. The coda also starts in D flat major, but as it is thematically related to the minuet, it unites the two contrasting sections of the movement. Both this piece and the minuet of the preceding quartet exhibit features characteristic of Beethoven's scherzos. Striking is the beginning of the andante of No. 2. It is limited to two parts only, thus recalling the distinctive "thinness" of Philipp Emanuel Bach's piano compositions. In this period, when true expression seemed more important to Haydn than a perfect balance between form and content, he was getting closer to the style of Johann Sebastian Bach's second son, and at the same time to that of his own storm-and-stress period.

In 1803, Haydn began his last string quartet, Op. 103 (Hob. III:83), in B flat major. He wrote only two movements, an *andante grazioso* and a minuet. These movements show complete technical mastery, but at the same time a certain lack of inventive power. Haydn was unable to add the initial movement and finale to these two middle pieces. The quartet remained unfinished, and was eventually published in 1806 as the master's swan song. As a humorous explanation and apology it has at the end of the minuet a reproduction of the visiting card that Haydn used during the last years of his life. On it was printed a quotation from his favorite four-part song "Der Greis" (The

Old Man): *Hin ist alle meine Kraft, alt und schwach bin
ich* (Gone forever is my strength, old and weak am I).

❋   ❋   ❋

The Symphonie Concertante, Op. 84 (Hob. I:105), for
violin, oboe, violoncello, and bassoon, accompanied by full
orchestra, was written in 1792 in London. In this work
Haydn revived traditions of the preclassic era. He was
mainly interested in the problem of contrasting a group
of concertante instruments consisting of high- and deep-
pitched strings and woodwind with the ripieno instruments
used to accompany it. During most of the time the four
soloists, who vary so greatly in technical possibilities, are
used together, or at least in the same way, rendering impracticable the development of a style that takes into
consideration the technical accomplishments of each individual instrument. Remarkable in the last movement are
the little recitative episodes of the violin, reminiscent
of Haydn's earliest symphonies, and certain nineteenth-
century romantic compositions. It is to be regretted that
this attractive work, like other concertantes of the late
eighteenth and nineteenth centuries (J. C. Bach's, C.
Stamitz', Mozart's *Sinfonies concertantes*; Beethoven's triple concerto; Brahms's double concerto), is performed so
seldom.

In 1796, Haydn wrote a concerto for the keyed trumpet
(Hob. VIIe:1). This is a trumpet with holes in the wall of
the tube which are closed by keys. As a rule there are five
such keys, which raise the pitch by successive semitones.
They are so arranged that the performer can play them
with his left hand while holding the trumpet in his right.
The invention of the keyed trumpet has been ascribed to
the Viennese Anton Weidinger, who is said to have constructed it in 1801, but the instrument is older than that, as
Haydn's concerto was written five years earlier. The composition reveals the characteristics of the new invention;
one looks in vain for the usual triad melodies. The concerto
is predominantly diatonic, though there are chromatic
passages even in the deeper register of the instrument.
Great demands are made on the nimbleness of the trumpet,

and in the allegro runs of sixteenth notes are not unusual. With youthful enthusiasm, the aged composer threw himself into the novel task, creating the finest solo concerto of his whole career and proving once more his flexibility and ability to absorb new ideas.

Despite Haydn's efforts, the keyed trumpet had no real success. The explanation may be the fact that the holes detracted greatly from the brilliant tone of the instrument. Accordingly it never succeeded in obtaining admittance to the symphonic orchestra. However, Haydn's work was edited in various arrangements for valve trumpet and piano[9] and is today in the repertoire of most trumpeters.

A review of Haydn's whole output in the field of the concerto forces one to admit that he showed no particular interest in this form of composition. The few masterworks among the concertos hardly make up for the number of routine compositions written for a single performance and never meant for wider circulation. This will not surprise anyone familiar with Haydn's personality. Unlike Mozart, he was no virtuoso. Neither on the piano nor on the violin was his technique particularly brilliant. Above all, his natural disposition was alien to that of a virtuoso. The rather dramatic gifts of the professional performer, which great virtuosos like Liszt, Paganini, and even Mozart possessed in abundance, were completely lacking in Haydn. His reserve made it impossible for him to become a success as a soloist, and while he progressed as a composer, his interest in the concerto form gradually faded. Most of Haydn's concertos were written during the 1750s and 1760s, the smallest number of them (though including the finest works) during the eighties and nineties.

At different periods of his lifetime Haydn composed a number of marches and dances, but he does not seem to have attributed great importance to them. The catalogue of 1805 mentions only two marches and omits the dances altogether.

Seven marches,[10] mostly written during the composer's last creative period and preserved in autograph, are known

[9] First by A. Goeyens (Brussels, 1929).
[10] Edited by H. C. R. Landon (Vienna, 1960–61).

today. One of them was written in London for the Prince of Wales (Hob. VIII:3), two were for the Derbyshire Cavalry Regiment (Hob. VIII:1, 2); the last march, the *Hungarischer National Marsch* (Hob. VIII:4) is dated 1802. These are very concise pieces, the longest of which consists of only forty-six measures. As the marching bands of the eighteenth century usually performed without music, it seemed advisable to keep down the length of the pieces they had to memorize. The marches are mostly in the key of E flat major and are scored for two clarinets (and/or oboes), two bassoons, and two horns, to which at times a trumpet and a serpent were added. The "March for the Royal Society of Musicians" (Hob. VIII:3 *bis*), written in 1792 for a banquet of the society, adds two flutes and strings. However, this piece is an arrangement of the "March for the Prince of Wales," scored for wind instruments only. The little marches, strongly rhythmical pieces of vigorous and virile character, enjoyed popularity in Haydn's lifetime, as is proved by the fact that one of them (Hob. VIII:6) in slightly changed form is played by the musical clock of 1793 (Hob. XIX:25).

Many minuets and German dances were written by Haydn for balls and dances. A contemporary author[11] goes even so far as to mention four hundred such pieces contributed by the composer. The earliest of them go back to the master's first two periods of composition, while the last and best were written in the nineties. Graceful utility music is provided in the six allemandes (Hob. IX:9) of the middle eighties. A climax was reached with the twelve minuets and twelve German dances (Hob. IX:11, 12)[12] for large orchestra which Haydn offered in the fall of 1792 to the Pensionsgesellschaft bildender Künstler Wiens (Pension Fund of Vienna's Artists) for their masked ball. It took place on November 25, the name day of St. Catherine, and the compositions were therefore called "Catherine

[11] C. Bertuch, *Bemerkungen auf einer Reise aus Thüringen nach Wien im Winter 1805–6* (Weimar, 1808). 12. Brief.

[12] Hob. IX:9 was edited by H. C. R. Landon (Vienna, 1906), Hob. IX:11 by E. F. Schmid (Leipzig, 1940), Hob. IX:12 by O. E. Deutsch (Leipzig, 1931).

Dances." These twenty-four pieces are jewels of musical inspiration pervaded by amiable humor and chiseled with exquisite understanding of the individual instruments' potentialities. Haydn, who, after the triumphs won in England, may have felt the reception given to him in Vienna to be somewhat cool, probably was eager to bring his art to the attention of the Viennese, and these dances seemed particularly suitable for such a purpose. That the composer attached significance to the dainty and unassuming pieces is proved by the various sketches he made for them.

*   *   *

The twelve London symphonies (Hob. I:93–104), composed between 1791 and 1795, plus an additional one, the Thirteenth or Oxford symphony (No. 92 of 1788), represent the climax of Haydn's symphonic output. Never before had he written orchestral works of equal value, and no other musician composed in quick succession so large a number of great symphonic masterpieces. Although each of these thirteen works has it own outstanding merits, a gradual improvement in quality may be noticed. The symphonies Nos. 99–104, written for the second sojourn in London, surpass, if that be possible, the Nos. 93–98, composed for the first visit. No others of Haydn's scores show such virtuosity of instrumentation or such delightful unorthodox treatment of musical forms and contrapuntal devices in the development sections. Remarkable is the imagination displayed by Haydn at such a comparatively unimportant place as the recapitulation in sonata form. Occasionally composers introduce an almost mechanical repetition of the exposition as soon as the development is finished. Haydn, on the other hand, presents the material of the first section in a new way, writing a recapitulation as rich in inspiration as the exposition itself. A last climax is often reached in the coda. This coda, far from being a mere "tail," develops into a final dramatic concentration of the thematic material. The whole nineteenth century, beginning with Beethoven and ending with Brahms, was able to draw rich inspiration from Haydn's last thirteen symphonies.

The mosaic style of the thematic development has become a matter of course; filling and accompanying voices enjoy the same privileges as the parts carrying the melody, for the same motives are used by all. The baroque division into leading instruments, whose parts are florid and ornamental, and subordinate instruments, whose function is that of giving a foundation to the evolutions of the others, reflects the social cleavage of the period into a ruling and a subservient class, a division that here has been abandoned entirely.

Hermann Kretzschmar called the Oxford symphony (No. 92 in G major) Haydn's "Eroica," as it is the first work to display the full perfection of Haydn's fifth period of composition. In its whole architecture it belongs to the works of the nineties rather than to the Paris symphonies, though it was actually composed in 1788. Tovey[13] is mistaken when he points out that the Oxford symphony "was written for the occasion of Haydn's receiving the Doctorate of Music at Oxford." The fact is that this symphony No. 92 written in 1789 for the Count d'Ogny but not known in England, was presented as a new work at the Oxford celebration.

The Oxford symphony displays thematic development in every measure, and all the devices of counterpoint are introduced to reveal new sides of the subjects again and again. The work is gay and carefree, but at the same time filled with dramatic excitement. The climax is reached in the brilliant finale, which shows so many different forms of its main theme that it seems hard to determine which is the original and which a variation. The score, laid out at first for an orchestra of only medium size, later was enlarged by the addition of trumpets and timpani.

Symphony No. 93, in D major, composed in 1791, starts with a slow introduction of lofty grandeur, its dramatic impact enhanced by frequent pauses. The *largo cantabile* of the second movement may have been in Beethoven's mind when he worked on the Pastoral symphony, but near the end Haydn intentionally destroys the deeply

---

[13] *Essays in Musical Analysis* (London, 1935–44), I, 143.

moving atmosphere by allowing the bassoon to break in
with a rather vulgar statement. The finale shows the combination of rondo and sonata form that Haydn liked so
much in his last period. Such a combination also is used in
the symphonies Nos. 94, 95, 100, 101, and 102, and it is
characteristic of the consummate mastery of the composer
that no two of these movements solve the problem in the
same way.

Symphony No. 94, in G major, known as the "Surprise"[14] and composed in 1791, owes its name to an episode in the andante of its second movement, which has a
folk-song character. Haydn introduced eight measures of
his theme at first piano, played by strings only, and then a
second time pianissimo. At the end of this repetition, when
the tone may be expected to fade out, quite suddenly a
fortissimo of the full orchestra, including the drums, sets
in. This sort of surprise had been used by Haydn before,
and the movement owes its popularity more to the graceful, simple melodic invention than to the little joke. The
andante displays a mixture of variation and three-part-song
form, as the freely constructed second variation in C minor
takes the place of the middle part. Haydn had the good
taste not to repeat in the individual variations the little
prank he introduced in the theme. In the coda, the childlike, naïve melody of the main subject suddenly assumes
an enigmatic character because of the romantic harmonies
of the stringed instruments used as an accompaniment
(measures 145–152). Here we reach the threshold of Beethoven's art.

The other movements match the andante in artistic perfection. In the slow introduction to the first movement,
Haydn boldly employs chromatic progressions of an almost
romantic fervor. The ensuing *vivace assai* built on three
subjects is worked out with the zest and ingenuity we have
learned to expect in these symphonies. Much more amusing

[14] An incomplete autograph is preserved in the University
Library, Tübingen. Some of the pages missing there are in the
Library of Congress, Washington, D. C. These sheets contain
the first version of the andante in which the "surprise" effect
has not yet been achieved.

than the "surprise" of the andante is a detail in the minuet. At the end of the second part (measures 39–40), a ridiculous snort and groan in the violoncellos and bassoons leads us back to the beginning of the main melody. This movement bears no relation to the graceful French minuet of the rococo period. It is a typical Austrian ländler, foreshadowing the waltz of the nineteenth century.

In the final rondo, too, the retransitions to the main theme show unusual humor and fantasy and a brilliant coda concludes this great movement.

The dramatic beginning in unison of symphony No. 95, in C minor, composed in 1791, reminds us of the storm-and-stress period. The lack of a slow introduction to the first movement, the frequent doubling by the strings of the parts of the woodwind instruments, and the baroque use of polyphonic devices in the finale are equally characteristic of an earlier phase in Haydn's creative output. The variations of the andante, however, displaying in their whole construction a great resemblance to the "surprise" movement of the preceding symphony, and the rather difficult violoncello solo in the trio of the minuet show that in Haydn's latest period old and new elements are blended together with perfect success.

The symphony No. 96, in D major, may well be the first number of the set Haydn composed in London. It is known as the "Miracle," a nickname not owing to aesthetic qualities (well deserved though it would be), but rather to a story told about the first performance. At the end of the concert, the applauding crowd rushed toward the platform to have a better view of the composer. At this moment a chandelier in the rear crashed down. Thanks to the enthusiasm the audience had shown, nobody was hurt, and exclamations were heard that a miracle had happened.[15]

In the vigorous first movement, a bold, truly Beethovian effect may be observed in the middle section, in which Haydn concludes a passage in F sharp major and, after a

[15] According to Landon, *Symphonies,* p. 535, the event happened in February 1795 at the premiere of symphony No. 103. Yet the nickname has been linked indissolubly with symphony No. 96.

pause, unexpectedly starts a half-tone higher, with a chord in G. The slow movement, on the other hand, seems to recapture the best spirit of rococo art, and its dainty charm and exquisitely soft pastel coloring bring Watteau's masterpieces to mind. Robust jocularity reigns in the minuet, while the trio presents a dance tune of poignant sweetness deeply rooted in Austrian folklore. The finale offers a brilliant *perpetuum mobile*, allowing Haydn to display his uncanny resourcefulness in achieving a variety of humorous effects while obstinately clinging to the same rhythm.

In the symphony No. 97, in C major, composed in 1792, the introduction to the first movement is intimately connected with the main part. The characteristic motive of its second measure returns all through the movement, the last time in the coda. Near the beginning of the development section, the strings toss backward and forward a little motive derived from the main subject. The "Jacob's ladder" effect in the finale of Beethoven's Eighth symphony (measures 458–469) is foreshadowed in this little episode. In the following variation movement, the unexpected forte entrance of trumpets and timpani in the second variation is particularly stirring. A gem outstanding even in this set of masterpieces is the minuet, in which Haydn displays his magical touch as orchestrator. Here the traditional repetitions are written out completely, introducing attractive little variations instead of mechanical reiteration. The same is true of the trio, incidentally one of the most typically Austrian pieces Haydn ever wrote. The finale of this symphony displays an obvious mirthfulness; near the end, however, in a dramatic move the composer introduces a passage imbued with the spirit of tragedy, taking the listener completely by surprise. Immediately afterward, cheerfulness is restored; the dark shades were used only to give a more effective background to the prevailing bright colors.

In the symphony No. 98, in B flat major, composed in 1792, the slow introduction in B flat minor anticipates the main subject of the following allegro (B flat major) in a way that was to become customary in romantic music. The *adagio cantabile* of the second movement, according to Tovey, might almost be called Haydn's "requiem for Mozart, the news of whose death had so deeply shocked him during his London visit." It certainly is an unusually serious piece, anticipating in its hymnlike character the prayer "Sei nun gnädig" in *The Seasons*. However, the last two movements once more sparkle with the composer's typical love of fun. The finale, which conjures up a hilarious operatic scene, achieves a particularly amusing effect by suddenly slowing up its brisk motion near the end. It is noteworthy that a manuscript of the symphony, loaned by the Royal College of Music to the British Museum, contains in bars 365–375 of the finale, arpeggios for the harpischord; Haydn, who liked to conduct from the keyboard instrument, apparently had them inserted for his own use.[16]

The symphony No. 99, in E flat major, composed in 1793 between the two trips to England, is the first symphony in which Haydn uses clarinets, though these instruments had been prescribed by him in such earlier compositions as the notturni with lire organizzate. How well he understood the possibilities of this wind instrument is shown in the very first measures of the score. The sonorous chalumeau register of the clarinet provides an effective bass for the stringed instruments. Daring modulations give this introduction a decidedly progressive character. In the main section of the movement, the second subject is of greater significance than the first, and a similar romantic preponderance of the subsidiary idea may be noted in the following adagio, one of the deepest and most stirring pieces written by Haydn. As in the preceding symphony, the mood changes completely with the beginning of the minuet. This scherzo-like movement and even more the finale employ all the devices of instrumentation and counterpoint to create pictures of uncontrollable gaiety. Thus Haydn could count on pleasing the exacting Londoners with the first symphony he planned to present to them after his return.

In the first movement of the symphony No. 100, in G

[16] Cf. Landon, op. cit., p. 580.

major, composed in 1794 and known as the Military symphony, a trio consisting of a flute and two oboes introduces the main subject; no other instruments are added for support. So revolutionary a treatment of the high woodwinds, which in the earlier symphonies almost never are used independently, shows that the aged Haydn did not cease experimenting and trying out new effects. The subsidiary subject bears a certain resemblance to both the main idea of the first movement of Mozart's great G minor symphony and to one of the most popular Austrian tunes of the nineteenth century, the *Radetzky March* by the elder Johann Strauss. Even the use of the first three notes of both Mozart's and Haydn's subjects in the respective development sections displays a striking similarity. The work owes its name to the allegretto of the second movement. The piece increases Haydn's ordinary symphonic orchestra by military instruments: triangle, cymbals, bass drum, and the penetrating C clarinet. In this composition he used the allegretto from his third lira concerto, changing only the orchestration and the end of the movement. Even the division of the violas used in the original composition is preserved in its adaptation for the Military symphony. The composer frequently prescribes the percussion instruments in piano and pianissimo, thus producing charming effects of color. Rather strange is the unaccompanied trumpet signal near the end of the movement, followed by a roll of the kettledrums, increasing from pianissimo to fortissimo. It can hardly be doubted that Haydn, in a purely romantic way, meant to express with this dramatic episode a certain poetical program. From here the way leads directly to the trumpet signals in Beethoven's *Leonore* overtures. The brisk final presto uses the same percussion instruments as the andante. It is distinguished by interesting modulations and contains several little replicas of the famous "surprise" from the symphony No. 94 which are hardly less effective than the original itself. Particularly amusing are measures 118–123. Two chords are played by violins and viola, first piano, then after a general pause, diminuendo, and finally after a second general pause, pianissimo. Before this charming effect can be fully grasped, the kettledrum crashes in with six powerful fortissimo beats. By omitting the third general pause, which the listener anticipates, Haydn set a sort of trap for his audience, the humorous effect of which nobody can miss.

The symphony No. 101, in D major, commonly known as "The Clock," was written in 1794. The presto of the first movement and its six-eight time are what one would expect in the finale of a symphony rather than in its initial movement. The andante introduces an accompaniment of bassoons and plucked strings that sounds like the ticktock of a big clock and is responsible for the symphony's nickname. This movement displays Haydn's favorite mixture of variation and rondo form, which so strongly impressed Beethoven that one finds traces of it even in the slow movement of his "Choral" symphony. In Haydn's andante, continual changes of the orchestration occur. Particularly attractive is the entrance of the charming main theme after the dramatic episode in G minor. Here the ticktock is taken over by a flute, so that a tiny clock seems to replace the big timepiece heard at the beginning. The trio of the succeeding minuet belongs to the type now frequently used by Haydn, which does not contrast with the preceding dance, but rather supplements it. Both sections are in the same key, a fact that has induced some conductors to omit the repetition of the minuet after the trio. It is hardly necessary to point out that such a procedure completely destroys the architecture of the movement. The finale, imbued with mellow joyfulness, shows a construction greatly resembling that of the andante. In spite of its prevailing light, gay character, the entrance of the main theme after the minor episode assumes the form of a double fugue in miniature. How solidly this finale is constructed may be gathered from the fact that the first three notes of the main subject are used throughout the movement, giving the greatest unity to the composition. One is reminded of the thematic "germ cell" that plays so important a part in the symphonies of Johannes Brahms.

In the symphony No. 102, in B flat major (composed in 1794), the slowly gliding chords of the introductory largo intoned by the wind instruments transport us to a world of mystery. A brisk allegro follows, its second subject once more revealing the aged composer's joy in experimentation. Haydn has the theme start on a fortissimo outcry. A general pause ensues, and then the rest of the melody is uttered piano. Also striking are the violent dissonances in the canonic episode of the development. The soul-stirring adagio displays an orchestration of unusual subtlety, introducing muted trumpets and muffled kettledrums. It is a simple piece imbued with serene faith, and it is not surprising that it was arranged as an anthem at a later date. Haydn himself used this adagio in F major a second time: in the piano trio in F sharp minor (Hob. XV:26), it serves as the middle movement. The hearty, robust minuet of the symphony has a romantic trio in which chromatic progressions express ardor and yearning that one would expect in a composition by Mozart rather than a piece by Haydn. The brilliant finale employs an old Croat folk tune as main subject. Near the end, the great musical humorist produces another of his delightful jokes. The first violin suddenly begins to stutter: it tries to present the main theme, but succeeds in uttering no more than its first few notes. These grow more and more confused, whereupon the chorus of attending instruments rudely breaks in, and with loud laughter carries the movement to an exuberant conclusion.

Among the many romantic and highly dramatic introductions that head the first movements of Haydn's London symphonies, the one written in 1795 for the symphony No. 103, in E flat major, "with the Drum Roll," is particularly remarkable. It starts with a completely unaccompanied long roll of the kettledrum. This mysterious first measure is followed by an impressive unison of bassoons, violoncellos, and double basses. Here Haydn wrote the basses an octave higher than the cellos, so that the two groups of instruments sound at the same pitch. Only in this way can the lonely majesty of the passage be expressed fully. This is another example of the special care that Haydn then bestowed on the problems of orchestration. In the succeeding *allegro con spirito* the composer uses a real waltz tune as a subsidiary subject, and a gay and warm spirit pervades the movement. Twice, however, reminiscences of the solemn adagio introduction are heard, and thus a new dimension seems to be added to the sparkling gaiety of the piece. The following andante is in variation form, using two themes of folk-songlike character which show a certain relationship to each other. The first theme is in C minor, the second in C major, and Haydn wrote variations on them alternately. Particularly delightful is the second C major variation, which has the oboes sound the theme while the bassoons offer a ponderous accompaniment and the flutes chime in like little bells. This *andante più tosto allegretto*, with its superb treatment of the variation form, is followed by a minuet that introduces in its second section an effective stretto of the main subject, showing that the use of polyphonic devices need not be restricted to the first and last movements of a symphony. The beginning of the finale is just as daring as that of the first movement. Two horns play an unaccompanied signal of the type later used by Schubert and Schumann. This horn theme is nothing but a counterpoint to the main idea, which is presently introduced by the first violin. (Incidentally, these two ideas have a striking resemblance to the beginning of the finale in Mozart's "Jupiter" symphony.) The whole movement is based entirely on the one main melody. Its first five notes—a variation of the old "sigh motive"—lend themselves particularly well to the contrapuntal work that Haydn uses extensively all through this masterly piece.

Haydn's last symphony, No. 104 in D major, composed in 1795, is sometimes known as his London symphony, though this name may be applied to any of the last twelve symphonies. The autograph preserved in the Staatsbibliothek, Berlin, bears the inscription (in English) "the 12th which I have composed in England." In writing this, Haydn may have felt that he was not only finishing the last symphony he had promised to compose for the English public, but that he also was completing his output in the field of orchestral composition. The first movement starts with a solemn adagio in D minor, after which the D major allegro section presents a warm, tender subject of Mozartean nature. It is typical of Haydn's art that a slightly modified repetition of the main idea is used instead of the subsidiary subject. There is also a contrasting melody near the end of the exposition, which at first seems to be quite insignificant. However, like Beethoven in later years, Haydn chooses as a foundation for his developing work the very theme that appeared least likely to attract his attention. The andante of the second movement is in three-part form, and here Haydn achieves greater coherence by using material from the first section for the contrasting *minore* of the middle part. The movement's sweetly poignant theme and its deeply moving coda once more bring Mozart to mind. The mood changes completely when we reach the zestful minuet in D major (with trio in B flat major). Here the accents on the last beats of measures and the general pause near the end, followed by a trill of the woodwind and strings, anticipate the scherzos of Beethoven. In the finale the composer employs two subjects, one based on the old English street song "Hot Cross Buns," the contrasting one imbued with tender longing. The main subject is accompanied by the deep drone of horns and violoncellos holding the tonic note D as a pedal point for long stretches, creating the illusion of a rustic dance tune played on a bagpipe.

Admiring the facets of Haydn's art displayed in these last symphonies, we feel that they fittingly serve as a final point in the gigantic structure erected by the composer's orchestral work.

*   *   *

The vocal compositions of Haydn's fifth period are on a level with his creations in the field of instrumental music. The English imprint is on most of these works, even on those written in Austria after he left England. Haydn gave a surprisingly large amount of his time to the writing of songs. Nevertheless, the creation of songs never became for him—or for that matter for Mozart or Beethoven either —a matter of great importance.

The first set of Haydn's *Six Original Canzonettas*, written in England to English words, was printed by Corri, Dussek and Company in London in 1794, a second set of six

English canzonettas the following year. In these songs, the inclusion of the vocal part in the right-hand part of the piano accompaniment, as exemplified in Haydn's first twenty-four German songs, is abandoned. The composer now uses a separate line for the voice part; his instrumental introductions become larger and more important, and the piano accompaniment is of greater significance. Occasionally it is obvious that Haydn was thinking in terms of the orchestra even when composing for the piano only. The influence of the aria in these songs is just as conspicuous as it is in Beethoven's *Adelaide*, for soprano with piano, written at about the same time. Haydn's use of coloratura and chromatic progressions, the wide range of the voice part, and the occasional influx of the dramatic spirit show the opera composer at work. However, it is not always the Italian opera, but occasionally, as in the "Sailor's Song," the simpler German Singspiel that influenced him. At the same time, Haydn still preferred the strophic arrangement, which he also had used in the first twenty-four German songs. "A Pastoral Song" and "She Never Told Her Love" belong among the more attractive pieces of the two English sets; for the latter, Haydn used a text from Shakespeare's *Twelfth Night*.

Two songs not included in the twelve canzonettas are settings of English words. "O Tuneful Voice" is based on a poem given to Haydn by Mrs. Hunter before his departure from England (see p. 162). It is to be wondered whether this almost tragic composition in the style of *opera seria* does not take the simple text a little too seriously. To Haydn's best pieces for voice and piano belongs "The Spirit's Song," again on a text by Anne Hunter. Apparently the author's romantic manner of conveying the idea of life after death struck a responsive note in the aging composer's mind. For once, this expressive composition is void of operatic influence; in its mysterious atmosphere and deep feeling it anticipates Schubert's Lied.

Yet Haydn's most successful song is his "Gott erhalte Franz den Kaiser," composed in 1797 as the Austrian national anthem. For more than a century this melody was used with at least a dozen different texts as the anthem of the Austro-Hungarian monarchy. In Germany, Haydn's tune has been employed for the patriotic song "Deutschland, Deutschland, über alles," and in the English-speaking countries as a church hymn.

In this work, folk song and art music came to a classical union. Hardly ever did a composer create with such simple means a work imbued with such fervor and solemnity. Like every tune of simple folk-song character, "Gott erhalte" resembles other melodies in certain details. Dr. Kuhač found analogies between Haydn's hymn and the Croat folk song "Vjutro runo," and came to the conclusion that the master's melody must be of Croat origin. Even if the Croat folk song were older than Haydn's anthem the melodic relationship would not prove anything, as similar slight resemblances may be discovered in a great number of other pieces that Haydn most certainly never saw. Tappert,[17] Friedländer,[18] and Botstiber[19] made lists of such "relations" and proved that some of the melodic successions of Haydn's song are also to be found in: a minuet from Sperontes' *Singende Muse an der Pleisse*; Hasse's *Pilgrime von Golgatha*; a rondeau for piano by Georg Philipp Telemann; a hymnbook from 1786; Mozart's violin sonata in C (K. 296) and his *Exultate jubilate* of 1773; a composition by Christoph Gottlieb Breitkopf; and Haydn's own setting of *The Seven Last Words*. (Even long after Haydn's death, Brahms used in his piano sonata in F minor a tune with a certain similarity.) This does not mean that Haydn studied all these works; it only shows that he succeeded in creating one of those basic melodies of which elements are to be found in works by the most different composers. This fundamental quality, which was reached only after long and arduous work (Haydn made many sketches to this short, uncomplicated song and they are

[17] *Musikalische Studien* (1868).
[18] Introduction to the volume of songs in the first Collected Edition (Leipzig, 1932).
[19] Vol. 3 of C. F. Pohl's *Joseph Haydn* (Leipzig, 1927).

preserved in the Vienna National Library), also accounts for its unparalleled success.

Inspired by Nelson's victory at Aboukir Bay in 1798, Haydn in 1800 wrote his aria for soprano or tenor and piano, "Lines from the Battle of the Nile." As in *Arianna a Naxos*, the piano part bears the character of an orchestral arrangement; thus Ludwig Landshoff's instrumentation of this piece is to a certain extent justified. The gay principal subject of the aria, characterizing the victorious hero, makes its appearance in the introductory recitative. Like an operatic scene by Gluck, "Lines from the Battle of the Nile" subordinates the music to the text. Consequently, the recitative, which also interrupts the continuous flow of the aria, is almost more important than the aria itself.

In London in 1795 Haydn wrote for Brigida Giorgi-Banti "Berenice que fai,"[20] for soprano accompanied by strings and woodwind, a grand concert aria full of impressive modulations and harmonic changes. Three years later he composed the soprano aria "Solo e pensoso"[21] on a sonnet by Petrarch. It starts with an *adagio cantabile* dispensing almost completely with wind instruments and leads to an allegretto in which the soloist and instruments (now including two clarinets) are offered ever greater opportunities for displaying their art.

Haydn's arrangements of Scottish and Welsh folk songs belong to a special group. Starting on this work in London in 1792, he continued it in Vienna, carrying it on even after his failing health made really creative work impossible. Haydn worked for three different English and Scottish publishers; at first for William Napier, then simultaneously for George Thomson and William Whyte. Robert Burns wrote new texts for some of the songs published by Thomson. Among the artists who worked at that time or afterward on similar lines were Pleyel, Koželuch, and Beethoven.

Between 1791 and 1805, Haydn produced no less than four hundred and forty-five arrangements of Scottish, Welsh, and Irish folk songs, a comparatively easy task

---

[20] Edited by A. Orel (Leipzig, 1937).
[21] Edited by H. C. R. Landon (Salzburg, 1961).

that he apparently found pleasant. The Napier arrangements[22] were printed in three lines only, the top one destined for the violin, the second (under which the text is placed) for the melody, the third for the figured bass. The two lower lines apparently are intended for singer and clavierist, the use of a cello to reinforce the bass being optional. The setting is rather thin here, requiring the addition of filling notes by the clavierist, but the Thomson and Whyte editions offer a different picture. In them, as a rule, a separate line is allotted to the singer's part; the two lines underneath contain the completely elaborated clavier part. In separate volumes, the violin and cello parts also are presented, and though they could be omitted in performance, and in all likelihood were used but rarely, they contribute considerably to the coloristic enrichment and the poetic interpretation of the songs. A novelty in these arrangements for both Thomson and Whyte are instrumental preludes and postludes, on which Haydn apparently bestowed particular care. Haydn's new versions attempt to enter into the spirit of the originals. The composer tried to preserve the austere character of the tunes; the use of harsh cross relations as well as a striving toward modal harmonies testify to his aim to recapture the flavor of this peculiar folk art.

Frequently Haydn arranged the same tune for various publishers, trying to solve the problem in different ways. In this connection the *Airs with Variations* of 1805 ought to be mentioned. In each of these six songs, the part of the singer is repeated unchanged while the accompaniment is altered in every stanza. These very late arrangements prove that the form interested the composer until the very end, and that he continued to strive for its improvement.

* * *

[22] Selected folk songs were edited by B. Engelke (Leipzig, 1927). One hundred Scottish songs arranged for Napier were edited by K. Geiringer in the Collected Edition, Series XXXII, Vol. 1 (Munich, 1961). See also K. Geiringer, "Haydn and the Folk Song of the British Isles," *Musical Quarterly* (1949).

In 1796, Haydn wrote two Italian chamber duets of Nina and Tirsi, "Saper vorrei" and "Guarda qui,"[23] using texts by C. F. Badini, the librettist of his London opera *L'anima del filosofo*. The compositions, which are set for soprano, tenor, and clavier, have the character of simple operatic duets. They make no particular demands on the singers' technical abilities and were apparently meant for music-making in the home. Quite different is the great tercet for two sopranos, tenor, and orchestra, "Pietà di me, benigni dei," probably written for Mrs. Billington: in it there is no lack of fast runs and wide leaps in the vocal parts. As a counterpart to the trio of singers, Haydn here introduces a concertant trio of English horn, French horn, and bassoon; its parts match those of the vocalists in virtuosity.

Haydn's thirteen songs for three or four voices and clavier[24] were begun in 1796 according to the testimony of the autograph in the Paris Conservatory. Griesinger contends that in 1801 Haydn told him that he wanted to write twenty-five of these pieces, but old age apparently made this impossible. He probably received the impulse to create these works in England, where part singing always had been popular. As a true instrumental composer, Haydn added piano accompaniments to his compositions. The simple, naturally flowing melodies—avoiding all virtuosity and closely following the intentions of the poet—and the complete lack of theatrical pathos, give these pieces a unique position among Haydn's vocal output. Full of humor are the trio "An den Vetter" (To the Cousin) with its quaint coloratura, and the quartet "Harmonie in der Ehe" (Harmony in Marriage), in which Haydn delights in mocking a meaningless marriage. A special joke can be found at the end of the delightful quartet "Die Beredsamkeit" (Eloquence). Here the last word, *stumm* (still), must not be sung, but should only be mouthed soundlessly by the singers, as Haydn prescribes in the autograph. The other extreme is marked by the powerful

[23] Edited by H. C. R. Landon (Vienna, 1960).
[24] Edited by P. Mies in the Collected Edition, Series XXX (Munich, 1958).

religious songs "Danklied zu Gott" (Song of Thanks to God) and "Abendlied zu Gott" (Evensong to God), pieces that, despite their having more the character of chamber music, well can stand comparison with the great choruses of *The Creation* and *The Seasons*. Haydn himself suggested that Friedrich Zelter should make an arrangement of the "Abendlied" for chorus, solo quartet, and pianoforte.

All of Haydn's rounds and canons[25] are products of his last period of composition. The famous *Ten Commandments*, ten individual canons, each setting one of the commandments to music, probably were written in England to German words between 1791 and 1795. Haydn sent the first of these rounds, using the words "Thy voice, O Harmony" (instead of the original "Du sollst an einen Gott glauben"), to Oxford University in 1792 as a sign of appreciation of the doctorate of music conferred upon him. The *Ten Commandments* frequently was printed, the first German edition being published by Breitkopf and Härtel, Leipzig, in 1810, the first English edition by Clementi, London, around 1812.

After Haydn's return to Vienna, the new interest he took in vocal music prompted him to write a substantial number of secular canons, of which forty-five have survived. He was very fond of these pieces and used fair copies, glazed and framed, as wall decorations in his study. After his death, these copies were bought by Prince Esterházy. They were kept for a time in the castle of Esterháza, but no longer can be traced. Breitkopf and Härtel, Leipzig, published forty-two of them in the year 1810, during which the *Ten Commandments* appeared in print.

These canons and rounds usually are for three or four parts, but pieces for two, five, six, seven, and eight voices occur. Particularly subtle is the three-part canon "Thy Voice, O Harmony," which may also be sung backward as a canon cancrizans. A further possibility is that of turning the score of this canon upside down; held in this way the canon may again be sung forward and backward. The canon "Das gröszte Gut" (entitled "The Best" in Whit-

[25] They were edited by O. E. Deutsch in the Collected Edition, Series XXXI (Munich, 1959).

taker's edition)[26] introduces an imitation at the third and fifth below; and there are several canons for two voices at the fifth below. They all show that Haydn's contrapuntal skill was considerable. In the seventh of the *Ten Commandments,* according to an unproved old story, he used a melody that he himself had taken from another composer, as if to poke fun at the seventh commandment, "Thou shalt not steal." The whole thing is based on an unconfirmed rumor, but it would be very much in keeping with Haydn's delightful sense of humor.

The texts of the rounds and canons are, following the classical tradition, often facetious and not always sensible; some of them are unintelligible, as Haydn liked to set to music brief verses he had found in extensive poems; taken out of their context, the verses are likely to make no sense. As early as 1810 the German edition changed many of Haydn's original texts[27] and this procedure unfortunately was continued, though in many cases the expurgated versions definitely are inferior to the originals. In particular the Latin words of Horace, the Italian of Federico (used also in the first aria of Pergolesi's *La serva padrona*), and the funny verses of Lessing belong among the best texts used for this kind of composition.

* * *

It has been contended that Haydn's four-act opera *L'anima del filosofo,* based on a book by Badini dealing with the Orpheus myth, and written in 1791 for London, is unfinished. This is not the case, as research done by Botstiber and myself as well as, more recently, Wirth and Landon has shown.[28] The error was caused by the fact that in 1805 Breitkopf and Härtel published a selection of eleven numbers from the unperformed work under the name of *Orfeo ed Euridice,* which, in spite of its pre-

[26] *Rounds and Canons by Haydn* (London, 1932).

[27] See O. E. Deutsch in *Zeitschrift f. Musikwissenschaft,* Vol. 15 (1932–33), p. 112 f.

[28] Cf. Hugo Botstiber, *Joseph Haydn* (Leipzig, 1927), p. 339 ff., and the commentary accompanying the LP recording of the work by the Haydn Society, Boston (1951).

tentious designation as a *dramma per musica*, was destined
for the concert hall. Apparently Haydn objected to seeing
in print the complete score of a work that no longer was
really his property, as he had sold it to Gallini (see p. 118).

L'anima del filosofo was the only opera in which Haydn
did not have to take into account the small group of singers
of Prince Esterházy's company. He was thus in a position
to make ample use of the chorus, which, as in Gluck's
operas, plays an important part in the dramatic events.
For instance, the fourth act (this is Haydn's only opera
in four acts) contains, besides recitatives and a short instrumental piece, six choral numbers but only a single
aria. In the third act too there are more choral numbers
than arias. Mixed choruses alternate with women's and
men's choruses. Also the tragic final scene of the work, in
which the bacchantes administer poison to Orpheus, and
the boat carrying the body of the singer founders in a
storm, is treated as a women's chorus interrupted by
short accompanied recitative. All through the work Haydn
alternates choral and solo numbers. Thus, the second act
starts with a gay songlike women's chorus (Ex. 19),

which is followed by a dialogue in secco recitative between Orfeo and Euridice. Thereafter, the chorus repeats
its initial song. The lovers again take over and ultimately
the two soloists cooperate with the chorus. The important
part assigned to the choruses, the tragic ending of the
opera, the more concise form in which most of the numbers are cast, and the stirring effect of some scenes (especially of the simple, deeply moving death-song of Euridice) show that Haydn was aiming at improving the
Neapolitan *opera seria* along the lines of Gluck's operatic
reform. Yet he must have encountered a serious obstacle
in the verbosity and tediousness of Badini's libretto. Be-

sides, he was not able to dispense completely with the *recitativo secco,* and some of the pieces, such as the conventional coloratura aria of the Spirit in the third act, definitely point back into the past. In spite of its many beauties, *L'anima del filosofo* certainly is not on a level with the composer's other great vocal and instrumental works of the same period. The work shows again that Haydn did not feel sufficiently at home in the composition of serious operas to free himself completely from the bondage of prevailing taste and to create real musical drama.

Haydn's last work for the stage was incidental music to an English tragedy, *The Patriot King, or Alfred and Elvida,* by Alexander Bicknell (1788), which was performed in 1796 in Vienna in a translation by J. W. Cowmeadow, as *Alfred oder der patriotische König,* but had little success and before long disappeared from the repertoire. Haydn composed for this drama a three-part "Chorus of Danes" for sopranos, tenors, and basses;[29] a recitative and aria for the Guardian Spirit, and a duet for Alfred and Odun, Earl of Devon. The chorus was published after Haydn's death with changed words and piano accompaniment as "Kriegerischer Chor" or "Siegerchor" (Martial Chorus or Victory Chorus). It is a showy, somewhat shallow piece also employing trumpets and timpani. The soprano aria "Ausgesandt vom Strahlenthrone" (Sent forth from the radiant throne) is in fact a dialogue between a heavenly and a terrestrial being. The Spirit sings accompanied by a sextet of clarinets, horns, and bassoons, and the woman who receives the celestial message answers with spoken words to instrumental accompaniment. Evidently it was Haydn's aim to establish a clear distinction between supernatural and human beings. The duet "Der Morgen graut, es ruft der Hahn" (Dawn breaks, the cock is crowing) presents a solemn melody accompanied by pizzicato strings. In the orchestral ritornelli, the cantilena likewise played pizzicato by the first violins is accompanied by a *violino principale* in the upper octave, achieving a remarkable coloristic effect. Haydn originally

[29] The elimination of the alto voice is equally characteristic of Haydn's two great oratorios written soon afterward.

planned to have a harp cooperate, but he left the respective staff in the score empty, deciding that the plucked strings sufficed to produce the desired effect.

As this music concludes Haydn's production for the stage, it seems appropriate to review his operatic output as a whole here. The memorandum with which Haydn in the 1760s accompanied his cantata *Applausus* contained the significant words: "If I have failed to guess the taste of the musicians, it must not be taken amiss, as I did not know the performers or the locality. My ignorance of these matters really has made the work hard for me." When he wrote the opera *La vera costanza* for Vienna, an attempt was made to choose singers other than those originally provided. Thereupon Haydn withdrew his opera with the indignant remark: "I know what and for whom I am writing." In the famous letter of 1787 to Roth in Prague, he gave the following reason for his refusal to have one of his earlier operas performed there: "All my operas are too closely connected with our personal circle (Esterháza in Hungary); they could never produce the proper effect, which I have calculated in accordance with the locality." These utterances, made at different periods, reflect the basic attitude natural to a composer of the eighteenth century writing in the style of the Italian opera. The personality of the performers and the place of performance always had to be taken into consideration. The virtuosity of the singers, the technical equipment of the stage, the beauty of the costumes and decorations, and the skill of the stage architect were factors the composer took into serious account. It is significant that after the failure to have *L'anima del filosofo* performed in London, Haydn did not attempt to have it staged elsewhere. With the enormous prestige he enjoyed, he certainly could have obtained a production in Austria or Germany, and it would not have been too difficult to get a release from the London owner.[30]

[30] In this respect the edition printed by Breitkopf and Härtel is significant: it does not reveal the sequence of numbers in the opera. Evidently Haydn wanted merely to present individual pieces, not a complete opera suitable for performance.

Although a certain dependence on outside conditions therefore is to be noticed in Haydn's operas, they by no means deserve the neglect meted out to them in our time. These operas are, it is true, not equal to the top achievements of Gluck and Mozart. Yet such comic and semicomic works as *La canterina, Lo speziale, L'incontro improvviso, Il mondo della luna, L'infedeltà delusa,* and, in particular, *Orlando paladino* are delightful compositions, offering rewarding tasks to the singers, and they are sure of effect if properly performed.

*   *   *

Around 1800, Haydn composed a *Te Deum* in C major[31] for the Empress Maria Theresia (second wife of Francis II). Although nearly forty years separate this work from the first *Te Deum*, written in the early 1760s, the two compositions resemble each other not only in the use of the same key, but also in many details, such as the characteristic combination of a melody to the words "In te Domine speravi" with a counterpoint to the words "Non confundar in aeternum." But the second *Te Deum* calls for a choir only and no solo voices. The orchestra is larger; the whole work is simpler and clearer than the earlier composition. Its expressive power is heightened by the introduction of the Gregorian melody of the *Te Deum* in the inner parts. In its concise structure and forceful language, this magnificent work counts among the aged Haydn's most significant contributions.

In the six Masses[32] written between 1796 and 1802 by order of Prince Esterházy, Haydn displayed the mastery

[31] The work was repeatedly printed: by Breitkopf and Härtel (Leipzig), Novello (London), and recently by Doblinger (Vienna).

[32] The *Missa in tempore belli* and the *Heiligmesse* were edited by H. C. R. Landon, K. H. Füssl, and C. Landon in the Collected Edition, Series XXIII:2 (Munich, 1958), the *Nelson Messe* by W. Weismann (Leipzig, 1931), the *Theresien Messe* by A. Schnerich (Augsburg, 1925), the *Creation Mass* by F. Habel (Augsburg, 1936), the *Harmonie Messe* by G. Göhler (Leipzig, 1909). Novello and Company (London) published organ scores of all six Masses.

that characterizes his other works of his last period. These works are:

No. 1, in C major (Novello No. 2), composed in 1796. Haydn wrote at the head of the score *Missa in tempore belli* (Mass in Wartime), as Napoleon, coming from Italy, at that time was threatening Vienna. In the Agnus Dei the use of trumpets and kettledrums emphasizes the war atmosphere, as does the fanfare of the wind instruments at the beginning of the "Dona nobis pacem."

No. 2, in B flat major (Novello No. 1), in Germany called *Heiligmesse* because of the use of the hymn "Heilig, heilig" by the contralto and tenor in the Sanctus. This Mass was composed in 1796 and dedicated to the memory of the monk Bernardus von Offida, who had been canonized the preceding year.[33]

No. 3, in D minor (Novello No. 3), Haydn's only Mass in a minor key. According to the autograph in the National Library, Vienna, it was composed in 1798 at Eisenstadt in fifty-three days (July 10–August 31). While Haydn worked on it, the news of the Battle of the Nile arrived. The striking use of the trumpets in the Benedictus is usually thought to be associated with the report of Nelson's decisive victory, which made a tremendous impression all over Europe.[34] The composition is known in Germany as the *Nelson Messe*, in England as the *Coronation* or *Imperial Mass*. In its orchestration no woodwind instruments are used, only brass, percussion, and stringed instruments.

No. 4, in B flat major (Novello No. 16), composed in 1799. It is known as *Theresien Messe*, probably after the Empress Maria Theresia, who was one of Haydn's patronesses and also a gifted singer.[35]

[33] The *Heiligmesse* usually is enumerated before the *Missa in tempore belli*, but as Haydn adopts the opposite order in his catalogue and Schnerich also considers that the treatment of the text in the C major Mass points to an earlier date of composition, the order has been reversed here.

[34] After Haydn's death, a chart of the Battle of the Nile was found among his papers.

[35] Schnerich's conjecture that the Mass was named after the singer Therese Rosenbaum-Gassmann does not seem very likely. On the other hand, the connection of the Mass with the Em-

No. 5, in B flat major (Novello No. 4), composed in 1801. As it introduces in the "Qui tollis" of the Agnus Dei a quotation from *The Creation*, this Mass is known as the *Creation Mass*.

No. 6, in B flat major (Novello No. 6), written in 1802. It is known as *Harmonie Messe* (Wind-Band Mass), probably because of its emphatic use of wind instruments.

The features of the older Masses still are preserved in these later works, but the distribution of the individual elements has changed and their connection has become tighter and more organic. The use of vocal solos is greatly reduced and their melodic line simplified in a classical manner. Instead of single voices, Haydn largely employs the solo quartet, the four voices of which are treated in a loose contrapuntal style, thus effectively contrasting with the plain tutti of the chorus, which predominantly are conceived on purely harmonic lines. On the whole the importance of polyphony is increased in these last Masses, and fugues are frequently introduced. The Credo of the *Nelson Messe* includes a canon at the fifth, and the Incarnatus of the *Heiligmesse* a three-part canon. Particularly impressive are the magnificent Credo fugue of the *Missa in tempore belli* and the "In gloria Dei" fugue of the *Heiligmesse*. Sketches for the latter prove the care that Haydn bestowed on it. In the earlier Masses, the instruments of the orchestra were used mainly to reinforce the vocal parts; in the works written after 1796, they frequently are employed independently, carrying melodies of their own. The choice of instruments reveals Haydn's joy in diversity: no two of the Masses have the same orchestral garb. The original version of the *Nelson Mass* prescribes three trumpets and timpani besides strings and concertizing organ, thus achieving a tonal language full of vigor and intensity. (Unfortunately, a more conventional orchestration was chosen for the printed edition, in which

---

press Maria Theresia established by tradition is not upheld by C. M. Brand, *Die Messen von Joseph Haydn* (Würzburg, 1941), who maintains that the work was written for the Princess Marie Hermenegild Esterházy and ought to be designated *Hermenegild Mass*.

one flute as well as two each of oboes, bassoons, and horns were added.) Likewise, the *Theresien Messe* calls only for two clarinets and two trumpets among the wind instruments. The most extensive orchestral body (two each of flutes, oboes, clarinets, bassoons, horns, trumpets, and timpani) is required in the *Harmonie Messe*, the last large work that Haydn completed. Truly romantic sound effects are achieved here by the woodwind; for example, the mysterious, soft employment of brass and timpani in the "Et incarnatus est" is exquisitely poetic. Of equal significance is the lovely Incarnatus in the *Creation Mass*, in which Haydn again introduces an organ solo. The delicate warbling and twittering provided here with the help of the flautino stop is intended to produce a pastoral effect. Beethoven uses a somewhat related idea in his *Missa Solemnis*. Haydn's main aim during this period was to furnish an adequate musical interpretation of his text; the composition tries to follow the Ordinary of the Mass in every detail and to deepen its expression. The occasions are becoming less and less frequent when Haydn's musicianship makes him oblivious to the dramatic possibilities of his subject. As an example of such neglect, the Incarnatus of the *Theresien Messe* should be mentioned. Its first part in B flat minor is followed by a second in D flat major. The mild, tender character of the second section is musically justified, but it hardly fits the words of the Crucifixus with which it is used. It is also noteworthy that in the same work Haydn omits to set to music the words "Et in unum Dominum Jesum Christum filium Dei unigenitum" despite their liturgical importance. But instances of excellent interpretation of the text in terms of music are far more frequent. The *Heiligmesse* contains a Crucifixus, the tragic expression of which could hardly be surpassed. In the Incarnatus of the *Missa in tempore belli*, Haydn, like Beethoven after him, uses the word *et* (and) in order to increase the dramatic suspense. The whole chorus sings it in a long, drawn-out forte based on a diminished seventh chord before the words "incarnatus est" sung in piano describe the miracle of the union of divinity with humanity in Christ. An anticipation of Beethoven also may be discerned in the menacing use of trumpets and timpani in the Agnus Dei of the same Mass. Beethoven's "prayer for inner and outer peace" is somewhat forecast in this deeply moving section. The use of brass instruments in the *Nelson Mass*, possibly Haydn's best-known Mass, gives its Benedictus a particularly brilliant and intense character. In this connection it may be pointed out that the inclusion of trumpet fanfares in the Mass is based on an old Austrian tradition. Christoph Strauss, a choirmaster of St. Stephen's Cathedral in Vienna, used it as early as 1631 in his *Missa veni sponsa Christi*. As in Haydn's late instrumental works, so in his late Masses, the influence of Mozart may be detected. A good example is provided by the Gratias of the *Theresien Messe*, which displays much of Mozart's grace and fervor.

Summarizing the results of the analysis of Haydn's church music, we notice that at first he used elements of style that had originated in various parts of Italy. Subsequently he succeeded in synthesizing these trends and creating, out of baroque and classical elements, with the help of simple, often folkloristic melodies, a language of his own, definitely of Austrian character. The type of sacred composition that thus was created from different building stones proved to be a solid foundation for the imposing edifice of nineteenth-century Mass composition.

*   *   *

In 1792, Haydn's chorus "The Storm," based on a text by John Wolcot—better known under his pen name of Peter Pindar—was performed in London. This work shows effective contrast between a realistic musical description of a storm (in G minor) and a melodious and flowing andante (in D major) expressing hope for the return of quiet. The contrast also is expressed in the instrumental coloring, as the trumpets, timpani, and trombones used in the first part are dismissed in the second section and the chorus is replaced by a quartet of soloists. This piece seems like a precursor of the thunderstorm in *The Seasons*, but the repetition of both sections, though certainly justified from a musical point of view, weakens its dramatic power.

The British Museum possesses an original manuscript by Haydn written in 1794 and entitled "Nor Can I Think My Suit Is Vain." This work consists of two numbers from an unfinished composition for solo voices, chorus, and orchestra. The words are taken from M. Nedham's poem "Neptune to the Commonwealth of England," which he used as an introduction to his English translation of John Selden's Latin treatise *Mare clausum*. The composition was undertaken at the request of the fourth Earl of Abingdon. But when Haydn found out that three other men before him, among them his former pupil Pleyel, had composed on the same subject, he lost interest in the work. Only the second and third of the seven stanzas of Nedham's poem were set. This torso—sometimes referred to as "Invocation to Neptune"—consists of the baritone aria of Neptune, "Nor can I think," brilliantly employing the woodwinds (including clarinets) and a vivid chorus, "Thy great endeavors." Originally Haydn seems to have planned to use two sopranos and two tenors for this number, but he changed his mind and employed a mixed chorus with four voices in the ordinary range.

The singularly expressive character of Haydn's music to *The Seven Last Words* always has been noticed. In 1788 the *Musikalische Realzeitung* wrote about the work: "We are able to guess in practically every note what the composer meant to convey by it." It was therefore an obvious idea to convert this instrumental composition into a vocal Passion piece by the introduction of voices. The first attempt in this direction was made by Joseph Friebert, a musician in the little city of Passau in south Germany. Haydn heard this arrangement in 1794, on his second trip to England. He did not approve of the new version, but was so interested in it that he decided to use it as a basis for a similar work of his own. The adaptation of the words was made by Gottfried van Sweiten, who in this work collaborated with Haydn for the first time. The new text, dealing with the sufferings of our Lord and the redemption of mankind, is lacking in action and is in complete conformity with the sentimental German oratorios of the second half of the eighteenth century, which were based on the story of the Messiah. Its content is altogether lyrical, and dramatic elements are eschewed as far as possible; apparently Ramler's *Tod Jesu* served van Swieten as a model. The librettist even appropriated episodes from that work, such as the gloomy and portentous text on the earthquake that concludes Haydn's work. Fortunately the stilted pomposity characteristic of so many German oratorio texts of the early eighteenth century hardly is noticeable in *The Seven Last Words.*

The autograph of the oratorio, preserved in the National Library, Budapest, plainly reveals the technique adopted by Haydn for his arrangement. He first had the original instrumental version copied by Elssler onto music paper ruled with a great many staves, only some of which were used. Then he himself started to insert the vocal parts and the new instruments, two clarinets and two trombones, into the score. At the same time, several minor changes were made in the original instrumentation. For instance, in order to increase the harsh grandeur of the introduction, Haydn omitted the flutes of the older version. An important addition to the vocal arrangement consists of a new number inserted between the fourth and fifth sonatas. It is a largo performed by wind instruments only. As a counterpart to the introduction, it once more expresses the prevailing tragic spirit by instrumental means. At the same time, the oratorio adopts a significant feature, each of its movements being preceded by the relevant utterance of the Saviour. The full chorus is employed to pronounce the "word" in simple recitation. Apart from these details, the original construction of the composition has not been changed. A chorus and a quartet of solo voices were added to the instrumental composition without any considerable alteration of the original music. Nevertheless, the text is mostly so well adjusted that the listener who is not informed about the genesis of *The Seven Last Words* is inclined to accept the work as an oratorio conceived in the normal way. Only occasionally are text and music incompatible. In the choral section of No. 6, for instance, the words "Woe ye wicked, woe ye blind" are accompanied by music imbued with an almost serene spirit. While the composer, inspired by the words "It is finished," expresses the confidence of mankind in the salvation through Jesus' sacrifice, the poet still is concerned with the drama of Golgotha. Either point of view is justified, but their combination certainly is unsatisfactory. Such shortcomings are, however, infrequent, and on the whole it is remarkable how admirably the poet follows the musician, though the peculiarities of the instrumental forms, such as the development and recapitulation sections, do not make his task an easy one.

The vocal version impresses the listener as a work fully realizing the composer's innermost intentions. Sandberger[36] feels that a large part of its success is owing to Friebert's work, as Haydn's arrangement, particularly in its first part, is strongly dependent on the model. However, we cannot help admiring Haydn's sure instinct and singular lack of prejudice in allowing himself to be guided by an artist of mediocre abilities at a time when he himself had reached the pinnacle of his creative output.

Very different from *The Seven Last Words* is the cantata *Die Erwählung eines Kapellmeisters* (The Election of a Conductor), which has often been attributed to Haydn, although no irrefutable proof of its authenticity has yet been provided. It is a caricature of the pompous cantatas in Neapolitan style intended to pay homage to an exalted person, a genre to which Haydn himself had contributed at an earlier period). In *The Election of a Conductor*, Minerva and Bacchus each present an aspirant for the post. Apollo sets their minds at rest by informing them that their two candidates—a conscientious scholar and a gay tippler—are really one and the same person, who accordingly is selected. *Die Erwählung eines Kapellmeisters* is written for three soloists, chorus, and small orchestra, and is made up of recitatives and *da capo* arias for the soloists, two ensémble numbers for the chorus only. The arias are full of coloratura and exhibit an old-fashioned style. The contrast between the pompous composition and the frivolous, rather silly text must have seemed extremely ludicrous to an eighteenth-century audi-

[36] *Zur Entwicklungsgeschichte von Haydns "Sieben Worten." Gesammelte Aufsätze* (Munich, 1921).

ence. All the performers had to do was to emphasize the contradictions between the words and music, and the assembled hearers, fully familiar with the weak points of the Neapolitan style, would enjoy the unpretentious work highly.

It is of interest that the exponents of the later romanticism, around the year 1900, looked with a very superior air, almost with contempt, at the early evidence of romantic feeling as displayed in Haydn's *The Creation* and *The Seasons.* I. F. Runciman[37] sums up his discussion of *The Creation* with the words: "After considering the songs, the recitatives, and the choruses in detail it really seems to contain very little. Perhaps it may be described as a third-rate oratorio, whose interest is largely historic and literary."

It no longer is necessary to apologize for Haydn's last two oratorios. Nevertheless, they do not enjoy in the English-speaking countries the position they deserve. Performances of *The Creation* are still relatively infrequent, and *The Seasons* is almost unknown even to many choral conductors. The great popularity that these oratorios enjoy in Austria and Germany is not paralleled in England and America, though in several respects the two works are more English than German.

Haydn had been among the audience of the great Handel Festival of 1791. He found a whole nation aroused by compositions offered in monumental performances. Compared with these concerts on a large scale, his own efforts of earlier years to entertain a small group of music lovers at Esterháza must have seemed to him almost insignificant. He desired intensely to write, as Handel had written, works meant for a whole nation. Different types of oratorios were used at that time in Austria and Germany, but none of them really satisfied the master. There was the Italian oratorio, which he had employed in his *Il ritorno di Tobia.* But Haydn was now reluctant to use a language foreign to the people for whom the composition was written, reluctant to commit himself to the formalism of this genre, with its weak arias and neglect of powerful choruses. There was, on the other hand, the contemplative, sentimental German

[37] *Old Scores and New Reading* (London, 1899), p. 92.

oratorio; but he had just finished the arrangement of *The Seven Last Words* and had no wish to lose himself again in tearful mellowness. Neither did he care for the dramatic type of German oratorio as cultivated by J. H. Rolle, which produced a sort of disguised sacred opera. After having written more than a dozen operas, Haydn felt too clearly that he never would give his very best in a work of predominantly dramatic character. There remained only one type of oratorio to which he really felt attracted, and that was again the oratorio of Handel, of the type exemplified by his *Israel in Egypt* and *L'allegro, il penseroso, ed il moderato*. The unorthodox construction of these works, the hymnic impetus of their choruses, and their strong feeling for nature deeply impressed Haydn, and he decided to follow the example of these great English oratorios rather than use a German model.

Also, a wholly suitable subject for his work was offered to Haydn in England. This was an oratorio text that Lidley had compiled from the contents of the first chapter of Genesis and the seventh and eighth books of Milton's *Paradise Lost*. According to tradition, this text, entitled "The Creation," originally had been destined for Handel himself. Haydn took the English libretto to Vienna, entrusting his friend Baron van Swieten with the translation. Van Swieten was certainly the right person for the task, as he had proved his skill with his work on *The Seven Last Words*, and moreover he was a great admirer of Handel. Therefore it is not surprising that the German text of "The Creation," based in its recitatives on the Vulgate, was in many respects akin to the texts of Handel's oratorios. Wherever it was possible, the powerful words of the Bible replaced the sentimental paraphrases used in German oratorios at that time. The old narrator was revived in the persons of three singers: the archangels Gabriel (soprano), Uriel (tenor), and Raphael (bass), who take turns in telling the story of the Creation. Most of all, the important share awarded to the chorus reminds us of the oratorios of Handel.

Van Swieten did not restrict himself to the arrangement of the text; the imperious baron also gave Haydn directions as to how to set the words to music. Far from resenting such tutoring, Haydn followed van Swieten's advice in most cases, and it cannot be denied that this was beneficial to the composition. What insight is revealed, for instance, by the baron's advice: " 'Let there be light' must be sung only once"!

Not only van Swieten's text, but also Haydn's music breathes the spirit of Handel. Haydn certainly did not copy the older master, but he found in the works of his great model an excuse for his tendency to abandon formulas accepted in his country. In Haydn's oratorio, chorus and soloists sometimes are used together, at other times alternate quickly; the form of the arias changes from number to number, but always is dependent on the text; the recitatives often assume the form of charmingly accompanied ariosos, displaying in their tone-paintings the composer's deep love of nature. All this is typical of Haydn's last period of composition, but it is doubtful that he would have dared to follow his instinct so completely, had it not been for the encouragement provided by Handel's oratorios. In his early cantatas, Haydn often subordinated the text to the music; in *Il ritorno di Tobia* they were treated as equals; finally, in *The Creation* and *The Seasons* the musical construction was determined by the substance of the text in the same way as it has been in all truly great oratorios before and after those of Haydn.

The apparently spontaneous freedom of expression in *The Creation* really is the product of an extraordinary intensity of work. Haydn now worked very slowly and carefully, first making sketches as Beethoven did after him. Of that easy reliance on sure instinct which his youthful works had revealed there is not a trace in *The Creation*.

The master used drafts for many works of this period, such as the last Masses and various marches, songs, and canons. None of these sketches is so extensive and so important as those of *The Creation*, twenty-three pages of which are preserved in the National Library, Vienna.[38] As they afford a valuable insight into the gradual shaping

[38] MSS. 16835 and 18987.

of Haydn's ideas, it seems appropriate to mention two characteristic instances.[39]

Particularly interesting are the sketches for the chorus "By thee with bliss," which in its final form presents only a shadowy foundation on which the swelling hymn of the two soloists is raised. Haydn did not arrive at this justly admired color effect at first inspiration. As originally conceived, this chorus was a lively movement opening with imitations and set in C minor, not C major. But Haydn did not let matters rest there, and the passage appears on another page of the sketches in C major. The soprano solo now occurs in its present form and the chorus is handled far more simply. In the margin Haydn appended the words, so indicative of his irrepressible sense of humor: "It is not good to be interesting," the obvious reasoning behind this comment being: This example proves that it is not good to write too complicated music. In fact, the final form of the chorus is far simpler than either of the sketches.

For the instrumental introduction to the oratorio, entitled "Representation of Chaos," two different sketches also exist. The passage for the first violin in the third and fourth measures, describing the boundless loneliness of lifeless chaos, is missing in the first sketch, and the ascending triplet-figure is not given the completely subdued coloring expressing infinite desolation. Haydn entrusts it to the first violin, horn, and clarinet, whereas he subsequently has it played by bassoon, viola, cello, and, occasionally, the second violin (which certainly sounds gentler than the first). The D flat major section merely is outlined in this first draft. The second sketch presents the first part of the introduction in practically the form in which we know it today, but the contrasting section in D flat major still lacks the significant accompaniment in sixteenth notes in the bassoon, which contributes so substantially to mellowing the austerity of the beginning. It also is characteristic that in measure forty-nine of the final version, Haydn has written a single ascending figure for the bassoon, whereas in

[39] Cf. K. Geiringer, "Haydn's Sketches for the 'Creation,'" *Musical Quarterly*, XVIII (1932).

the sketch he had put an ornate flourish, twice as long, for the clarinet. The composer worked steadily toward the simplification of expression, banning all rococo affectation from his work.

One of the greatest numbers in the score of *The Creation* is this very first one, describing Chaos. Zelter, the friend of Goethe, called it "the crown on a God's head." The romantic touch in these dark harmonies full of chromatic passing notes and suspensions is unmistakable, and Tovey even goes so far as to compare them to the music of Wagner's *Tristan und Isolde.* He suggests moreover, that Haydn, who had met the astronomer Herschel, may have heard about the evolution of the cosmos out of chaos, and that these ideas inspired him to write his overture. The economy of the composer's thematic work deserves greatest admiration. The first twenty measures of this prelude in C minor describing the sadness of Chaos are based on the stepwise descending "sigh motive." As soon as the idea of cosmic life is introduced, the gentle key of D flat major sets in, and with it in the woodwind an ascending instead of the former descending motive. Such monumental simplicity largely is responsible for the piece's overwhelming effect. The following recitative and chorus contain the famous passage "And there was light," with its change from C minor to C major, and from piano to forte. A hundred years later, Richard Strauss, in his *Also sprach Zarathustra,* described the mighty appearance of the sun with similar means of expression. The ensuing "Now vanish," is one of the many numbers of this score in which Haydn connects a soloist with the chorus, displaying in these mixed pieces an unrivaled fantasy and variety of form. Here the chorus repeatedly sings the words "A new created world springs up at God's command." Whenever the words "a new created world" recur, Haydn changes the harmony. No. 3, Raphael's recitative "And God made the firmament," contains some of the innumerable descriptions of nature in which *The Creation* excels. Storm, lightning, thunder, rain, hail, snow, and, later on, a whole menagerie of mammals, birds, fishes, and insects—all this Haydn's orchestra describes with a great sense of humor.

He, who clung to nature and all earthly things more fervently than most other composers, fully succeeded in reflecting the youthful purity of the newly created universe. So sure was Haydn of the expressive power of his music that his descriptions always precede the explaining text. A powerful solo by Gabriel with a choral accompaniment concludes the second day of the Creation. No. 6, Raphael's aria "Rolling in foaming billows," is partly modeled on Italian examples. It is not free from ornamental coloratura, and its key sequences are reminiscent of those used in instrumental music. Nevertheless, the text predominates over the form here too, and an equal number of musical sections corresponds to the four pictures of the poem (ocean, mountains, river, and brook). The lovely, purely lyrical aria of Gabriel, "With verdure clad," contrasts very effectively with the majestic chorus "Awake the harp." The simple, terse first ten measures of the recitative "In splendor bright," describing the sunrise, belong among Haydn's greatest inspirations. The melody is lifted slowly stepwise through the interval of a tenth. In almost every measure a fresh instrument is added to the orchestra until the delicate pianissimo has been changed into an overwhelming fortissimo. The chorus with a trio of the soloists, "The heavens are telling," ends the first part of *The Creation*. It is one of the best-known pieces of the score, but its popularity ought not to induce the conductors of small choruses to perform it as a separate piece with the omission of the solo voices, as this procedure deprives the composition of much of its charm.

The second part of the oratorio begins with the fifth day of the Creation, when the animals come to life. In the coloratura aria of Gabriel "On mighty pens," the cooing sounds of the pigeons are particularly well imitated by the bassoons and violins. A stroke of genius is found in No. 16, which begins as a recitative, but presently assumes the character of an arioso. At the words "Be fruitful and multiply," divided violas, violoncellos, and double basses are employed to express mysterious saturation and abundance. Here it is imperative that the double basses should play the lowest notes F_1, E_1, D_1, and C_1, as prescribed by

Haydn, for the usual transposition of this passage an octave upward is likely to nullify the majestic effect he intended. In No. 19, "The Lord is great and great His
might," the three soloists join in praise of the Almighty,
the chorus supporting them in an exuberant paean. The
recitative "Straight opening her fertile womb," (No. 21),
takes us to the sixth day of the Creation and with it to a
further extension of the zoological cast of characters. Here,
Haydn's resourcefulness in the invention of effects of color
is matched only by his economy in their employment. The
aria of Uriel, "In native worth" (No. 24), deals with the
achievement of the seventh day, the creation of the first
human couple. Its proud bearing expresses the optimistic
attitude toward mankind which Haydn shared with many
great spirits of the eighteenth century, the age of human-
ism and enlightenment. The end of the second part of the
oratorio consists of two great choruses in the same key,
based partly on identical words ("Achieved is the glorious
work") and music, but separated by a trio for the soloists,
the result being a sort of three-part form. The second of
these choruses contains a double fugue of Handelian dignity and simplicity.

The third part of *The Creation* is dedicated to the praise
of the Creation through the first human beings, Adam
(bass) and Eve (soprano), who now replace the archangels Gabriel and Raphael. In the E major introduction
to this part, Haydn uses three flutes accompanied by the
pizzicato of the strings. This intensely romantic description
of the early morning seems to anticipate the beginning of
the prelude to Wagner's *Lohengrin*. The duet and chorus
"By thee with bliss" (No. 30) already has been mentioned
in connection with the sketches for the oratorio. With its
approximately four hundred measures, it is one of the longest, and at the same time one of the most inspired and
powerful, numbers of the entire work. In a way it marks
the end of the oratorio, as the succeeding love duet between Adam and Eve displays a slightly incongruous and
commonplace character. Its ostentatious show in the *style
galant* seems better suited to a rococo Singspiel than an
oratorio based on the Bible and Milton's great epic. The

very last number, a prayer of thanks for solo quartet (the only number of the score in which a contralto solo is prescribed) and chorus, culminates in a mighty double fugue that brings the work to an imposing conclusion. Better than any personal document, *The Creation* testifies to the breadth of Haydn's inner world. In this work, childlike naïveté, joy in the world of the senses, and gentle humor are combined with profound faith, nobility of expression, and hymnlike fervor. The diversity inherent in this spiritual landscape may account for the strong echo that the work, since its first performance, has evoked in the hearts of listeners.

Soon after the completion of *The Creation*, Haydn started on another big vocal composition, on which he worked up to the year 1801. Again, van Swieten adapted the text from an English poem, James Thomson's *The Seasons*, printed in four sections in 1726, 1727, 1728, and 1730. This work, filled with gay optimism, describes with an abundance of detail the beauties of nature; any kind of dramatic action is completely absent from it. The poem offers a continuous series of images full of picturesque variety, and these provide an excellent foundation for a musical libretto. Van Swieten showed a certain attitude of independence toward the original work. He eliminated philosophical and historical details while emphasizing Thomson's tender lyrical observations of nature. The English poet's fundamental attitude, however, that of depicting the seasons with love and deep understanding but without any attempt to establish a relationship with human emotions, has been preserved by van Swieten. Thomson's work and the baron's adaptation do not present subjective feelings, but only objective descriptions. The exaggerated praises of the "merry shepherd," the "gay herd," and the wonderful "daughters of nature" all breathe the shallow playfulness of rococo art.

The English poem did not furnish van Swieten with any suggestions for the arrangement of the text into recitatives, arias, choruses; in this regard he again displayed a thorough understanding of the possibilities of musical setting, and particularly an appreciation of Haydn's specific tal-

ents. Far less successful was the arranger in transforming
the unhappy ending of Thomson's "Winter," in which the
wanderer perishes in the cold. But the baron had just as
little appreciation of the beauties of nature in wintertime
as Thomson himself, and accordingly he moved the scene
from the open air to a peasant's house, where the soloists
and chorus perform two pieces. For this episode, van
Swieten used texts written by other poets: "The Spinning
Song" by Gottfried August Bürger and a little poem by
Christian Felix Weisse (based on a French text by Madame Favart) which Johann Adam Hiller had employed
thirty years earlier in his Singspiel "Liebe auf dem Land."
But as the playful tune of the Singspiel seemed to the
baron unsuitable for the conclusion of an oratorio, he made
a sudden about-face and boldly ventured into the realm
of symbolism. Comparing the seasons in nature to the seasons of human life, he came to the conclusion that virtue
alone can lead to eternal happiness. The vision of Paradise
assures a dignified ending to the work. However, it cannot
be denied that the heterogeneous elements of van Swieten's
"Winter" do not blend well.

Again, the baron was not satisfied with merely writing
the libretto. Just as he had done when working on *The
Creation,* he advised Haydn on how to set the words to
music. Max Friedländer, the German musicologist, owned
the copy of van Swieten's libretto that Haydn had made
the basis of his composition.[40] The pages of the manuscript
were folded, and in the margin the baron had noted hints
for the benefit of the composer. For instance, he remarked
near the end of "Spring": "I believe that at the words
'God of Light! Hail Gracious Lord' a key strikingly different from the one used in the preceding 'Song of Joy' would
make a good effect and contribute to the solemn and devout character of the utterance." The highly effective
change from D major to B flat major in the majestic invocation of the Lord near the end of "Spring" thus is intimated. It is well known that Haydn disliked certain sections
of the text of *The Seasons,* and he particularly resented

[40] See Max Friedländer, "Van Swieten und das Textbuch zu
Haydns Jahreszeiten," *Jahrbuch Peters* (1909).

van Swieten's suggestions of inserting little tone-paintings and genre scenes into the music. As stated earlier in this book, the composer remarked: "This Frenchified trash was forced upon me." But the librettist should not be blamed too severely for having done the "forcing." Although van Swieten was no great poet, his text furnished Haydn with an abundance of musical possibilities, and even the notorious episode of the croaking frogs in "Summer" by no means disgraces the composition. The composer's complaint about the unpoetical chorus "Joyful, joyful the liquor flows," is equally unjustified. This piece gave him a chance to introduce a typically Austrian note into the work, and even if the words are neither dignified nor poetic, the finished number ranks among the jewels of the score. This is a case of the great and naïve musician Haydn versus the reflective aesthete Haydn, and we must be grateful to van Swieten for having encouraged the former rather than the latter.

Haydn used sketches[41] for _The Seasons_ as he had in the case of _The Creation_. He emphasized again and again how strenuous the work was, and he must be admired all the more in that the finished product displays no signs of the toil and labor involved in its making. The apparently easy flow of the musical language is really the result of a strain on the composer's every nerve.

It cannot surprise us that _The Creation_ and _The Seasons_, having been conceived in quick succession, display frequent similarities. Haydn again uses a solo trio consisting of Simon, a farmer (bass); Lucas, a countryman (tenor); and Jane, Simon's daughter (soprano), instead of the traditional solo quartet. The free, unorthodox construction of the sections is particularly marked in the later work. It seems to be, in effect, a succession of four loosely connected cantatas, and many editions (among them the first one) do not carry the designation "oratorio" at all.

As in _The Creation_, the introductions to the different parts of the work express a poetical program. The art of description is so highly developed that some of the instru-

[41] See G. Schünemann, "Ein Skizzenblatt Joseph Haydns," _Die Musik_, VIII/16.

mental pieces tell a story of their own, after which the ensuing vocal number carries on the account from where the instrumental introduction left off. These instrumental numbers rank among the very best sections of the score.

The first part of *The Seasons*, called "Spring," opens with an overture "expressing the passage from winter to spring." Here the master orchestrator asserts himself. The icy terror of winter is described by a menacing unison of the strings at the start and subsequently by syncopations and sforzati, as well as by the threatening voices of trombones and timpani. Later, the instruments toss to each other a high-spirited new subject (measure 56); clearly, spring is on its way and a more transparent instrumentation suggests the melting of the ice.

The overture to *The Seasons* is followed by one of those recitatives with highly expressive orchestral accompaniments in which this composition so excels. The lovely chorus of peasants, "Come gentle spring" (No. 2), uses in its middle section alternate groups of women and men, providing an effective contrast to the full chorus employed at the beginning and end of the number. In other sections of the oratorio, too, Haydn at times has divided his mixed chorus in order to obtain greater variety of color. The succeeding aria of Simon (No. 4) displays the same attractive simplicity as the chorus. The bass describes the plowman tilling his field and whistling a folk tune, which the piccolo intones in the few instrumental measures after the first stanza. It is none other than the theme of the andante in Haydn's Surprise symphony; even farmers were presumed to know it at that time. Two mighty ensemble numbers constitute the second half of "Spring." The prayer for a blessing of the fields (No. 6) reveals Haydn's art in having soloists and chorus alternate or cooperate, thus building up a musical texture of greatest diversity. It starts with a rapturous solo of the soprano, later joined by tenor and chorus, extolling the beauties of the fields in bloom. After a jubilant ending in D major, the chorus boldly intones a hymn to the Creator in the solemn key of B flat major. A short section for the solo trio leads to an imposing choral fugue imbued with the ingenious majesty of the choruses in *Messiah.* In this piece, Haydn gives special prominence to the first three notes of his subject and they are used in the second half of the fugue in a very effective augmentation. The analogy with some of his own symphonic movements is obvious.

"Summer" starts with an introduction "representing the idea of morning twilight." The anxieties and fears of the night are described at first in order to create a dark background for the light, cheerful atmosphere of the following scenes. It is interesting to note that Haydn intended this passage in its original form to sound even more mournful. The old manuscript score, which belonged to the Tonkünstlersocietät in Vienna, and shows a version of the instrumentation earlier than the one in the first printed edition, used no violins at all in this number. The melody of the strings was confined to the violas and basses, an idea that Brahms later used in his *Requiem.* As soon as the "crested harbinger of the day with lively note the shepherd wakes," the amusing oboe solo effectively dispels the gloomy mood of the beginning. The vision of sunrise (No. 11) is equal, if not superior, in value to the parallel description in *The Creation.* Haydn depicts the ascent of the sun with the help of instruments, solo voices, and chorus, and the device of chromatic modulation is most impressively employed. It takes the composer, who begins the movement piano, six measures only to reach the climax, and in these few measures, urging, growing, driving, and expansion are expressed, which we would expect in the work of a youth rather than in that of a man of almost seventy. After the jubilant chorus to the sun, a striking contrast is created by the cavatina (No. 13) of Lucas, painting a most realistic picture of languid prostration with the help of muted strings, flute, and oboe. The ensuing recitative and aria (Nos. 14 and 15) of Jane are inserted as a retarding element before the cataclysm of the thunderstorm, announced by scary pizzicatos in the strings and two ominous timpani rolls. Of the storm choruses that Haydn composed, the one in "Summer" is not only the last but also certainly the greatest. Its first part describes with striking realism the uproar of nature, its second section, a fugue with a lamenting subject, the distress of frightened mankind. A disaster and its reflection in the human heart are depicted in colors of sublime grandeur. For the second time in the course of "Summer" the composer introduces a dark, almost tragic element in order to produce a change in the predominantly optimistic gaiety of the composition. The last trio and chorus of this section is an idyll very different from the majestic endings of "Spring" and "Winter." The dramatic episode of the thunderstorm is over, and beast and man enjoy the return of peace. Here Haydn presents some of his most charming nature studies: the lowing of cows, the chirping of crickets, the croaking of frogs, and the ringing of evening bells. How delightful is all this "Frenchified trash," and how beautifully it fits into the score. Evening has come, the stars shine, and the country people go to sleep. In delicate pianissimo the rustic scene reaches its tranquil end.

If this conclusion of "Summer" is reminiscent of the slow movement of a symphony, the following "Autumn" contains many numbers recalling a scherzo. The instrumental introduction "indicating the husbandman's satisfaction at the abundant harvest" presents a graceful tune reflecting a happiness that Haydn, who spent most of his life in the country, must often have experienced at harvest time. This introduction originally was much longer. The score of the Tonkünstlersocietät contained, after measure 30 of this piece, twenty-four measures that Haydn later cut. The composer always avoided drawing out a composition unnecessarily if he could achieve the same effect with fewer notes. The ensuing trio with chorus (No. 20), praising industry, was, as Haydn himself admitted, composed very reluctantly because of its pedantic text; yet the vivid fugue placed in its center imbued the philistine phrases with life and spirit. The succeeding duet (No. 22) expresses the tender affection between the young peasant Lucas and the farmer's daughter Jane. The words of both are sung to the same melody, thus making the close connection of the couple obvious. This piece, with its coloratura passages and two changes of time, recalls to some extent the form of the grand Italian arias. The *style galant* of the rococo period is in evidence in this pastoral scene, and it would not be surprising if in spite of, or rather because of, its ostentatious show of artless simplicity, Lucas and Jane were replaced by Damon and Phyllis.

There follow various scenes devoted to hunting. We see dogs flushing birds, then a battue aimed at killing hares, and finally a stag hunt. Haydn, who loved hunting, here creates a composition full of verve and color. Four French horns, the traditional interpreters of hunting scenes, are used to excellent effect. The fact that this piece begins in D and ends in E flat is characteristic of the composer's daring inspiration. The best is, however, yet to come: the final chorus of "Autumn," depicting the merrymaking after the gathering of the grapes. The orchestra, ultimately reinforced by triangle and tambourine, greatly contributes to the exhilarating scene, and one is reminded of old Dutch paintings showing lusty peasants dancing, drinking, shouting. Haydn's musical portraits are, however, typically Austrian in character, and in their earthy vigor they are far removed from the coy lovers described earlier. He does not hesitate to depict the effect of wine on the merry tipplers, relying on his own observations in wine-growing country.

The instrumental introduction to "Winter," depicting the thick fogs at the approach of that season, resembles "Representation of Chaos" in *The Creation*, written in the same key, C minor. It is interesting that this stirring piece originally was longer. In the manuscript score of the Tonkünstlersocietät, a sequence of nineteen measures is found which in the printed version is replaced by measures 11 and 12 only; obviously the introduction as originally planned had forty-nine instead of thirty-one measures. This again is a proof of Haydn's tendency to concentrate his composition as much as possible. The eighteenth century did not feel any appreciation for the beauties of outdoor life in winter, and thus Haydn, after describing the desolation and danger threatening the wanderer in icy expanses guides him into a hospitable farmhouse with obvious relief. A delightful genre picture unfolds, with the girls spinning and singing under Jane's leadership. The combination of the whirring and humming noise of the wheels in the instrumental accompaniment with the simple, ingratiating melody of the voices has left its traces in the spinning song of Wagner's *Flying Dutchman,* written forty years later. The next number, which is separated from the spinning song only by a recitative of eight measures, is again for solo soprano and chorus. The droll story of the conceited lord who is taken in by the "honest country lass" is treated like a number in a German Singspiel, and is so completely different from the preceding piece that an entire change in the means of expression could not have provided a greater variety of effects.

Once more the mood of the oratorio becomes serious. The author draws a parallel between winter and old age, and the thought of the imminence of death leads him to the hope of God's mercy. As this final number marks the climax of the whole work, the chorus is subdivided into two groups, and the marked use of brass instruments (three horns, three trumpets, three trombones) enhances the grandeur of this conclusion. The antiphonal questions and answers exchanged between the trio of soloists and the two choruses remind us of the ideas expressed in *The Magic Flute*: "But who shall dare those gates to pass?" "The man whose life was incorrupt." "And who the holy hill ascend?" "The man whose tongue was void of guile." A short, though very impressive Amen brings the work to a majestic ending.

Looking at the work as a whole, we find that van Swieten's libretto furnished just the right basis for Haydn. The objective description of nature was transformed through music into pure expression, and it may well be that a more emotional text would have hampered rather than inspired the composer. The glaringly optimistic attitude of the text is put into correct balance by the music, which creates countless shadings in the bright colors and brings them into relief by stressing darkness wherever possible. Thus, "Summer" not only offers the catastrophic thunderstorm, but also starts with an introduction conjuring up the mood of an anguished, sleepless night. Against this somber background, the ensuing scenes radiate greater sparkle. In "Winter," the labored text becomes fully convincing in the composition, leading us through gloom to gaiety, and finally to feelings of gratitude to the Almighty. Thus through the magic of his genius Haydn transformed the libretto's rather superficial cheerfulness into strongest artistic expression.

CONCLUSION

Unbroken homogeneity and steadiness of purpose were basic features of Haydn's nature. Throughout his artistic career, he entered no dead-end streets, and no real rebounds are noticeable. Though the direction of his progress may change at times, Haydn constantly moves forward, and every inch of territory captured by him is being preserved and cultivated. Thus, through more than half a century his art steadily gains in significance.

The composer by no means started as a pioneer; his point of departure was the very place occupied by his predecessors. When he turned from the rococo idiom toward that of sensibility, the change of style was heralded years in advance and achieved step by step. By the time he attained full maturity, the rococo lightness purified in the fiery tide of the storm-and-stress and deepened by the impact of earlier masterworks, had changed into noble popularity. Out of *galant*, expressive, and baroque elements, Haydn evolved a classical synthesis, but he still moved forward, and the last phase in his artistic growth again revealed stronger emphasis on subjective and expressive features.

A powerful nature averse to dualism is expressed in Haydn's music. Even in an early symphony (No. 31 of 1765) he achieved a thematic connection between the beginning and the end. He often avoided the use of a contrasting second subject in the sonata form and replaced it by one growing out of the main idea. At the same time, the development section became more concise, eschewing the employment of new thematic material. In his vocal arias, Haydn similarly confined the middle section to subject matter introduced in the first part.

The composer's manuscripts clearly reveal his steadfastness. Unlike Mozart, who at times broke off in the midst of a composition, he completed almost every work he started. His composing progressed slowly and steadily. "I never was a fast worker," he remarked to Griesinger, "and always composed carefully and diligently." As a rule he worked out his compositions in his mind before committing them to paper and produced very clear manuscripts. This does not quite apply to the works of the opera composer who, forced to meet a performance deadline, often had to make alterations in the course of rehearsals. By and large, however, Haydn's autographs exhibit but few changes. In his last creative period the composer seems to have relied on sketches. He was aware that his work was listened to by the entire musical world, and he aimed to give it the definitive shape that would remain valid through changing times. Again and again the aged composer stirringly expressed his hope "not wholly to die," but to live on in his music.

The admiration given Haydn in his lifetime was largely the result of his peculiar development. As the young composer's work revealed no pioneering or unusual features, it did not offend anyone; on the other hand, the greater significance of his idiom was bound to attract attention. Thus Haydn laid the foundation of his fame in the 1760s. Thenceforth the growth and expansion of his spiritual world occurred at so slow a pace that even the enemies of progress found it possible to follow him. The mature master then captured all hearts by the humor and the noble popularity of his idiom. Thanks to these irresistible qualities, such provoking features as concentrated thematic elaboration, daring modulations, and instrumental devices pointing toward the future were accepted, without protest. On the other hand, the very gaiety and naturalness of his idiom, combined with unbroken homogeneity, earned Haydn the disdain of the romantic era. The scarcity of discordant and ambiguous moods in his music made people look down on "good old Papa Haydn." Only in the twentieth century, when romantic ideals began to lose their hold on artistic thinking, did a true appreciation of Haydn's greatness become possible.

Haydn was endowed with a truly mundane spirit. Healthy sensuality pervaded his nature. He was a shrewd observer who watched everything around him with clear, sharp eyes and never-failing interest. His feeling for nature was deep, far deeper than Mozart's, perhaps even than Beethoven's. He loved to hunt and fish; he was conversant with the habits of many creatures, and it is significant that as a crowning achievement in his life's work he praised the creation in its smallest as well as largest manifestations. The "Laus Deo" at the foot of almost every Haydn autograph is enhanced to outsized proportions in *The Creation*.

Out of Haydn's love for the beauties of our world grew the gaiety and affirmative spirit apparent throughout all his creative periods. At first constrained by modish *galant* precepts, they assumed their rightful place as soon as Haydn embraced the expressive style. To counterbalance the dark passion of the *Sturm und Drang*, he often was, as he himself stated, "seized by uncontrollable humor." Even in his advanced age, this gaiety did not desert him. Nurtured by his noble humanity and a victorious optimism maintained through all the vicissitudes of a long and arduous life, this radiant joyfulness again and again manifested itself, and Haydn considered it his mission to let his fellow beings share in this unique gift. This was touchingly expressed in the letter he wrote a few years before his death to admirers in the German town of Bergen:[1] "Often when contending with obstacles of every sort that interfered with my work, often when my powers both of body and mind were failing and I felt it a hard matter to persevere on the course I had entered on, a secret feeling within me whispered: 'There are but few contented and happy men here below; grief and care prevail everywhere; perhaps your labors may one day be the source from which the weary and worn, or the man burdened with affairs, may derive a few moments' rest and refreshment.' What a powerful motive for pressing onward!"

[1] See p. 193.

A CHECKLIST OF HAYDN AUTOGRAPHS

(The dates added in parentheses were affixed to the manuscripts by the composer himself.)[1]

Piano Sonatas: The Bibliothèque du Conservatoire, Paris, owns Hob. XVI:18 (fragm.), 20 (1771), and 21–23 (1773). Nos. 19 (1767) and 29 (fragm.) are in a private collection in Switzerland; No. 45 (1766) in the British Museum, London; No. 26 (1776) in the Westdeutsche Bibliothek, Marburg; No. 49 (1790) in the Stadtbibliothek, Vienna; No. 52 (1794) in the Library of Congress, Washington, D. C.

Piano Variations: The F minor variations Hob. XVII:6 (1793) are in the New York Public Library.

Pieces for Musical Clocks: The Westdeutsche Bibliothek, Marburg, owns Hob. XIX:9, 10, 17, 18, 27, 29, 30, and 32; the Gesellschaft der Musikfreunde, Vienna, Nos. 11 and 28. No. 16 (1789) is at Jindřichův Hradec, Czechoslovakia; No. 31 in a private collection in Switzerland.

Piano-Trios: Hob. XV:5 (fragm.) and 9 (1785) are in the Westdeutsche Bibliothek, Marburg; No. 7 (1785) in a private collection in England; No. 30 (fragm.) in the Heinemann Foundation, New York; No. 31 (1795) was formerly in the possession of Stefan Zweig.

Baryton Trios: The National Library, Budapest, owns Hob. XI:2 (fragm.), 5 (fragm.), 10 (fragm.), 53 (1767), 60–61 (fragm.), and 109. In the Bibliothèque du Conservatoire, Paris, are the fragments of 79 and 80;

---

[1] Haydn had the habit of replacing the first digit with a line above the remaining numerals, thus writing, for instance, 762 instead of 1762.

in the Universitäts Bibliothek, Tübingen, the fragments of 40, 41, and 42 (1767). At Stanford University, Palo Alto, Calif., is No. 24 (1766); in the Zentral Bibliothek, Zürich, the fragments of No. 57 (1768). Walter Johnson, New York, owns No. 106 (1772); Nos. 68 and 69 (fragm.) are in a private collection in Sweden; No. 105 (1772) was formerly in the collection of the publishing house Artaria in Vienna.

Trios for Wind and String Instruments: The trios for 2 flutes and violoncello Hob. IV:1, 2 (1794) are in the Deutsche Staatsbibliothek, Berlin. The trio for horn, violin, violoncello Hob. IV:5 (1767) was formerly the property of E. Speyer, Ridgehurst, England.

String Quartets: The Gesellschaft der Musikfreunde, Vienna, owns the twelve Quartets Op. 17 (1771) and Op. 20 (1772); the Westdeutsche Bibliothek, Marburg, preserves Op. 42 (1785) and Op. 54/2 (fragm.). Op. 54/3 (fragm.) is in the Universitäts Bibliothek, Tübingen; Op. 64/1 (1790) in the British Museum, London; Op. 64/2 (1790) belongs to Gregor Piatigorsky, Beverly Hills, Calif.; Op. 64/3 (1790) to the Rychenberg Stiftung, Winterthur; Op. 64/6 (1790) to the Library of Congress, Washington, D. C.; Op. 64/5 (1790) is in a private collection in Bavaria. Op. 71/1–3 and Op. 74/1–3 are in the Deutsche Staatsbibliothek, Berlin. Fragments from Op. 76/3 are dispersed over various libraries; Op. 77 (1799) is in the National Library, Budapest; Op. 103 belongs to Broude Brothers, New York.

Clavier Quartet: The National Library, Budapest, owns the quartet for clavier, 2 violins, and violoncello Hob. XIV:4 (1764).

Larger Chamber Music Ensembles: The Prince Harrach Collection, Vienna, owns a fragment of the sextet Hob. II:15 (1760); the Universitäts Bibliothek, Tübingen the sextet Hob. II:23; the National Library, Budapest, the octet Hob. II:16 (1760), and the notturno No. 3 Hob. II:27. Formerly in the possession of Oscar Mez, Freiburg, was the notturno No. 7, Hob. II:31 (1790).

Concertos: The Hessische Landesbibliothek, Darmstadt, owns the clavier concerto Hob. XVIII:1 (1756); the Gesellschaft der Musikfreunde, Vienna, the horn concerto Hob. VIId:3 (1762) and the trumpet concerto Hob. VIIe:1 (1796); the National Bibliothek, Vienna, the cello concerto Hob. VIIb:2 (1783); the National Library, Budapest, the lira concerto Hob. VIIh:3 (fragm.); the Westdeutsche Bibliothek, Marburg, the symphonie concertante Hob. I:105 (1792).

Marches and Dances: The National Library, Budapest, possesses the marches Hob. VIII:1 (1795) and Hob. VIII:4 (1802), the sixteen minuets (for pianoforte) Hob. IX:3 and the twelve German dances (for pianoforte) Hob. IX:12. The Bibliothèque du Conservatoire, Paris, has the march Hob. VIII:6; the Haydn House, Eisenstadt, the marches Hob. VIII:2 (1795) and Hob. VIII:7 (fragm.); the Royal Society of Musicians, London, the march Hob. VIII:3 (1792); the Monastery Seitenstetten, Austria, the twelve minuets Hob. IX:1; the Universitäts Bibliothek, Tübingen, six minuets Hob. IX:5 (1776).

Symphonies: The National Library, Budapest, owns Hob. I, Nos. 7 (1761), 12 (1763), 13 (1763), 21–24 (1764), 29–31 (1765), 35 (1767), 42 (1771), 45–47 (1772), 54 (1774), 57 (1774), 61 (1776), 63 (fragm.), 100 (1794). The Deutsche Staatsbibliothek, Berlin, has Nos. 85 (fragm.) and 104 (1795); the Universitäts Bibliothek, Tübingen, Nos. 28 (1765), 53 (fragm.), 56 (1774), 94 (1791), 102 (1794); the Westdeutsche Bibliothek, Marburg, No. 55 (1774); the British Museum, London, Nos. 40 (1763), 95 (1791), 96 (1791), 103 (1795); the Fitzwilliam Museum, Cambridge, England, No. 89 (1787); the Kungliga Musikaliska Akademien, Stockholm, No. 49 (1768); the Bibliothèque Nationale, Paris, Nos. 83 (1785), 86 (1786), 87 (1785), 92 (1789); the Bibliothèque du Conservatoire, Paris, No. 82 (1786), the collection Floersheim-Koch, Muzzano, Switzerland, No. 84 (1786); the Library of Congress, Washington, D. C., Nos. 90 (1788), 94 (sketch to 2d movement); in a private collection in the U.S.A. is No. 91 (1788). The heirs of Stefan Zweig own No. 97 (1792). The present whereabouts of Nos. 9 and 93 (1791) as well as of five symphonies—Nos. 50 (1773), 73 (1781), 98 (1792), 99 (1793), 101 (1794)—which belonged to the Preussische Staatsbibliothek, Berlin, are not known.

Overtures: The Bibliothèque du Conservatoire, Paris, owns *Acide e Galatea* and *La vera costanza* (1777); the Deutsche Staatsbibliothek, Berlin, *L'incontro improvviso;* the British Museum, London, *Orlando paladino* (1782); the Royal College of Music, London, *Armida* (1783); the Westdeutsche Bibliothek, Marburg, *L'anima del filosofo;* the Universitäts Bibliothek, Tübingen, Hob. Ia:7 (1777). The present whereabouts of *L'isola disabitata* (formerly Preussische Staatsbibliothek, Berlin) is not known.

Lieder, Arias, and Solo Cantatas: The National Bibliothek, Vienna, has "Gott erhalte," that of Budapest, "Auch die Sprödeste"; the Westdeutsche Bibliothek, Marburg, "Der schlaue Pudel." A number of Scottish songs are in the Bibliothèque du Conservatoire, Paris, and the British Museum, London. The National Library, Budapest, owns "Quando la rosa," "Agl' a monti," "Ah tu non senti" (1786), "Un cor si tenero" (1787), "Se tu mi sprezzi" (1788), "Infelice sventurata" (1789), "Da che penso" (1790), "D'una sposa maschinella," "Lines from the Battle of the Nile" (1798); the Stadt Bibliothek, Vienna, "Chi vive amante" (1787), "Berenice che fai" (1795); the Bibliothèque du Conservatoire, Paris, "Solo e pensoso" (1798); the British Museum, London, "Guarda qui" (1796).

Duets, Parts Songs, and Canons: "Guarda qui" (1796) is in the British Museum, London; the three- and four-part songs are in the Bibliothèque du Conservatoire, Paris; the "Zehn Gebote der Kunst" in the Gesellschaft der Musikfreunde, Vienna. Individual canons and sketches to canons are in various libraries.

Operas: The National Library, Budapest, owns: *La marchesa Nepola* (1762, fragm.), *Acide* (1762, fragm.),

La canterina (1766), *Lo speziale, Le pescatrici* (1769),
L'infedeltà delusa, Il mondo della luna (fragm.), *La
fedeltà premiata* (1780, fragm.), chorus of the Danes
from *Alfred* (1796); the Universitäts Bibliothek, Tübingen, possesses *Acide* (fragm.), the Westdeutsche Bibliothek, Marburg, parts of *Alfred*, most of *L'anima del
filosofo* (1791), the third act of *Orlando Paladino*, and
fragments of *La vera costanza*; the Deutsche Staatsbibliothek, Berlin, has fragments of *La fedeltà premiata*
and *Il mondo della luna*; the Royal College of Music,
London, the greatest part of *Armida* (1783). The first
two acts of *Orlando Paladino* (1782) are in the British
Museum, London. Fragments from *Acide* and *Il mondo
della luna* are in the Paris libraries. A fragment from
Armida is at Harvard University, Cambridge, Mass.,
"Ein Tag der allen Freuden bringt" from *Philemon und
Baucis* in the Sibley Library, Rochester, N. Y.; other
short fragments are in various libraries of Vienna, Basle,
and Paris.

Smaller Church Works: The *Salve Regina* in E major
(1756) is in the Hessische Landesbibliothek, Darmstadt;
that in G minor (1771) in the Universitäts Bibliothek,
Tübingen. The small "Alleluja" is in the Haydn Museum,
Eisenstadt.

Masses: The National Library, Budapest, owns the *Missa
in tempore belli* (1796) and fragments of the *Great
Organ Mass* and the *Mass of St. Cecile*. The National
Bibliothek, Vienna, possesses the *Nelson Mass* (1798)
and the *Theresien Mass* (1799); the Westdeutsche Bibliothek, Marburg, the incomplete manuscript of the
Missa Sancti Nicolai (1772); the Deutsche Staatsbibliothek, Berlin, the *Missa Celensis* (1782), the Gesellschaft
der Musikfreunde, Vienna, the *Short Organ Mass*, the
Bayrische Staatsbibliothek, Munich, the *Creation Mass*
(1801), and the Bibliothèque du Conservatoire, Paris,
the *Harmonie Messe* (1802).

Cantatas and Oratorios: The Deutsche Staatsbibliothek,
Berlin, owns the cantata *Destatevi o miei fidi* (1763), a
second Esterházy cantata, and sketches to the *Seasons*;

the Gesellschaft der Musikfreunde, Vienna, possesses the *Applausus* (1768) and parts of *Il ritorno di Tobia*; the National Library, Budapest, has "Svanisce in un momento" (1784) composed for this oratorio, the chorus "The Storm" (1792), and the partly autograph manuscript of the *Seven Words*; in the British Museum, London, is a partly autograph manuscript of the chorus "Der Sturm" (German text), as well as "Nor can I think" and "Thy great endeavours" from *Invocation of Neptune* (1794). The Library of Congress, Washington, D. C., has from the cantatas for Prince Esterházy, "Qual dubbio omai," "Se ogni giorni," and "Saggio il pensier." The National Bibliothek, Vienna, has sketches for the *Creation*.

BIBLIOGRAPHY

ABBREVIATIONS USED IN BIBLIOGRAPHY

ActaM	*Acta Musicologica*
DTOe	*Denkmäler der Tonkunst in Oesterreich*
ML	*Music and Letters*
MQ	*Musical Quarterly*
PJ	*Jahrbuch Peters*
PMA	*Proceedings of the Musical Association*
SIMG	*Sammelbände der Internationalen Musikgesellschaft*
StzMW	*Studien zur Musikwissenschaft*
ZfM	*Zeitschrift für Musik*
ZfMW	*Zeitschrift für Musikwissenschaft*

Abert, H. "Joseph Haydns Klavierwerke," *ZfMW*, II and III (1920–21).

—— and O. Jahn. *Mozart*. Leipzig, 1920–21.

Adler, G. "Die Wiener klassische Schule," *Handbuch der Musikgeschichte*, 2d ed. Leipzig, 1920.

—— "Haydn and the Viennese Classical School," *MQ*, XVIII (1932).

—— "Joseph Haydn," *Festrede*. Vienna, 1909.

Alberti-Radanowicz, E. "Das Wiener Lied von 1789–1815," *StzMW*, X (1923).

Albrecht, O. E. *A Census of Autograph Music Manuscripts of European Composers in American Libraries*. Philadelphia, 1953.

Altmann, W. *Handbuch für Streichquartettspieler*. Berlin, 1928.

Arnold, J. F. *Joseph Haydn.* Erfurt, 1810.

Artaria, F. *Verzeichnis der musikalischen Autographe von Joseph Haydn.* Vienna, 1893.

—— and H. Botstiber. *Joseph Haydn und das Verlagshaus Artaria.* Vienna, 1909.

Bartha, D. "Zur Abstammung Joseph Haydns," *ActaM*, VII (1935).

—— *Joseph Haydn. Gesammelte Briefe und Aufzeichnungen.* Kassel, 1965.

—— and L. Somfai, *Haydn als Opernkapellmeister.* Budapest, 1960.

—— *See* Szabolcsi.

Becker, C. F. *Joseph Haydn.* Leipzig, 1832.

Bernhardt, R. "Gottfried van Swieten," *Der Bär* (1930).

Beyle, M.-H. (pseudonyms: L. A. C. Bombet and Stendhal) *Lettres écrites de Vienne, en Autriche, sur le célèbre compositeur Joseph Haydn.* Paris, 1814.

Blume, F. "Haydns Persönlichkeit in seinen Streichquartetten," *PJ*, XXXVII (1931).

Botstiber, H. *See* Artaria, *Joseph Haydn* . . . ; Pohl, *Joseph Haydn.*

Brand, C. M. *Die Messen von Joseph Haydn.* Berlin, 1939.

Brenet, M. *Haydn.* Paris, 1909, London, 1926.

Breton, J. Le. *Notice historique sur la vie et les ouvrages de Joseph Haydn.* Paris, 1822.

Bücken, E. "Musik des Rokoko und der Klassik," *Handbuch der Musikwissenschaft*, V. Potsdam, 1927.

Burkat, L. "Haydn's Symphonies: A Collation," *Music Library Association Notes*, Series I, 1942.

Burney, C. *The Present State of Music in Germany, the Netherlands.* . . . London, 1773.

Carpani, G. *Le Haydine.* Milan, 1812.

Cobbett, W. W., ed. *Cyclopedic Survey of Chamber Music.* 2 vols. London, 1929, 1930.

Conrat, H. "Joseph Haydn und das kroatische Volkslied," *Die Musik*, XIV (1904–5).

Cunningham, P. *See* Wallace.

Dab, K. "Schubert's indebtedness to Haydn," *ML*, XXI (1940).

Daffner, H. *Die Entwicklung des Klavierkonzerts bis Mozart.* Leipzig, 1908.

Dale, K. *See* Scott article on Haydn . . .

Dent, E. *Alessandro Scarlatti.* London, 1905.

Deutsch, O. E. Preface to his edition of Haydn's *12 Deutsche Tänze für Orchester.* Leipzig, 1930.

—— "Haydn's Kanons," *ZfMW*, XV (1932).

—— "Haydn's Hymn and Burney's Translation," *Musical Review*, IV (1943).

Diemand, A. "Haydns Korrespondenz mit dem Fürsten K. E. zu Oettingen-Wallerstein," *Ztschr. d. histor. Vereins f. Schwaben*, XCV.

Dies, A. C. *Biographische Nachrichten über Joseph Haydn.* Vienna, 1810.

Edgcumbe, R. (second Earl of Mount Edgcumbe) *Musical Reminiscences of an Old Amateur.* 4th ed. London, 1834.

Edwall, H. R. "Ferdinand IV and Haydn's Concertos for the *Lira Organizzata*," *MQ*, XLVIII (1962).

Einstein, A. *Mozart: His Character, His Work.* New York, 1945.

—— *See* Gyrowetz.

Engel, H. *Die Entwicklung des deutschen Klavierkonzertes von Mozart bis Liszt.* Leipzig, 1927.

Engl. J. E. *Haydns handschriftliches Tagebuch des 2. Aufenthaltes in London.* Leipzig, 1909.

Feder, G. *Bemerkungen über die Ausbildung der klassischen Tonsprache in der Instrumentalmusik Haydns.* Report of the 8th Congress of the Intern. Musicol. Soc. New York, 1961.

—— "Zur Datierung Haydnscher Werke" in Hoboken *Festschrift*. Mainz, 1962.

Fellerer, K. G. "Zum Joseph Haydn Bild im frühen 19. Jahrhundert" in Hoboken *Festschrift*. Mainz, 1962.

Fétis, E. *Biographie universelle des musiciens*. Brussels, 1839.

Fischer, W. "Zur Entwicklungsgeschichte des Wiener klassischen Stils," *StzMW*, III (1915).

—— "Instrumentalmusik," Adler's *Handbuch der Musikgeschichte*. Berlin, 1929.

—— Preface to *DTOe*, XIX:2 (1912).

Framery, N. *Notice de Joseph Haydn*. Paris, 1810.

Fröhlich, J. *Joseph Haydn*. Edited with an introduction by A. Sandberger. Regensburg, 1936.

Fruchtman, E. "The Baryton: Its History and Its Music Re-examined," *ActaM*, XXXIV (Jan.–June, 1962).

Gardiner, W. *Music and Friends*. London, 1838–53.

Geiringer, K. *Joseph Haydn*. Potsdam, 1932.

—— "Das Haydn Bild im Wandel der Zeiten," *Die Musik*, XXIV (1932).

—— "Haydn's Sketches for *The Creation*," *MQ*, XVIII (1932).

—— "Joseph Haydn," *Thompson's International Cyclopedia of Music and Musicians*. New York, 1939.

—— "Haydn as an Opera Composer," *PMA*, LXVI (1939–40).

—— "Joseph Haydn," Grove's *Dictionary of Music and Musicians*. 4th ed. London, 1940. (New article in this work.)

—— "The Operas of Haydn," *Musical America* (1940).

—— "Haydn and the Folk Song of the British Isles," *MQ* (1949).

—— *Joseph Haydn*. Mainz, 1959.

—— "The Small Sacred Works by Haydn in the Esterházy Archives at Eisenstadt," *MQ* (1959).

—— "Eigenhändige Bemerkungen Haydns in seinen Musikhandschriften," Hoboken *Festschrift*. Mainz, 1962.

Gerber, E. K. *Neues Lexikon der Tonkunst.* Leipzig, 1790–92. (Article on Joseph Haydn.)

Gotwals, V. "The Earliest Biographies of Haydn," *MQ* (1959).

—— "Haydn's Last Will and Testament," *MQ* (1961).

—— *Joseph Haydn: Eighteenth-Century Gentleman and Genius.* Madison, Wis., 1963.

Greilsamer, L. "Le Baryton du Prince Esterházy," *SIMG*, VI (1910).

Griesinger, G. A. *Biographische Notizen über Joseph Haydn.* Leipzig, 1810.

Gyrowetz, A. *Biographie.* 1848. Newly edited by A. Einstein in *Lebensläufe deutscher Musiker.* Leipzig, 1915.

Haas, K. "Haydn's Marches," *The Score* (1950).

Haas, R. "Die Musik in der Wiener deutschen Stegreifkomödie," *StzMW*, XII (1925).

—— *W. A. Mozart.* Potsdam, 1933. 2d ed., 1950.

Hadden, J. C. *George Thomson: His Life and Correspondence.* London, 1898.

—— *Haydn.* Revised ed. London, 1934.

Hadow, W. H. *A Croatian Composer.* London, 1897.

Hárich, J. *Esterházy Musikgeschichte im Spiegel der zeitgenössischen Textbücher.* Eisenstadt, 1959.

—— "Das Repertoire des Opernkapellmeisters Joseph Haydn" in *Haydn Yearbook,* Vol. I (1962).

Hase, H. v. *Joseph Haydn und Breitkopf und Härtel.* Leipzig, 1909.

Haydn, J. "Jubiläumsfeier," *Kongressbericht.* Vienna, 1909.

—— *Haydn Yearbook.* Ed. H. Singer, K. H. Füssl, St. Harpner, and R. Landon, Vienna, 1962 ff.

—— *Katalog der Gedächtnisausstellung.* Vienna, 1932.

Heuss, A. "Die Kaiserhymne," *ZfMW*, I (1918).

Hoboken, A. van. *Joseph Haydn: thematisch-bibliographisches Werkverzeichnis.* Vol. I. Mainz, 1957.

—— *Discrepancies in Haydn Biographies.* Washington, D. C., 1962.

Hopkinson, C., and C. B. Oldman. "Thomson's Collections of National Songs with special reference to the contribution of Haydn and Beethoven," *Edinburgh Bibliographical Society Transactions,* II (1940).

—— "Haydn's Settings of Scottish Songs in the Collections of Napier and Whyte," *Edinburgh Bibliographical Society Transactions* (1954).

Horányi, M. *Das Esterházysche Feenreich.* Budapest, 1959.

Hughes, R. S. M. "Haydn at Oxford," *ML* (1939).

—— "Dr. Burney's Championship of Haydn," *MQ,* XXVII (1941).

—— *Haydn.* London, 1950.

Jacob, H. E. *Joseph Haydn.* Hamburg, 1952.

Jahn, O. *See* Abert, *Mozart.*

Jančik, H. *Michael Haydn.* Vienna, 1952.

Karajan, T. v. *Joseph Haydn in London.* Vienna, 1861.

Kelly, M. *Reminiscences.* London, 1826.

Kinker, J. *Ter nagedachtenis von Joseph Haydn.* Amsterdam, 1810.

Kobald, C. *Joseph Haydn. Bild seines Lebens und seiner Zeit.* Vienna, 1932.

Korzak, F. "Luigi Tomasini." Unpublished dissertation, Vienna, 1952.

Krehbiel, H. E. *Music and Manners in the Classical Period.* New York, 1896.

—— *See* Thayer.

Kretzschmar, H. *Führer durch den Konzertsaal.* Leipzig, 1887–1921.

—— "Haydns Jugendsymphonien," *PJ,* XV (1908).

Krienitz, W. "78 neue Haydn Symphonien," *Allgemeine Musikzeitung,* LX (1932–33).

Kuhač, F. *Josip Haydn.* Zagreb, 1880.

Lachmann, R. "Die Haydn Autographen der Staatsbibliothek zu Berlin," *ZfMW,* XIV (1932).

Landon, H. C. R. "On Haydn's Quartets of Opera 1 and 2," *Music Review* (1952).

—— *The Symphonies of Joseph Haydn.* London, 1955.

—— "Haydn and Authenticity: Some New Facts," *Music Review* (1955).

—— and J. P. Larsen. "Haydn" in *Die Musik in Geschichte und Gegenwart*, Vol. V. Kassel, 1956.

——, comp. and tr. *The Collected Correspondence and London Notebooks of Joseph Haydn.* London, 1959.

—— "Haydn's Marionette Operas" in *Haydn Yearbook*, Vol. I (1962).

Lang, P. H. "Haydn and the Opera," *MQ*, XVIII (1932).

—— *Music in Western Civilization.* New York, 1941.

Larsen, J. P. Replies to A. Sandberger's articles, *Actam*, VIII (1936), IX (1937).

—— *Die Haydn-Überlieferung.* Copenhagen, 1939.

—— *Drei Haydn Kataloge in Faksimile.* Copenhagen, 1941.

—— "Zu Haydns künstlerischer Entwicklung" in Fischer *Festschrift.* Innsbruck, 1956.

—— *See* Landon, "Haydn" (1956).

Laurencie, L. de la. "L'apparition des oeuvres d'Haydn à Paris," *Revue de Musicologie*, XVI (1932).

Lorenz, F. *Haydns, Mozarts, und Beethovens Kirchenmusik.* Breslau, 1866.

Luithlen, V. "Haydn Erinnerungen . . ." in Hoboken *Festschrift.* Mainz, 1962.

Major, E. "Ungarische Tanzmelodien in Haydns Bearbeitung," *ZfMW*, II (1920).

Mayer, S. *Brevi notizie . . . di Giuseppe Haydn.* Bergamo, 1809.

Mencik, H. "Einige Beiträge zur Haydn Biographie," *Musikbuch für Oesterreich*, VI. Vienna, 1909.

—— "Haydns Testamente," *Die Kultur* (Vienna, 1909).

Mozart, W. A. *See* Anderson.

Neukomm, K. "18 mois de la vie de Haydn," *Revue et Gazette musicale de Paris*, XXI (1854).

Neurath, H. "Das Violinkonzert in der Wiener klassischen Schule," *StzMW*, XIV.

Nohl, L. *Musikerbriefe*. Leipzig, 1867. (For English translation *see* Wallace.)

—— *Haydn*. New edition by A. Schnerich. Leipzig, 1931.

Nowak, L. *Joseph Haydn*. Vienna, 1951. 2d ed., 1959.

—— *Ein Haydn-Autograph und sein Schicksal*. Biblos, 1954.

Oldman, C. B. *See* Hopkinson.

Orel, A. "Katholische Kirchenmusik," Adler's *Handbuch der Musikgeschichte*. Berlin, 1929.

Parke, W. T. *Musical Memoirs, comprising an account of the general state of music in England, 1784–1830*. London, 1830.

Philips, H. *Musical and Personal Recollections*. London, 1864.

Pohl, C. F. *Mozart und Haydn in London*. Vienna, 1867.

—— *Joseph Haydn*. Berlin, 1875 and 1882. 3d vol. by H. Botstiber, Leipzig, 1927.

Radcliffe, P. "The Piano Sonatas of Joseph Haydn," *Music Review* (1946).

Reich, W. *Joseph Haydn*. Lucerne, 1946.

Reichardt, J. F. *Vertraute Briefe*. Amsterdam, 1810.

Reissmann, A. *Joseph Haydn*. Berlin, 1880.

Riehl, W. H. *Musikalische Charakterköpfe*. Stuttgart, 1862.

Riemann, H. *Handbuch der Musikgeschichte*, II, 3. 2d ed. Leipzig, 1922.

—— Prefaces to *Denkmäler deutscher Tonkunst in Bayern*, 2d series, III:1, VII:2, VIII:2.

Rochlitz, J. F. *Für Freunde der Tonkunst*. Leipzig, I, 1824; IV, 1832.

Rosenbaum, J. C. *Diary, 1797–1822*. Manuscript in National Library, Vienna. Ser. nov., 194–204.

Rutz, H. *Joseph Haydn*. Munich, 1953.

Saint-Foix, G. de. "Les manuscrits et les copies d'oeuvres de Joseph Haydn à la Bibliothèque du conservatoire," *Revue de Musicologie*, XV (1931).

—— "Haydn and Clementi," *MQ*, XVIII (1932).

Sandberger, A. "Zur Entwicklungsgeschichte von Haydns 'Sieben Worten,'" *Gesammelte Aufsätze*. Munich, 1921.

—— "Zur Geschichte des Haydnschen Streichquartetts," *Gesammelte Aufsätze*. Munich, 1921.

—— "Neue Haydniana," *PJ*, XL (1933).

—— "Zu Haydns Repertoire in Eisenstadt und Esterház," *PJ*, XL (1933). *See also* Sandberger's articles and Larsen's replies in *ActaM* and *ZfMW* (1935–37).

—— "Ein unbekannter Brief von Joseph Haydn," *ZfM* (1938).

—— *See* Fröhlich.

Sandys, W., and S. A. Forster. *The History of the Violin*. London, 1864.

Schering, A. *Geschichte des Oratoriums*. Leipzig, 1911.

Schmid, A. *Joseph Haydn und Nicolo Zingarelli*. Vienna, 1847.

Schmid, E. F. "Joseph Haydn und die Flötenuhr," *ZfMW*, XIV (1932).

—— "Joseph Haydn," *Ein Buch von Vorfahren und Heimat des Meisters*. Kassel, 1934.

—— "Franz Anton Hoffmeister und die 'Göttweiger Sonaten,'" *ZfM*, CIV (1937).

—— "Joseph Haydns Jugendliebe," in Fischer *Festschrift*. Innsbruck, 1956.

Schnerich, A. *Messen-Typus von Haydn bis Schubert*. Vienna, 1893.

—— *Messe und Requiem seit Haydn und Mozart*. Vienna, 1909.

—— "Textliche Versehen in Messen Haydns," *Kongressbericht*. Vienna, 1909.

—— "Zur Geschichte der früheren (und späteren) Messen Haydns," *Zeitschr. d. internationalen Musikgesellschaft*, XIV, XV (1912–14).

Schnerich, A. *Joseph Haydn und seine Seudung.* 2d ed. Vienna, 1926.

—— See Nohl, *Haydn.*

Scott, M. M. "Haydn's 83," *ML*, XIII (1931).

—— "Haydn in England," *MQ*, XVIII (1932).

—— "Haydn Relics and Reminiscences in England," *ML*, XIII (1932).

—— "Haydn's Op. 2 and 3," *PMA*, LXII (1935–36).

—— "Mi-Jo Haydn," *Monthly Musical Record*, LXIX (1939).

—— "Haydn, Fresh Facts and Old Fancies," *PMA*, LXVIII (1941–42).

—— "Some English affinities and associations of Haydn's songs," *ML*, XXV (1944).

—— and K. Dale. Article on Haydn in *Grove's Dictionary of Music and Musicians*, 5th ed. London, 1954.

Seeburg, F. v. *Joseph Haydn.* Regensburg, 1912.

Silverstolpe, F. S. *Negra aterblikar.* Stockholm, 1841.

Smith, C. Sprague. "Haydn's Chamber Music and the Flute," *MQ*, XIX (1933).

Somfai, L. *Evolution of Haydn's String Quartets* (in Hungarian). Haydn Emlékére, Budapest, 1960, p. 295 ff.

—— Joseph Haydn. *Sein Leben in Zeitgenössischen Bildern.* Kassel, 1966.

—— See also Bartha.

Sondheimer, R. "G. B. Sammartini," *ZfMW*, III (1920–21).

—— *Haydn: A Historical and Psychological Study based on his Quartets.* London, 1951.

Strunk, O. W. "Haydn's Divertimenti for Baryton, Viola, and Bass," *MQ*, XVIII (1932).

—— "Haydn," in *From Bach to Stravinsky*, edited by D. Ewen. New York, 1933.

—— "Notes on a Haydn Autograph," *MQ*, XX (1934).

Szabolcsi, B., and D. Bartha. *Haydn Emlékére.* Budapest, 1960.

Taylor, J. *Records of My Life*. London, 1832.

Tenschert, R. *Joseph Haydn*. Berlin, 1932.

Thayer, A. W. *The Life of Beethoven*. Revised by H. E. Krehbiel. New York, 1921.

Therstappen, H. J. *Joseph Haydn's sinfonisches Vermächtnis*. Wolfenbüttel, 1941.

Thompson, O., and G. W. Harris, eds. *International Cyclopedia of Music and Musicians*. New York, 1939.

Torrefranca, F. "Le origini della Sinfonia," *Rivista Musicale Italiana*, XX (1913), XXII (1915).

Tovey, D. F. *Essays in Musical Analysis*. 7 vols. London, 1935–44.

—— Article on Haydn's chamber music. In Cobbett, *q.v.*

Townsend, P. D. *Joseph Haydn*. London and New York, 1884.

Valkó, A. "Haydn Magyaroszági Müködése a Levéltári Akták Tükrében" in *Kodály Zoltán 75. Születésnapjára*, Budapest, 1957, and Part II of *Haydn Emlékére*, Budapest, 1960.

Vécsey, J. *Haydn Compositions in the Music Collection of the National Széchényi Library, Budapest*. Budapest, 1960.

Wallace, Lady G. M., tr., and P. Cunningham, ed. Nohl's *Letters of Distinguished Musicians*. London, 1857–59.

Wendschuh, L. *Über Haydns Opern*. Rostock, 1895.

Willett, T. E. "A Study of Haydn's Piano Sonatas." Unpublished thesis, Urbana, Illinois, 1946.

Wirth, H. *Joseph Haydn als Dramatiker*. Wolfenbüttel, 1941.

—— Preface to the recording of Haydn's *L'anima del filosofo*, Boston, 1951.

Wurzbach, C. *Joseph Haydn und sein Bruder Michael*. Vienna, 1862.

Wyzewa, T. "A propos du centenaire de Haydn," *Revue des deux mondes* (Paris, 1909).

—— and G. de Saint-Foix. *Mozart*. Paris, 1912.

INDEX OF COMPOSITIONS